Alive
The Final Evolution

3

Story by Tadashi Kawashima
Art by Adachitoka

Translated and adapted by
Anastasia Moreno

Lettered by
North Market Street Graphics

Ballantine Books • New York

A Del Rey Trade Paperback Original

Alive volume 3 copyright © 2004 by Tadashi Kawashima and Adachitoka
English translation copyright © 2008 by Tadashi Kawashima and Adachitoka

Published in the United States by Del Rey Books, an imprint of The Random House Publishing Group, a division of Random House, Inc., New York.

DEL REY is a registered trademark and the Del Rey colophon is a trademark of Random House, Inc.

Publication rights arranged through Kodansha Ltd.

First published in Japan in 2004 by Kodansha Ltd., Tokyo

ISBN 978-0-345-49937-0

Printed in the United States of America

www.delreymanga.com

9 8 7 6 5 4 3 2 1

Translator/Adapter—Anastasia Moreno
Lettering—North Market Street Graphics

Contents

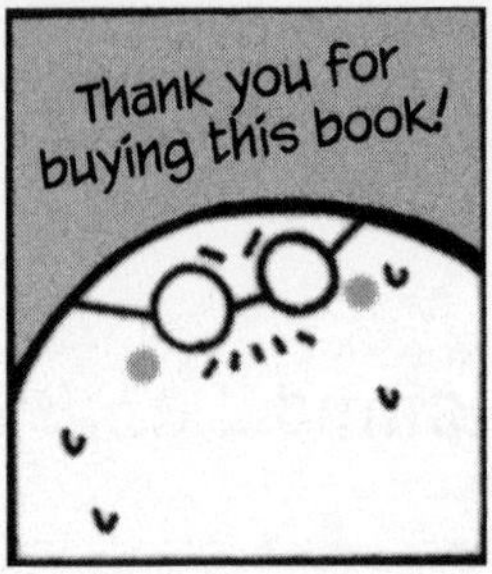
Thank you for buying this book!

Tadashi Kawashima

I am here now because I was able to avoid a nervous breakdown (LOL)

Thank you ♡

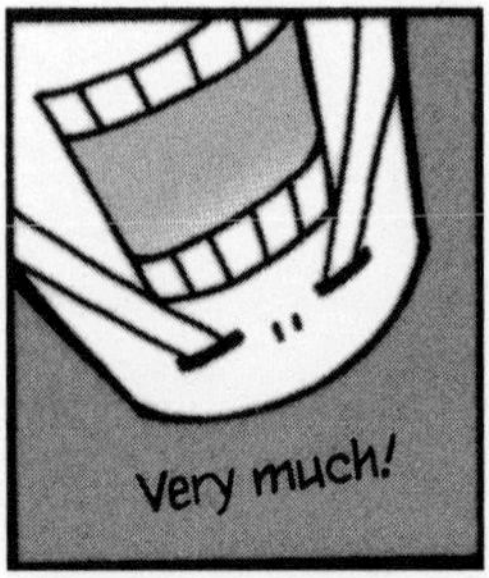
Very much!

Adachitoka

The model for the rabbit in this issue is, of course, Stew.

Honorifics Explained

Throughout the Del Rey Manga books, you will find Japanese honorifics left intact in the translations. For those not familiar with how the Japanese use honorifics and, more important, how they differ from American honorifics, we present this brief overview.

Politeness has always been a critical facet of Japanese culture. Ever since the feudal era, when Japan was a highly stratified society, use of honorifics—which can be defined as polite speech that indicates relationship or status—has played an essential role in the Japanese language. When addressing someone in Japanese, an honorific usually takes the form of a suffix attached to one's name (example: "Asuna-san"), is used as a title at the end of one's name, or appears in place of the name itself (example: "Negi-sensei," or simply "Sensei").

Honorifics can be expressions of respect or endearment. In the context of manga and anime, honorifics give insight into the nature of the relationship between characters. Many English translations leave out these important honorifics and therefore distort the feel of the original Japanese. Because Japanese honorifics contain nuances that English honorifics lack, it is our policy at Del Rey not to translate them. Here, instead, is a guide to some of the honorifics you may encounter in Del Rey Manga.

-san: This is the most common honorific and is equivalent to Mr., Miss, Ms., or Mrs. It is the all-purpose honorific and can be used in any situation where politeness is required.

-sama: This is one level higher than "-san" and is used to confer great respect.

-dono: This comes from the word "tono," which means "lord." It is an even higher level than "-sama" and confers utmost respect.

-kun: This suffix is used at the end of boys' names to express familiarity or endearment. It is also sometimes used by men among friends, or when addressing someone younger or of a lower station.

-chan: This is used to express endearment, mostly toward girls. It is also used for little boys, pets, and even among lovers. It gives a sense of childish cuteness.

Bozu: This is an informal way to refer to a boy, similar to the English terms "kid" and "squirt."

Sempai/
Senpai: This title suggests that the addressee is one's senior in a group or organization. It is most often used in a school setting, where underclassmen refer to their upperclassmen as "sempai." It can also be used in the workplace, such as when a newer employee addresses an employee who has seniority in the company.

Kohai: This is the opposite of "sempai" and is used toward underclassmen in school or newcomers in the workplace. It connotes that the addressee is of a lower station.

Sensei: Literally meaning "one who has come before," this title is used for teachers, doctors, or masters of any profession or art.

-[blank]: This is usually forgotten in these lists, but it is perhaps the most significant difference between Japanese and English. The lack of honorific means that the speaker has permission to address the person in a very intimate way. Usually, only family, spouses, or very close friends have this kind of permission. Known as *yobisute,* it can be gratifying when someone who has earned the intimacy starts to call one by one's name without an honorific. But when that intimacy hasn't been earned, it can be very insulting.

Alive

③

Writer/ Tadashi Kawashima
Artist/ Adachitoka

contents

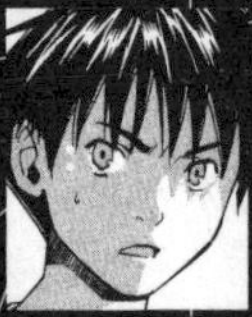

Taisuke Kanou

High school student weak in fights, but with a strong sense of justice. During "Nightmare Week," acquired a supernatural power to control heat. Currently on a journey to find Hirose and Megumi.

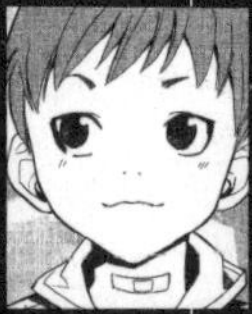

Yuta Takizawa

Little boy traveling with Taisuke. Speaks like an adult, but has a deep, emotional scar resulting from witnessing his mother's suicide.

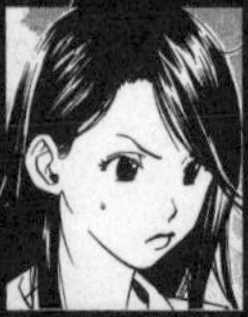

Youko Kanou

Taisuke's older sister and also school nurse. Strong-willed woman who raised Taisuke after their parents died.

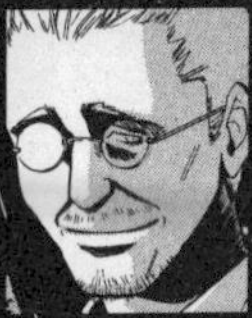

Shigeki Katsumata

Former detective, and a leader type amongst the "comrades" with supernatural powers. His thoughts and intent are unclear, but seems to be manipulating Hirose.

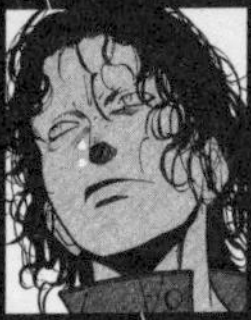

Takumi Yura

One of Katsumata's "comrades." Controls highly pressurized air bubbles and claims to be a leader of humans, but slaughters people mercilessly. Has frizzy hair and wears coveralls.

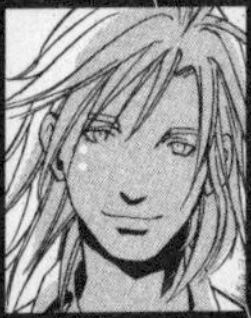

Kenichirou Morio

One of Katsumata's comrades. Controls wind to create sharp blades of air like a *kamaitachi* to slice humans. Ordered by Katsumata to kill Taisuke.

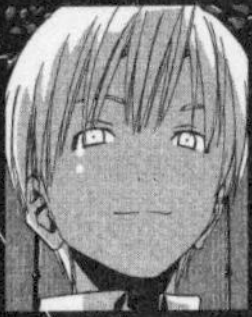

Yuichi Hirose

Taisuke's close friend. He used to be weak and shy, but changed personalities after he acquired supernatural powers, and kidnapped Megumi. Accompanies Katsumata.

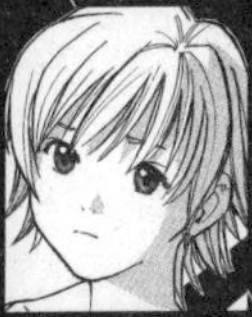

Megumi Ochiai

Taisuke's childhood girl friend. She always ends up arguing with Taisuke because she worries about him so much. Kidnapped by Hirose and confined in the house.

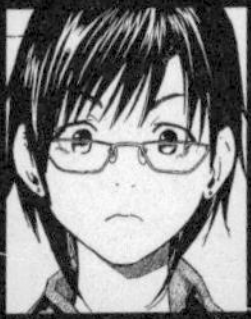

Kyouko Amamiya

Passionate reporter of a weekly magazine. Opposes the editorial policy of focusing on gossip and far-fetched occult material, and investigates the string of incidents related to the mass suicides.

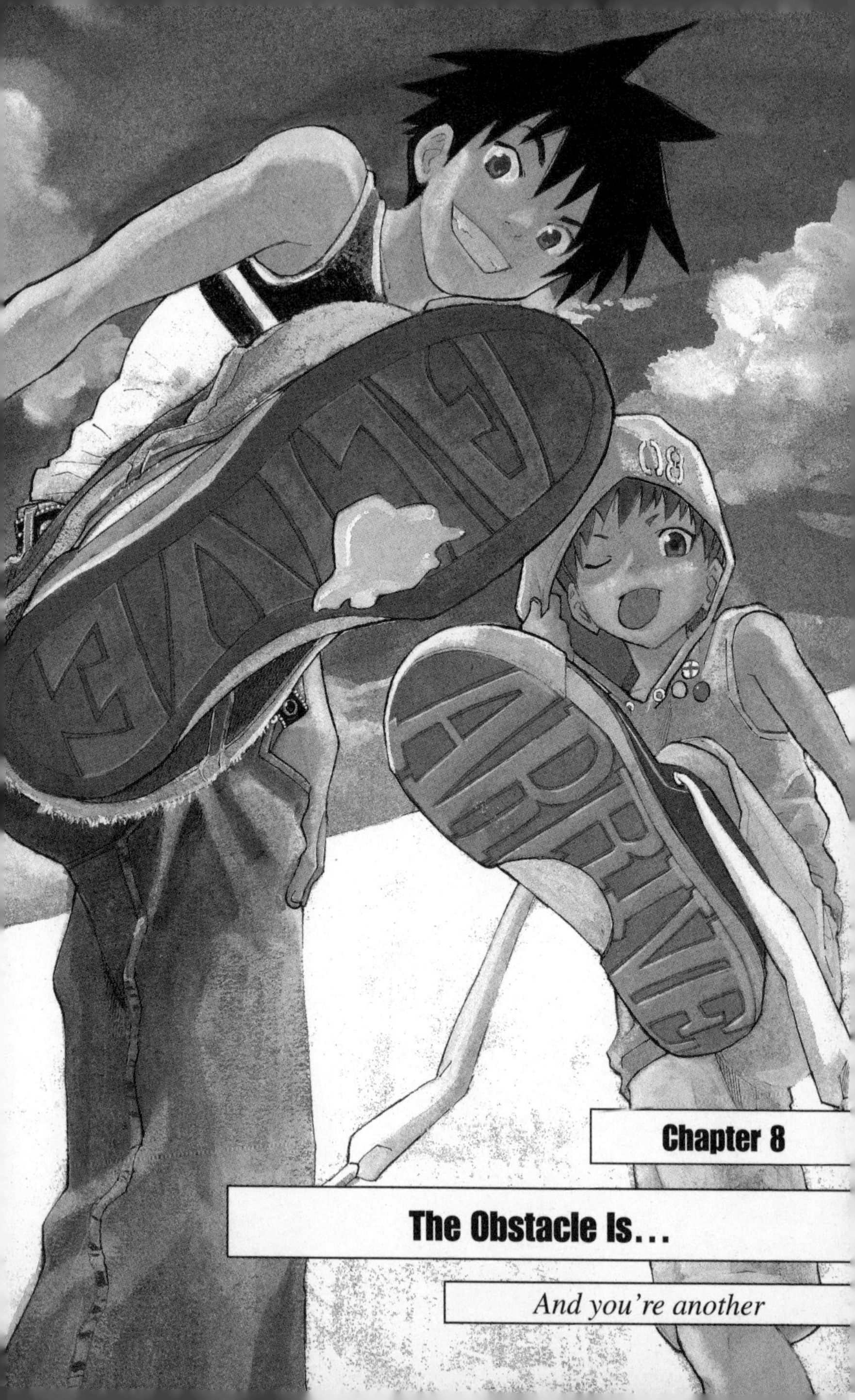
Chapter 8
The Obstacle Is...
And you're another

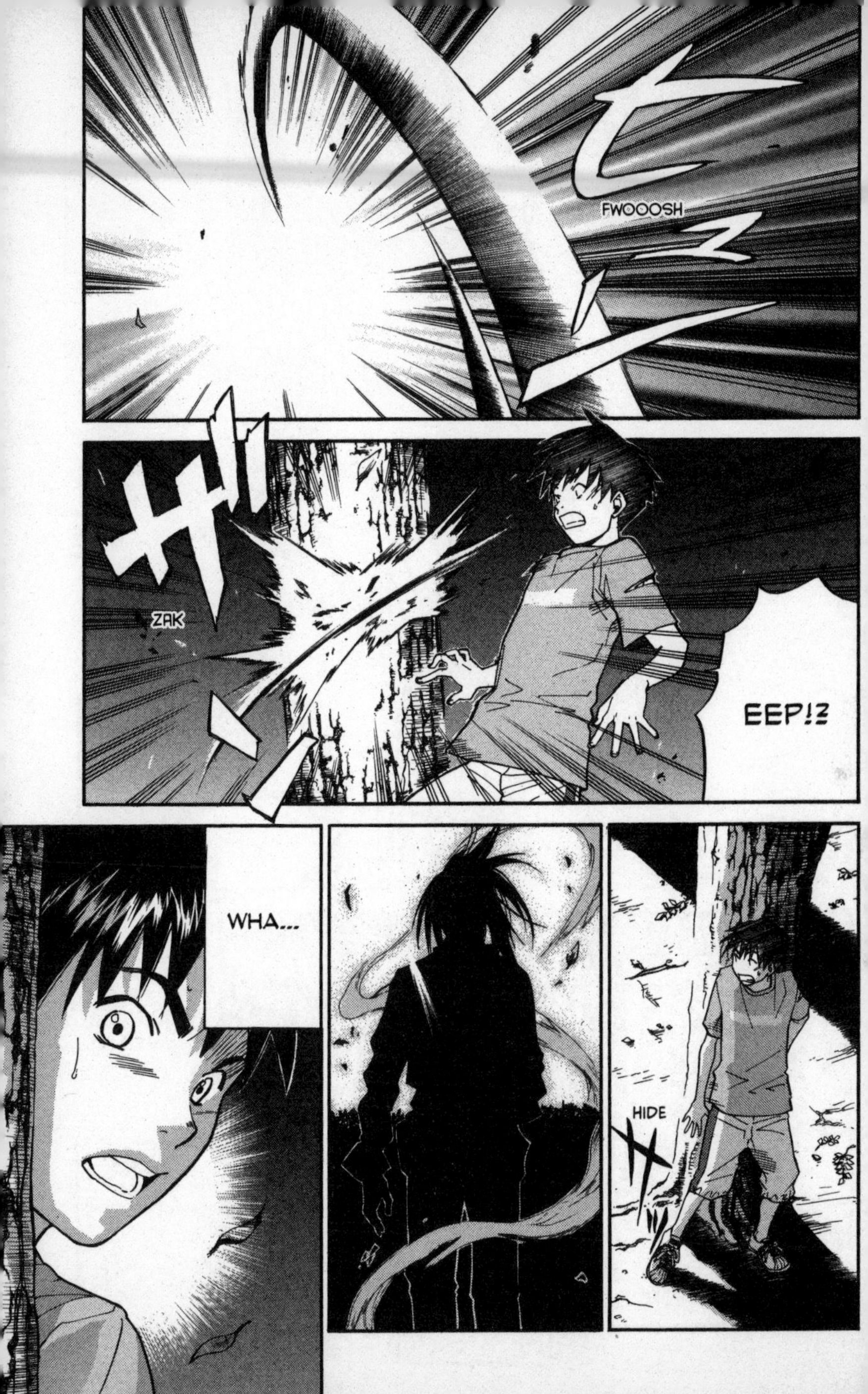
FWOOOSH
ZAK
EEP!?
HIDE
WHA...

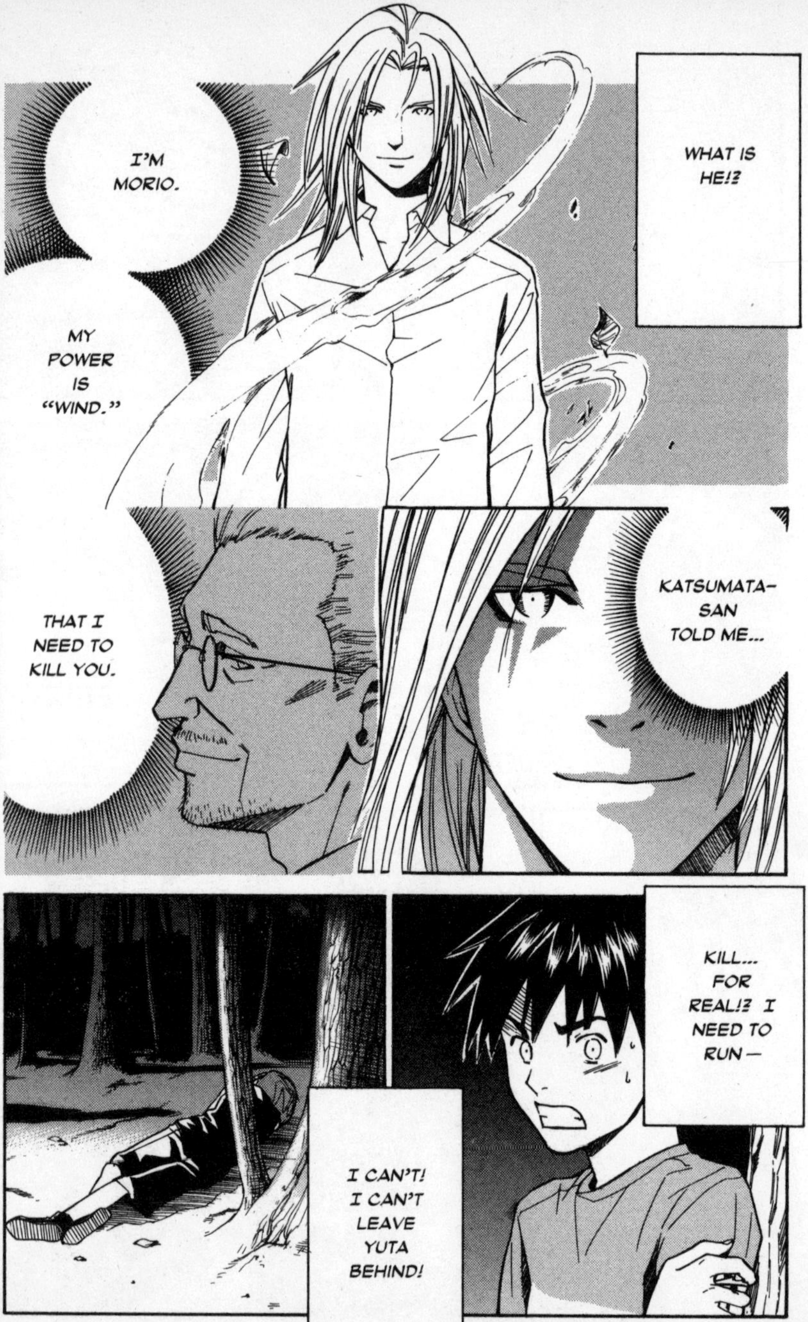
WHAT IS HE!?
I'M MORIO.
MY POWER IS "WIND."
KATSUMATA-SAN TOLD ME...
THAT I NEED TO KILL YOU.
KILL... FOR REAL!? I NEED TO RUN—
I CAN'T! I CAN'T LEAVE YUTA BEHIND!

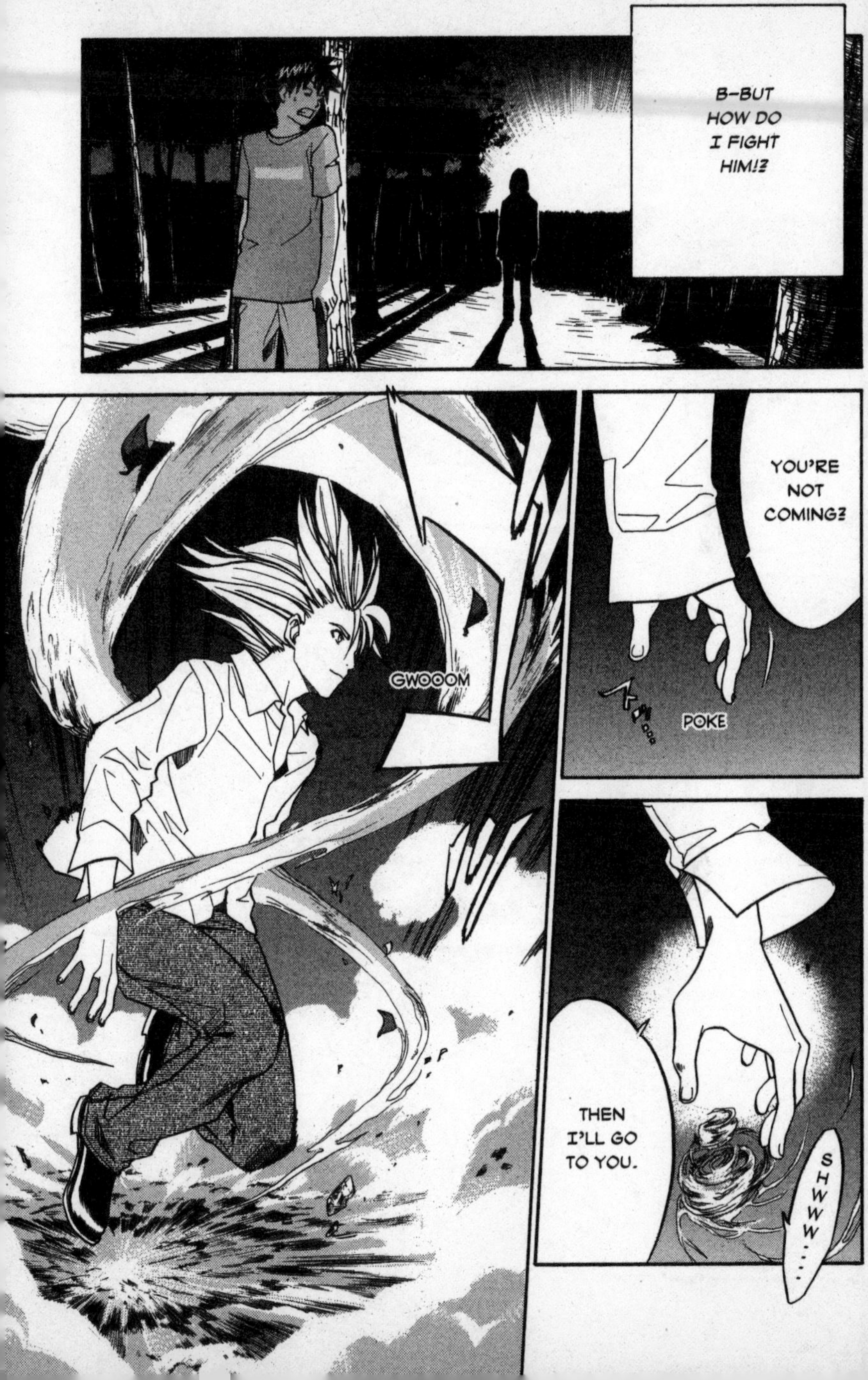
B–BUT HOW DO I FIGHT HIM!?
YOU'RE NOT COMING?
POKE
THEN I'LL GO TO YOU.
SHWWW....
GWOOOM

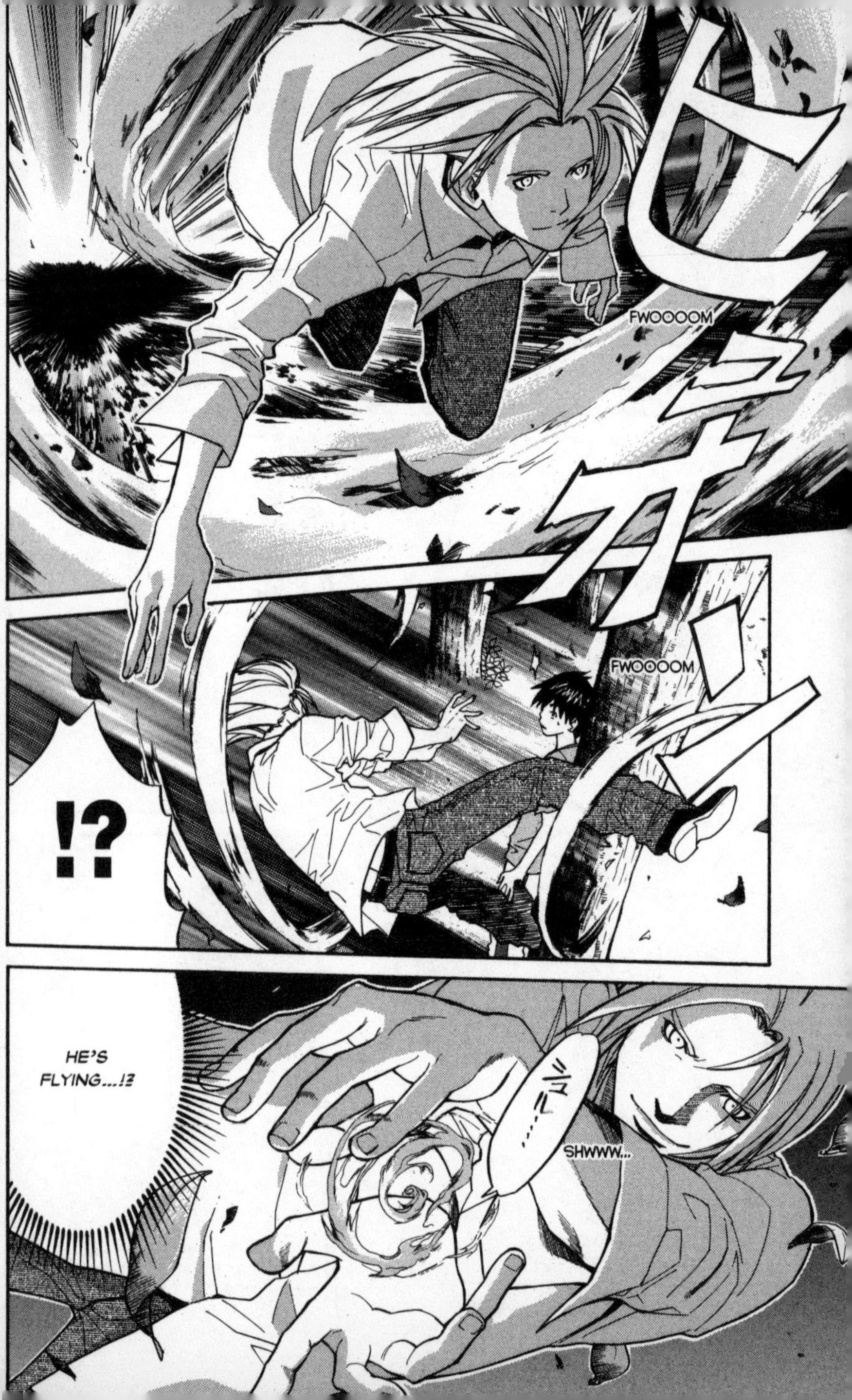
FWOOOOM
FWOOOOM
!?
SHWWW...
HE'S FLYING...!?

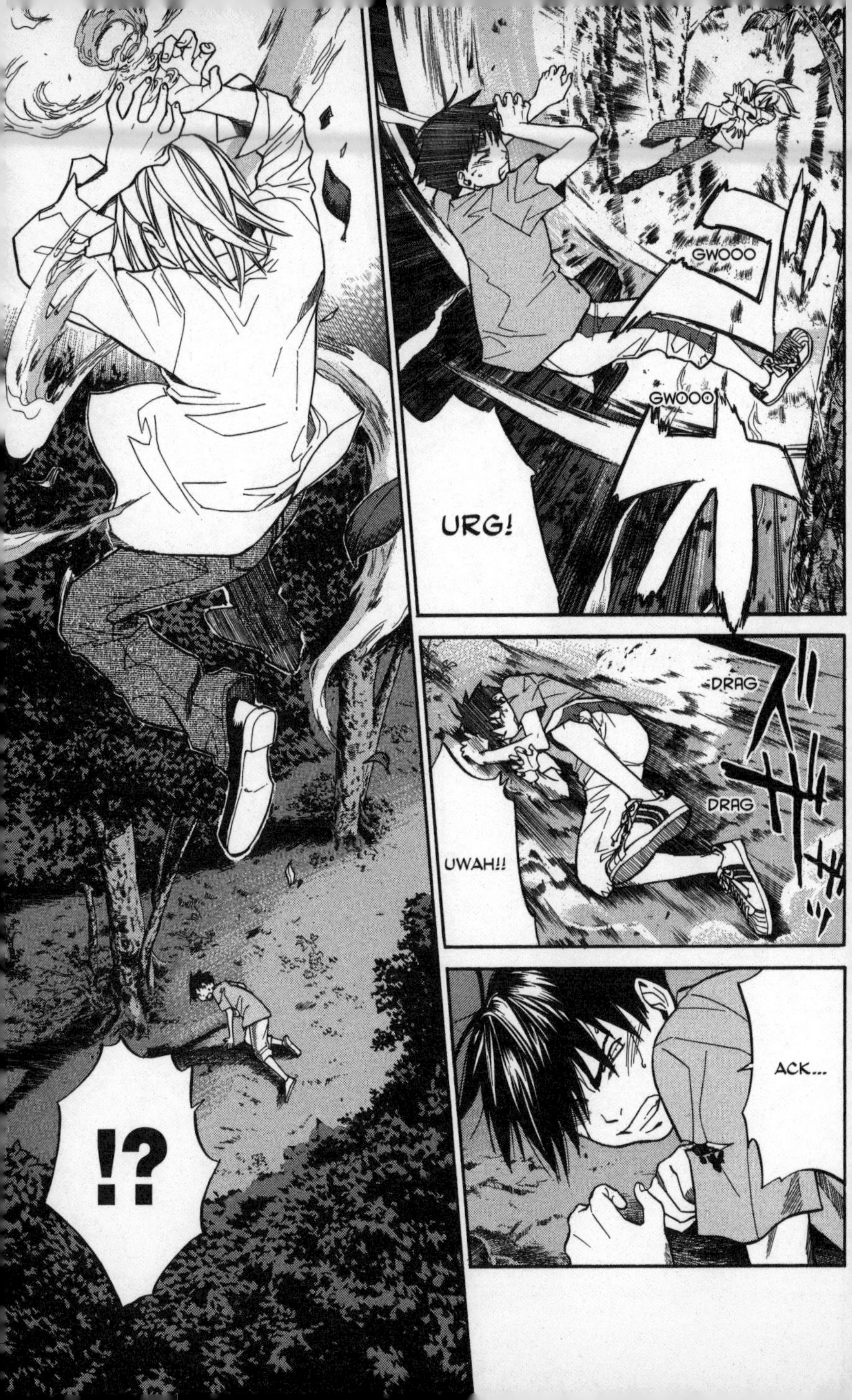
GWOOO
GWOOO
URG!
DRAG
DRAG
UWAH!!
ACK...
!?

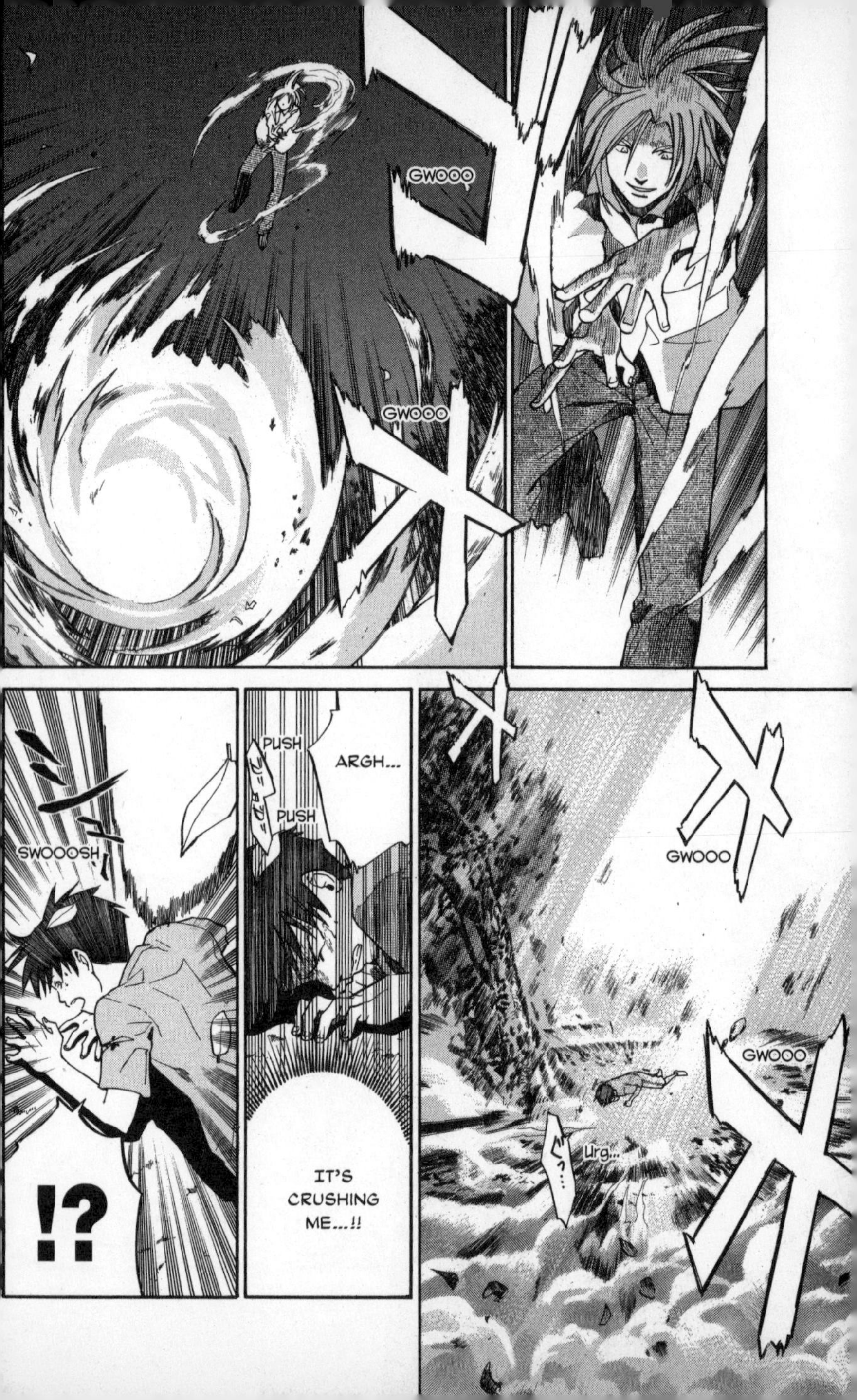
GWOOO
GWOOO
GWOOO
GWOOO
Urg...
ARGH...
PUSH
PUSH
IT'S CRUSHING ME...!!
SWOOOSH
!?

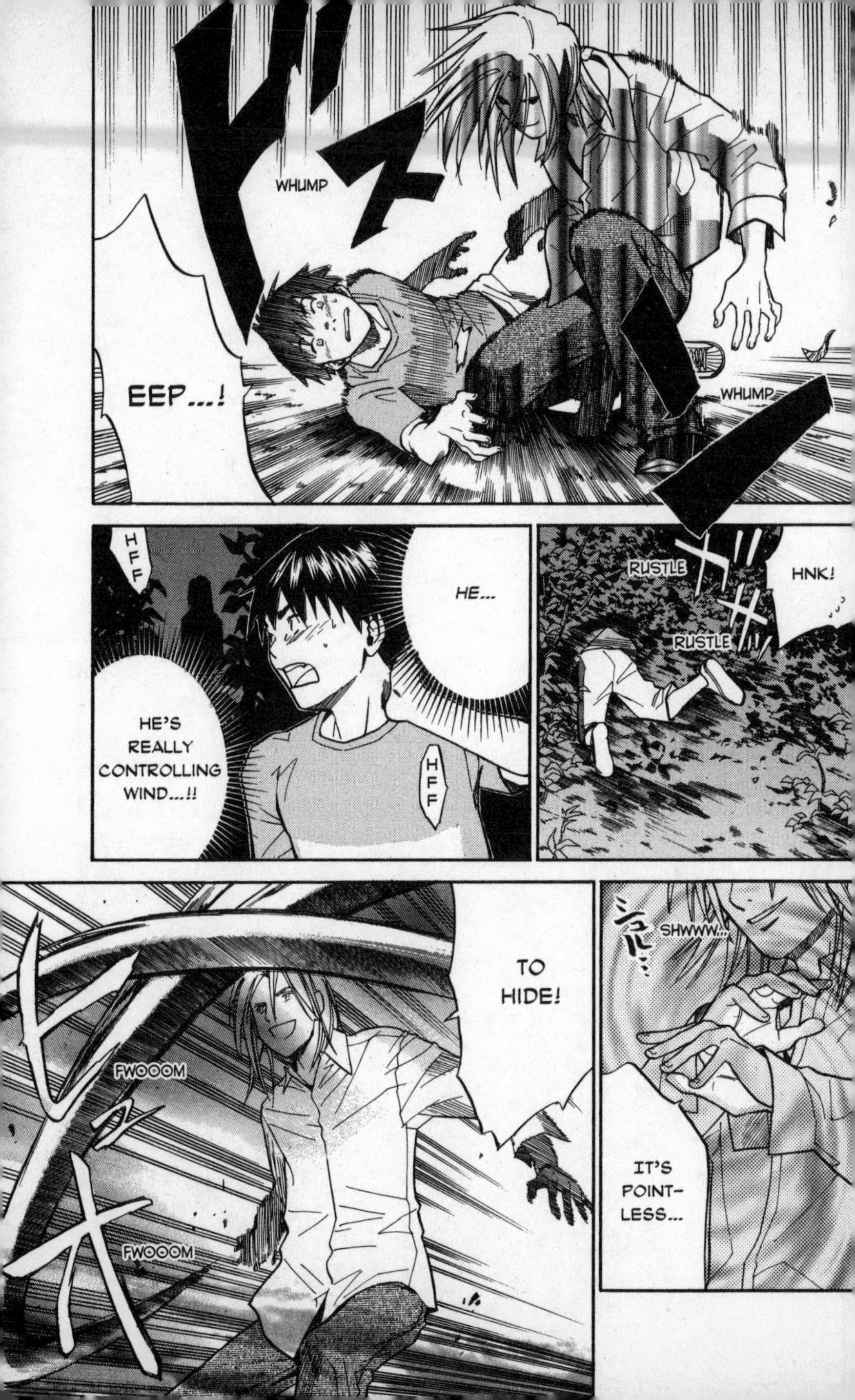
WHUMP
WHUMP
EEP...!
HNK!
RUSTLE
RUSTLE
HE...
HFF
HE'S REALLY CONTROLLING WIND...!!
HFF
SHWWW...
IT'S POINT-LESS...
TO HIDE!
FWOOOM
FWOOOM

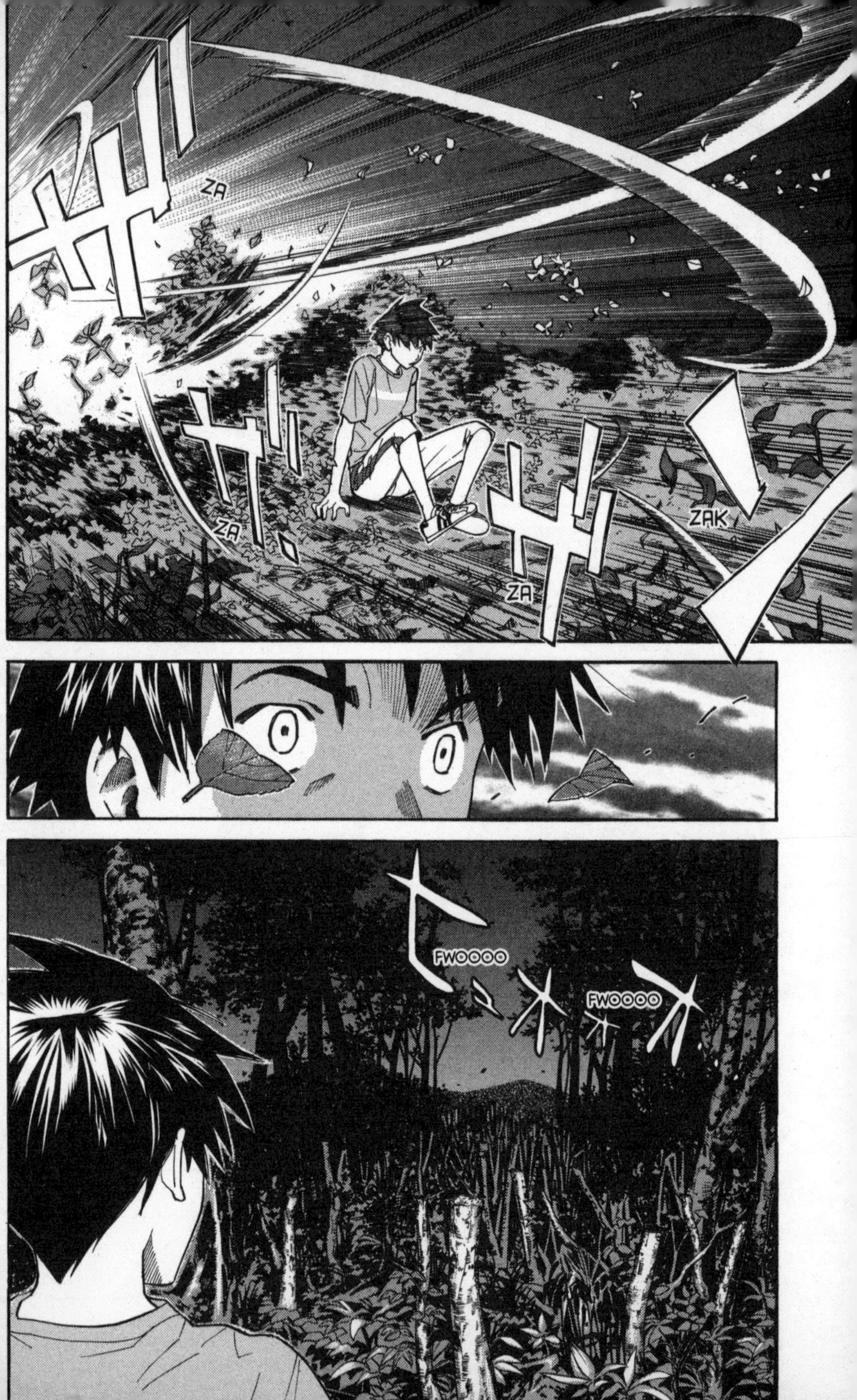
ZAK
ZA
ZA
ZA
FWOOOO
FWOOOO

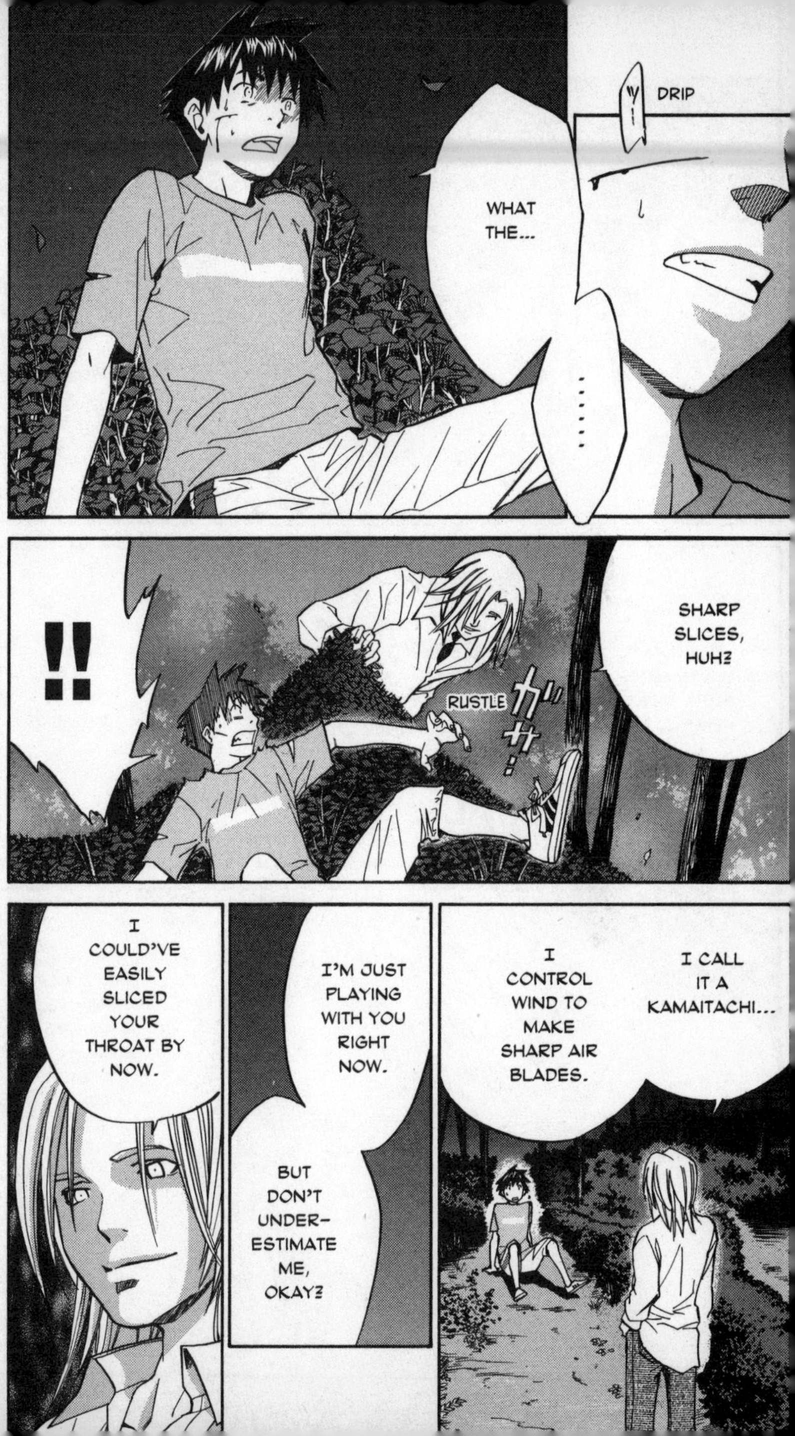
DRIP
WHAT THE...
......
SHARP SLICES, HUH?
RUSTLE
!!
I CALL IT A KAMAITACHI...
I CONTROL WIND TO MAKE SHARP AIR BLADES.
I'M JUST PLAYING WITH YOU RIGHT NOW.
BUT DON'T UNDER-ESTIMATE ME, OKAY?
I COULD'VE EASILY SLICED YOUR THROAT BY NOW.

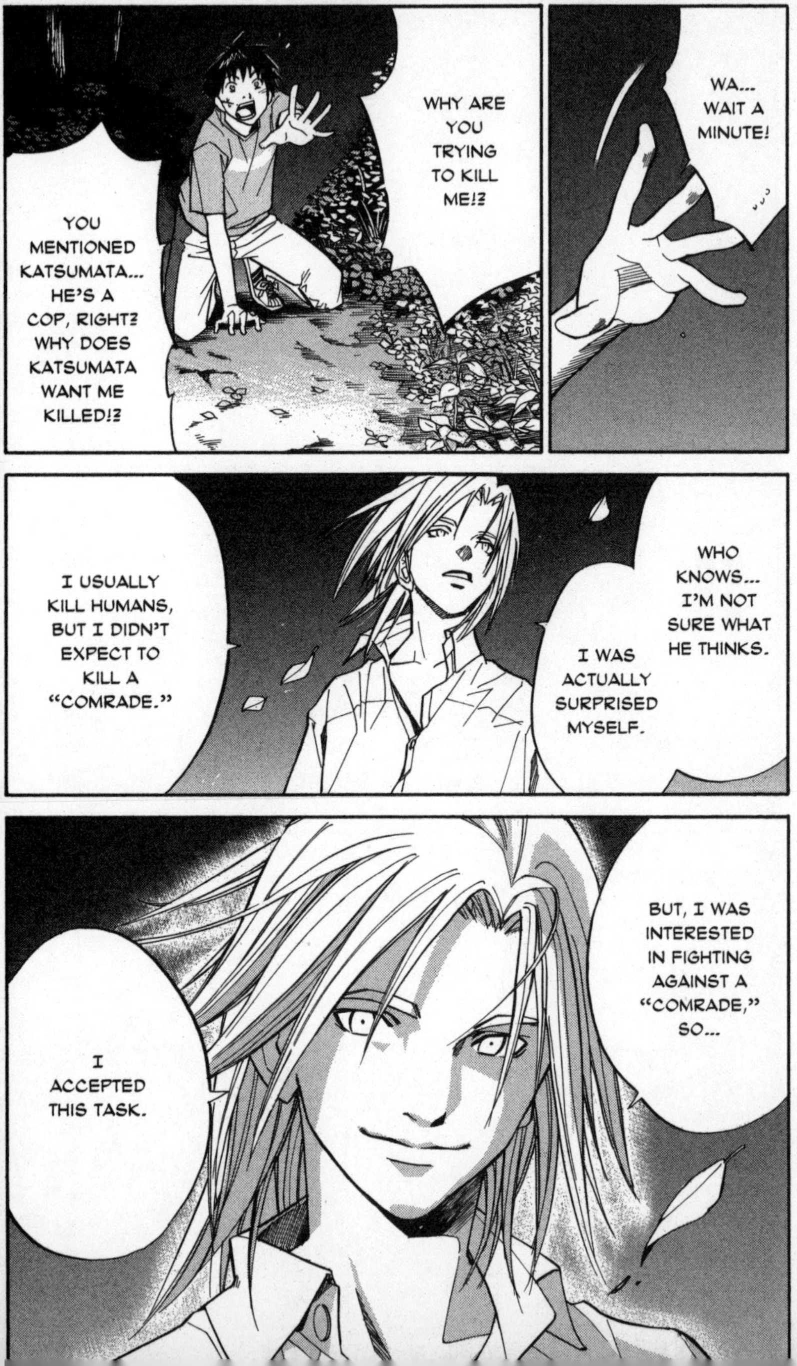
WA... WAIT A MINUTE!
WHY ARE YOU TRYING TO KILL ME!?
YOU MENTIONED KATSUMATA... HE'S A COP, RIGHT? WHY DOES KATSUMATA WANT ME KILLED!?
WHO KNOWS... I'M NOT SURE WHAT HE THINKS.
I WAS ACTUALLY SURPRISED MYSELF.
I USUALLY KILL HUMANS, BUT I DIDN'T EXPECT TO KILL A "COMRADE."
BUT, I WAS INTERESTED IN FIGHTING AGAINST A "COMRADE," SO...
I ACCEPTED THIS TASK.

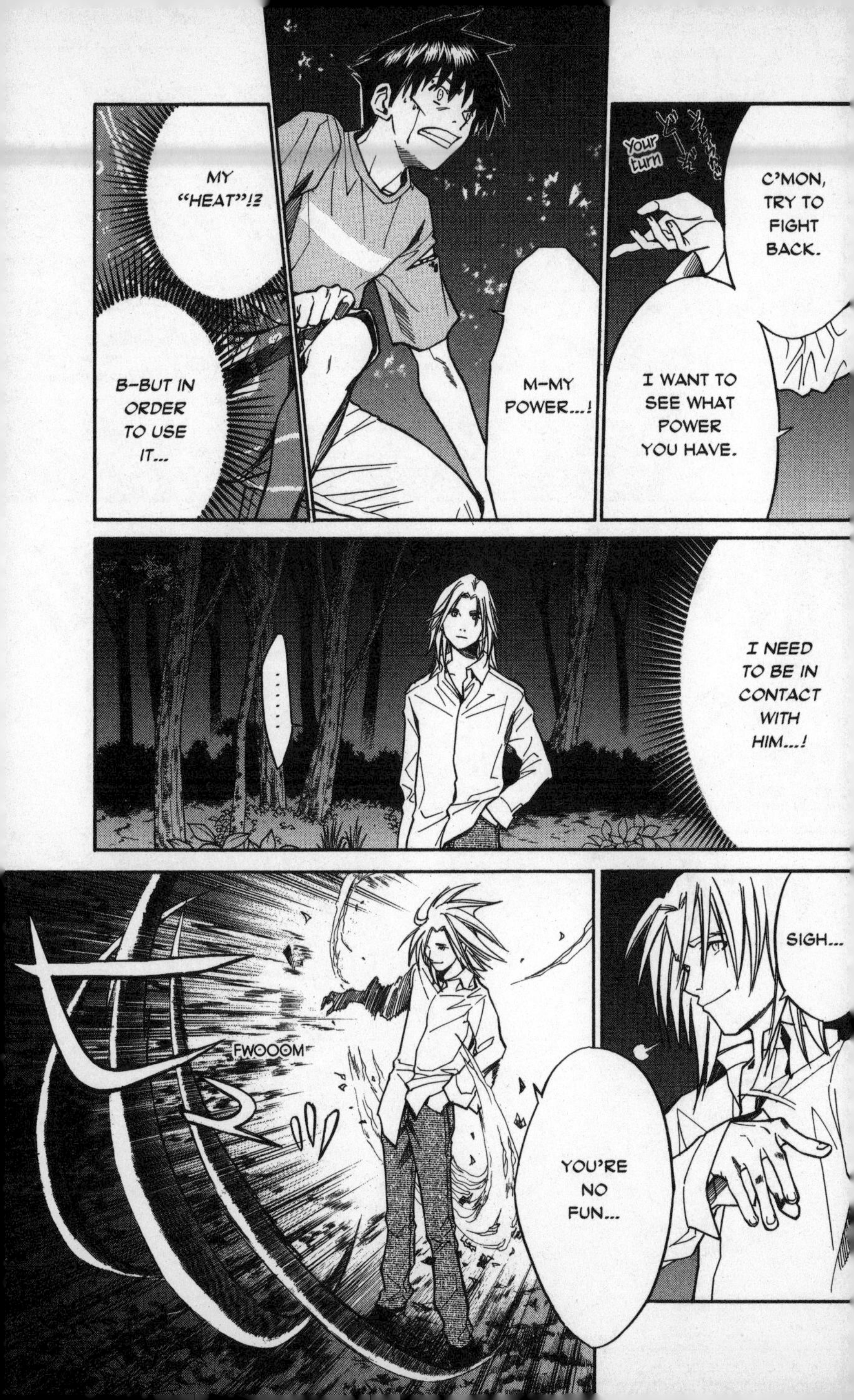
Your turn
C'MON, TRY TO FIGHT BACK.
I WANT TO SEE WHAT POWER YOU HAVE.
M-MY POWER...!
MY "HEAT"!?
B-BUT IN ORDER TO USE IT...
I NEED TO BE IN CONTACT WITH HIM...!
......
SIGH...
YOU'RE NO FUN...
FWOOOM

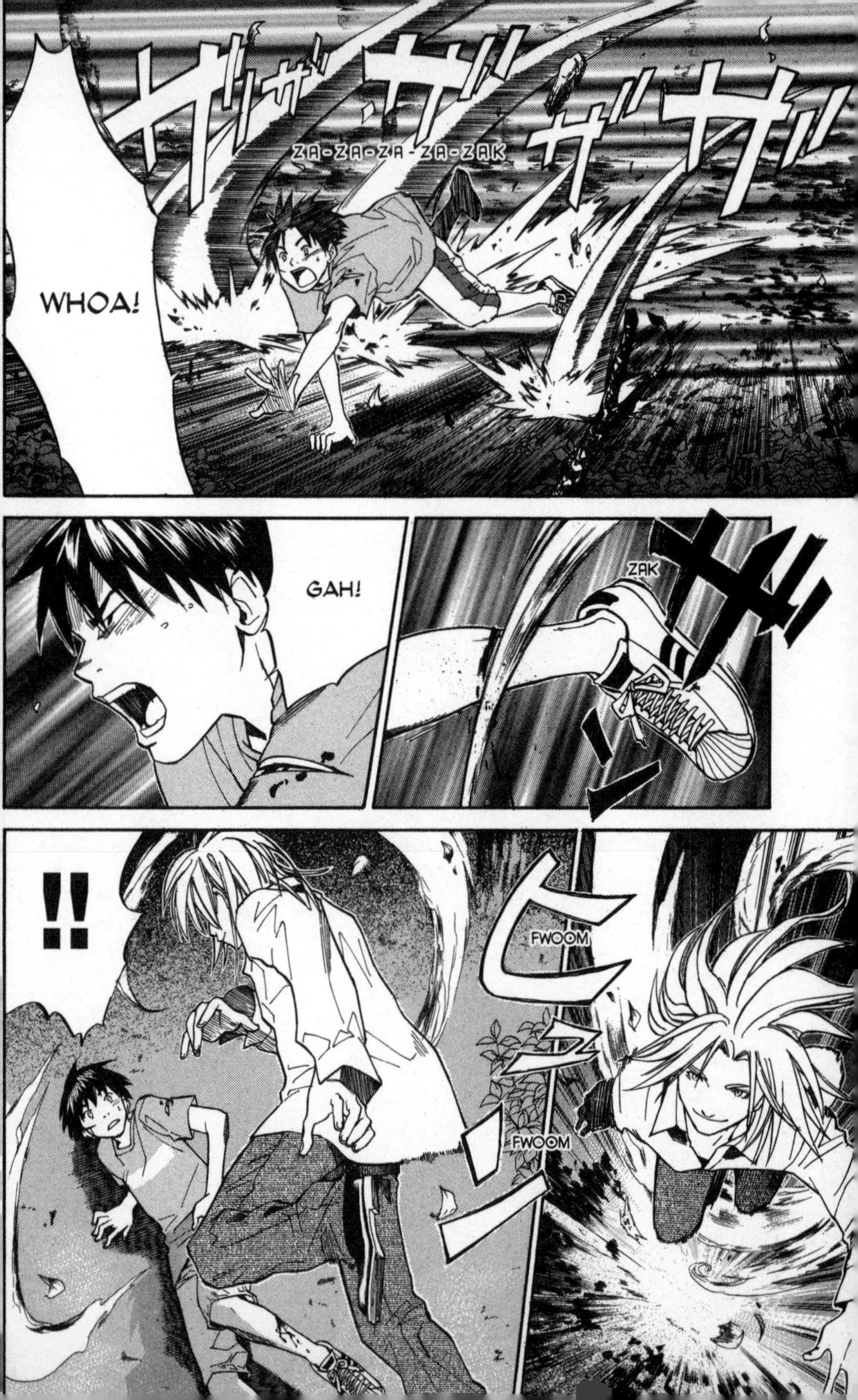
ZA-ZA-ZA-ZA-ZAK
WHOA!
ZAK
GAH!
FWOOM
FWOOM
!!

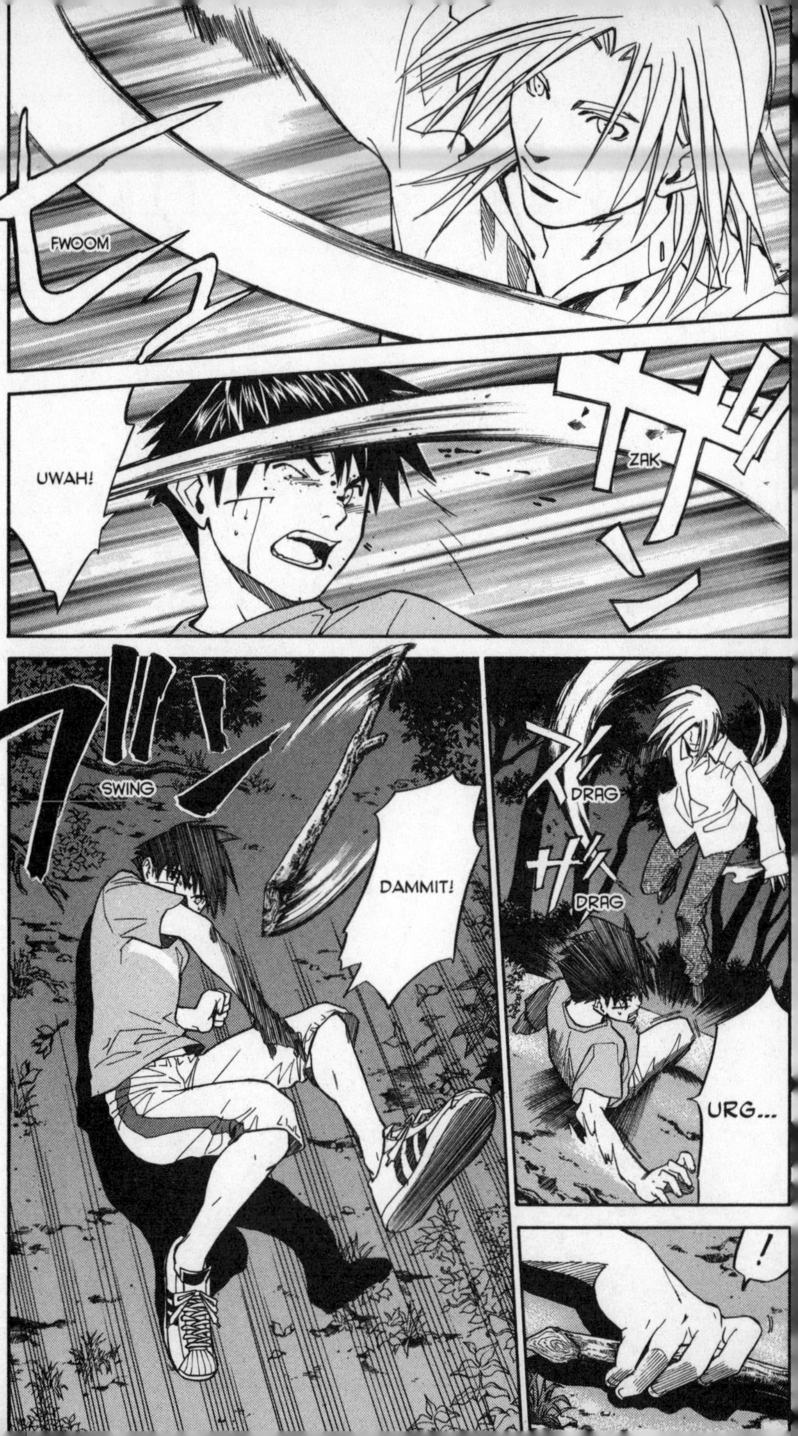
FWOOM
ZAK
UWAH!
SWING
DAMMIT!
DRAG
DRAG
URG...
!

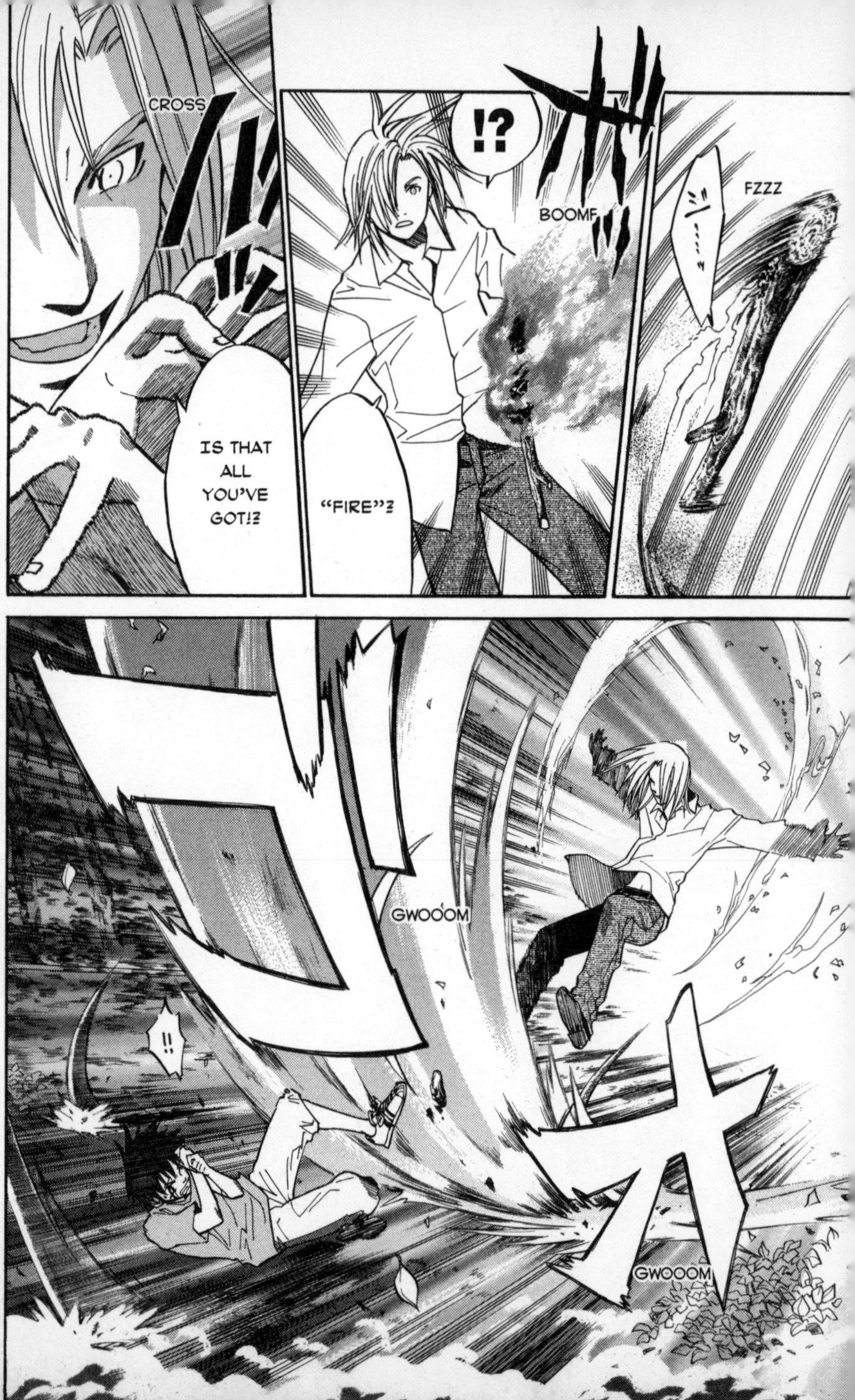
FZZZ
!?
BOOMF
"FIRE"?
CROSS
IS THAT ALL YOU'VE GOT!?
GWOOOM
!!
GWOOOM

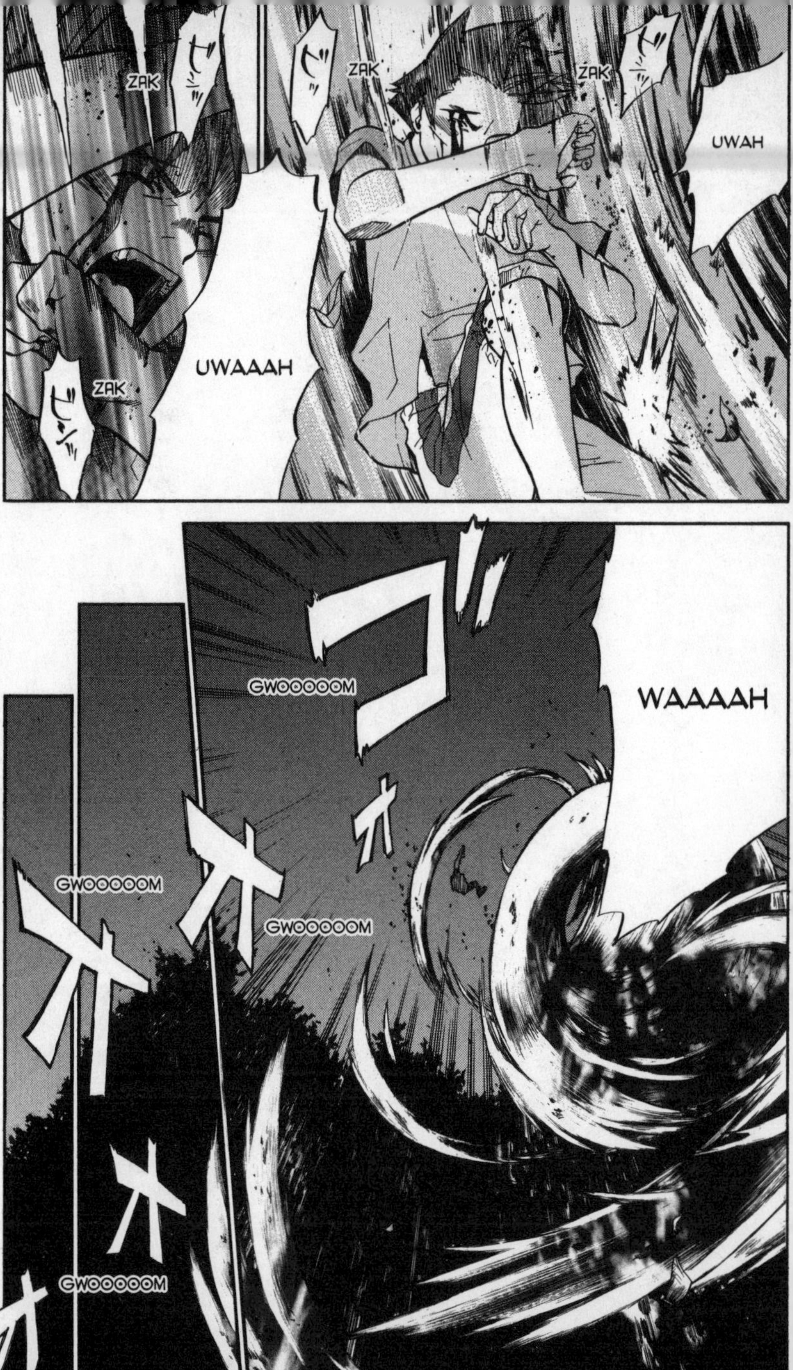
UWAH
ZAK
ZAK
ZAK
UWAAAH
ZAK
WAAAAH
GWOOOOOM
GWOOOOOM
GWOOOOOM
GWOOOOOM

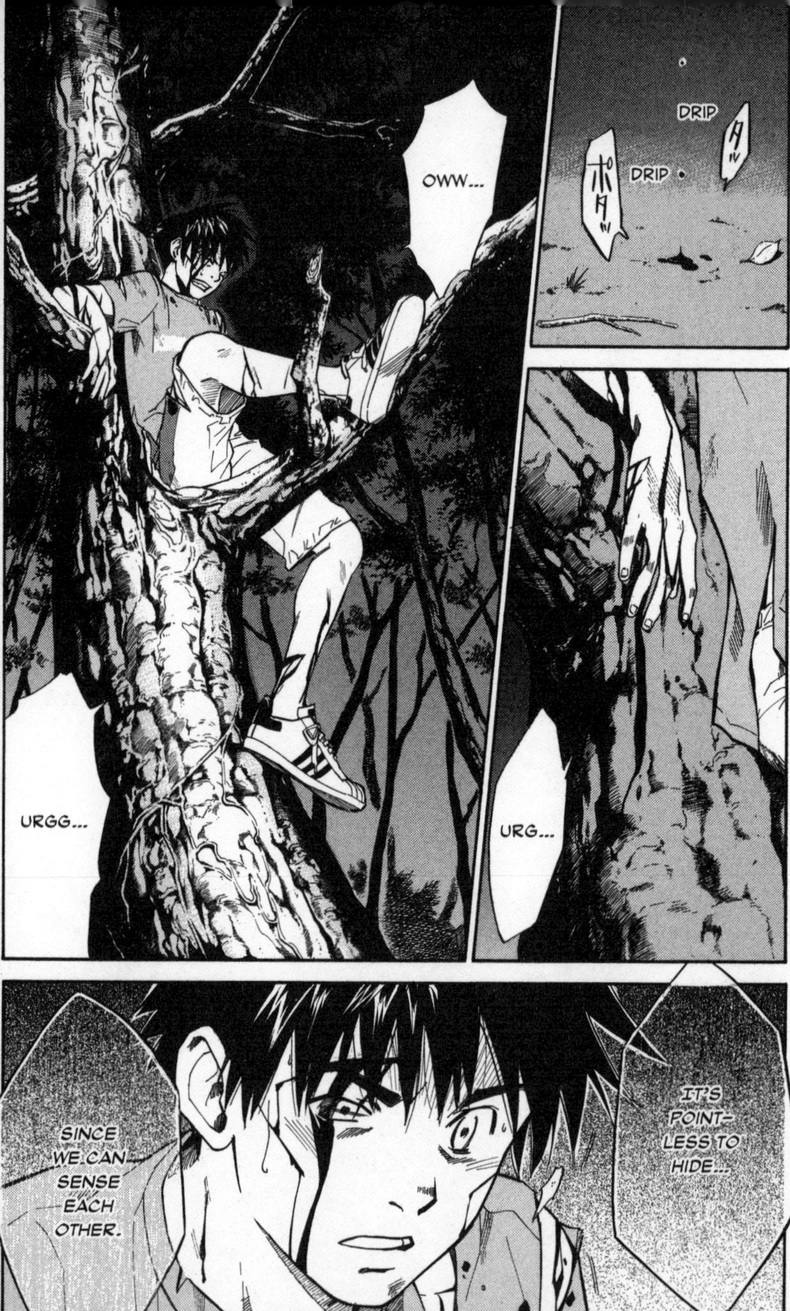
DRIP
DRIP
URG...
OWW...
URGG...
IT'S POINTLESS TO HIDE...
SINCE WE CAN SENSE EACH OTHER.

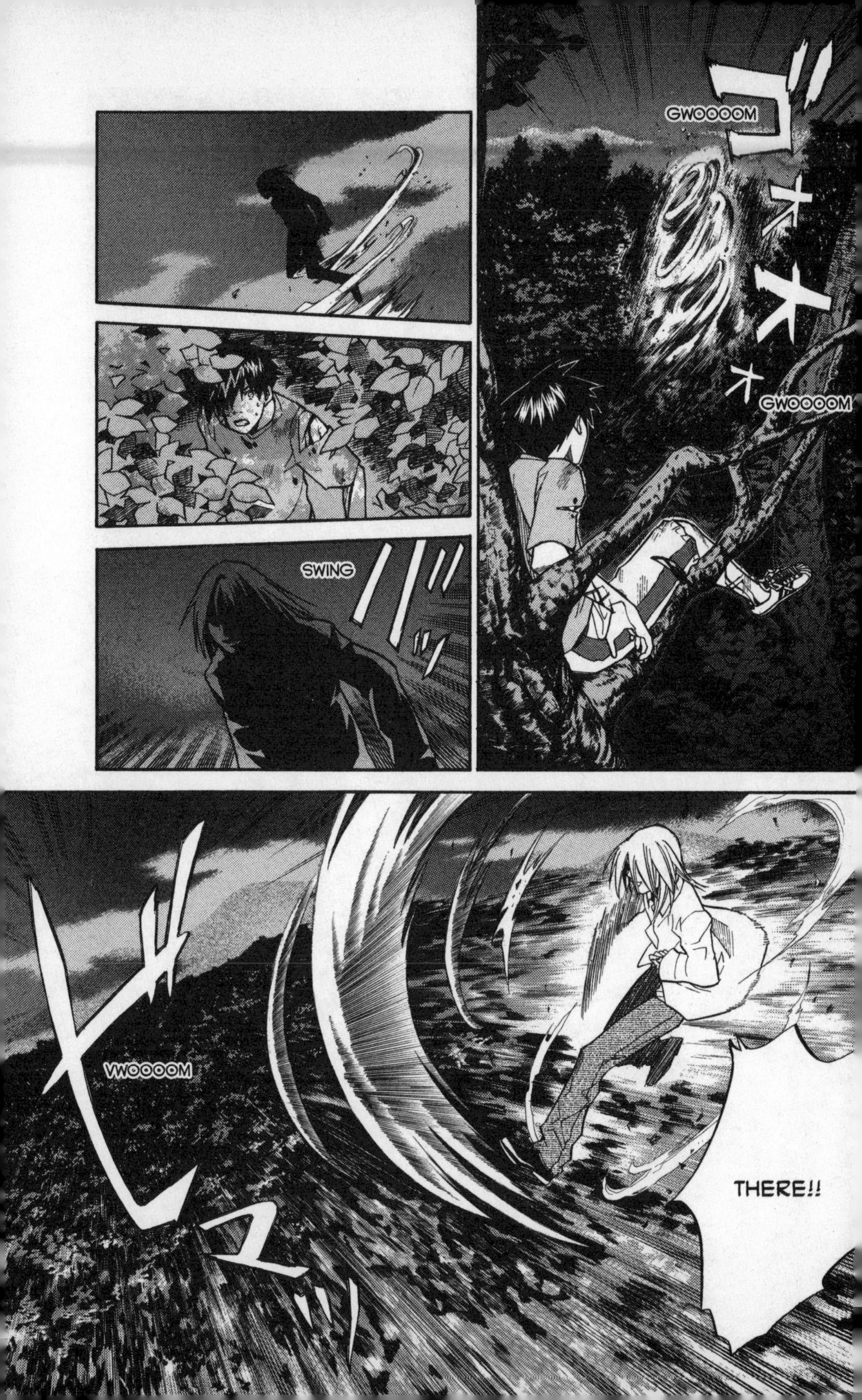
GWOOOOM
GWOOOOM
SWING
THERE!!
VWOOOOM

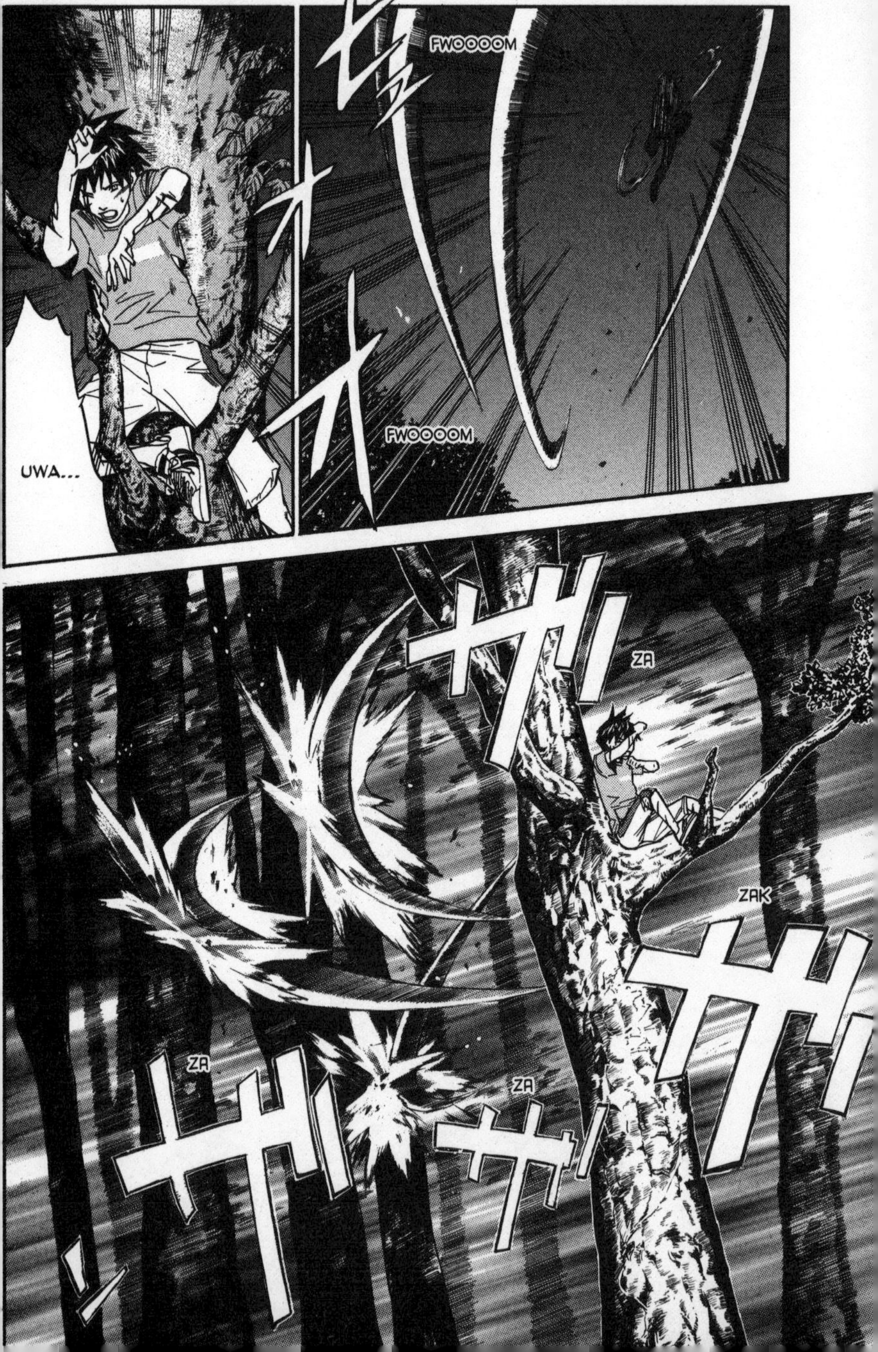
FWOOOOM
FWOOOOM
UWA...
ZA
ZAK
ZA
ZA

WAAAAAA

CRACK

AAAAAAAAH

CRACK!

!?

AH...

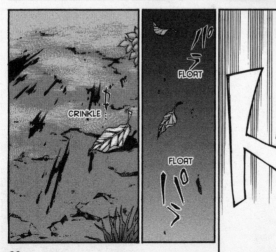

CRINKLE

FLOAT

FLOAT

WHUMP

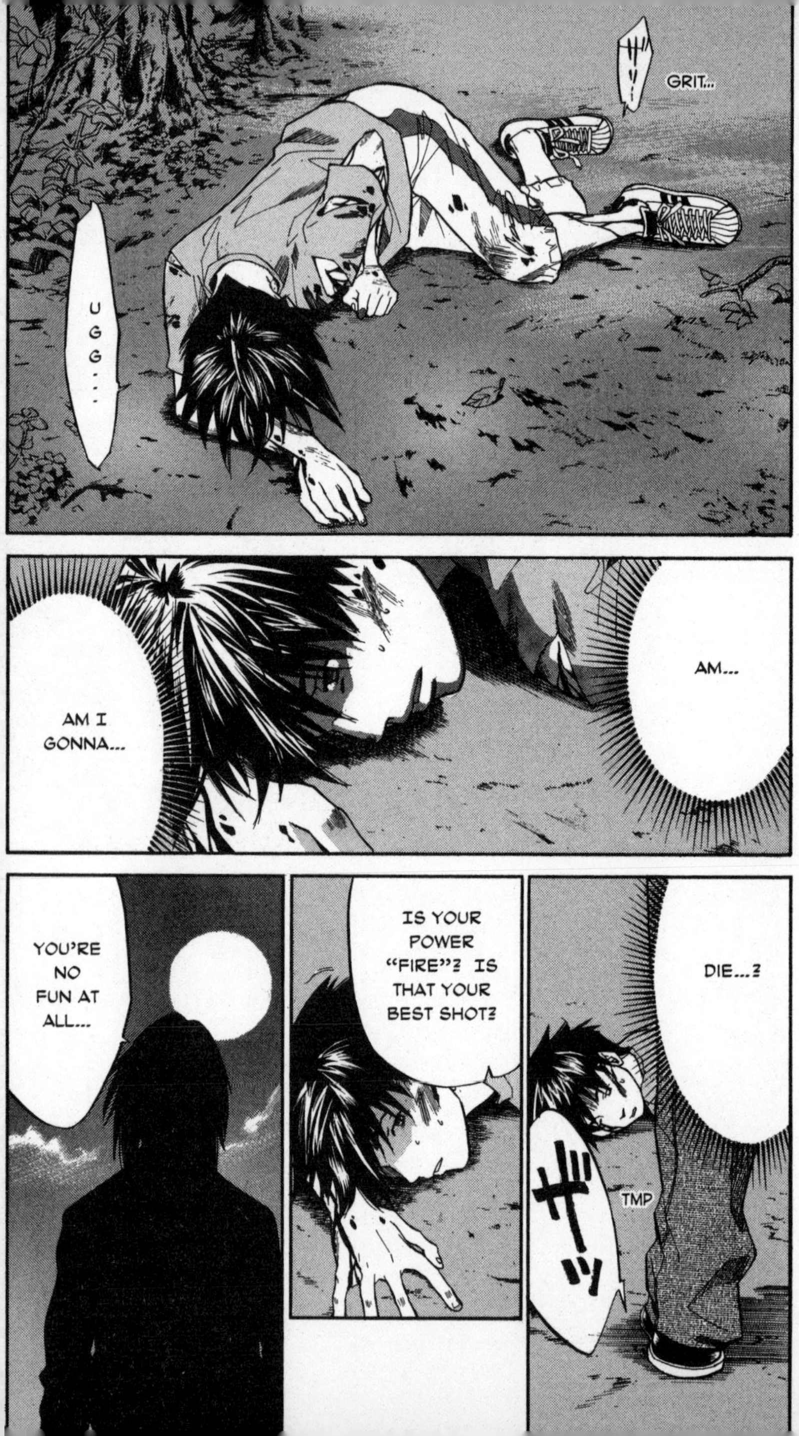

GRIT...
UGG...
AM...
AM I GONNA...
DIE...?
ザッ
TMP
IS YOUR POWER "FIRE"? IS THAT YOUR BEST SHOT?
YOU'RE NO FUN AT ALL...

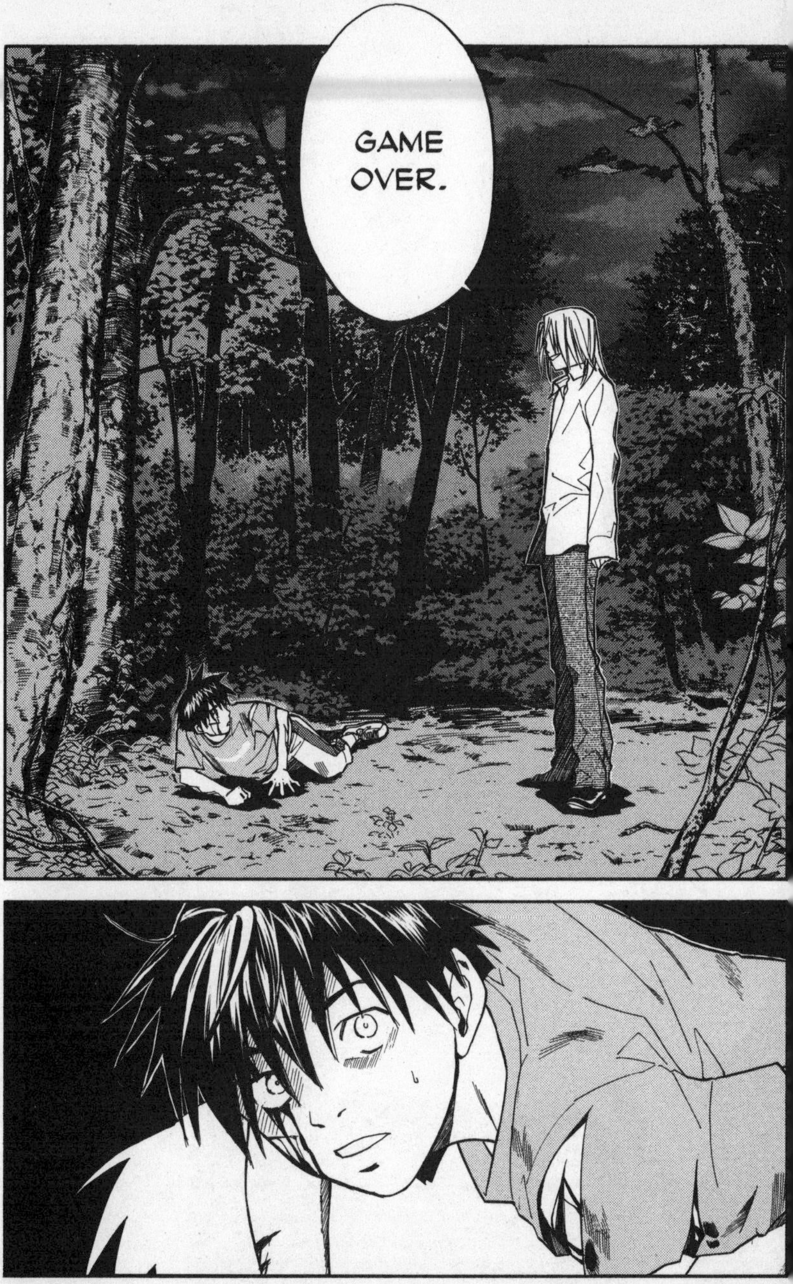
GAME OVER.

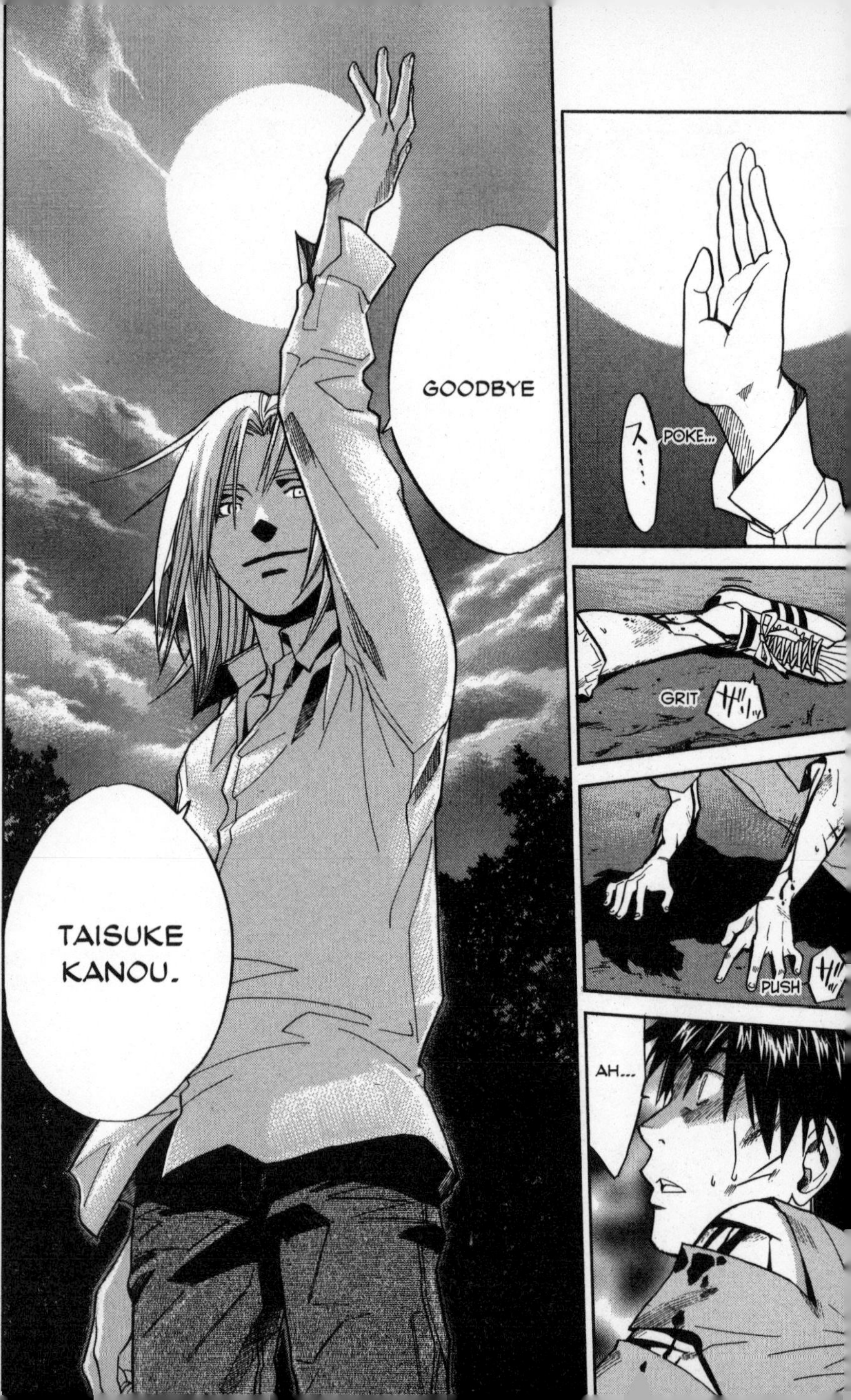

ス…
POKE...
GRIT
ザリッ
PUSH
AH...
GOODBYE
TAISUKE KANOU.

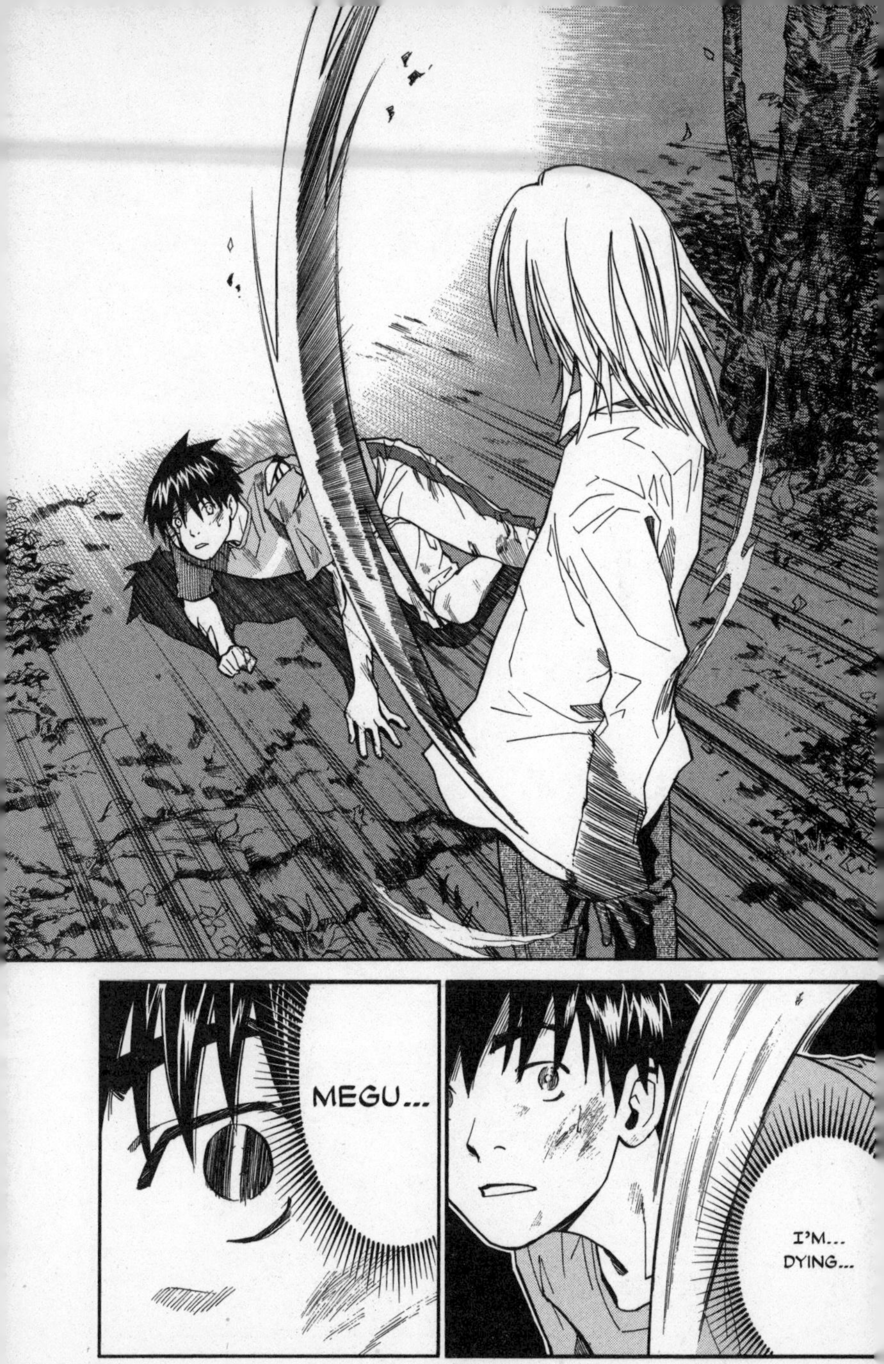
I'M... DYING...
MEGU...

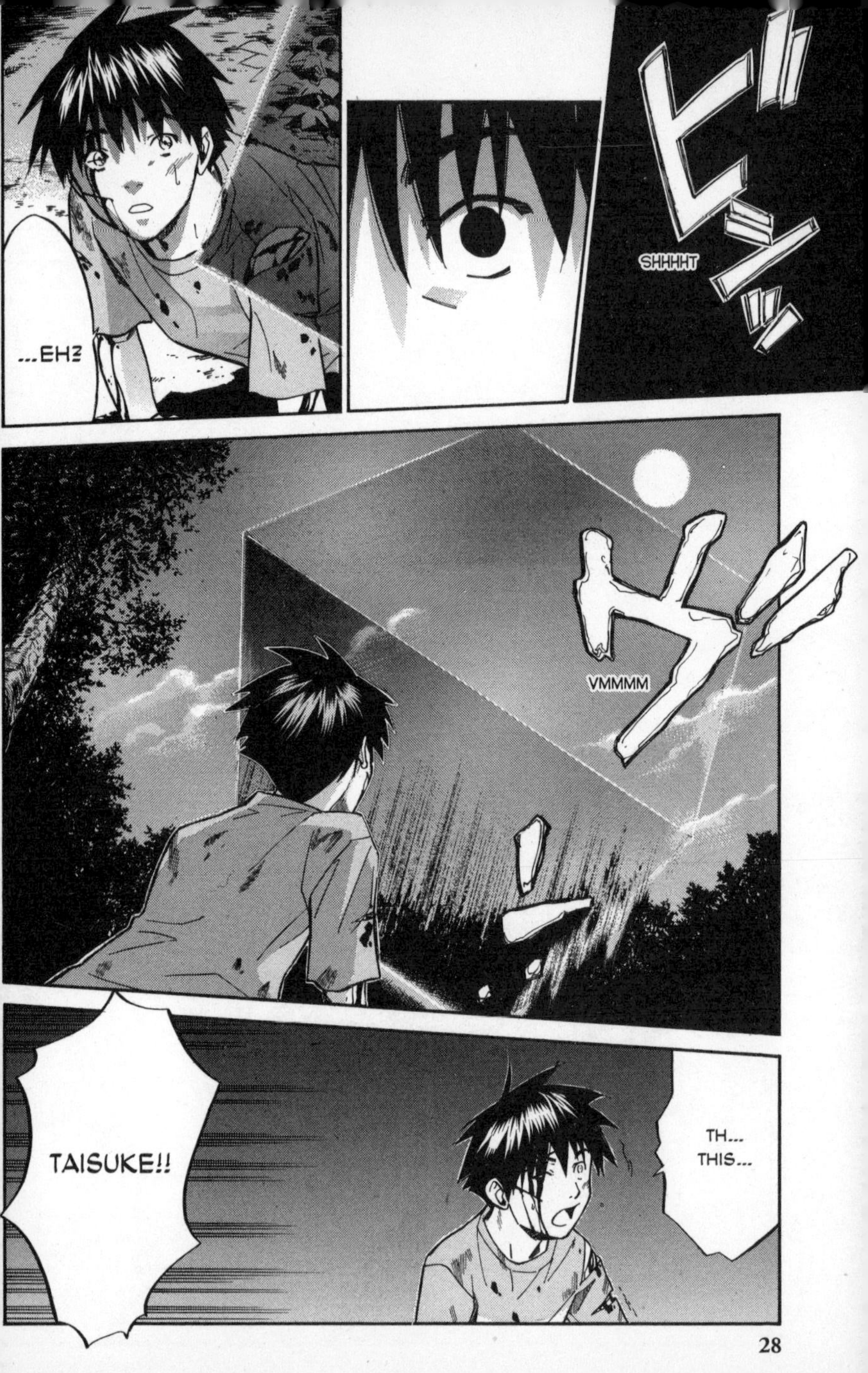
SHHHHT
...EH?
VMMMM
TH... THIS...
TAISUKE!!

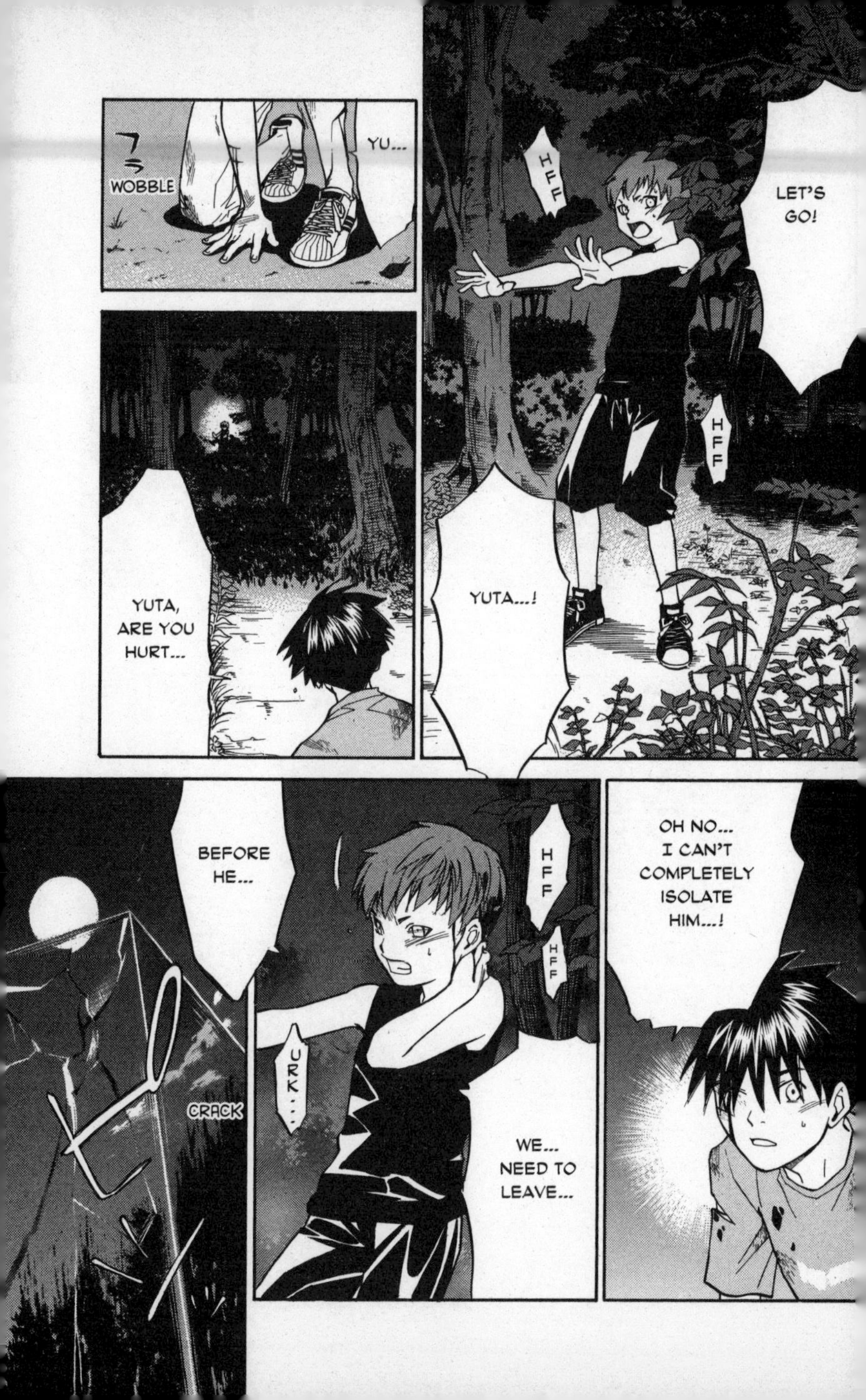

LET'S GO!
HFF
HFF
YUTA...!
YU...
WOBBLE
YUTA, ARE YOU HURT...
OH NO... I CAN'T COMPLETELY ISOLATE HIM...!
HFF
HFF
BEFORE HE...
URK...
WE... NEED TO LEAVE...
CRACK

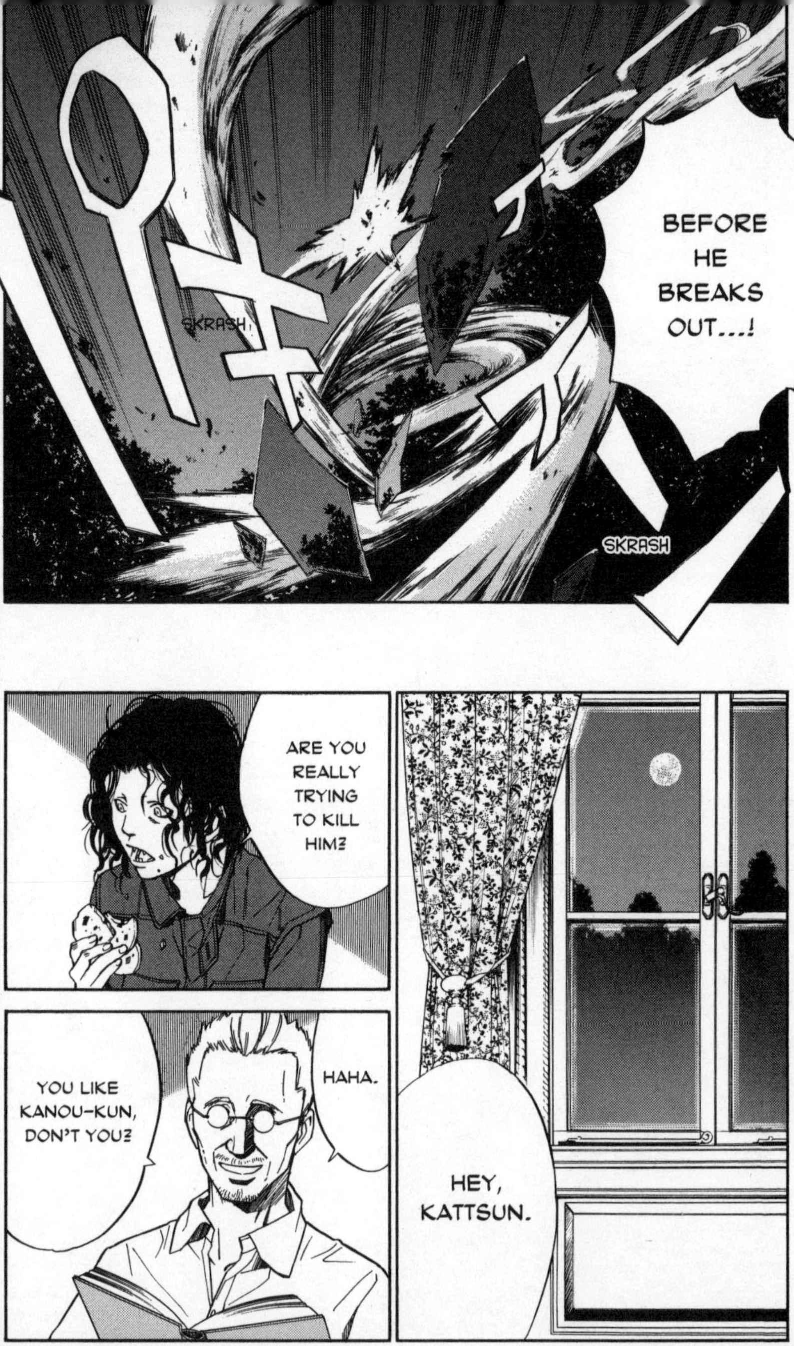
BEFORE HE BREAKS OUT...!
SKRASH
SKRASH
HEY, KATTSUN.
ARE YOU REALLY TRYING TO KILL HIM?
HAHA.
YOU LIKE KANOU-KUN, DON'T YOU?

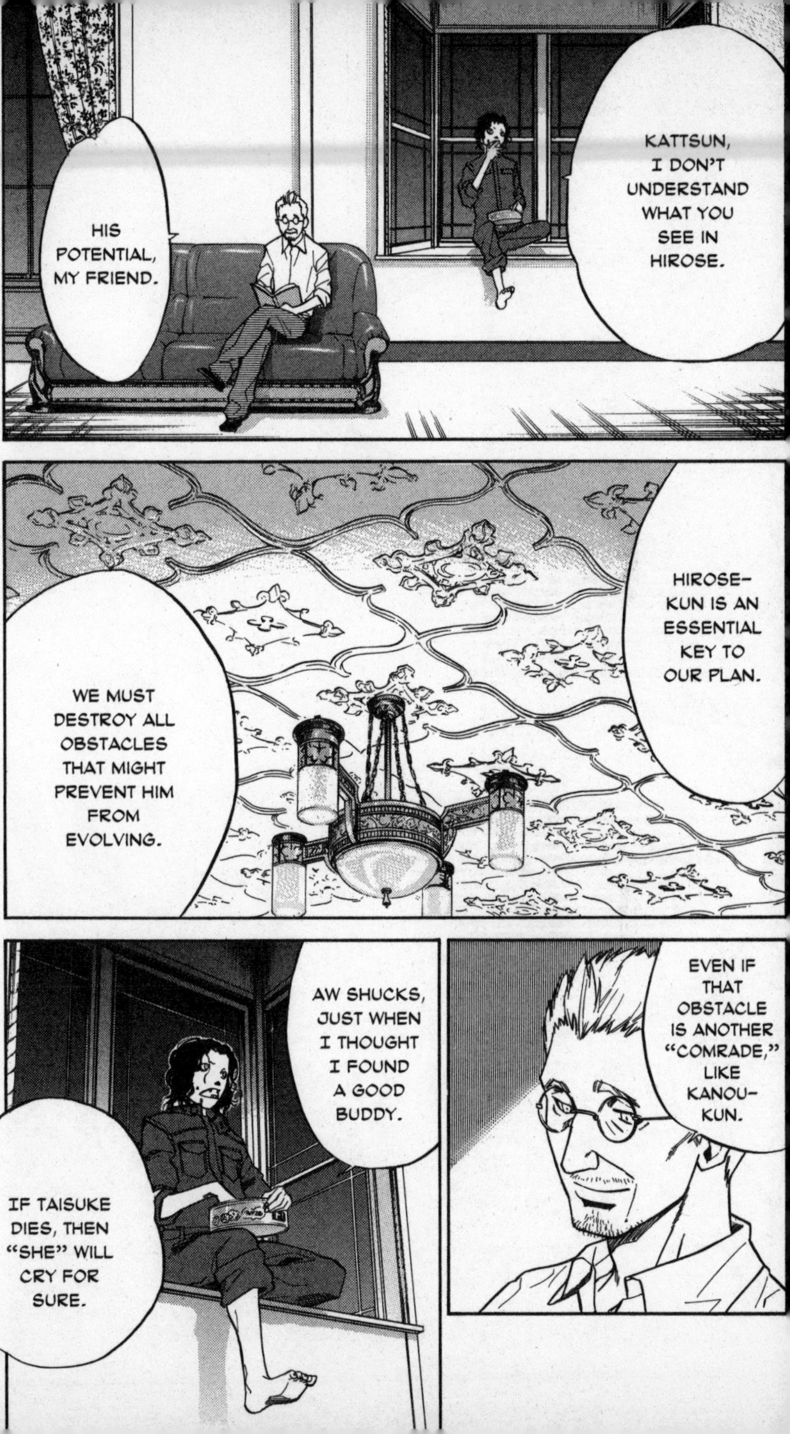
KATTSUN, I DON'T UNDERSTAND WHAT YOU SEE IN HIROSE.
HIS POTENTIAL, MY FRIEND.
HIROSE-KUN IS AN ESSENTIAL KEY TO OUR PLAN.
WE MUST DESTROY ALL OBSTACLES THAT MIGHT PREVENT HIM FROM EVOLVING.
EVEN IF THAT OBSTACLE IS ANOTHER "COMRADE," LIKE KANOU-KUN.
AW SHUCKS, JUST WHEN I THOUGHT I FOUND A GOOD BUDDY.
IF TAISUKE DIES, THEN "SHE" WILL CRY FOR SURE.

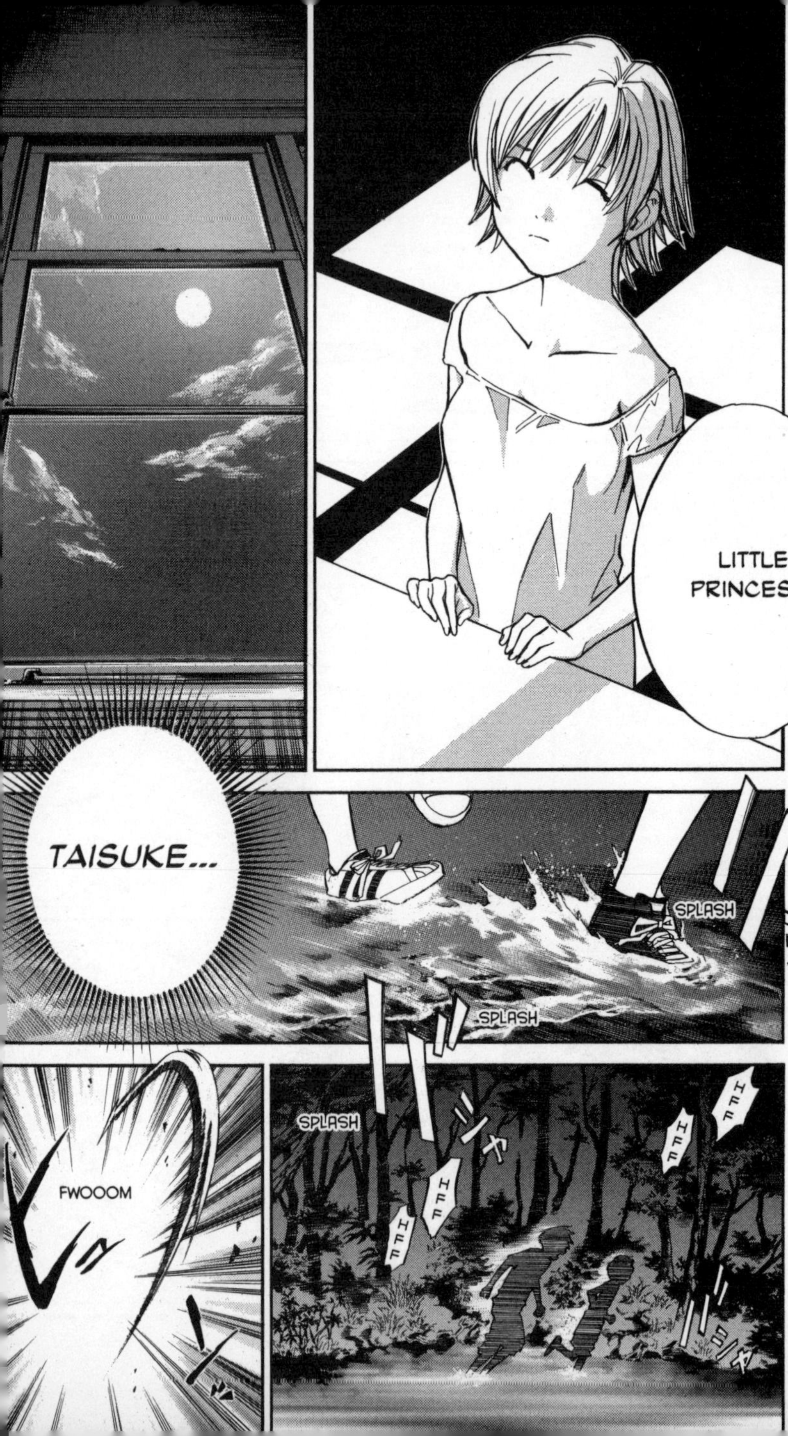
LITTLE PRINCESS!
TAISUKE...
SPLASH
SPLASH
HFF HFF
HFF HFF
SPLASH
HFF HFF
FWOOOM

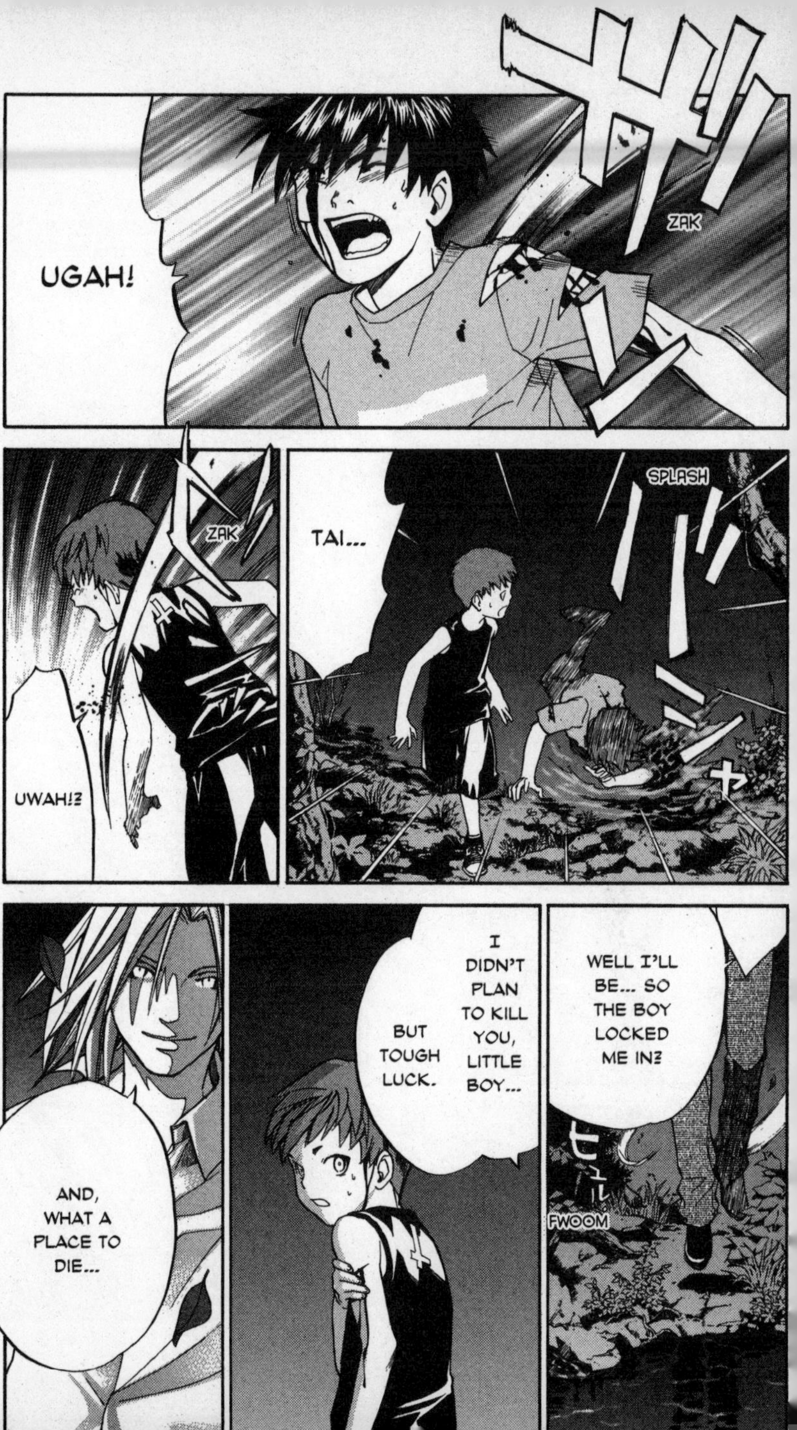
ZAK
UGAH!
SPLASH
TAI...
ZAK
UWAH!?
WELL I'LL BE... SO THE BOY LOCKED ME IN?
FWOOM
I DIDN'T PLAN TO KILL YOU, LITTLE BOY...
BUT TOUGH LUCK.
AND, WHAT A PLACE TO DIE...

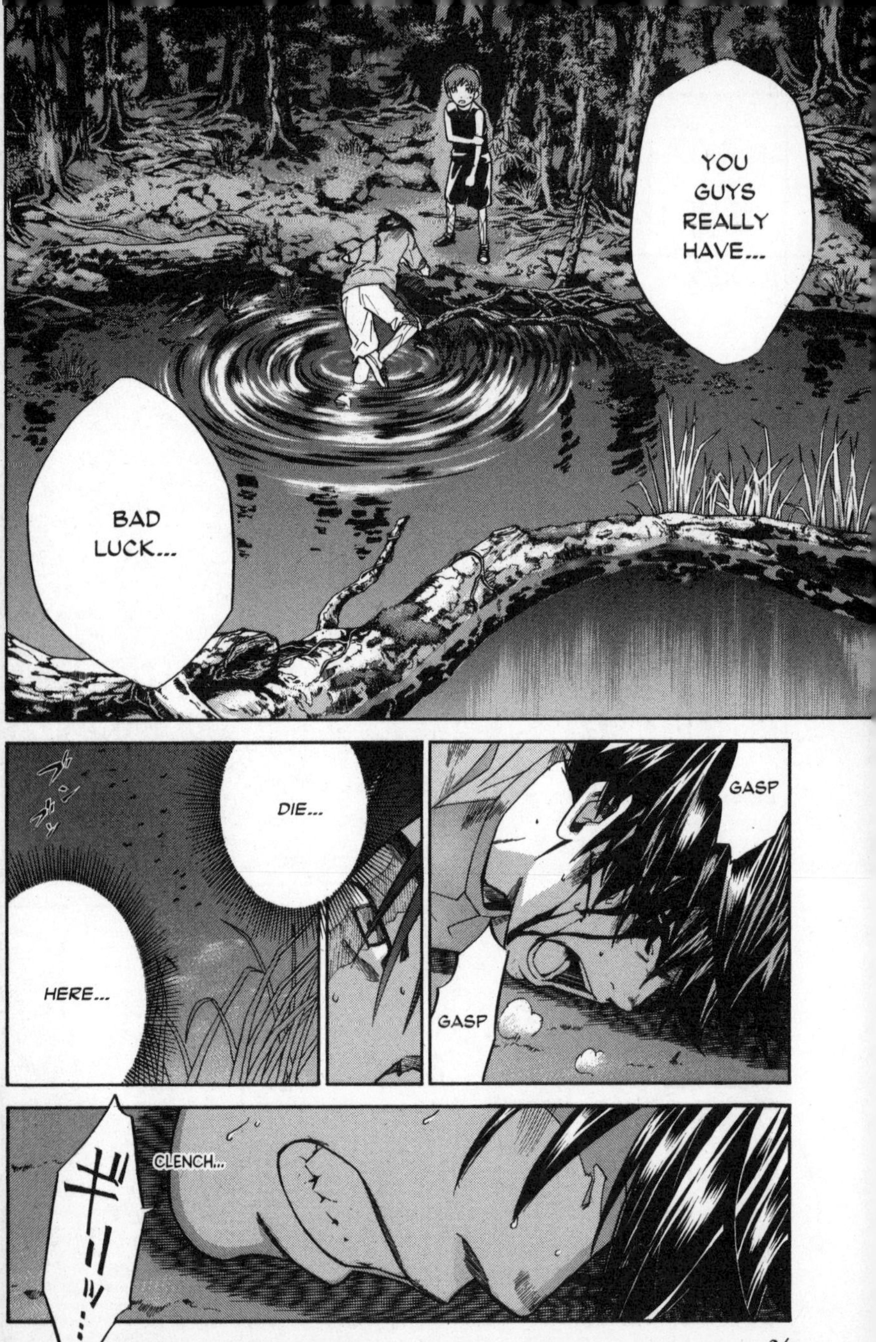
YOU GUYS REALLY HAVE...
BAD LUCK...
GASP
GASP
DIE...
HERE...
CLENCH...
ギリッ…

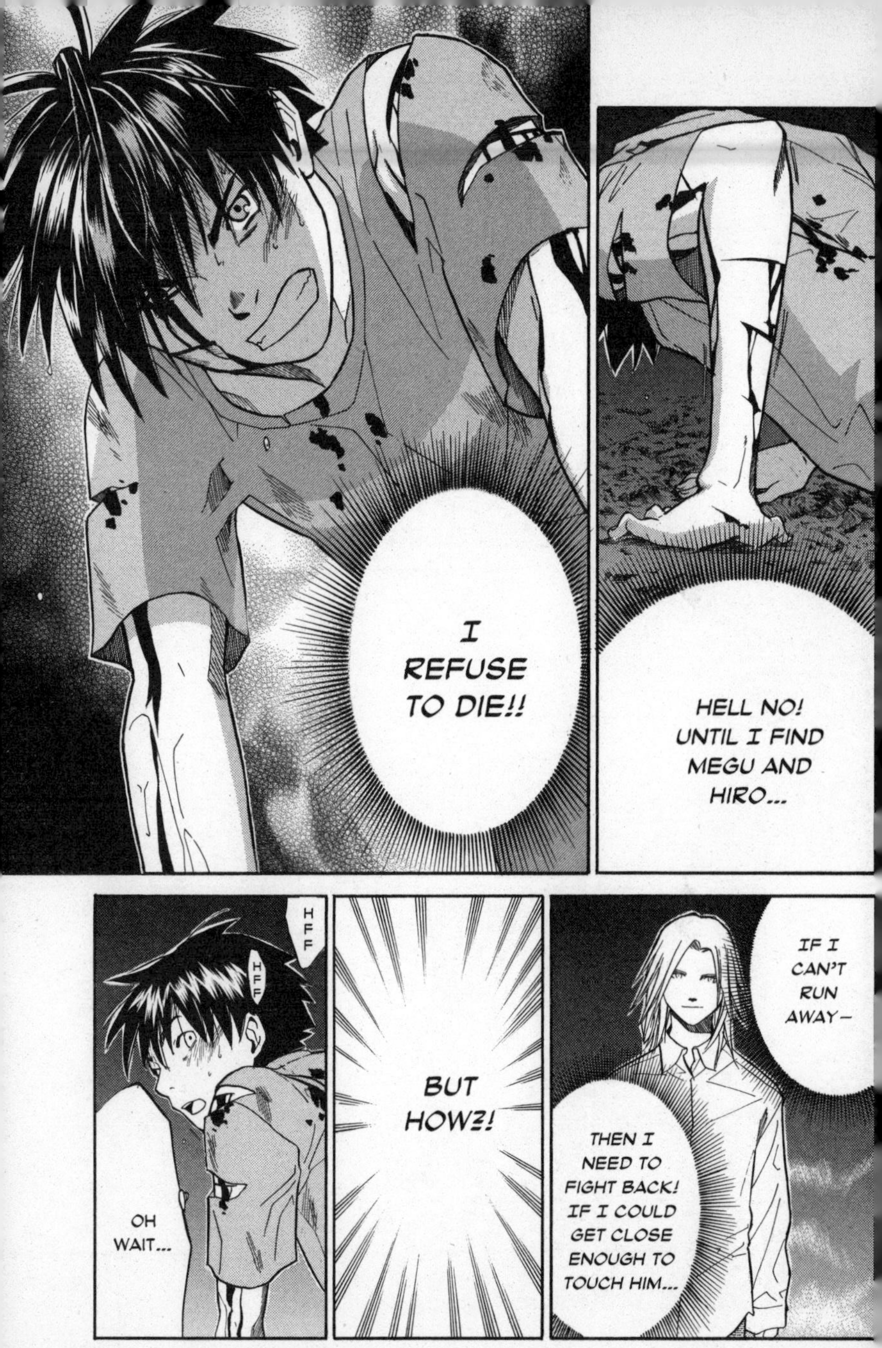
HELL NO! UNTIL I FIND MEGU AND HIRO...
I REFUSE TO DIE!!
IF I CAN'T RUN AWAY—
THEN I NEED TO FIGHT BACK! IF I COULD GET CLOSE ENOUGH TO TOUCH HIM...
BUT HOW?!
HFF
HFF
OH WAIT...

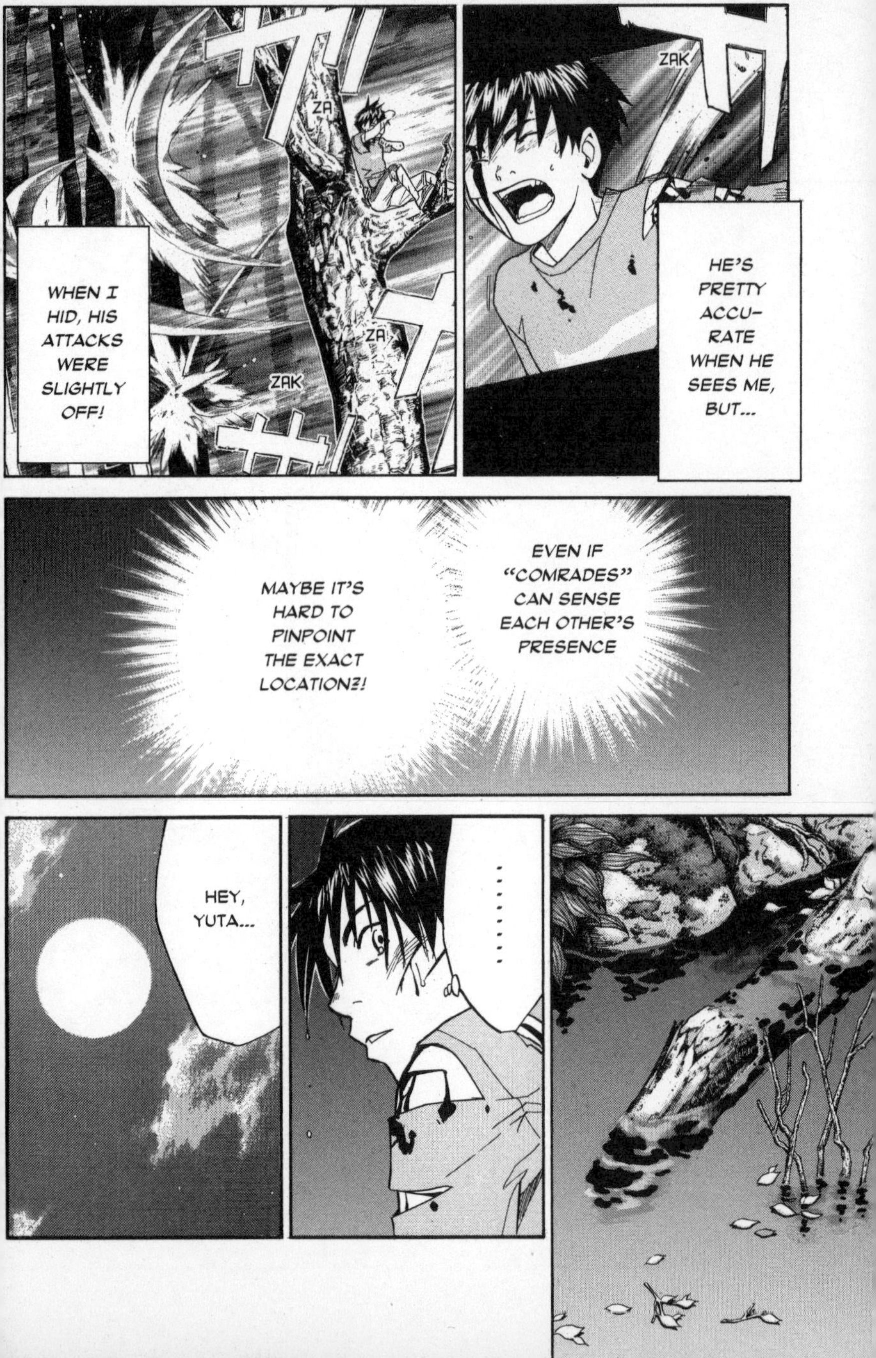
ZAK
HE'S PRETTY ACCURATE WHEN HE SEES ME, BUT...
ZA
ZA
ZAK
WHEN I HID, HIS ATTACKS WERE SLIGHTLY OFF!
EVEN IF "COMRADES" CAN SENSE EACH OTHER'S PRESENCE
MAYBE IT'S HARD TO PINPOINT THE EXACT LOCATION?!
......
HEY, YUTA...

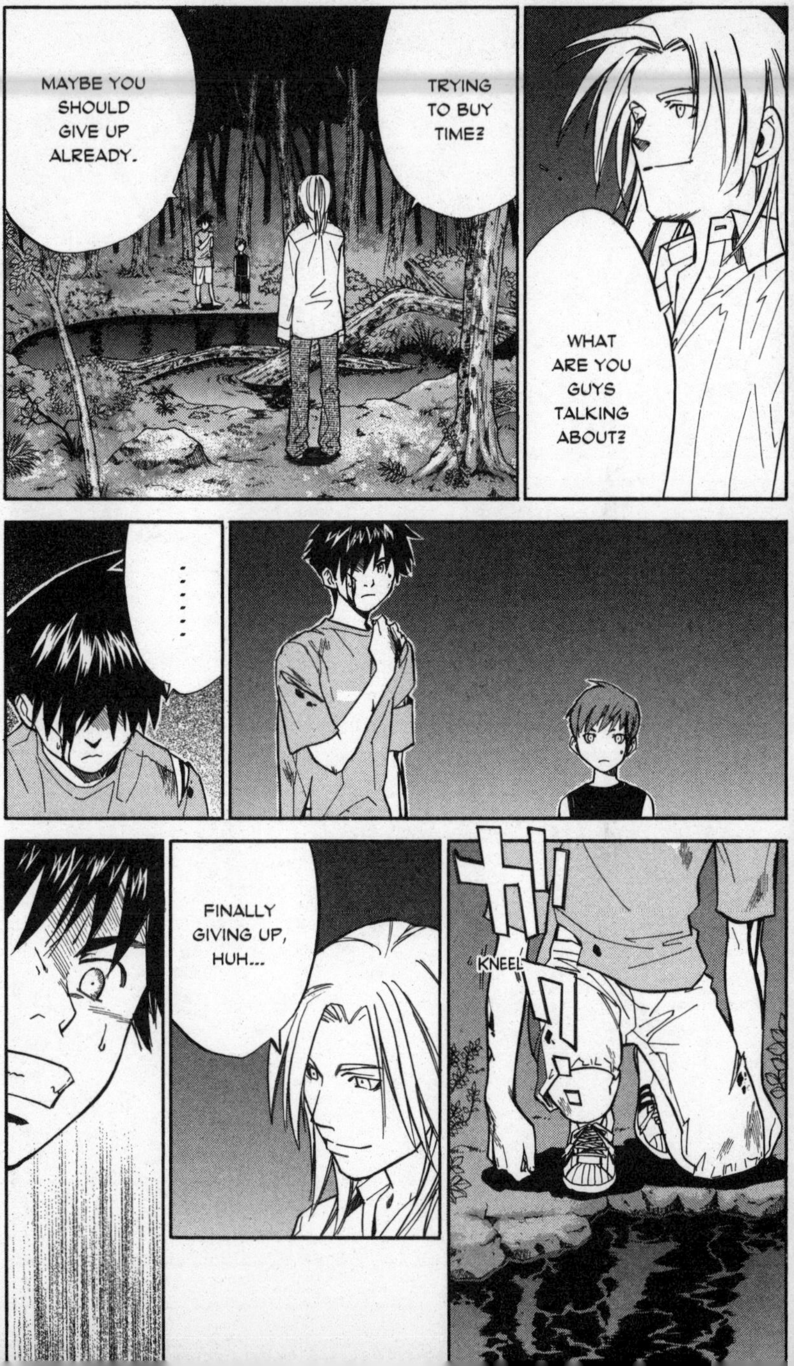
WHAT ARE YOU GUYS TALKING ABOUT?
TRYING TO BUY TIME?
MAYBE YOU SHOULD GIVE UP ALREADY.
......
KNEEL
FINALLY GIVING UP, HUH...

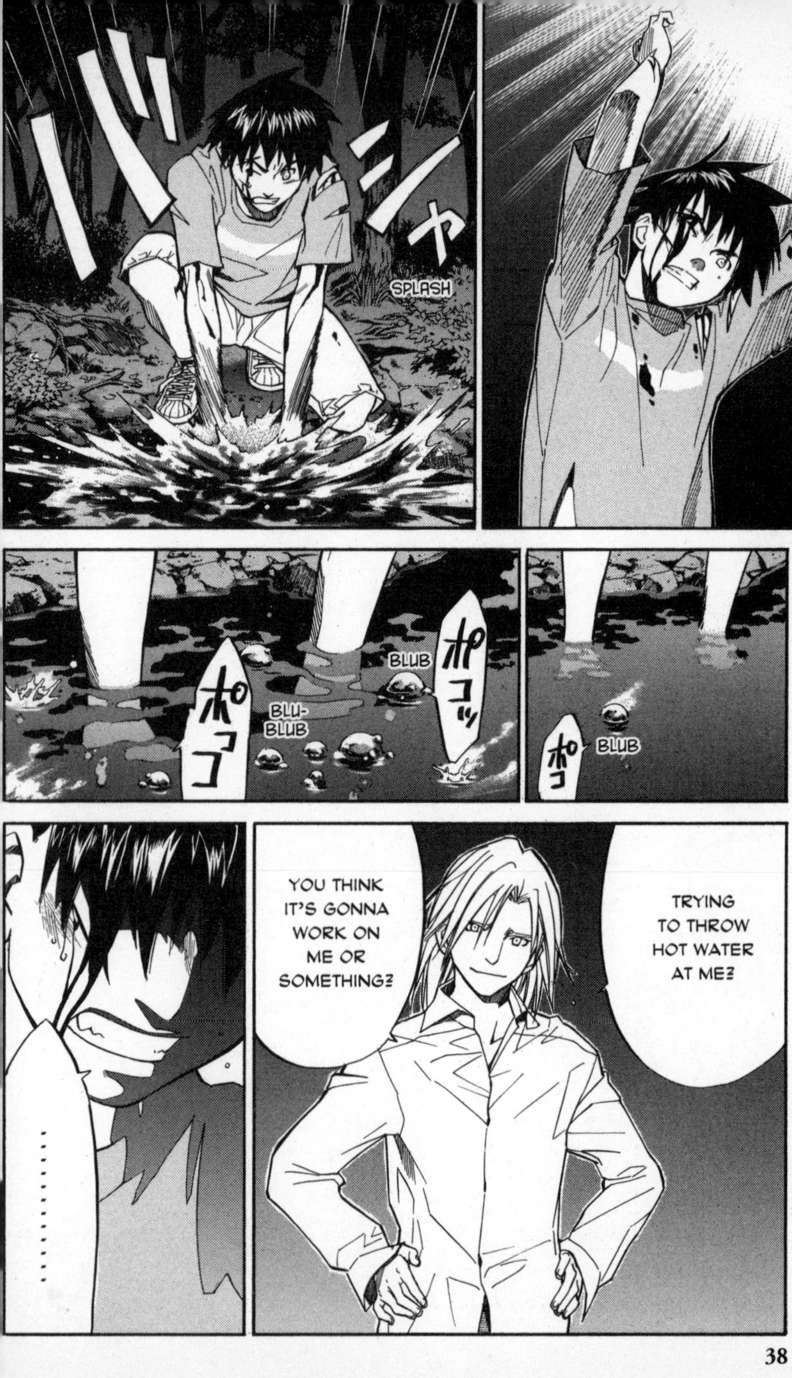
バシャ
SPLASH
ポコ
BLUB
ポコッ
BLUB
BLU-BLUB
ポコ
TRYING TO THROW HOT WATER AT ME?
YOU THINK IT'S GONNA WORK ON ME OR SOMETHING?
......

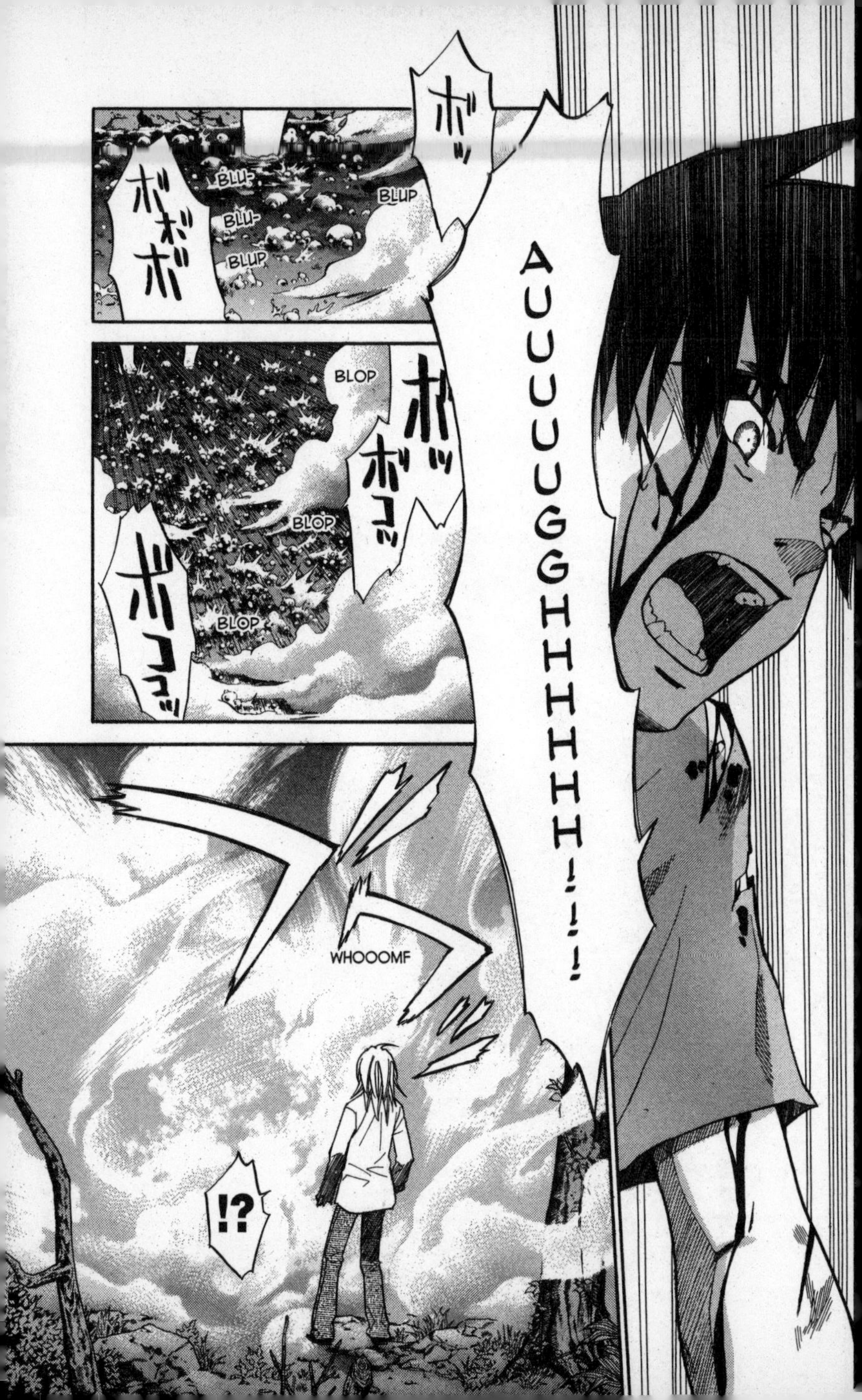
AUUUUUGHHHHH!!!
ボッ
BLUP
BLU-
BLU-
BLUP
ボボボ
ボッ
ボコッ
BLOP
BLOP
ボコココッ
BLOP
WHOOOMF
!?

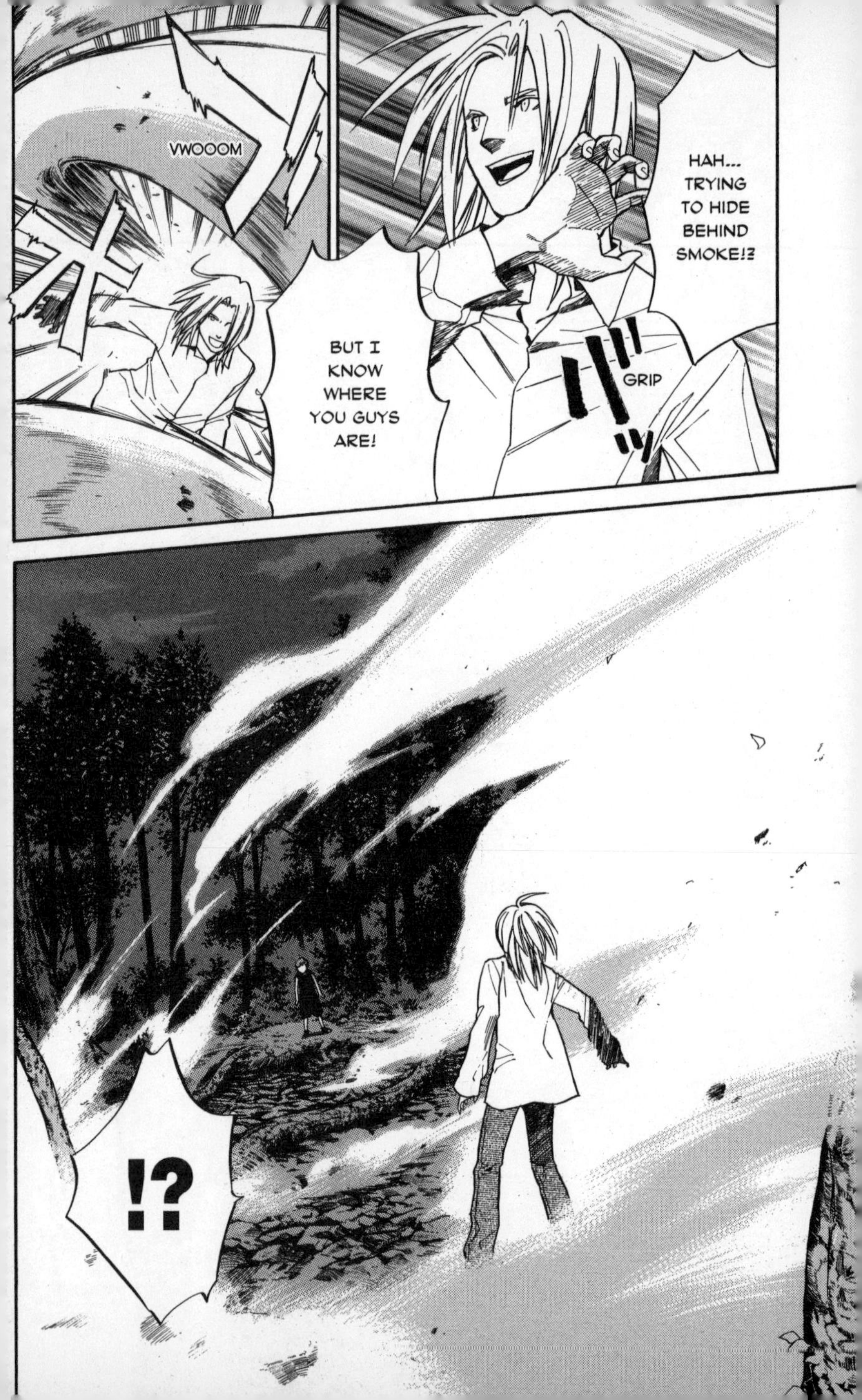
HAH... TRYING TO HIDE BEHIND SMOKE!?
GRIP
BUT I KNOW WHERE YOU GUYS ARE!
VWOOOM
!?

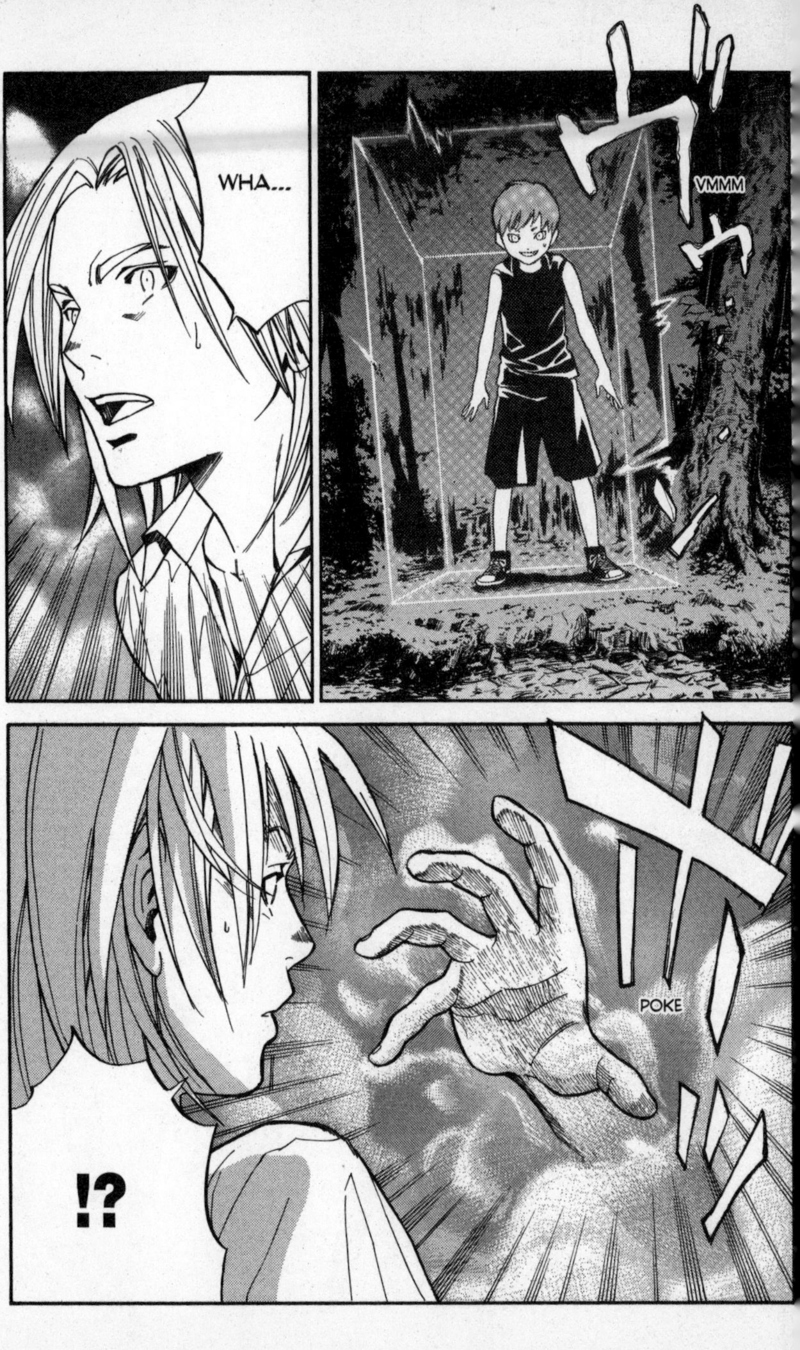
VMMM
WHA...
POKE
!?

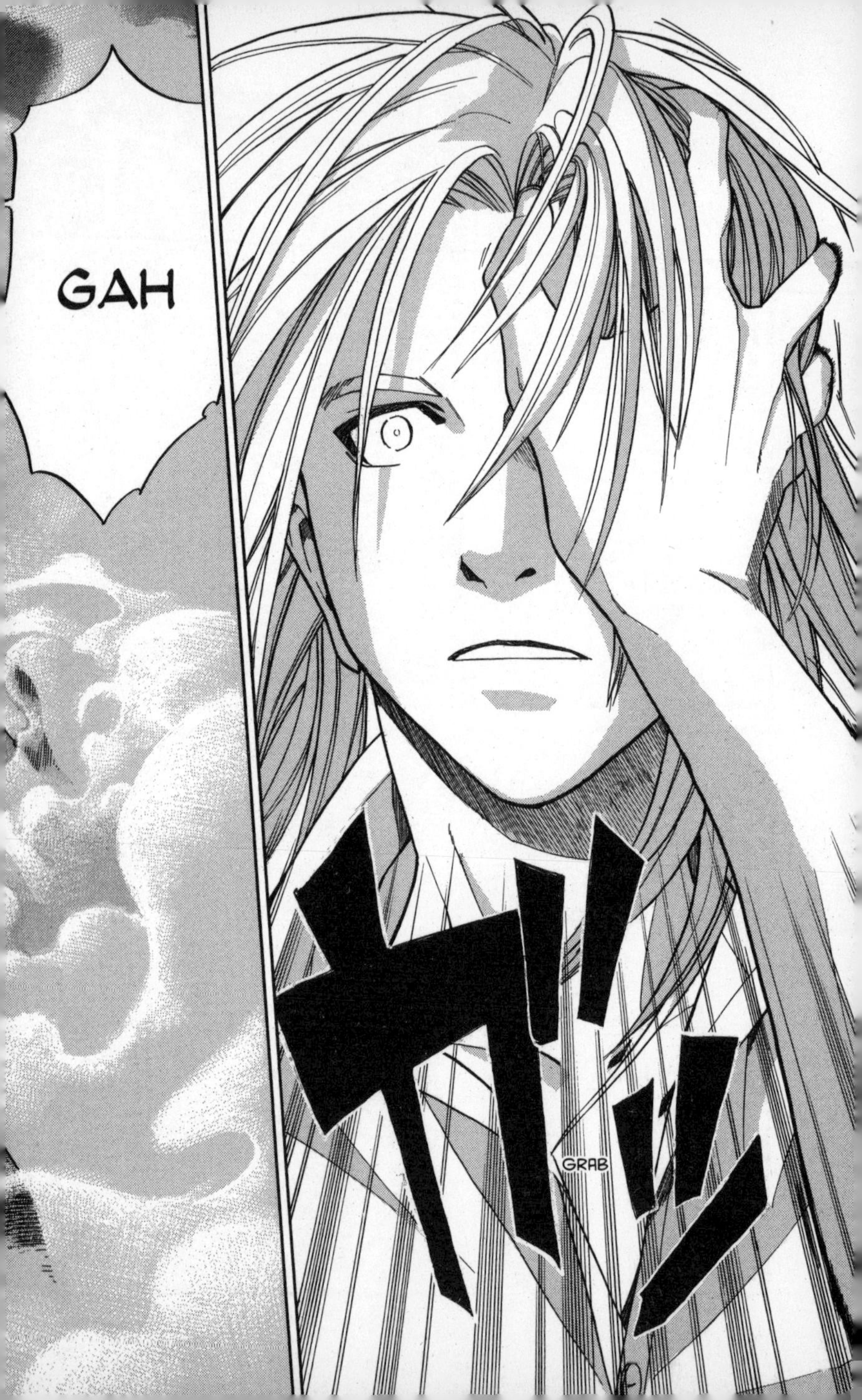
GAH
GRAB

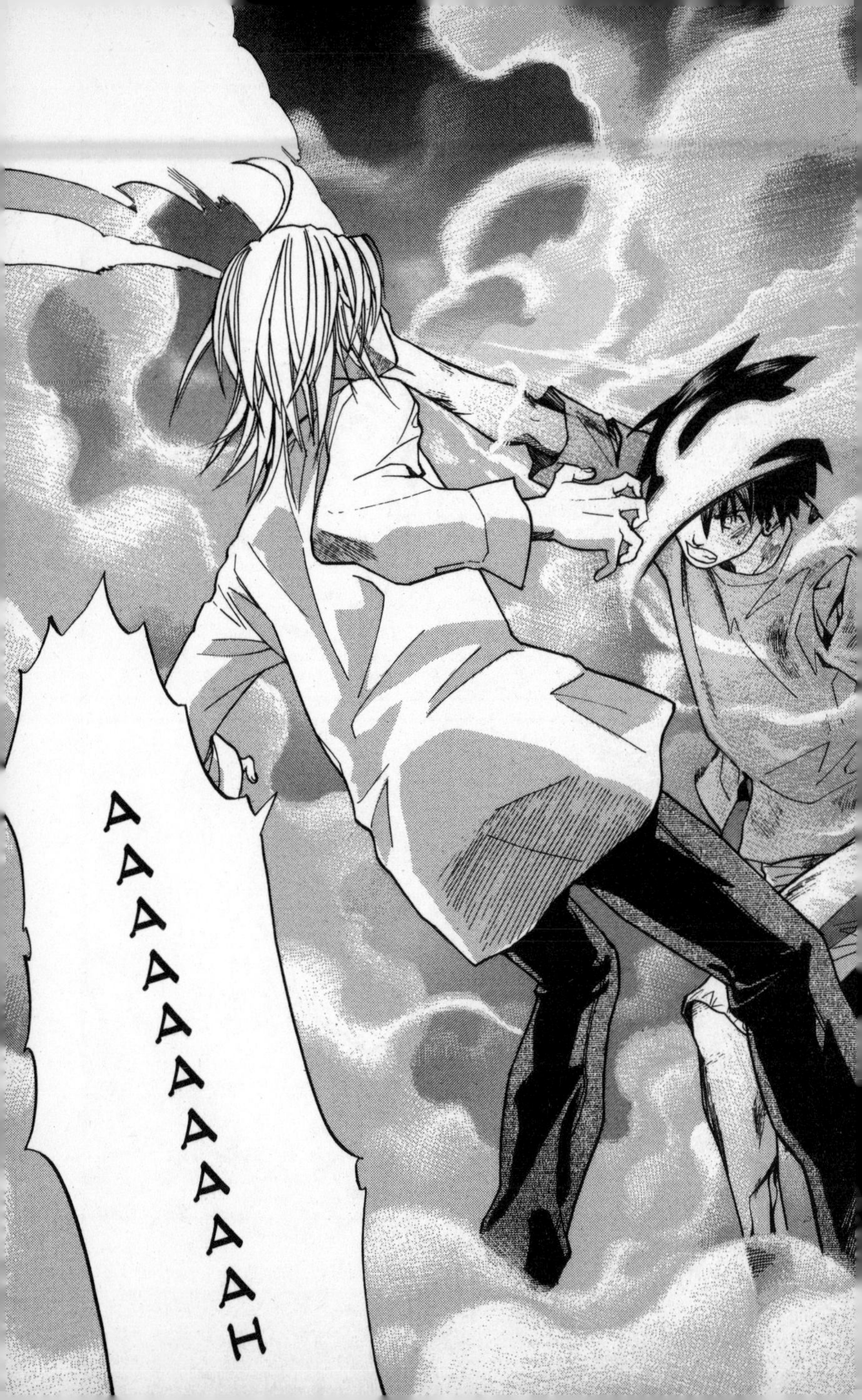
AAAAAAAAAH

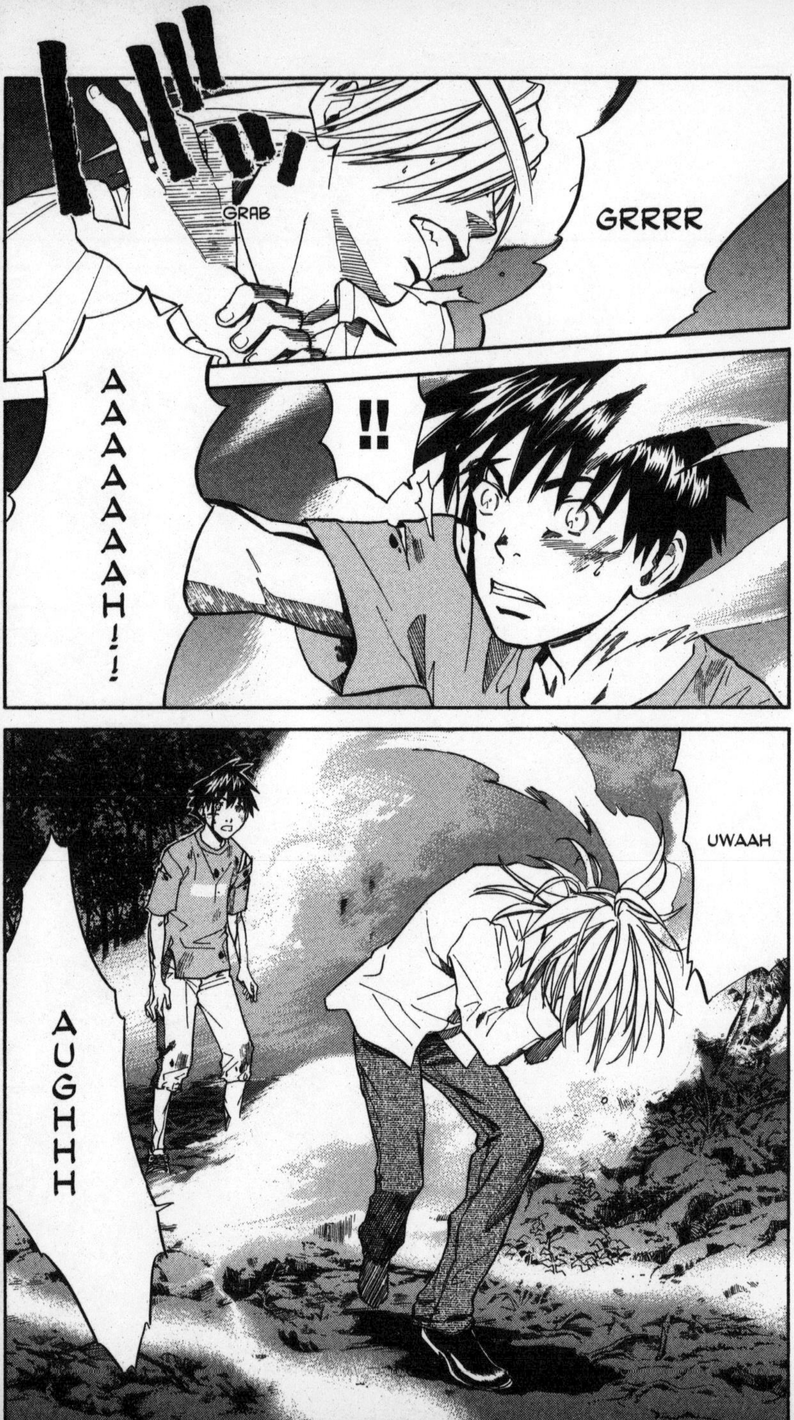
GRRRR
GRAB
!!
AAAAAAAAH!!!
UWAAH
AUGHHH

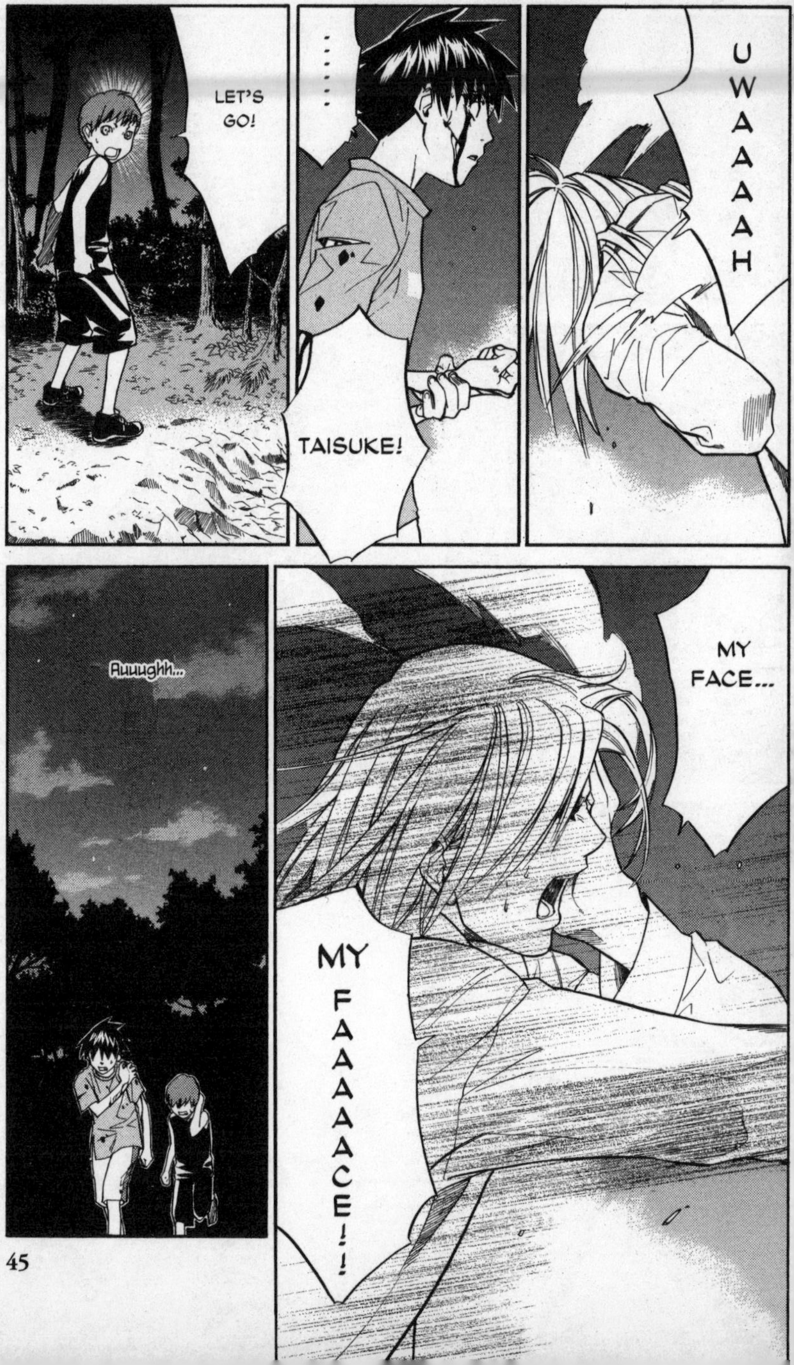
UWAAAAAH
......
TAISUKE!
LET'S GO!
MY FACE...
MY FAAAAAACE!!
Auuughh...

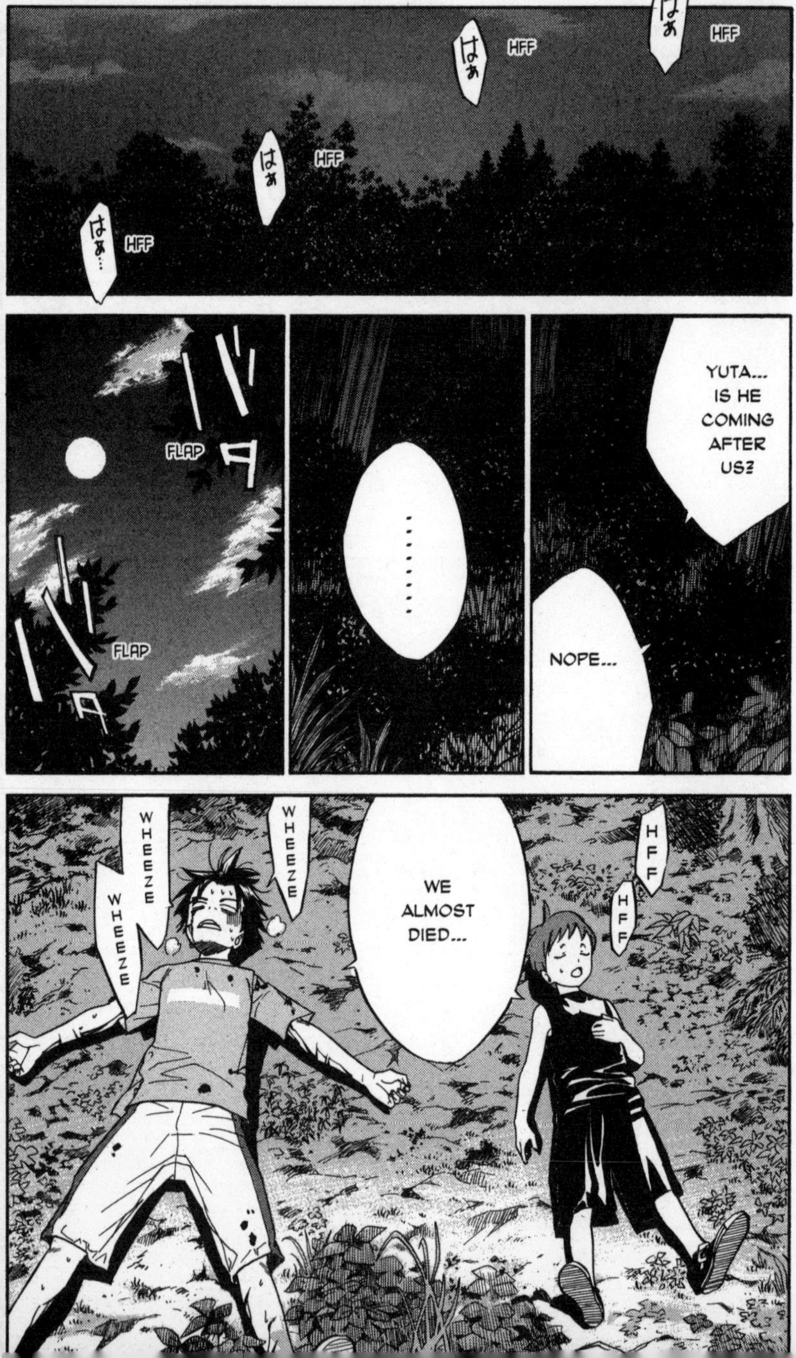
はぁ
HFF
はぁ
HFF
はぁ
HFF
はぁ…
HFF
YUTA... IS HE COMING AFTER US?
NOPE...
......
バタ
FLAP
バタ
FLAP
HFF
HFF
WE ALMOST DIED...
WHEEZE
WHEEZE
WHEEZE
WHEEZE

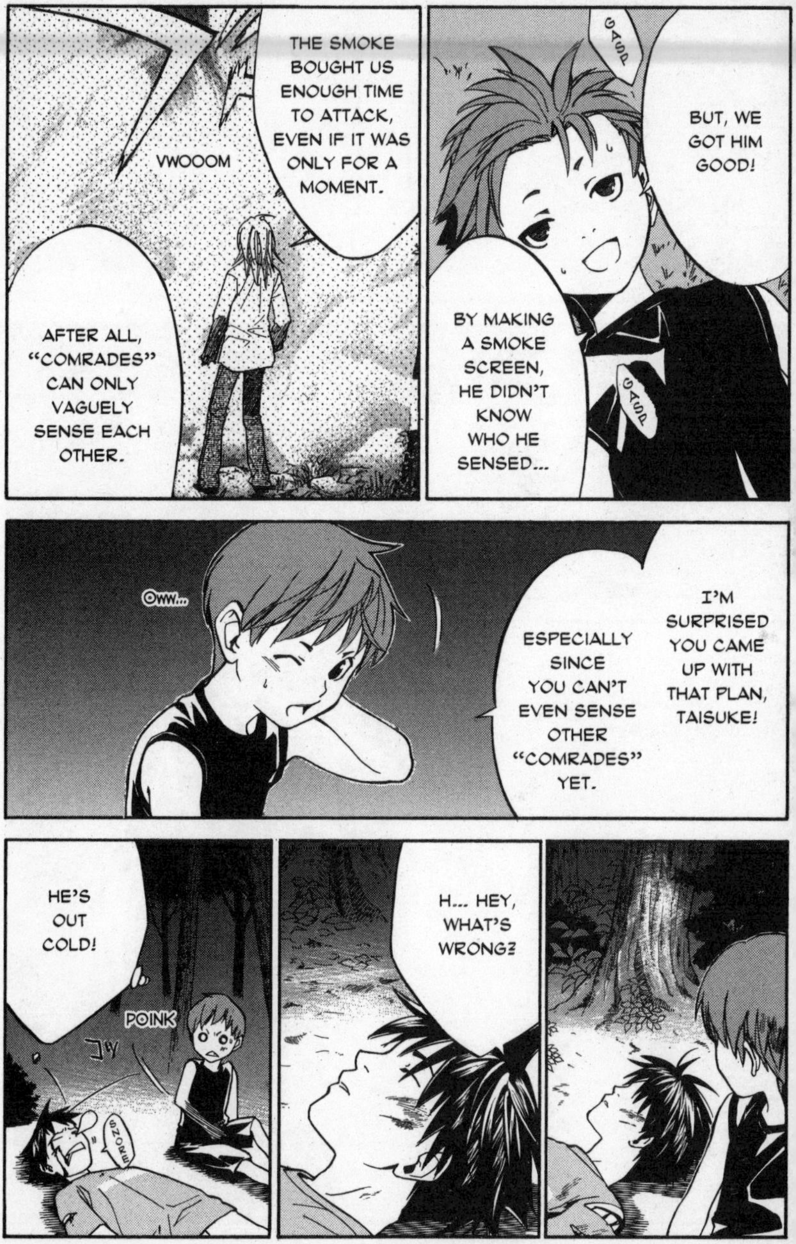
GASP
BUT, WE GOT HIM GOOD!
BY MAKING A SMOKE SCREEN, HE DIDN'T KNOW WHO HE SENSED...
GASP
THE SMOKE BOUGHT US ENOUGH TIME TO ATTACK, EVEN IF IT WAS ONLY FOR A MOMENT.
VWOOOM
AFTER ALL, "COMRADES" CAN ONLY VAGUELY SENSE EACH OTHER.
I'M SURPRISED YOU CAME UP WITH THAT PLAN, TAISUKE!
ESPECIALLY SINCE YOU CAN'T EVEN SENSE OTHER "COMRADES" YET.
Oww...
H... HEY, WHAT'S WRONG?
HE'S OUT COLD!
POINK
SNORE

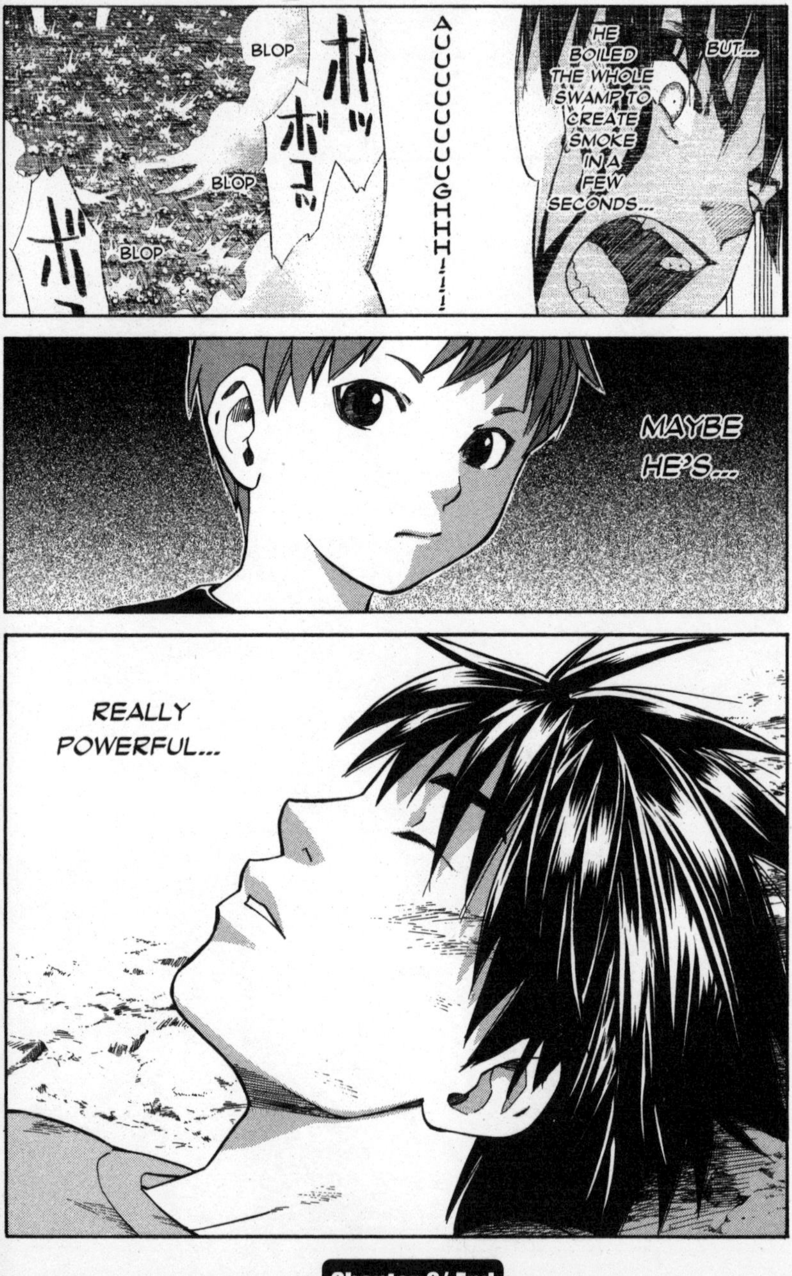
BUT...
HE BOILED THE WHOLE SWAMP TO CREATE SMOKE IN A FEW SECONDS...
AUUUUUUUUUGHHH!!!!
ボッ
ボコッ
BLOP
BLOP
BLOP
MAYBE HE'S...
REALLY POWERFUL...

Chapter 8/ End

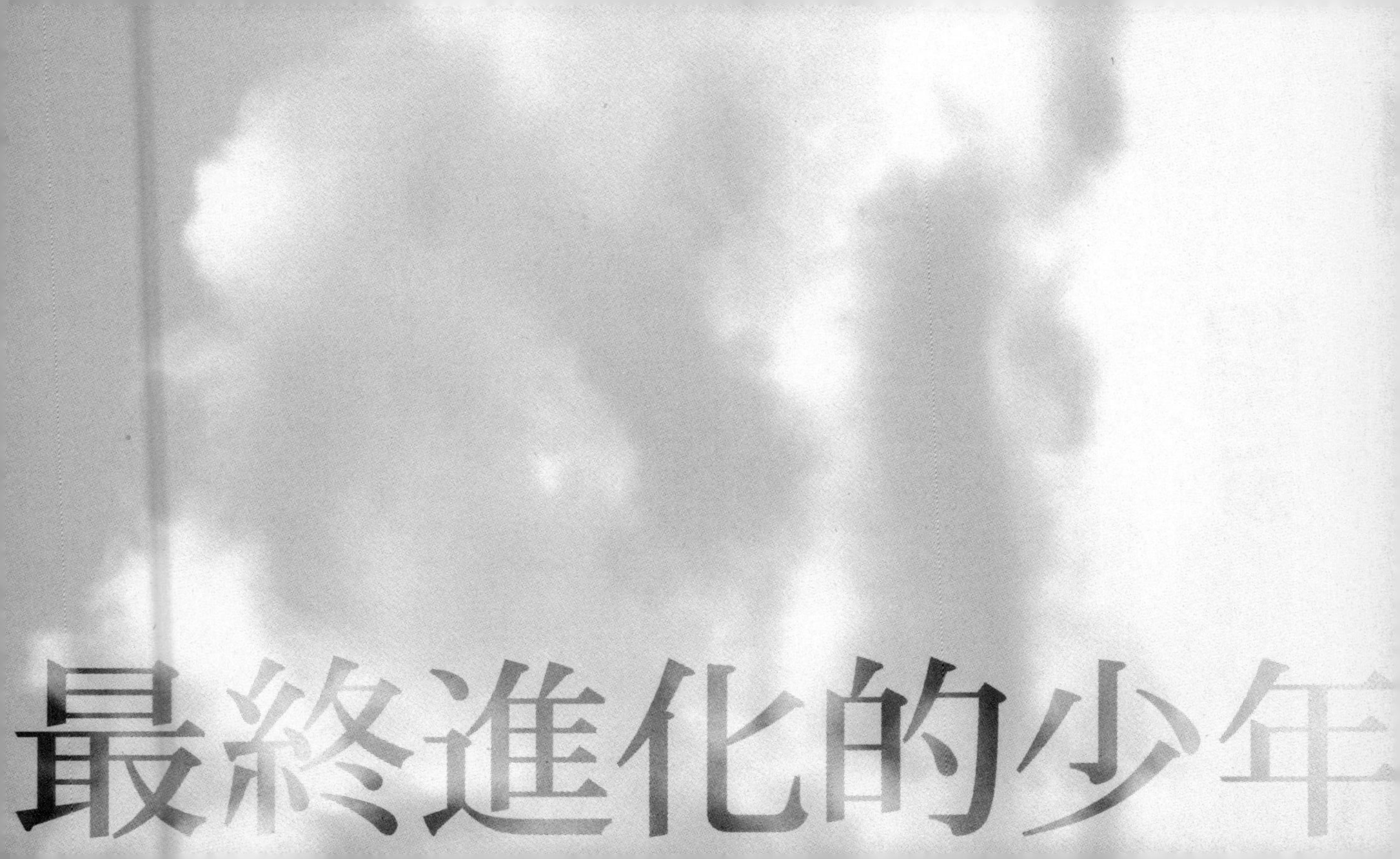
最終進化的少年

Alive

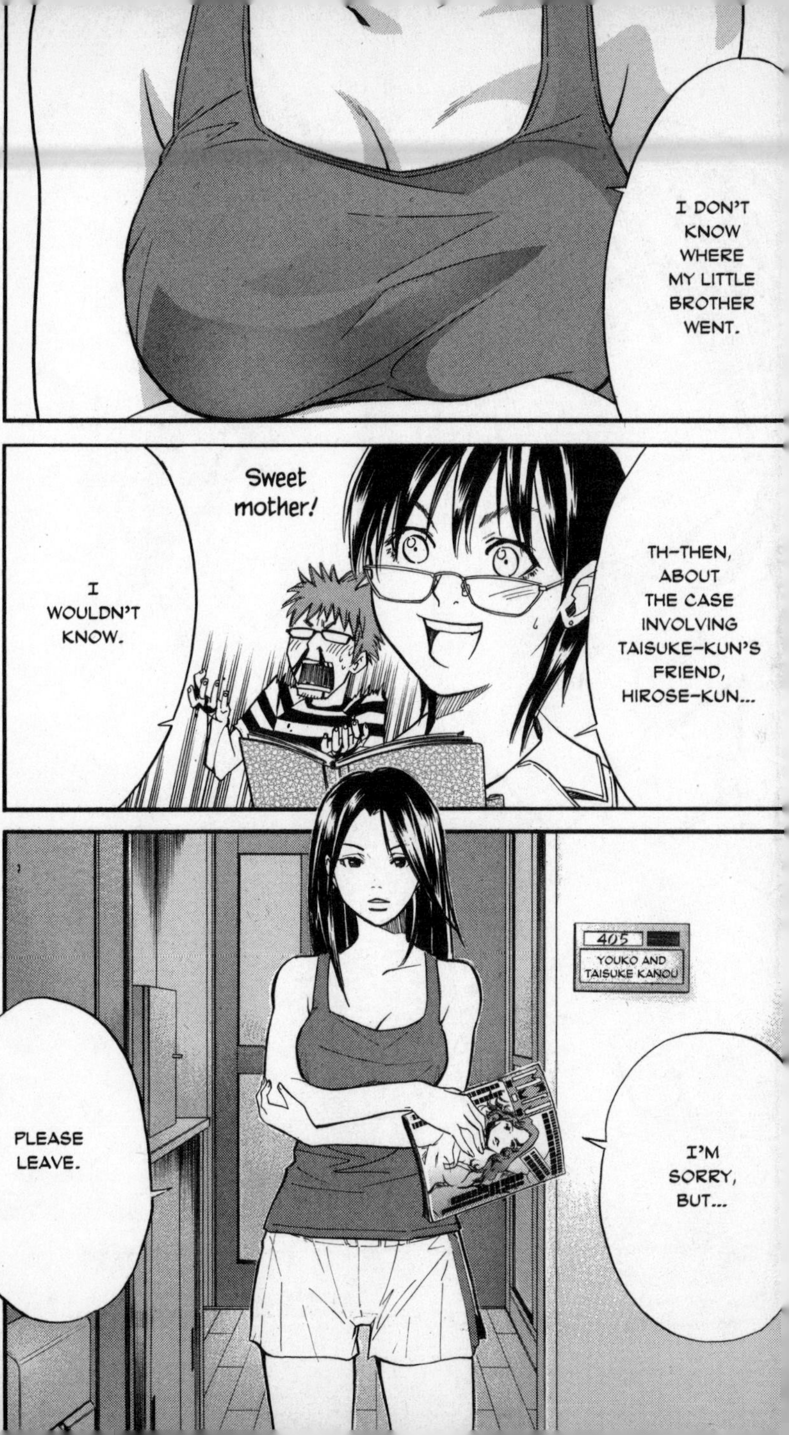
I DON'T KNOW WHERE MY LITTLE BROTHER WENT.
TH-THEN, ABOUT THE CASE INVOLVING TAISUKE-KUN'S FRIEND, HIROSE-KUN...
Sweet mother!
I WOULDN'T KNOW.
405
YOUKO AND TAISUKE KANOU
I'M SORRY, BUT...
PLEASE LEAVE.

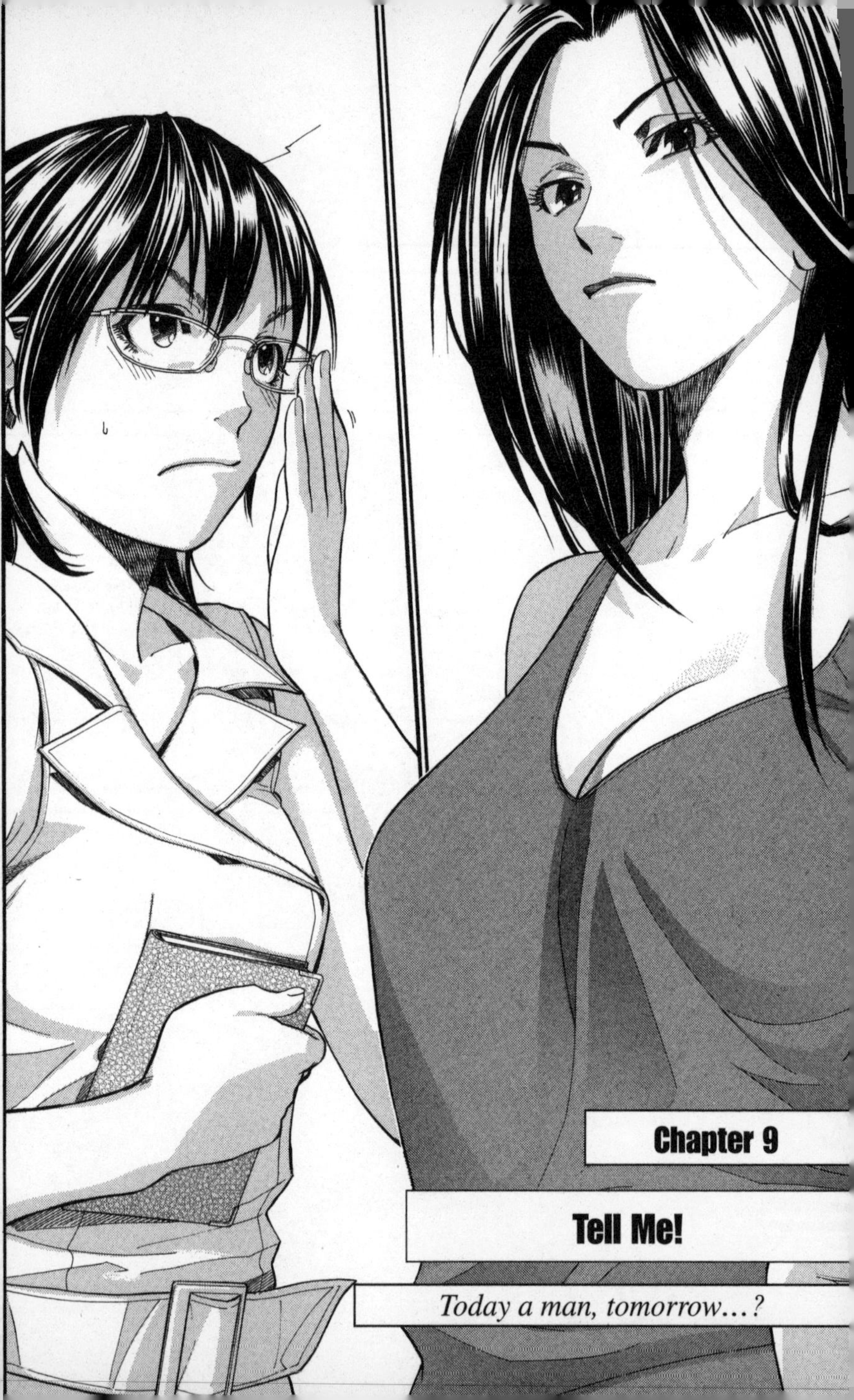
Chapter 9
Tell Me!
Today a man, tomorrow…?

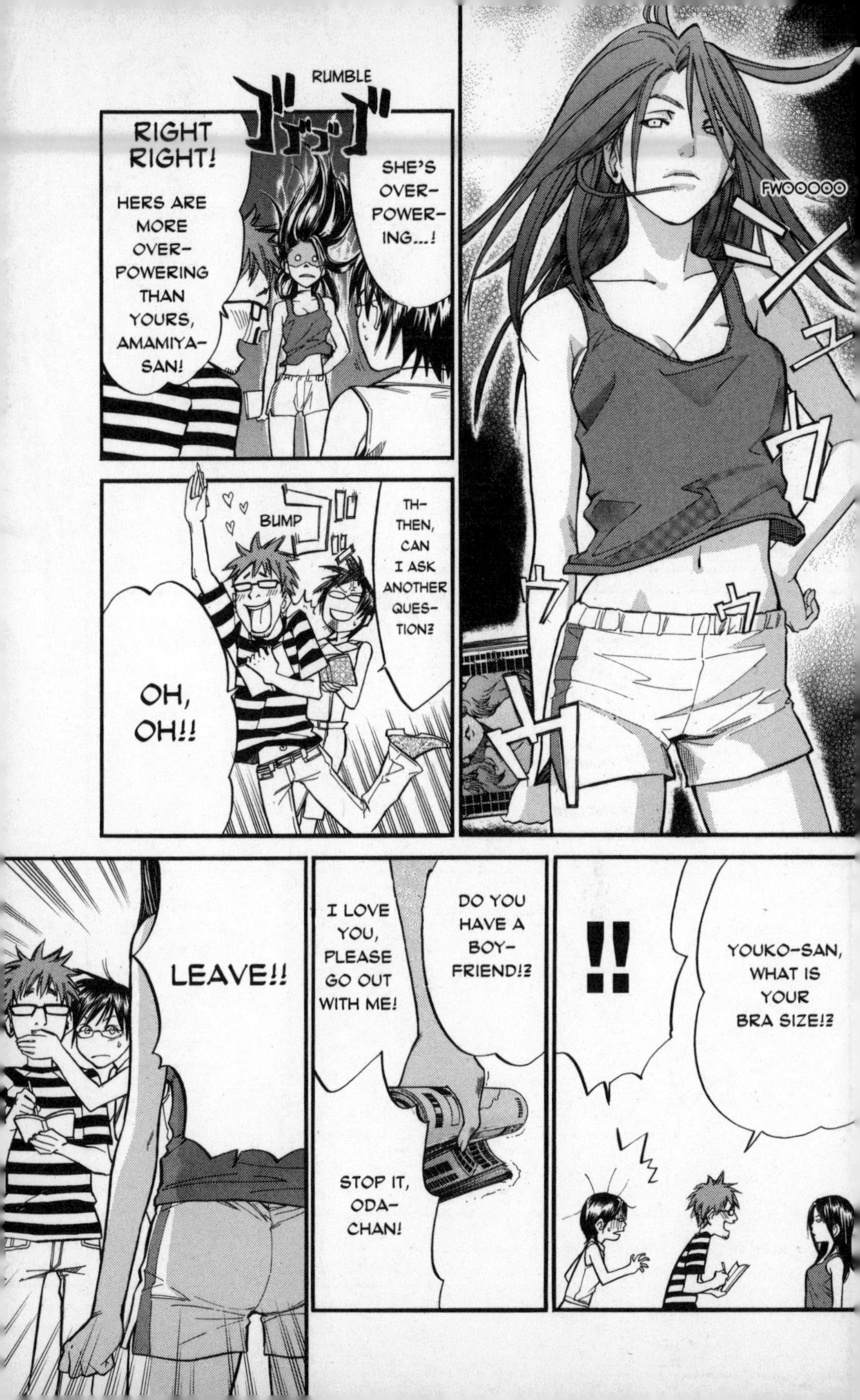
FWOOOOO
SHE'S OVER-POWER-ING...!
RUMBLE
RIGHT RIGHT!
HERS ARE MORE OVER-POWERING THAN YOURS, AMAMIYA-SAN!
TH-THEN, CAN I ASK ANOTHER QUES-TION?
BUMP
OH, OH!!
YOUKO-SAN, WHAT IS YOUR BRA SIZE!?
!!
DO YOU HAVE A BOY-FRIEND!?
I LOVE YOU, PLEASE GO OUT WITH ME!
STOP IT, ODA-CHAN!
LEAVE!!

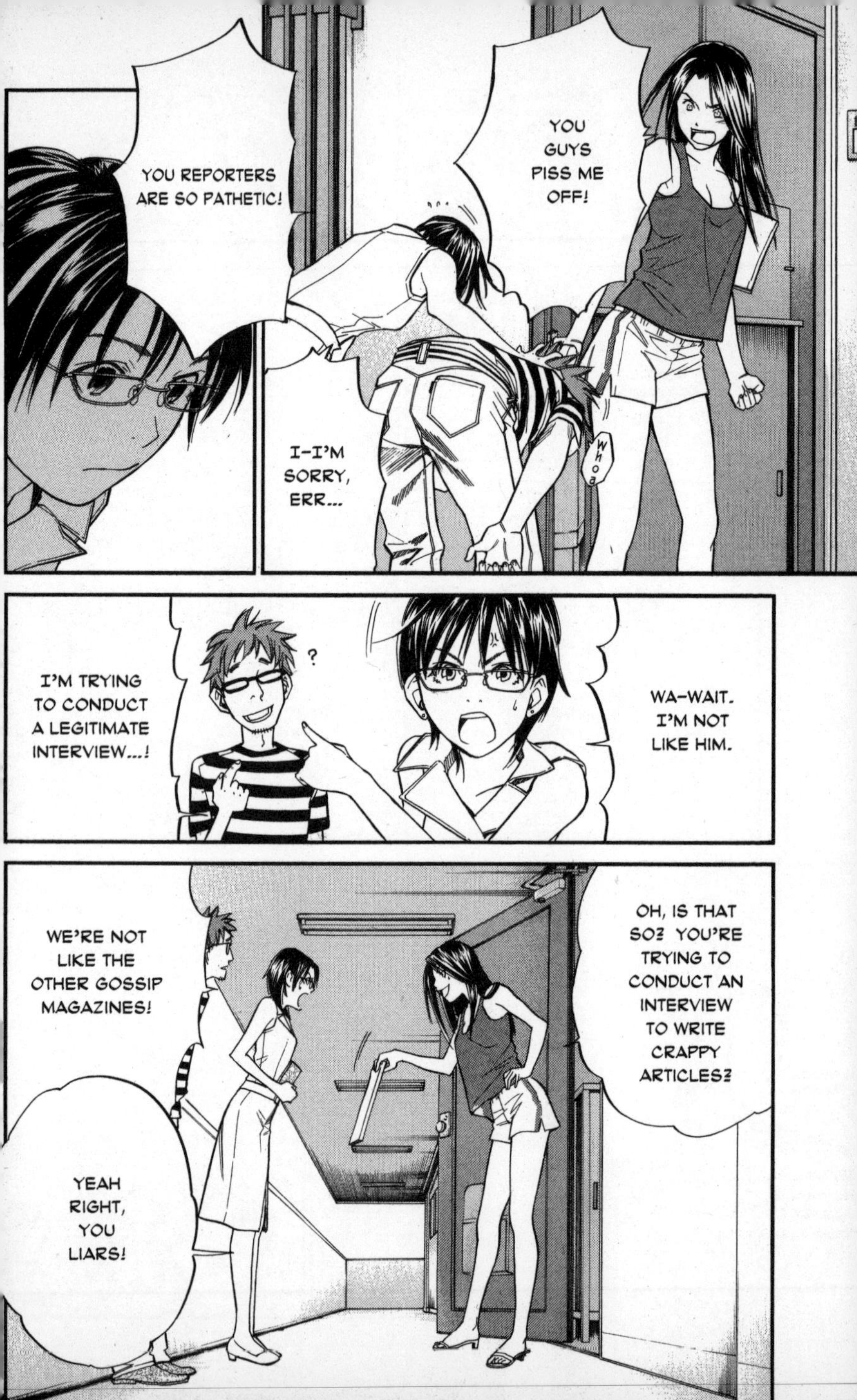
YOU GUYS PISS ME OFF!
Whoa
I-I'M SORRY, ERR...
YOU REPORTERS ARE SO PATHETIC!
WA-WAIT. I'M NOT LIKE HIM.
?
I'M TRYING TO CONDUCT A LEGITIMATE INTERVIEW...!
OH, IS THAT SO? YOU'RE TRYING TO CONDUCT AN INTERVIEW TO WRITE CRAPPY ARTICLES?
WE'RE NOT LIKE THE OTHER GOSSIP MAGAZINES!
YEAH RIGHT, YOU LIARS!

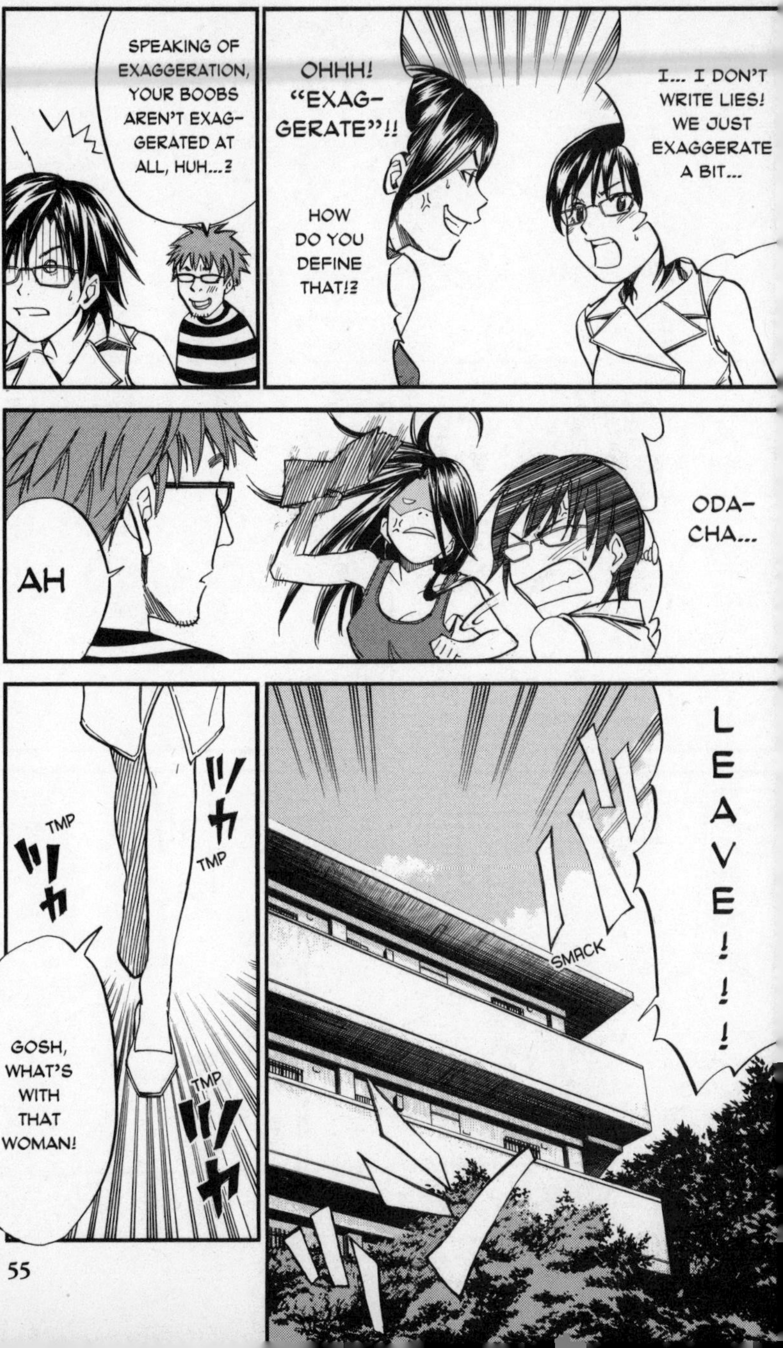
I... I DON'T WRITE LIES! WE JUST EXAGGERATE A BIT...
OHHH! "EXAG-GERATE"!!
HOW DO YOU DEFINE THAT!?
SPEAKING OF EXAGGERATION, YOUR BOOBS AREN'T EXAG-GERATED AT ALL, HUH...?
ODA-CHA...
AH
LEAVE!!!
SMACK
TMP
TMP
TMP
GOSH, WHAT'S WITH THAT WOMAN!

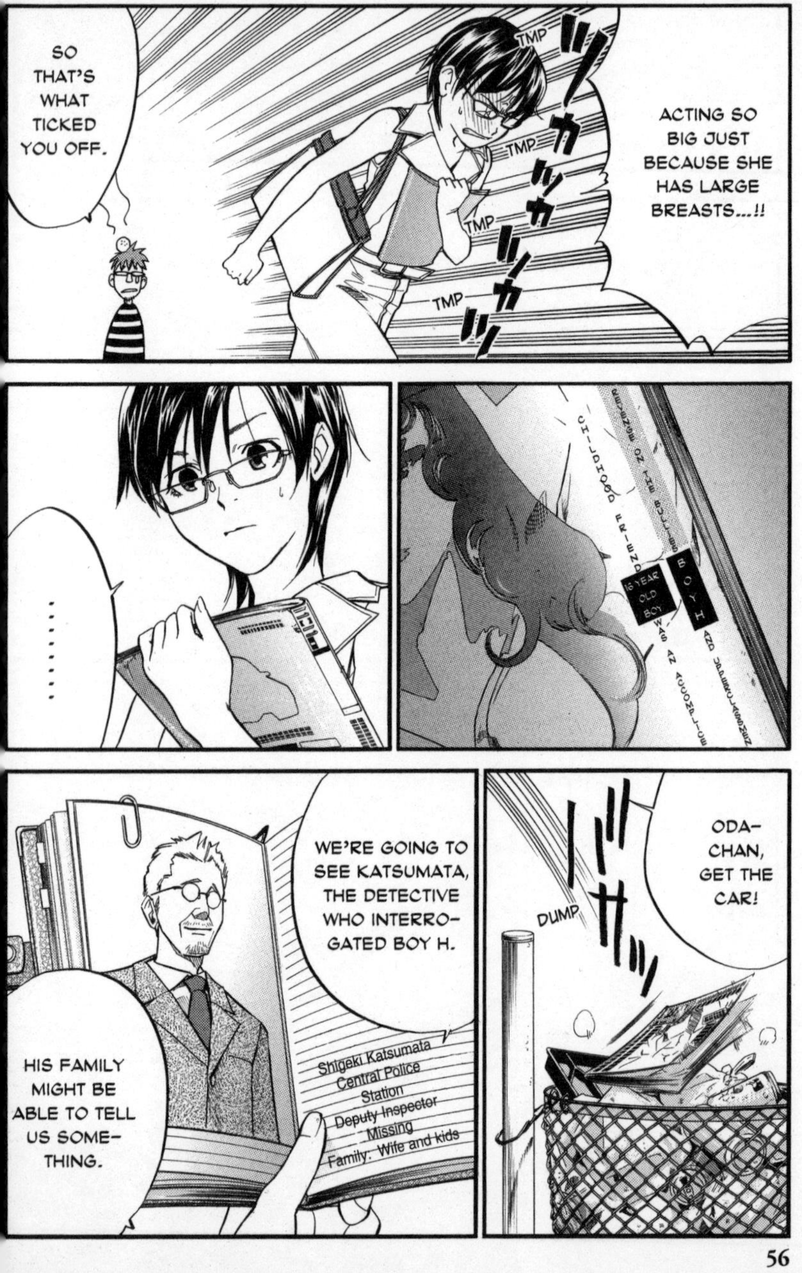
TMP
TMP
ACTING SO BIG JUST BECAUSE SHE HAS LARGE BREASTS...!!
TMP
TMP
SO THAT'S WHAT TICKED YOU OFF.
REVENGE ON THE BULLIES
CHILDHOOD FRIEND
BOY H
16 YEAR OLD BOY
WAS AN ACCOMPLICE
AND UPPERCLASSMEN
......
ODA-CHAN, GET THE CAR!
DUMP
WE'RE GOING TO SEE KATSUMATA, THE DETECTIVE WHO INTERRO-GATED BOY H.
HIS FAMILY MIGHT BE ABLE TO TELL US SOME-THING.
Shigeki Katsumata
Central Police Station
Deputy Inspector
Missing
Family: Wife and kids

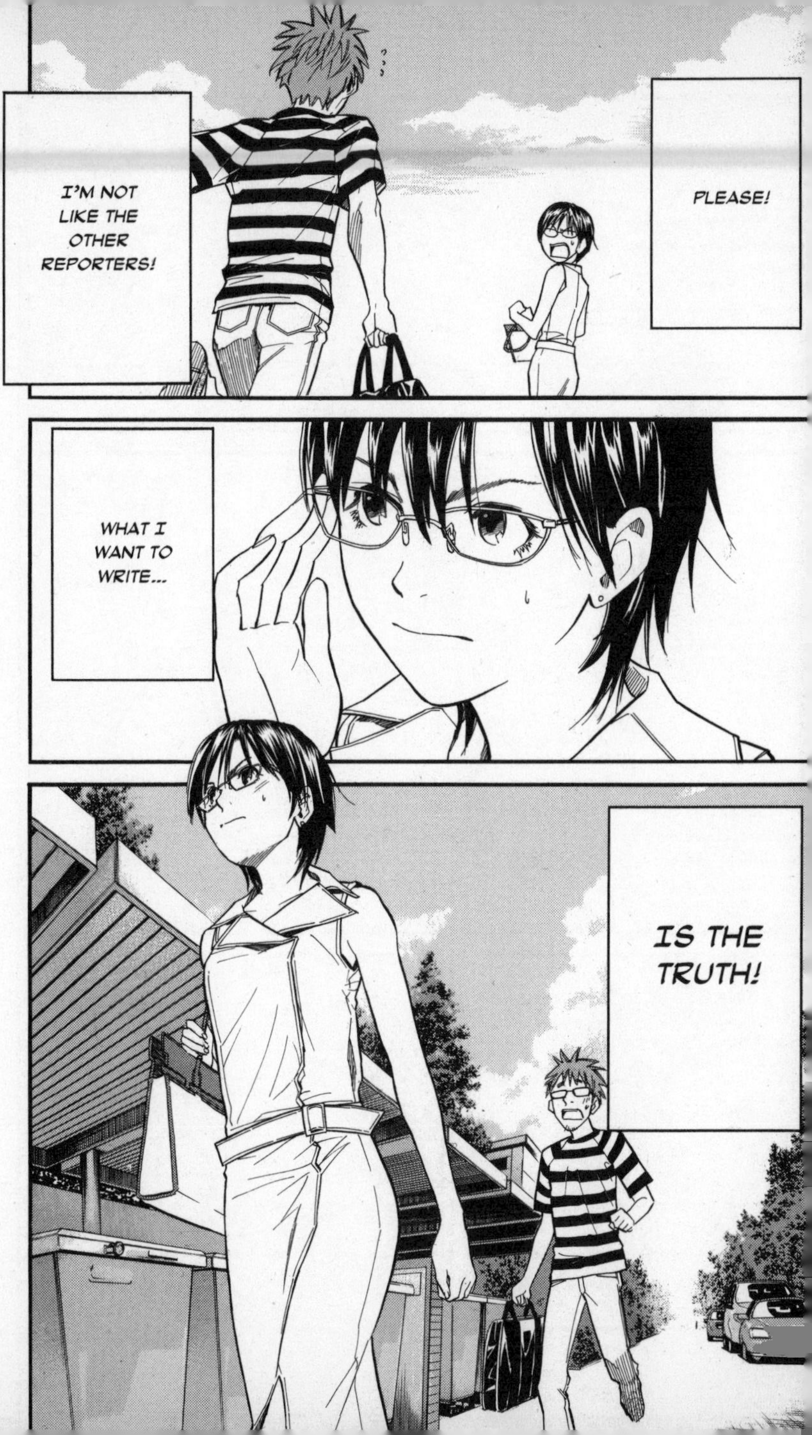
PLEASE!
I'M NOT LIKE THE OTHER REPORTERS!
WHAT I WANT TO WRITE...
IS THE TRUTH!

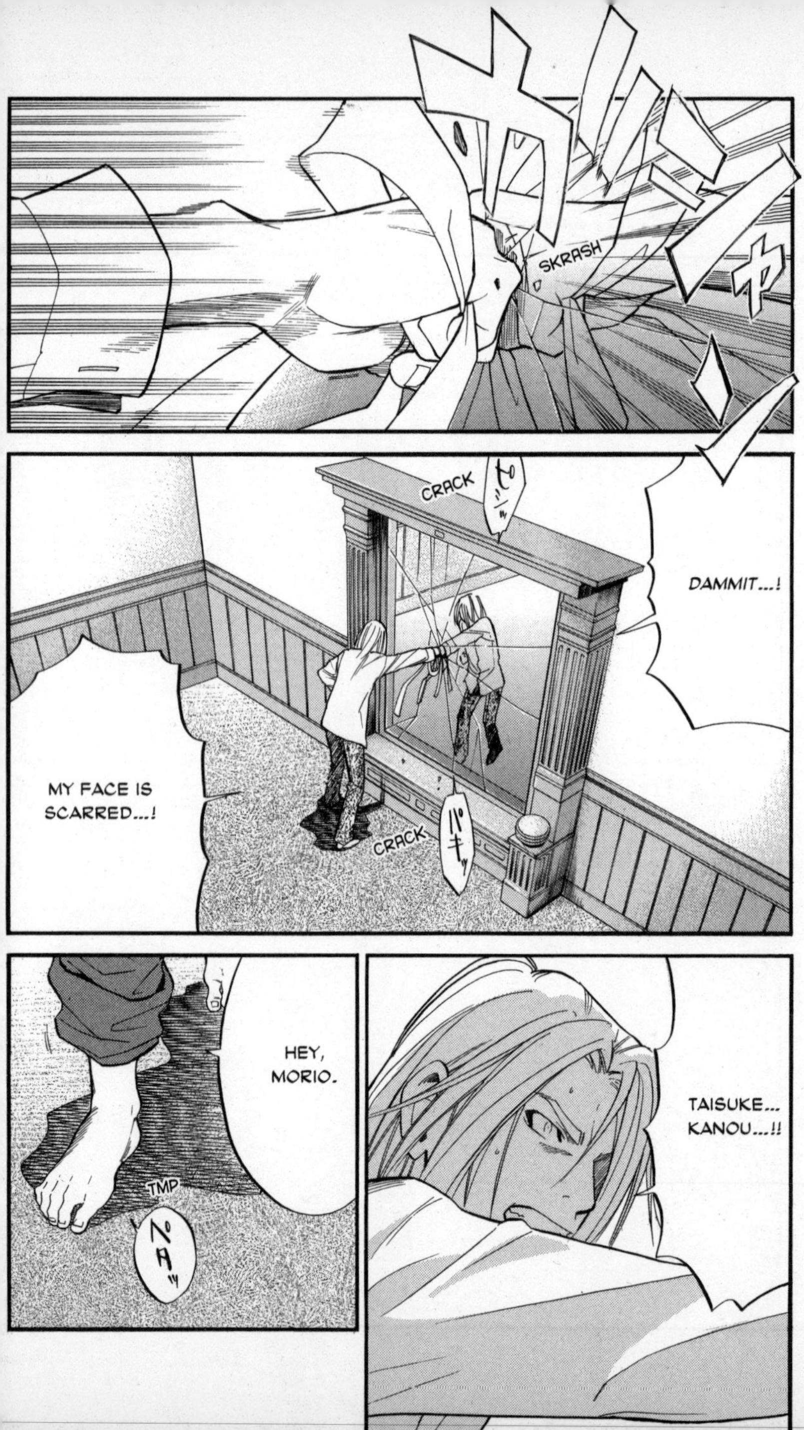
SKRASH
DAMMIT...!
CRACK
MY FACE IS SCARRED...!
CRACK
TAISUKE... KANOU...!!
HEY, MORIO.
TMP

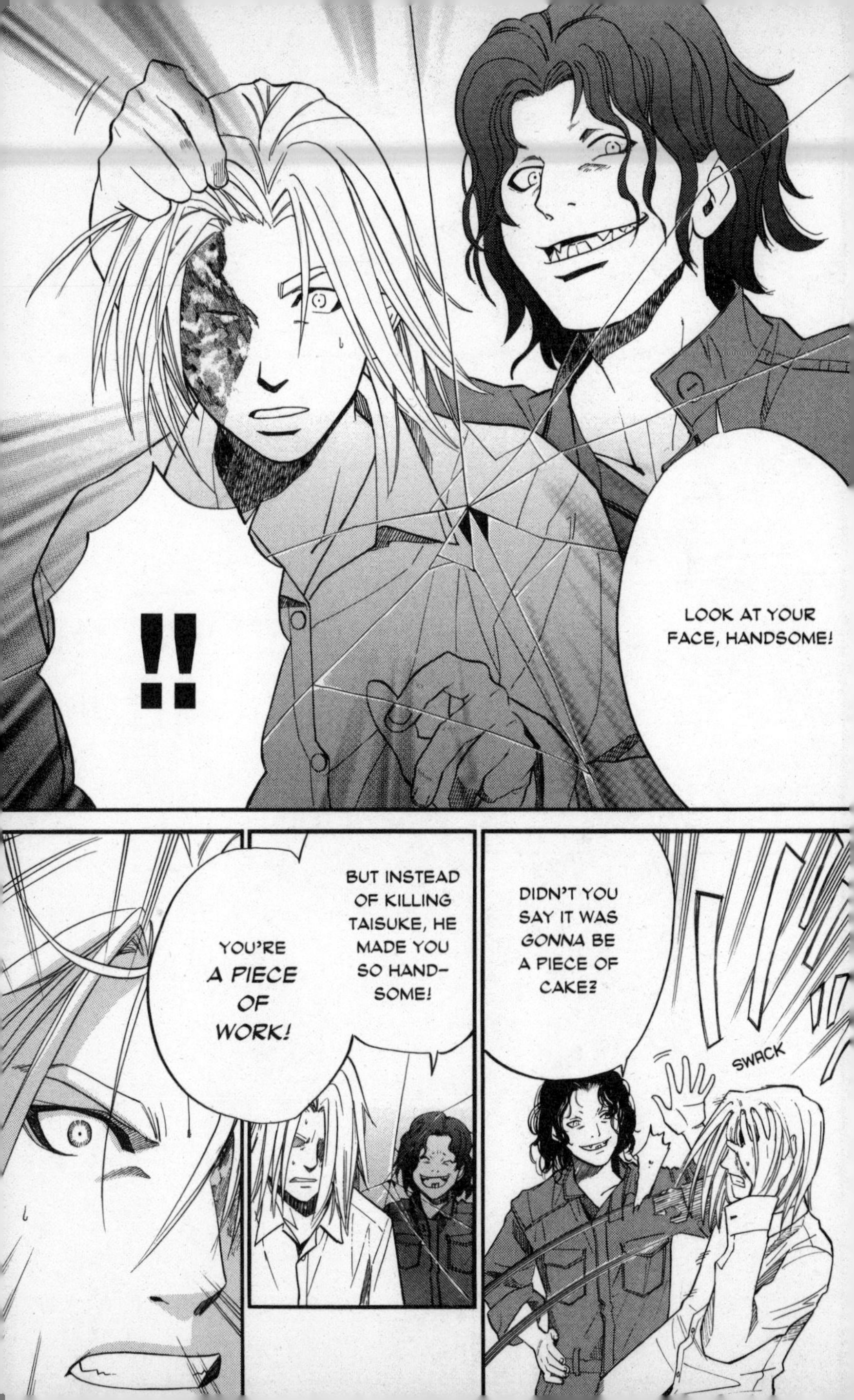
LOOK AT YOUR FACE, HANDSOME!
!!
DIDN'T YOU SAY IT WAS GONNA BE A PIECE OF CAKE?
SWACK
BUT INSTEAD OF KILLING TAISUKE, HE MADE YOU SO HAND-SOME!
YOU'RE A *PIECE OF WORK!*

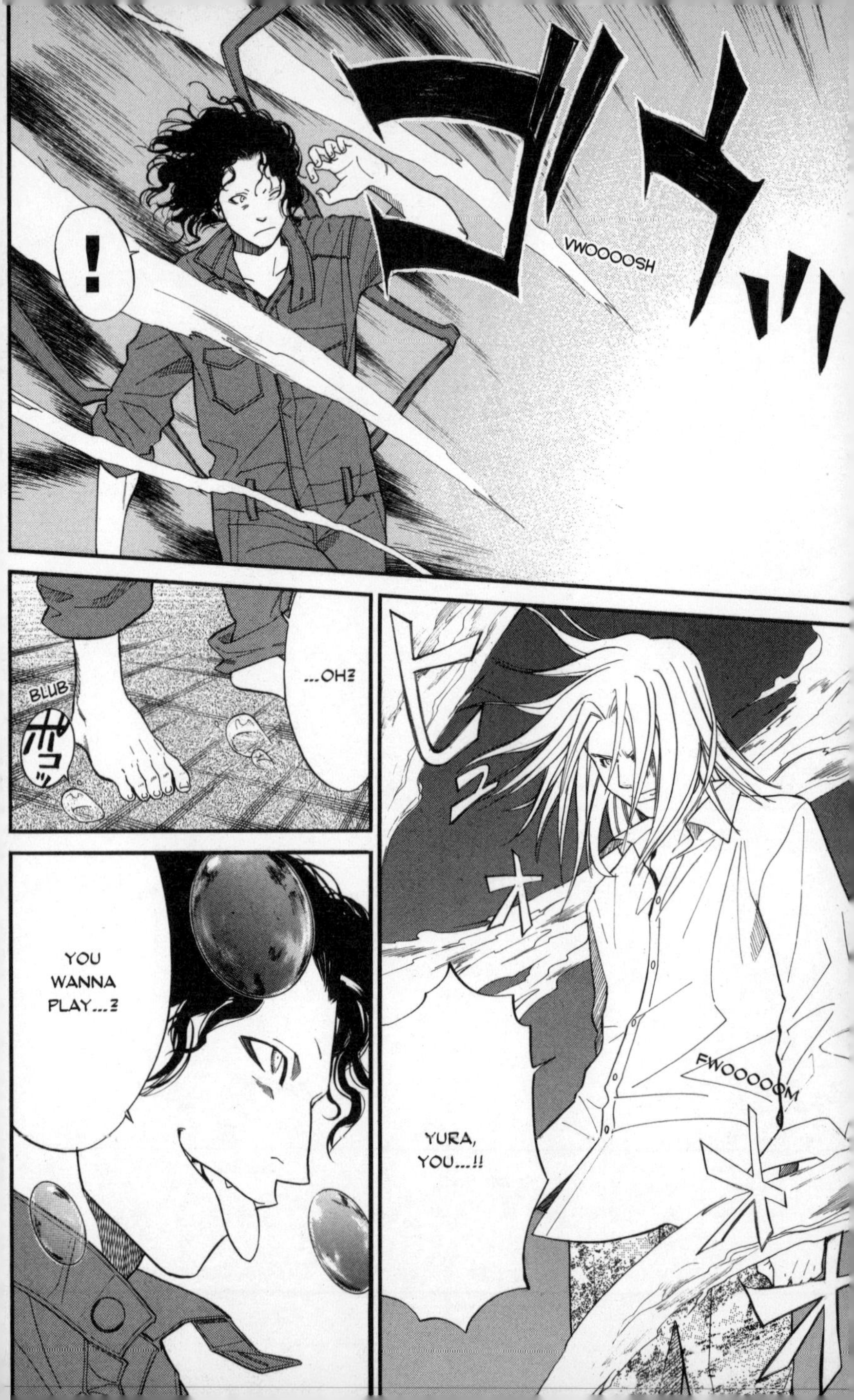
!
VWOOOOSH
FWOOOOOM
YURA, YOU...!!
...OH?
BLUB
YOU WANNA PLAY...?

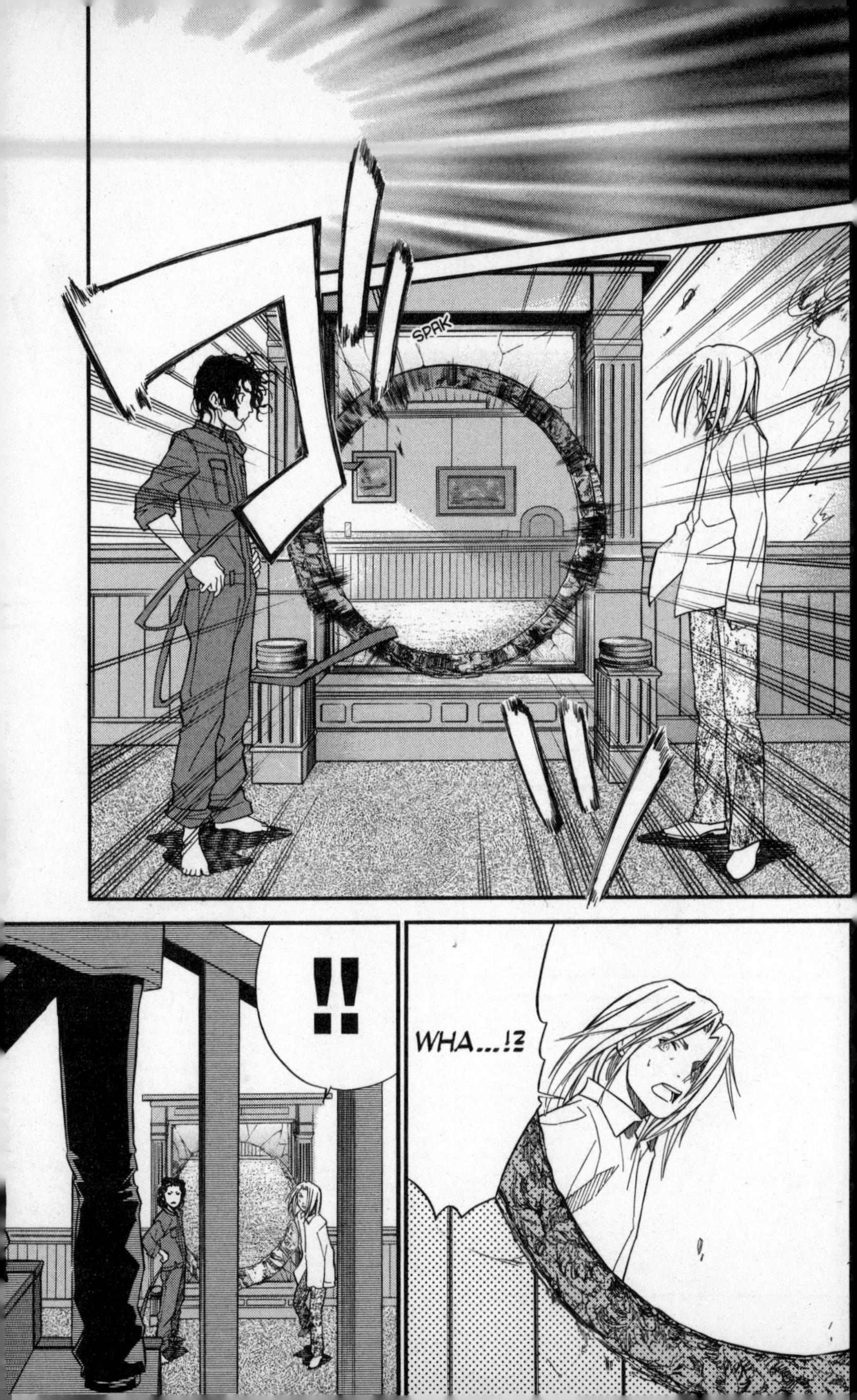
SPAK
WHA...!?
!!

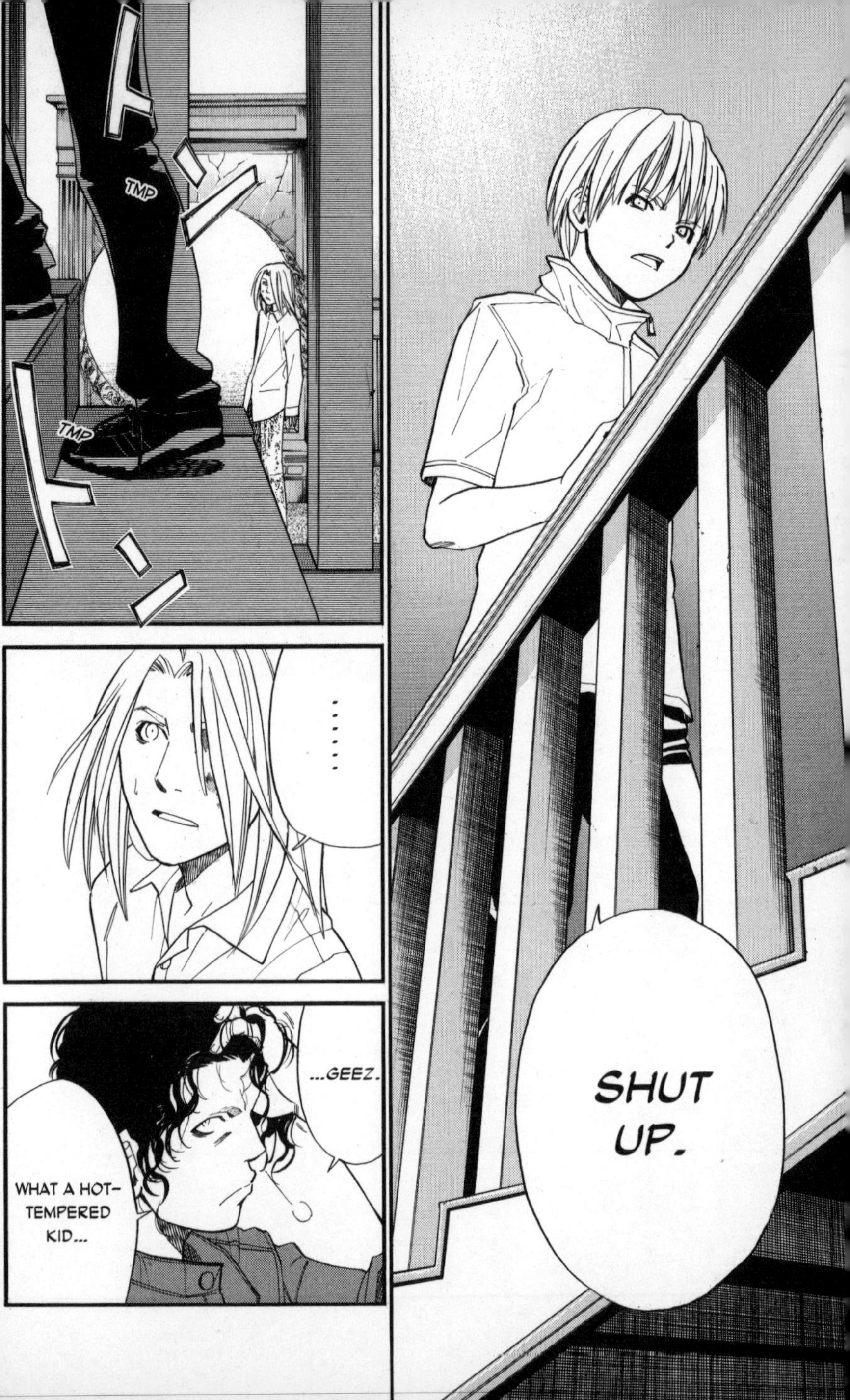
SHUT UP.
TMP
TMP
......
...GEEZ.
WHAT A HOT-TEMPERED KID...

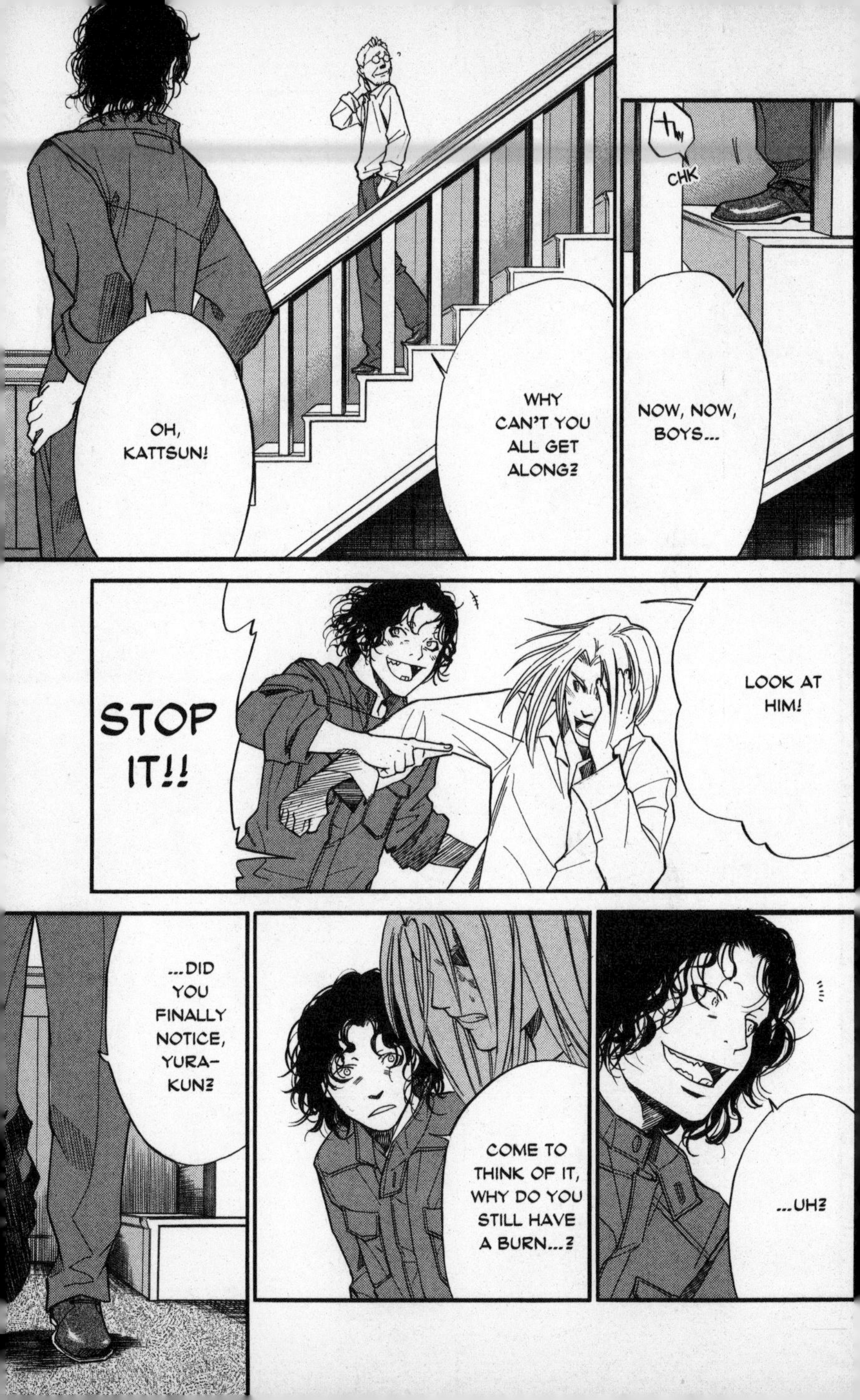
CHK
NOW, NOW, BOYS...
WHY CAN'T YOU ALL GET ALONG?
OH, KATTSUN!
LOOK AT HIM!
STOP IT!!
...UH?
COME TO THINK OF IT, WHY DO YOU STILL HAVE A BURN...?
...DID YOU FINALLY NOTICE, YURA-KUN?

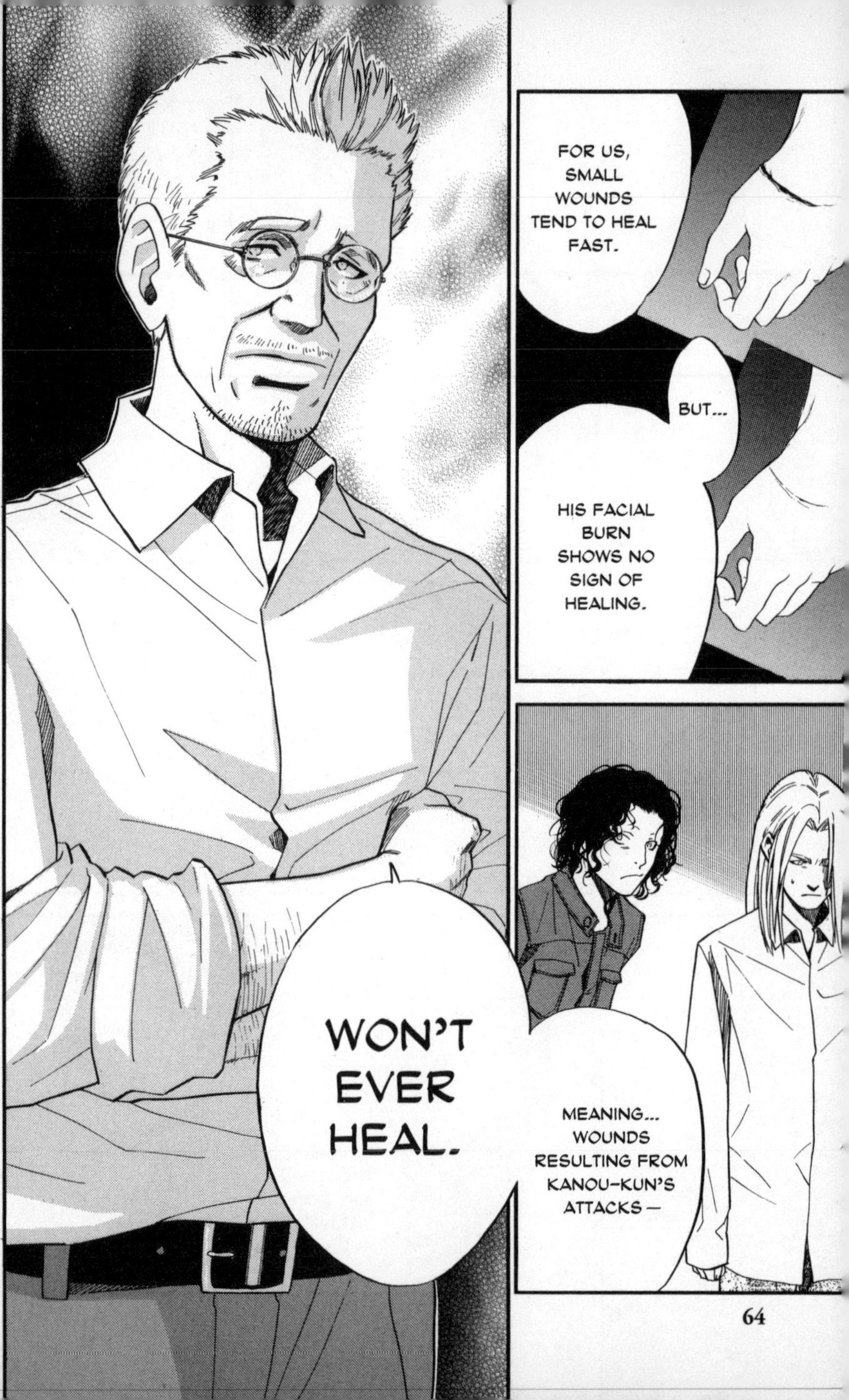
FOR US, SMALL WOUNDS TEND TO HEAL FAST.
BUT...
HIS FACIAL BURN SHOWS NO SIGN OF HEALING.
MEANING... WOUNDS RESULTING FROM KANOU-KUN'S ATTACKS—
WON'T EVER HEAL.

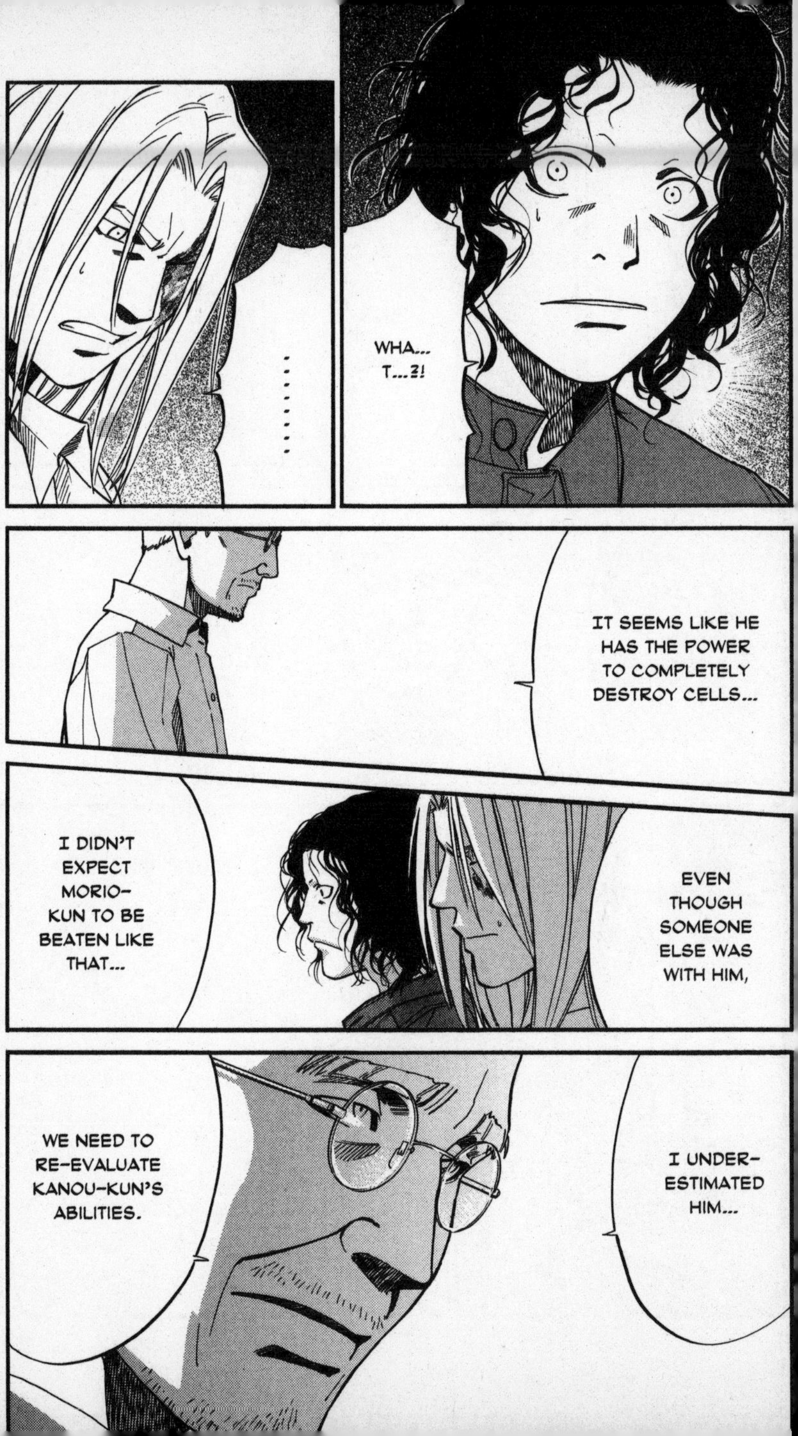
WHA... T...?!
......
IT SEEMS LIKE HE HAS THE POWER TO COMPLETELY DESTROY CELLS...
EVEN THOUGH SOMEONE ELSE WAS WITH HIM,
I DIDN'T EXPECT MORIO-KUN TO BE BEATEN LIKE THAT...
I UNDER-ESTIMATED HIM...
WE NEED TO RE-EVALUATE KANOU-KUN'S ABILITIES.

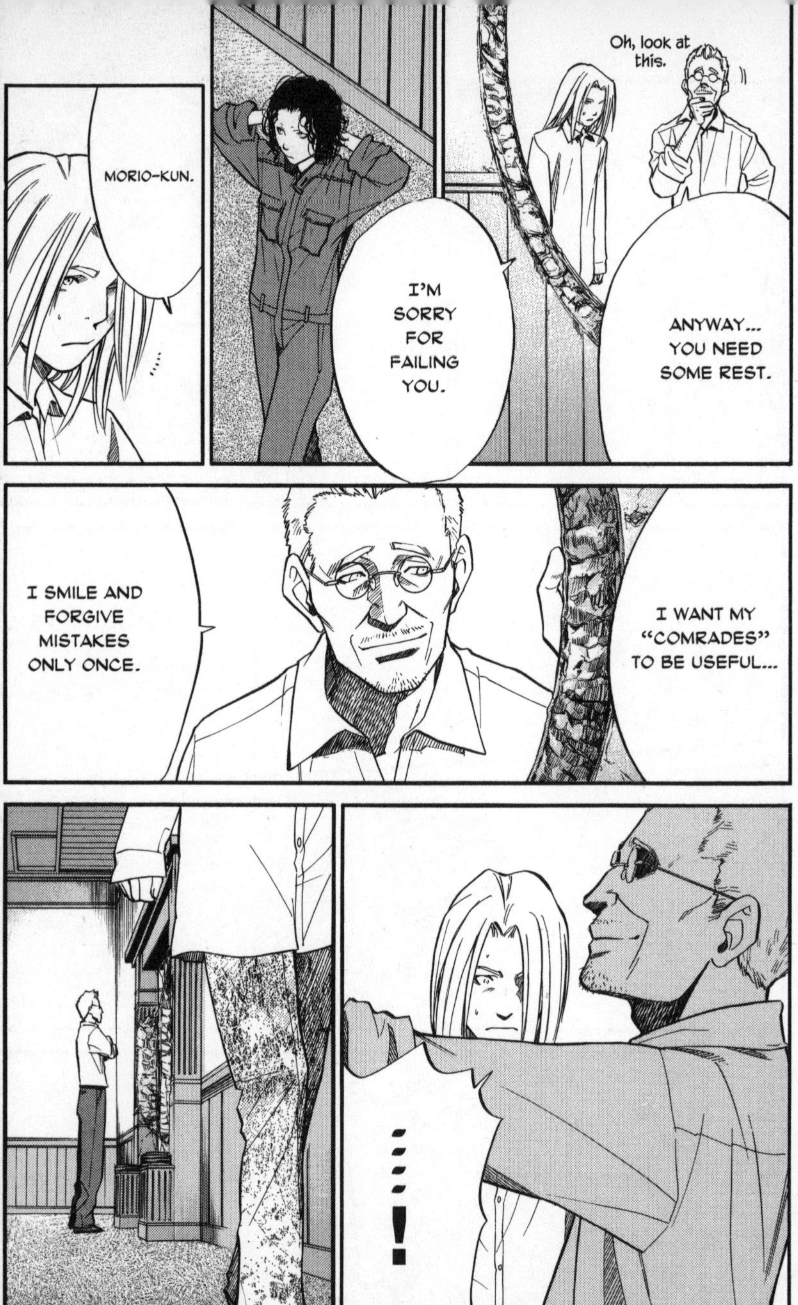
Oh, look at this.
ANYWAY... YOU NEED SOME REST.
I'M SORRY FOR FAILING YOU.
MORIO-KUN.
.....
I WANT MY "COMRADES" TO BE USEFUL...
I SMILE AND FORGIVE MISTAKES ONLY ONCE.
...!

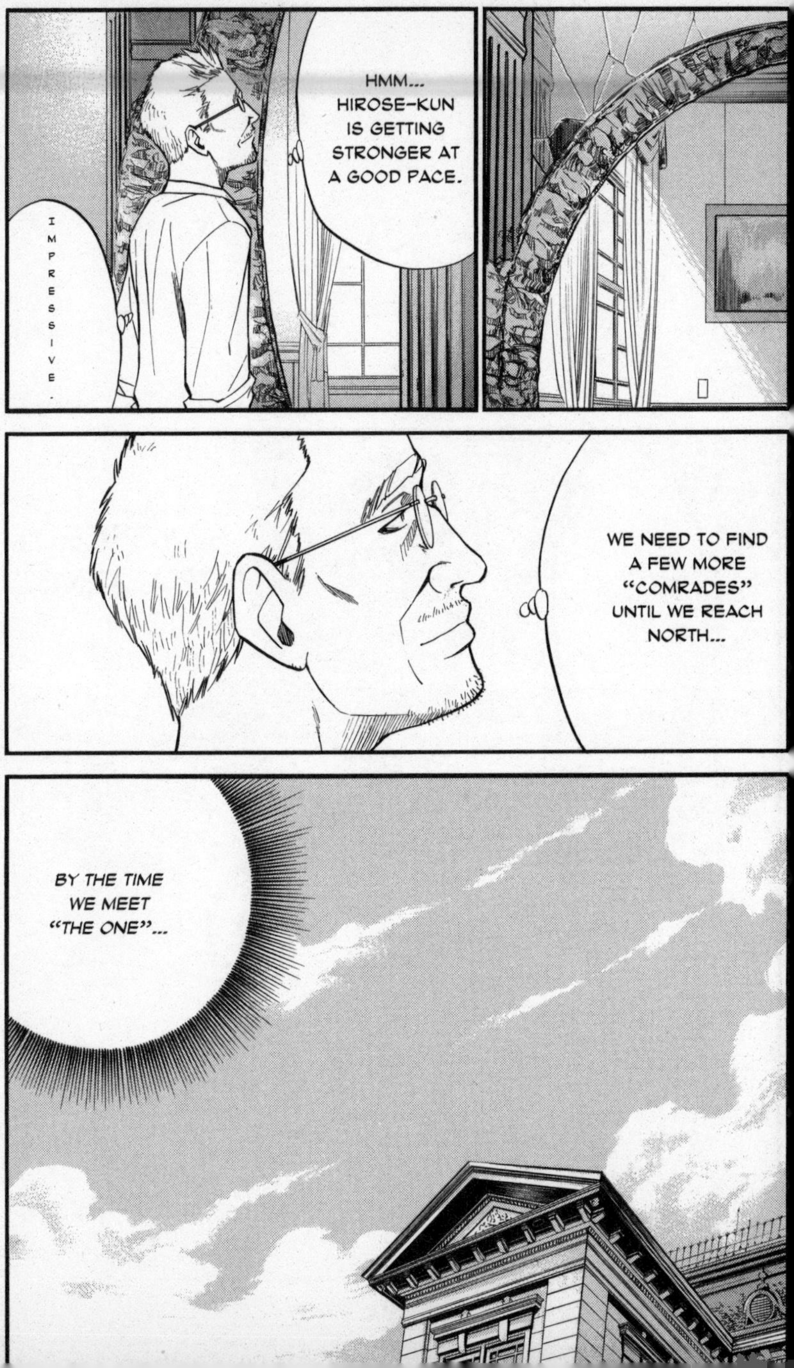
HMM... HIROSE-KUN IS GETTING STRONGER AT A GOOD PACE.
IMPRESSIVE.
WE NEED TO FIND A FEW MORE "COMRADES" UNTIL WE REACH NORTH...
BY THE TIME WE MEET "THE ONE"...

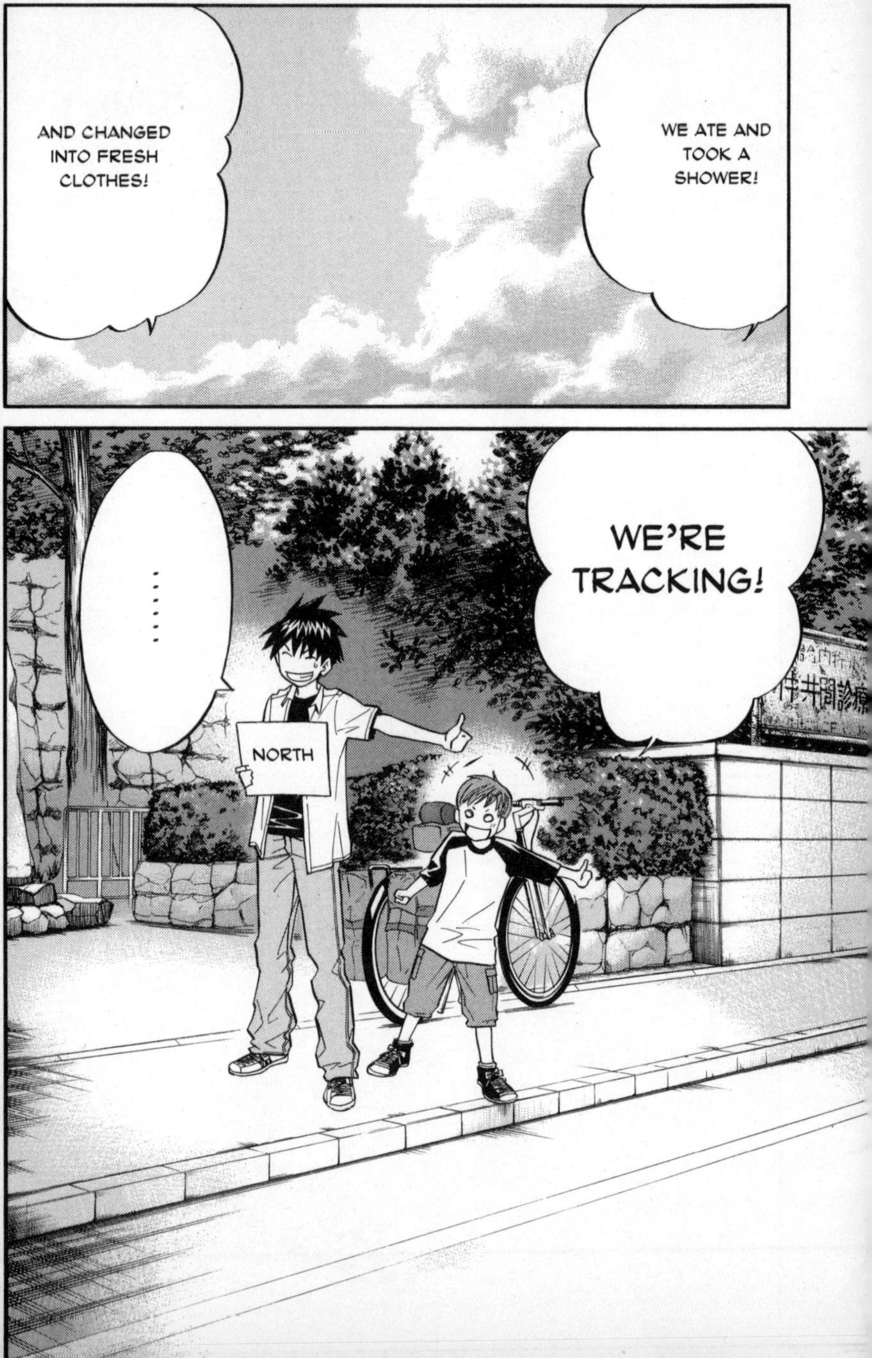
WE ATE AND TOOK A SHOWER!
AND CHANGED INTO FRESH CLOTHES!
WE'RE TRACKING!
NORTH
......

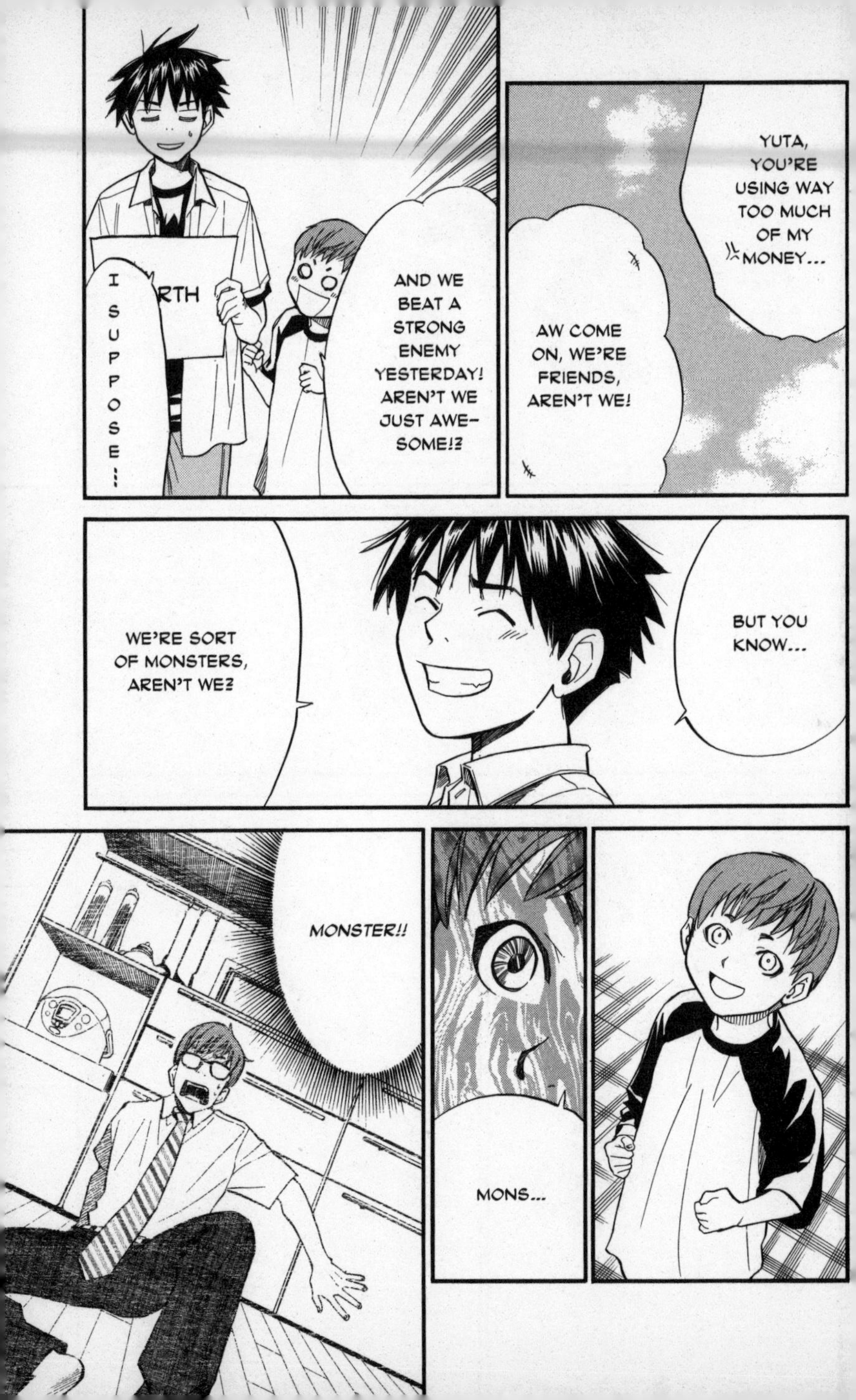
YUTA, YOU'RE USING WAY TOO MUCH OF MY MONEY...
AW COME ON, WE'RE FRIENDS, AREN'T WE!
AND WE BEAT A STRONG ENEMY YESTERDAY! AREN'T WE JUST AWE-SOME!?
I SUPPOSE!!
BUT YOU KNOW...
WE'RE SORT OF MONSTERS, AREN'T WE?
MONS...
MONSTER!!

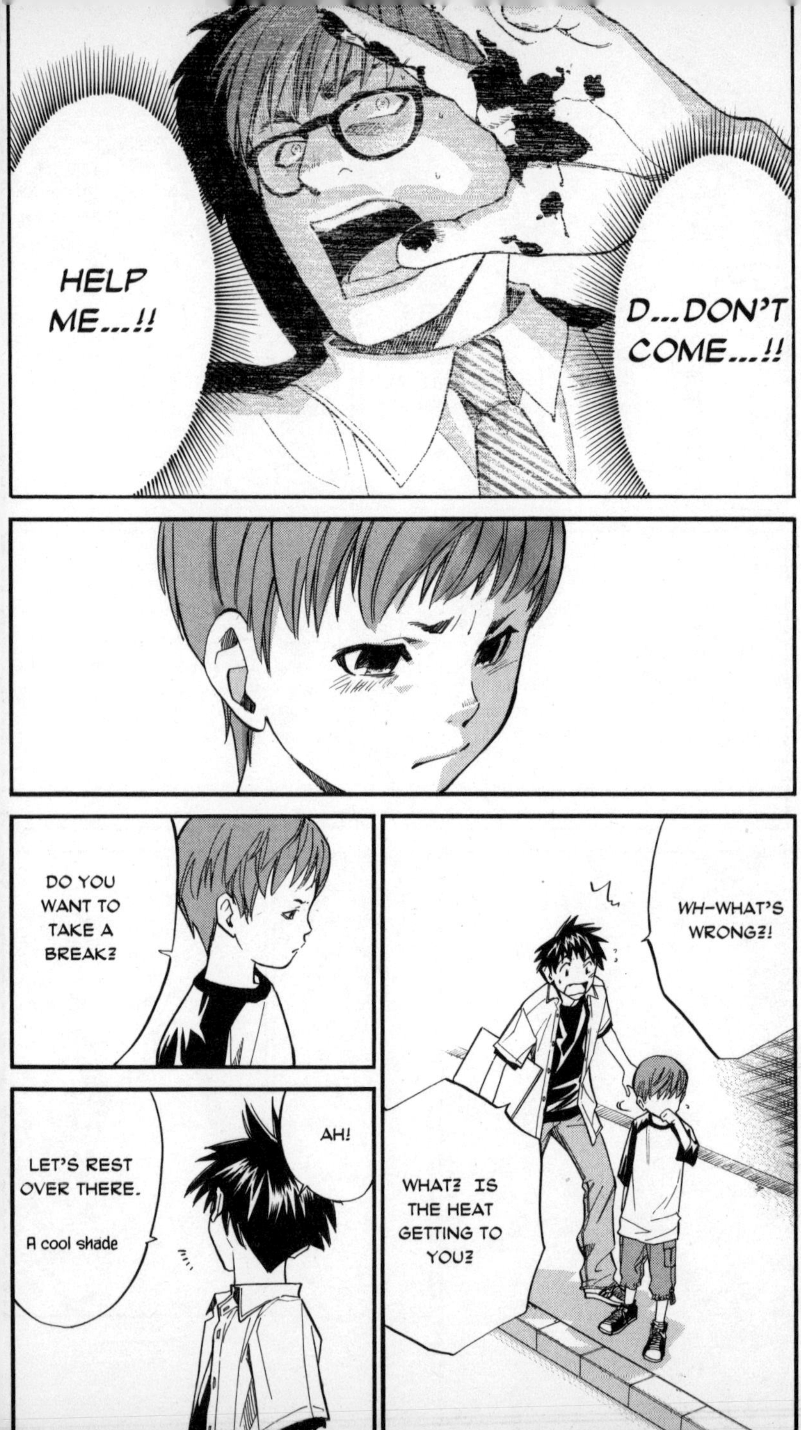
D...DON'T COME...!!
HELP ME...!!
WH-WHAT'S WRONG?!
WHAT? IS THE HEAT GETTING TO YOU?
DO YOU WANT TO TAKE A BREAK?
AH!
LET'S REST OVER THERE.
A cool shade

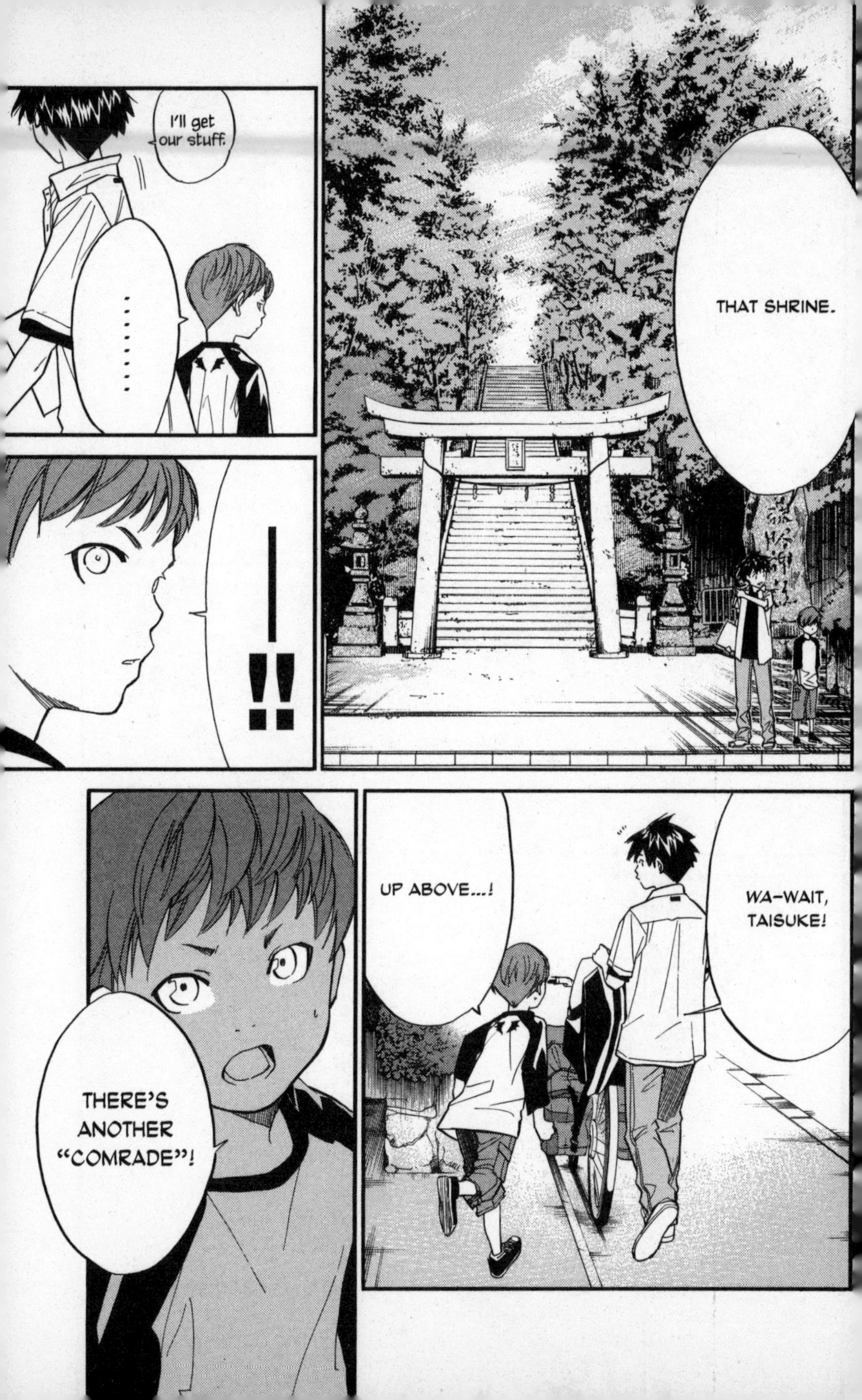
THAT SHRINE.
I'll get our stuff.
......
—!!
WA-WAIT, TAISUKE!
UP ABOVE...!
THERE'S ANOTHER "COMRADE"!

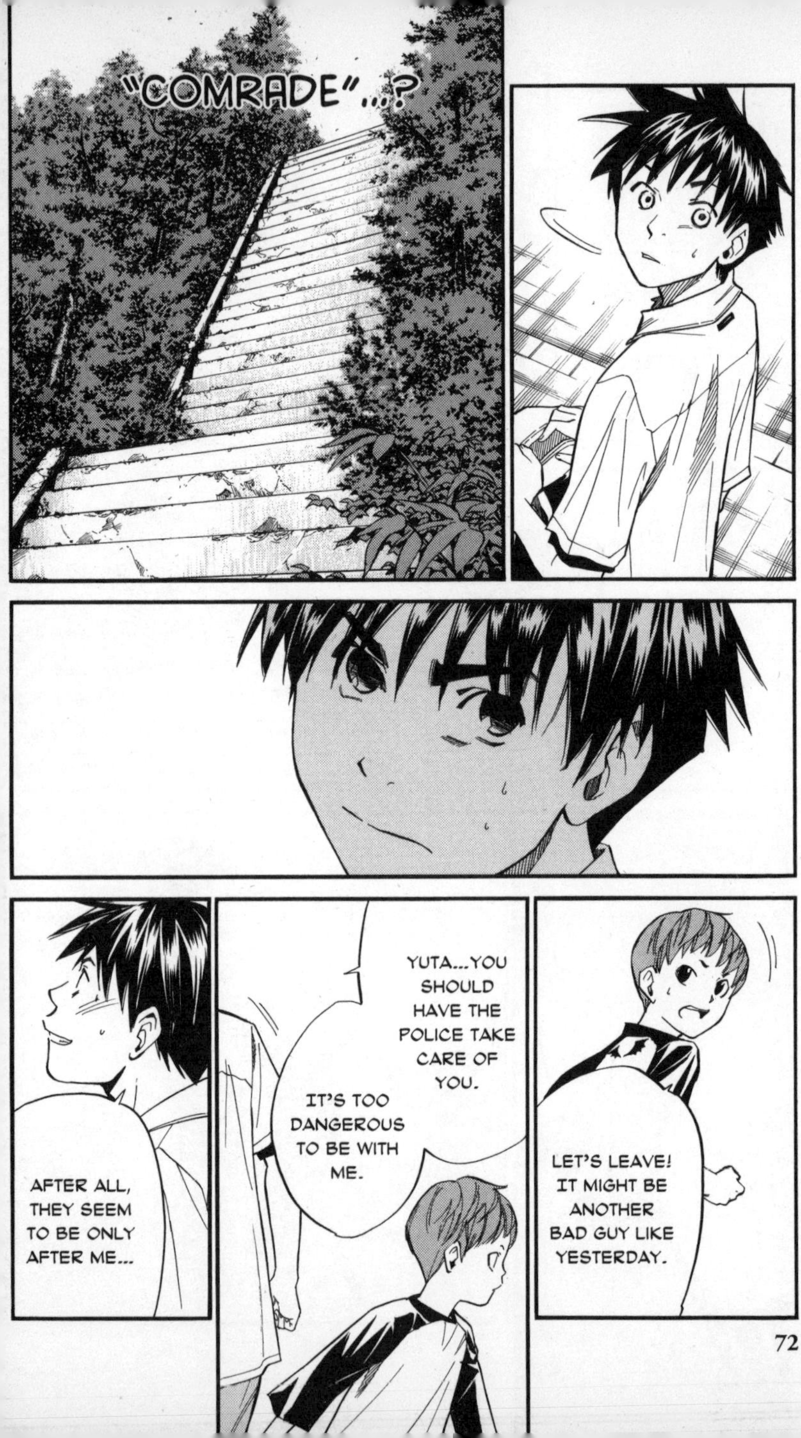
"COMRADE"...?
LET'S LEAVE! IT MIGHT BE ANOTHER BAD GUY LIKE YESTERDAY.
YUTA...YOU SHOULD HAVE THE POLICE TAKE CARE OF YOU.
IT'S TOO DANGEROUS TO BE WITH ME.
AFTER ALL, THEY SEEM TO BE ONLY AFTER ME...

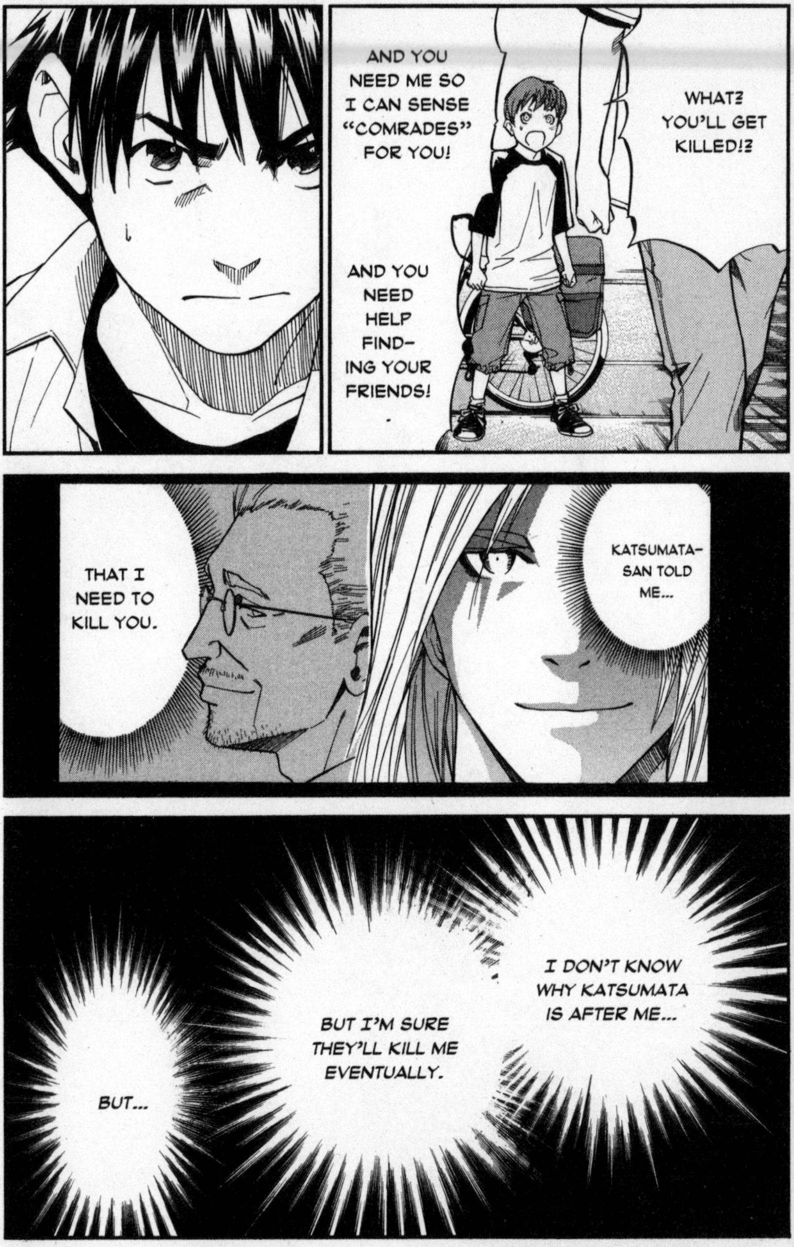
WHAT? YOU'LL GET KILLED!?
AND YOU NEED ME SO I CAN SENSE "COMRADES" FOR YOU!
AND YOU NEED HELP FIND-ING YOUR FRIENDS!
KATSUMATA-SAN TOLD ME...
THAT I NEED TO KILL YOU.
I DON'T KNOW WHY KATSUMATA IS AFTER ME...
BUT I'M SURE THEY'LL KILL ME EVENTUALLY.
BUT...

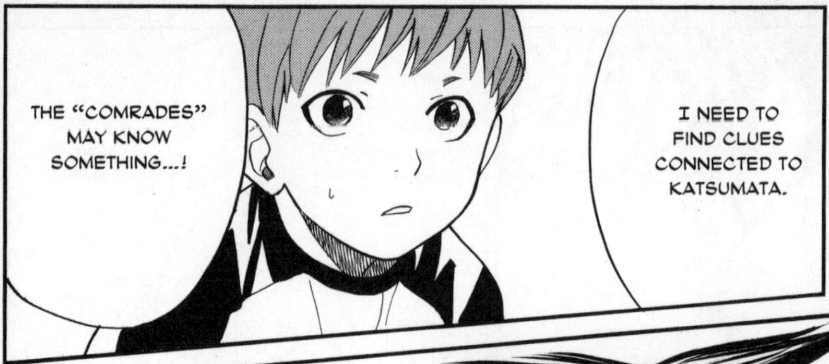
I NEED TO FIND CLUES CONNECTED TO KATSUMATA.
THE "COMRADES" MAY KNOW SOMETHING...!
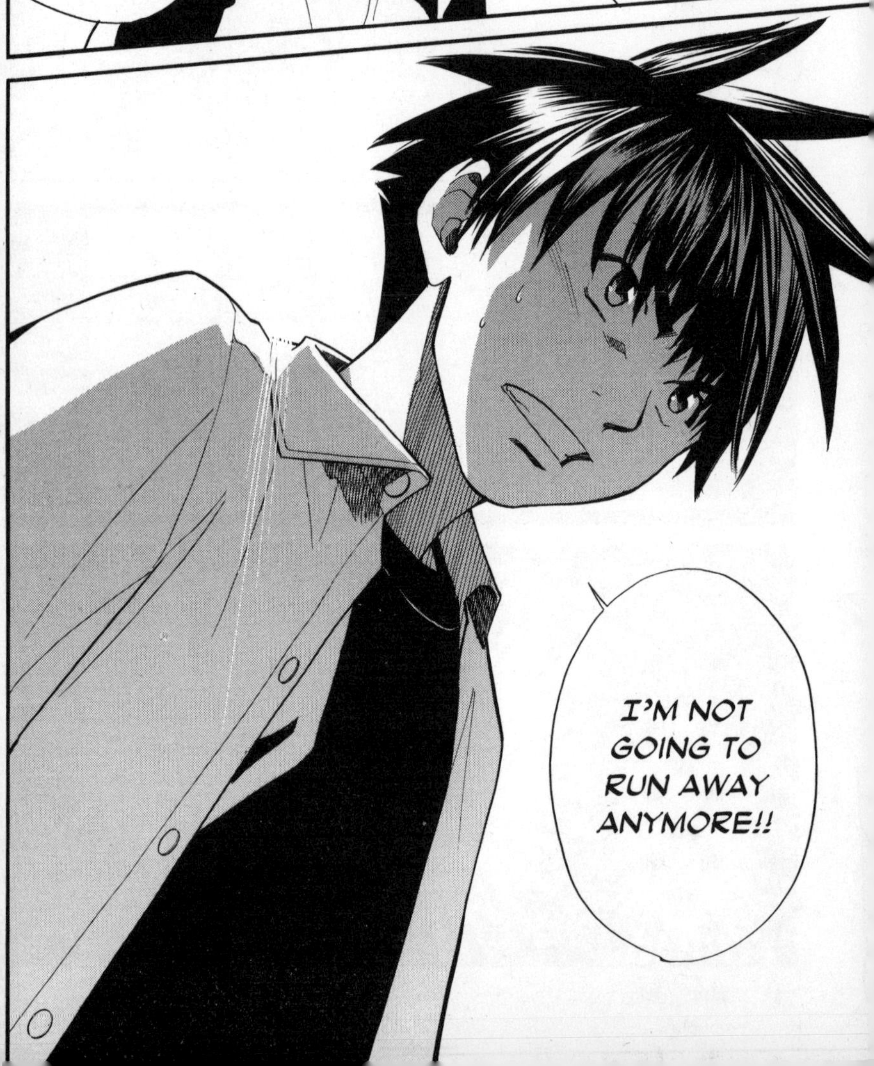
I'M NOT GOING TO RUN AWAY ANYMORE!!

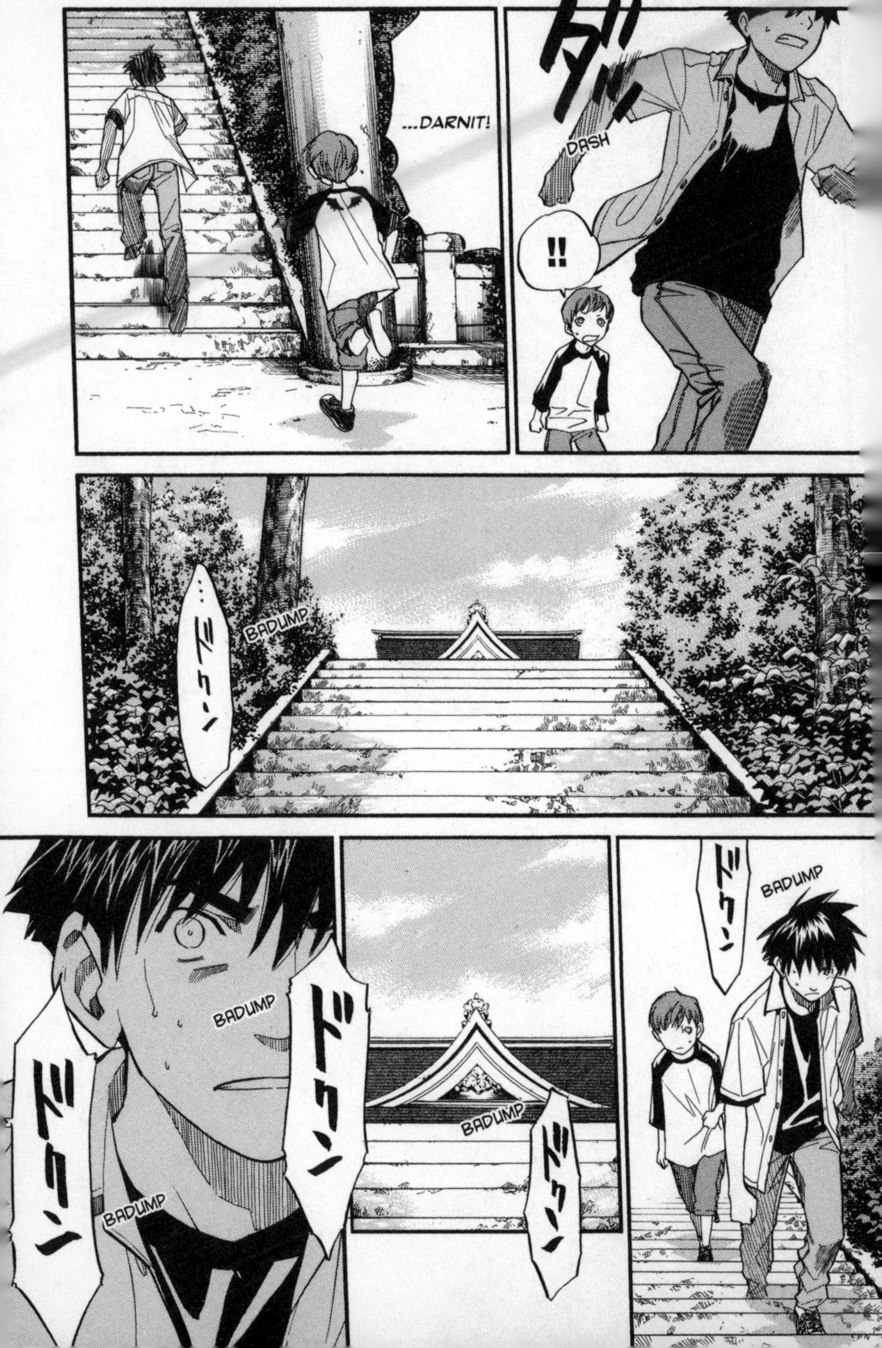
ダッ
DASH
!!
...DARNIT!
...ドクン
BADUMP
ドクン
BADUMP
ドクン
BADUMP
ドクン
BADUMP
ドクン
BADUMP

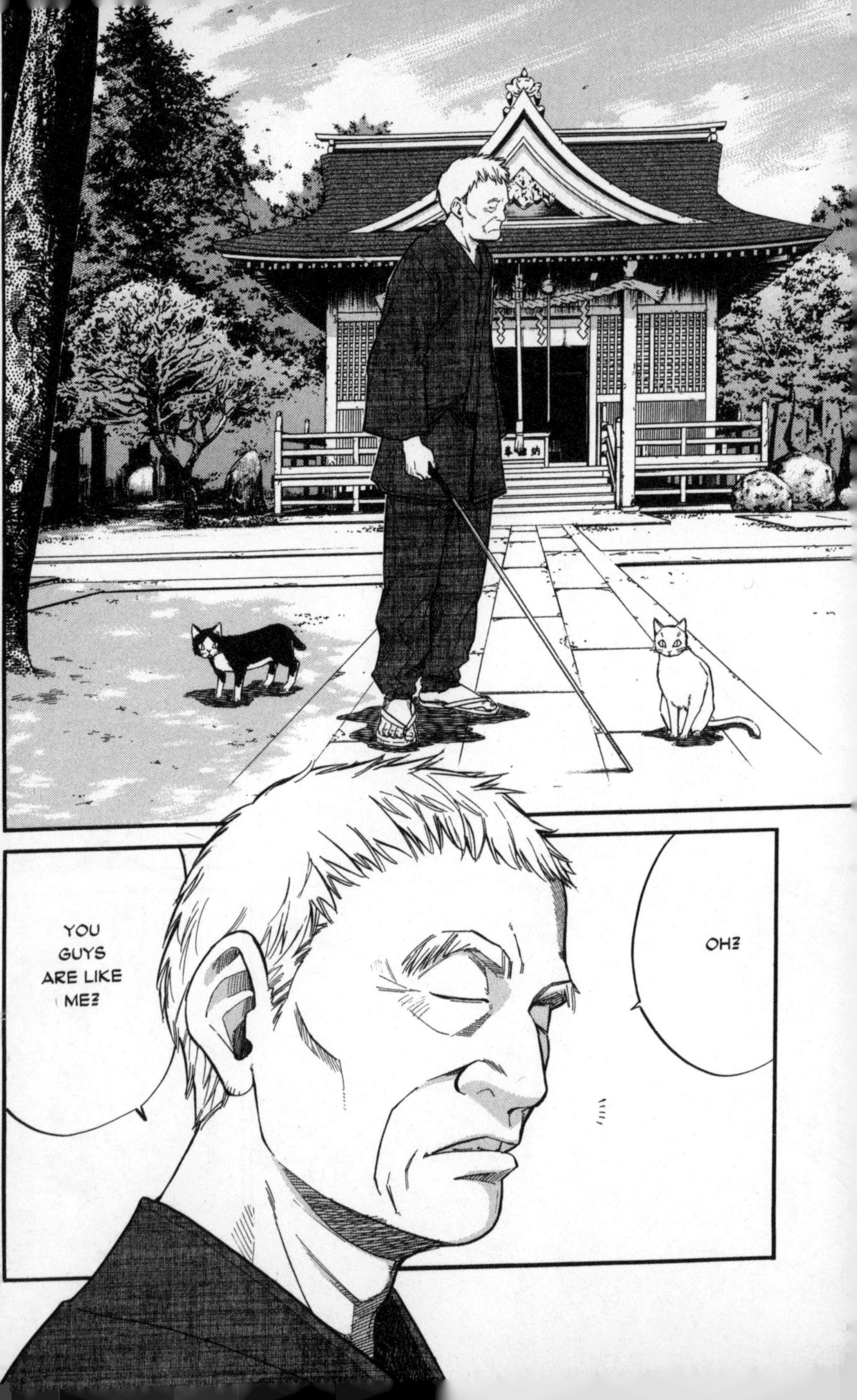
OH?
YOU GUYS ARE LIKE ME?

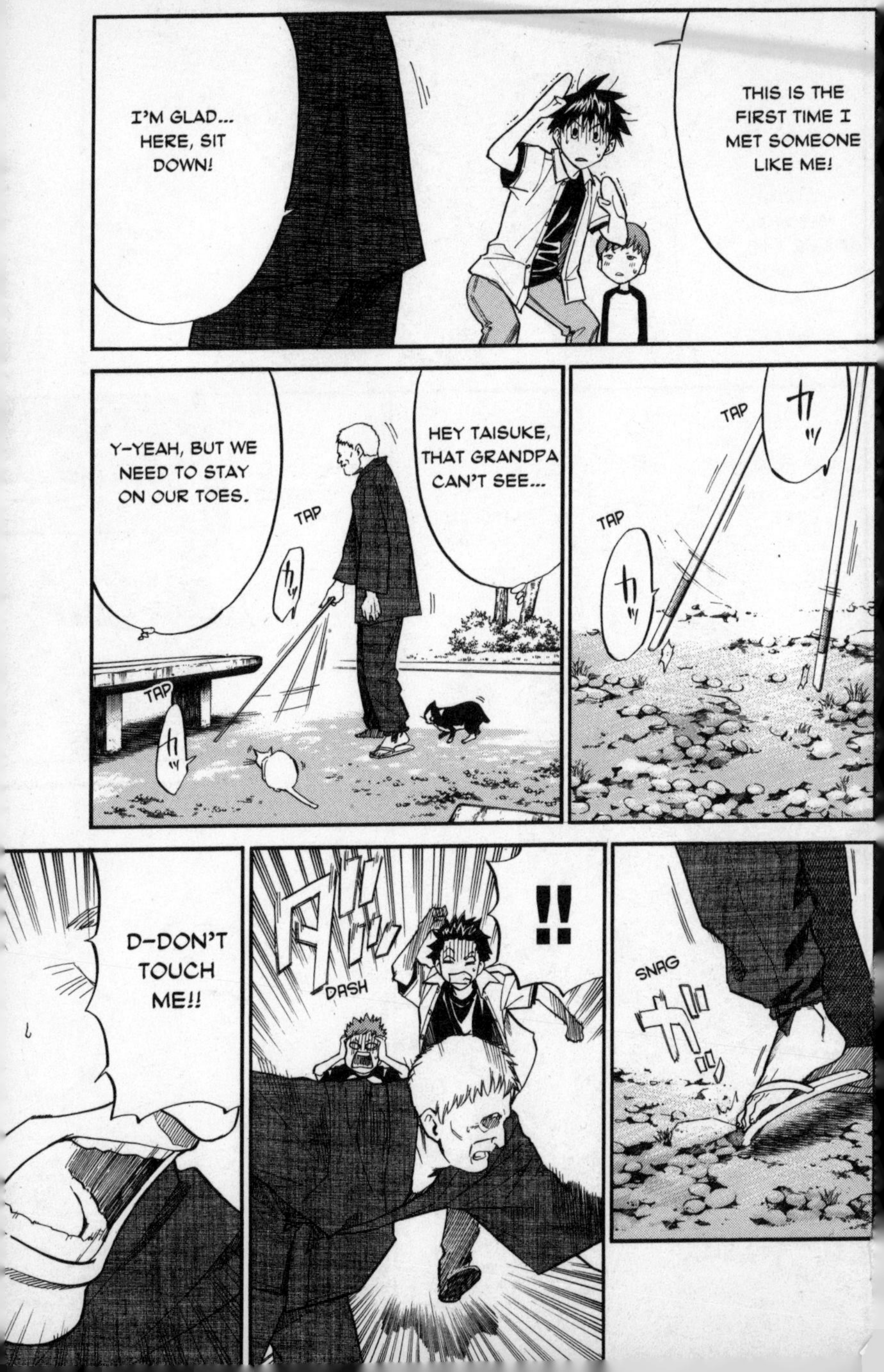
THIS IS THE FIRST TIME I MET SOMEONE LIKE ME!
I'M GLAD... HERE, SIT DOWN!
TAP
カッ
TAP
カッ
HEY TAISUKE, THAT GRANDPA CAN'T SEE...
TAP
カッ
Y-YEAH, BUT WE NEED TO STAY ON OUR TOES.
TAP
カッ
SNAG
ガッ
!!
ダッ
DASH
D-DON'T TOUCH ME!!

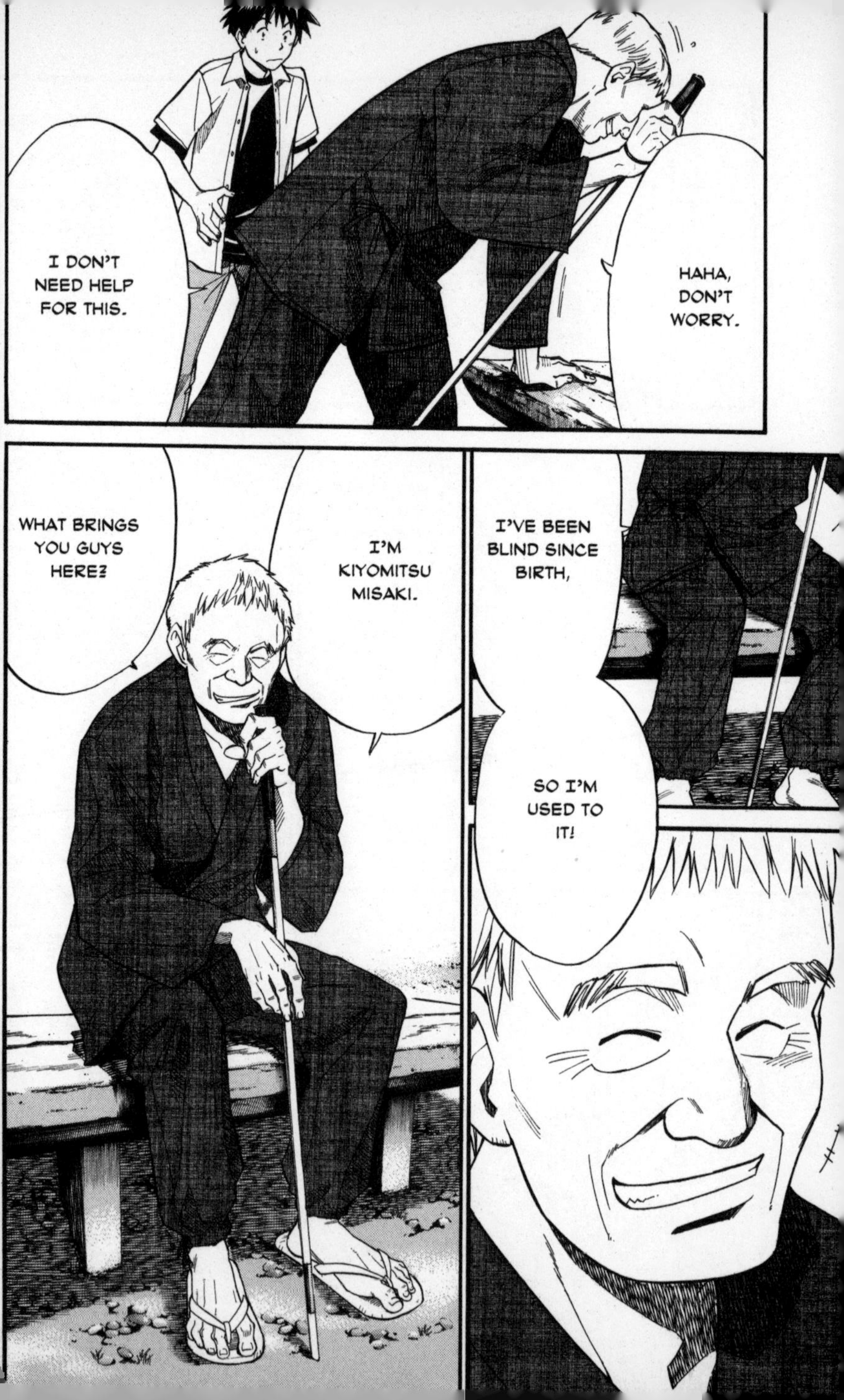
HAHA, DON'T WORRY.
I DON'T NEED HELP FOR THIS.
I'VE BEEN BLIND SINCE BIRTH,
SO I'M USED TO IT!
I'M KIYOMITSU MISAKI.
WHAT BRINGS YOU GUYS HERE?

THAT GRANDPA PROBABLY ISN'T PART OF KATSUMATA'S GANG.

There, there

Y-YEAH, TRUE.

I guess I feel safe, sort of...

THERE

THERE

POWER?

OH, THAT...

ERRR... WHAT IS YOUR POWER, GRANDPA?

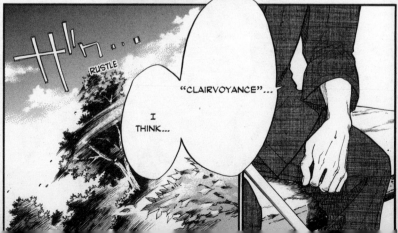

RUSTLE

"CLAIRVOYANCE"...

I THINK...

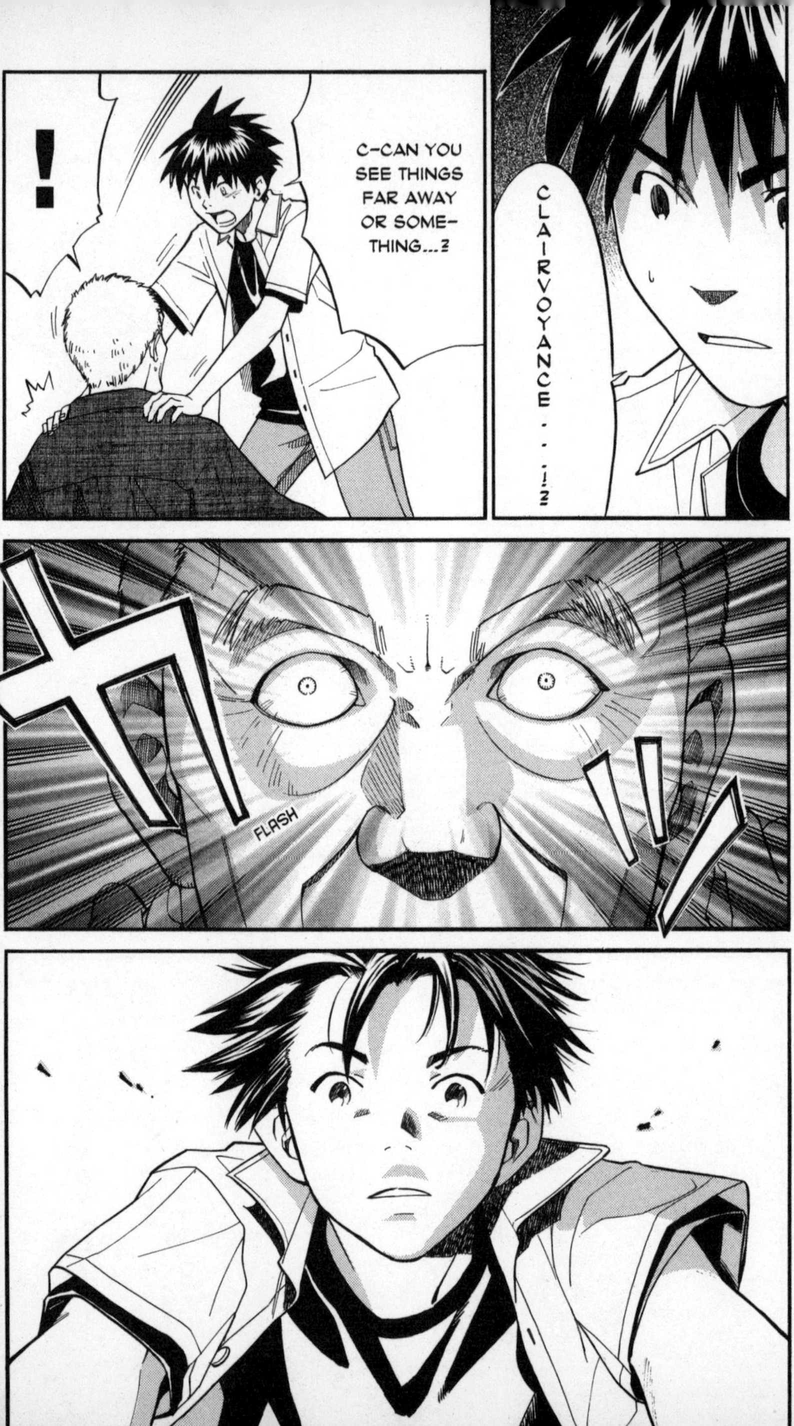
CLAIRVOYANCE...!?
!
C-CAN YOU SEE THINGS FAR AWAY OR SOME-THING...?
FLASH

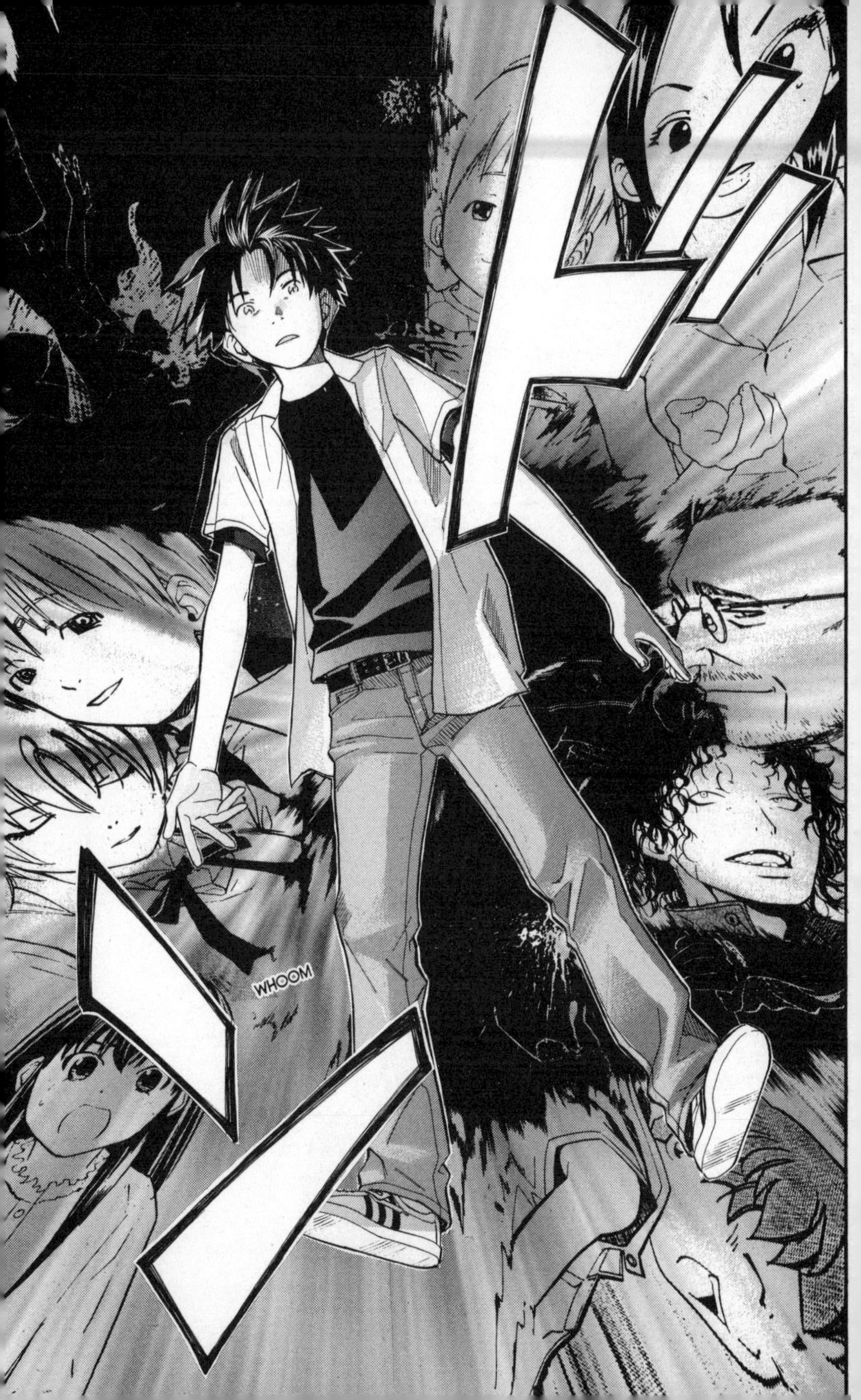
WHOOM

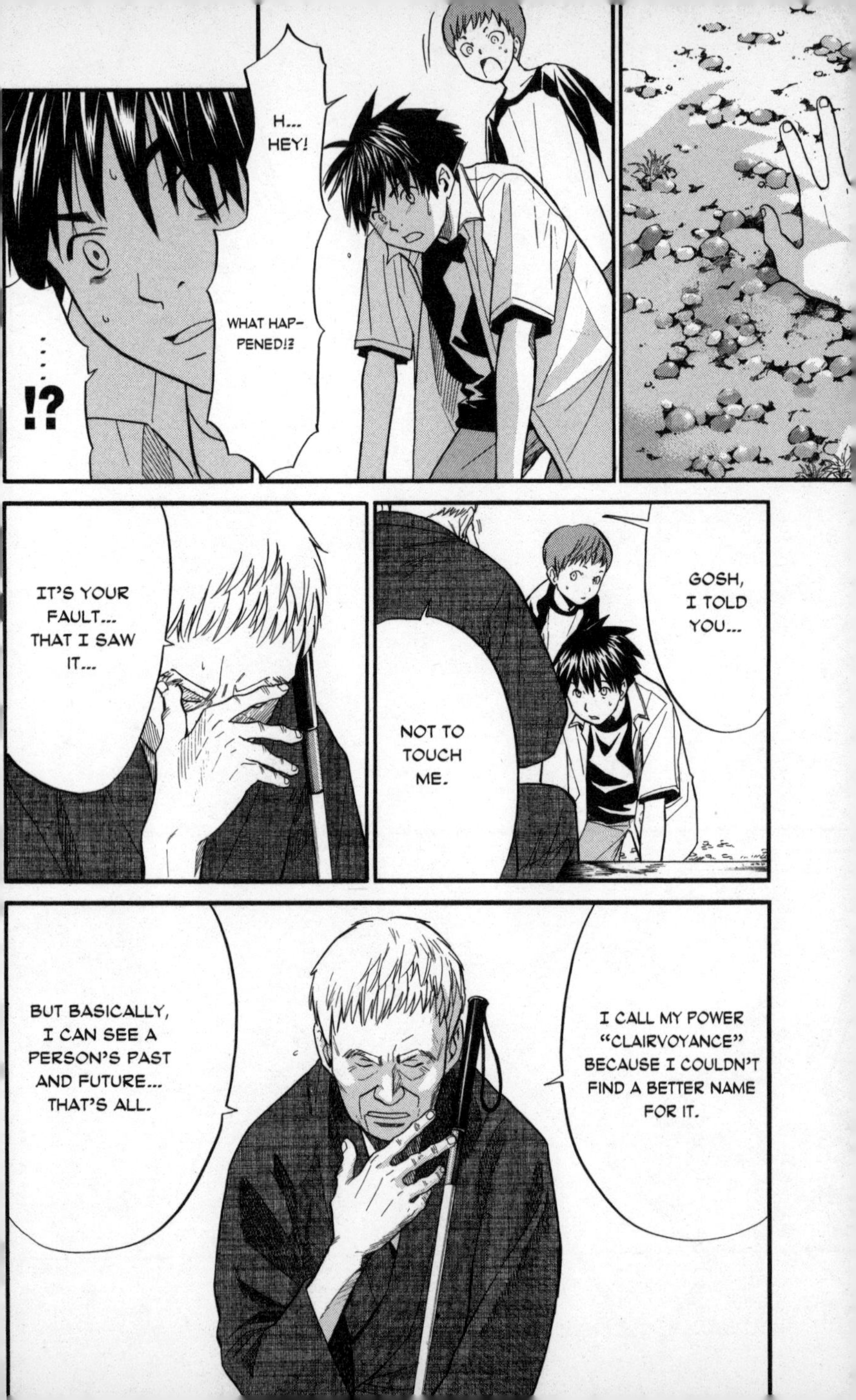
H... HEY!
WHAT HAP-PENED!?
...!?
GOSH, I TOLD YOU...
NOT TO TOUCH ME.
IT'S YOUR FAULT... THAT I SAW IT...
I CALL MY POWER "CLAIRVOYANCE" BECAUSE I COULDN'T FIND A BETTER NAME FOR IT.
BUT BASICALLY, I CAN SEE A PERSON'S PAST AND FUTURE... THAT'S ALL.

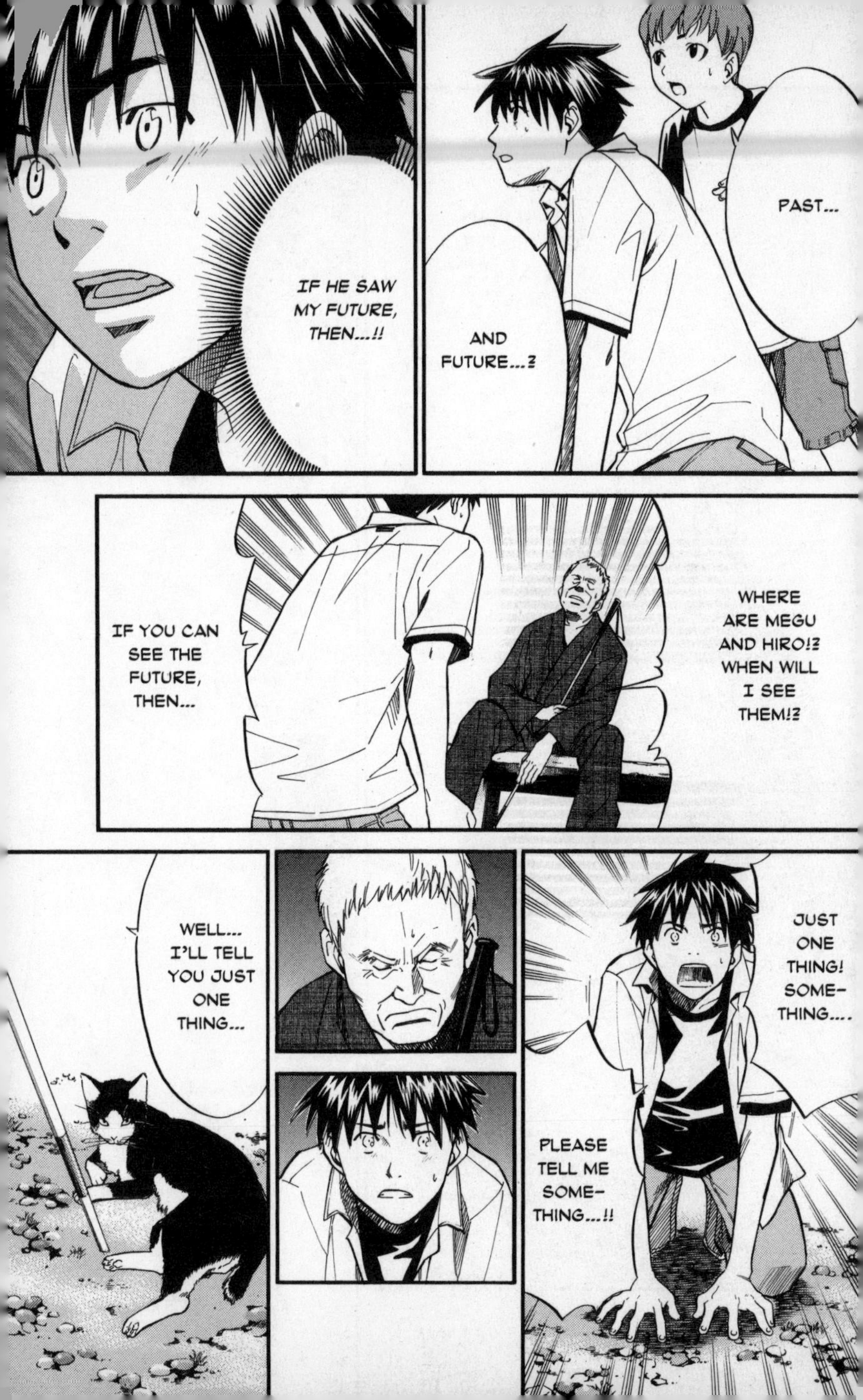
PAST...
AND FUTURE...?
IF HE SAW MY FUTURE, THEN...!!
WHERE ARE MEGU AND HIRO!? WHEN WILL I SEE THEM!?
IF YOU CAN SEE THE FUTURE, THEN...
JUST ONE THING! SOME-THING....
PLEASE TELL ME SOME-THING...!!
WELL... I'LL TELL YOU JUST ONE THING...

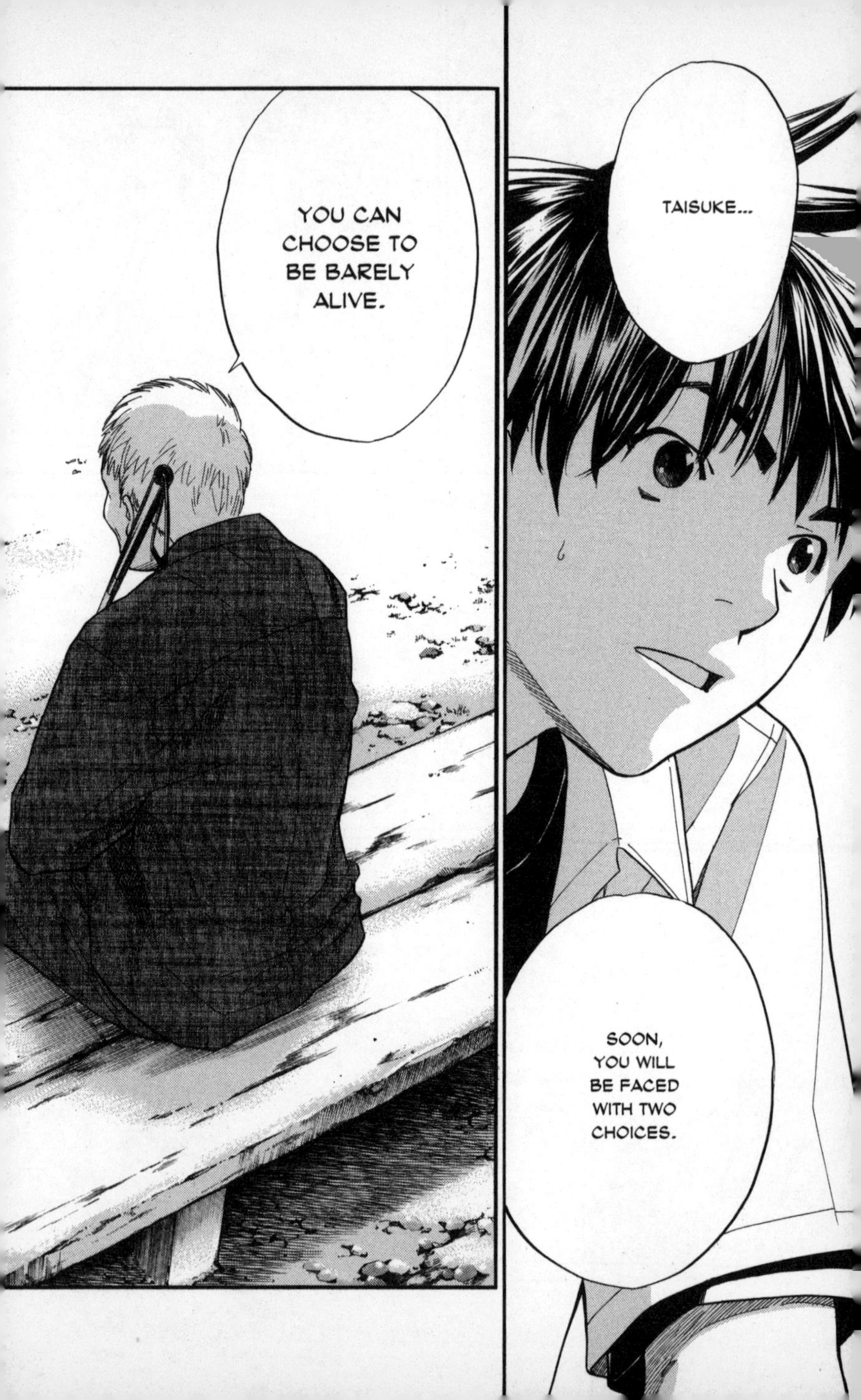
TAISUKE...
SOON, YOU WILL BE FACED WITH TWO CHOICES.
YOU CAN CHOOSE TO BE BARELY ALIVE.

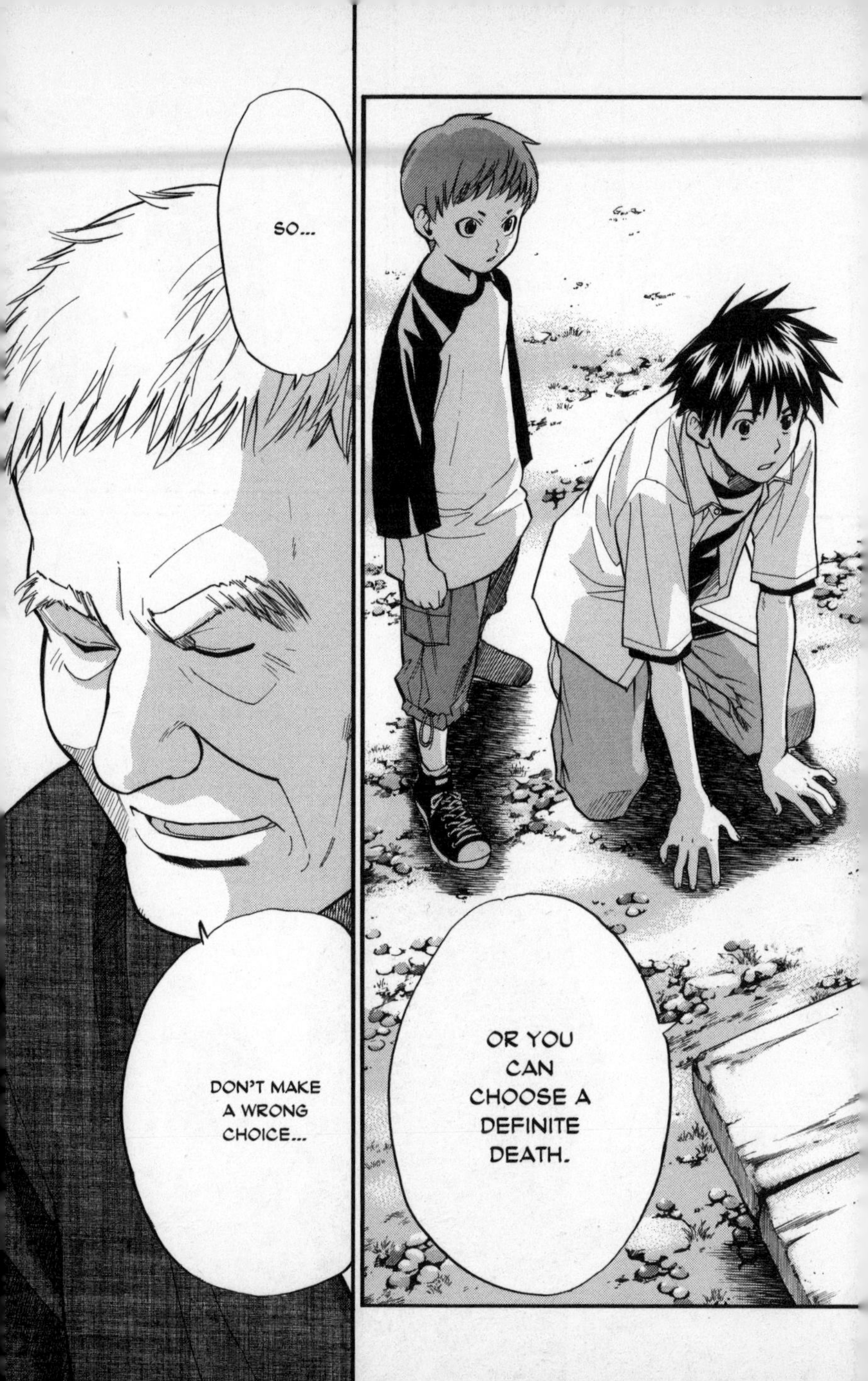
OR YOU CAN CHOOSE A DEFINITE DEATH.
SO...
DON'T MAKE A WRONG CHOICE...

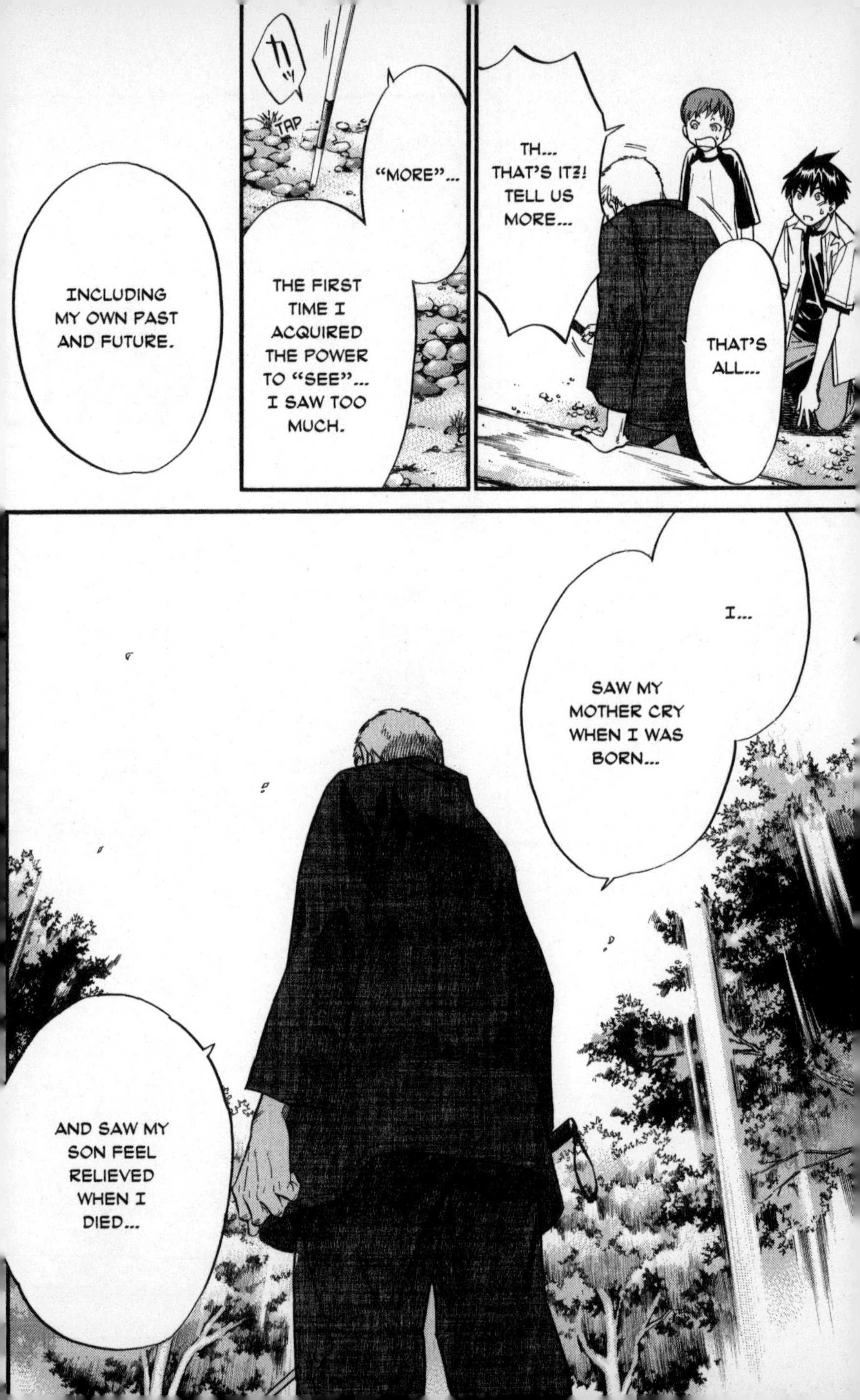
TH... THAT'S IT?! TELL US MORE...
THAT'S ALL...
カツ
TAP
"MORE"...
THE FIRST TIME I ACQUIRED THE POWER TO "SEE"... I SAW TOO MUCH.
INCLUDING MY OWN PAST AND FUTURE.
I...
SAW MY MOTHER CRY WHEN I WAS BORN...
AND SAW MY SON FEEL RELIEVED WHEN I DIED...

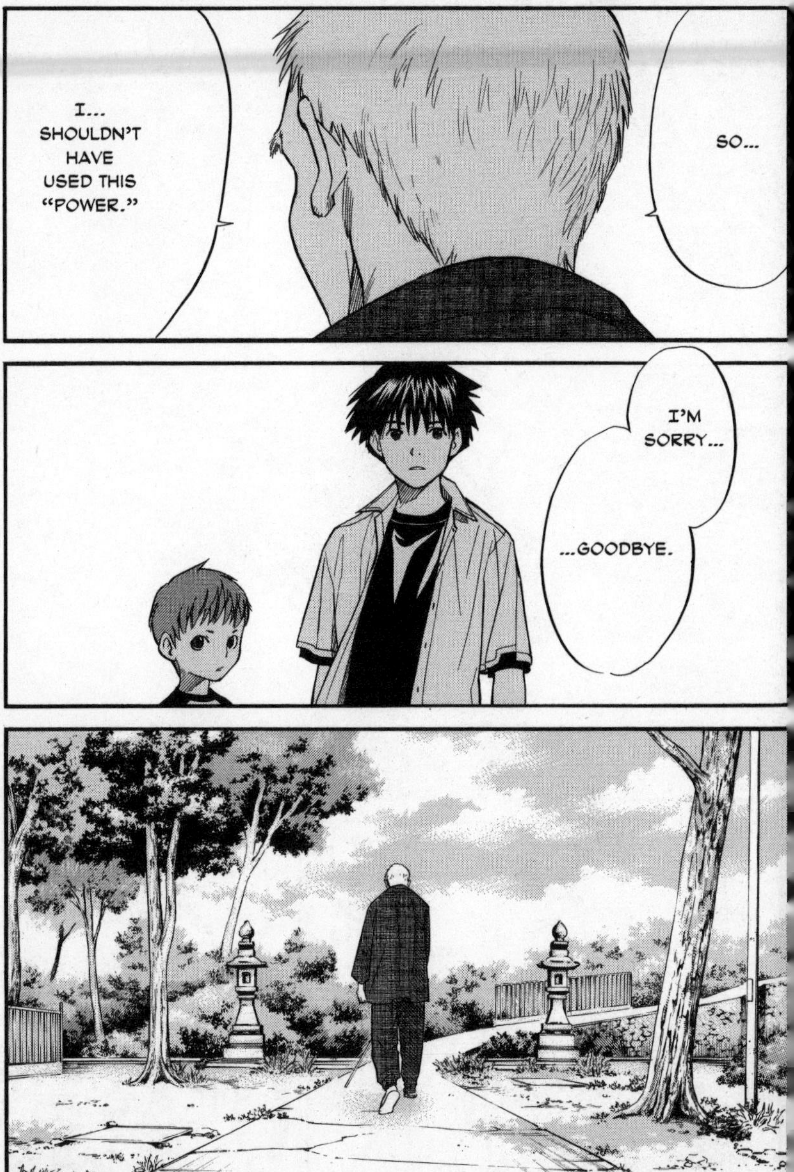
SO...
I... SHOULDN'T HAVE USED THIS "POWER."
I'M SORRY...
...GOODBYE.

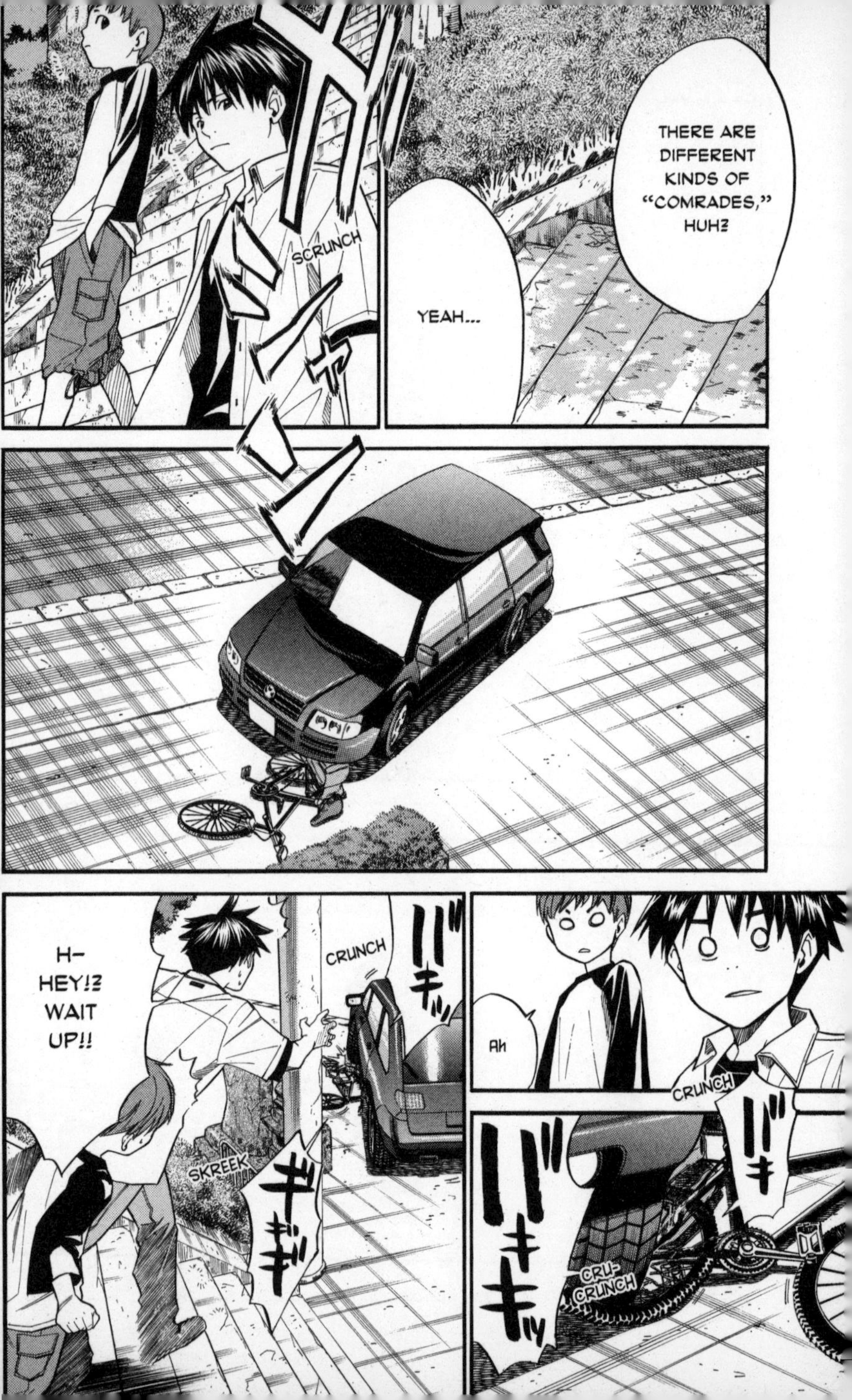
THERE ARE DIFFERENT KINDS OF "COMRADES," HUH?
YEAH...
SCRUNCH
Ah
CRUNCH
CRU-CRUNCH
CRUNCH
H-HEY!? WAIT UP!!
SKREEK

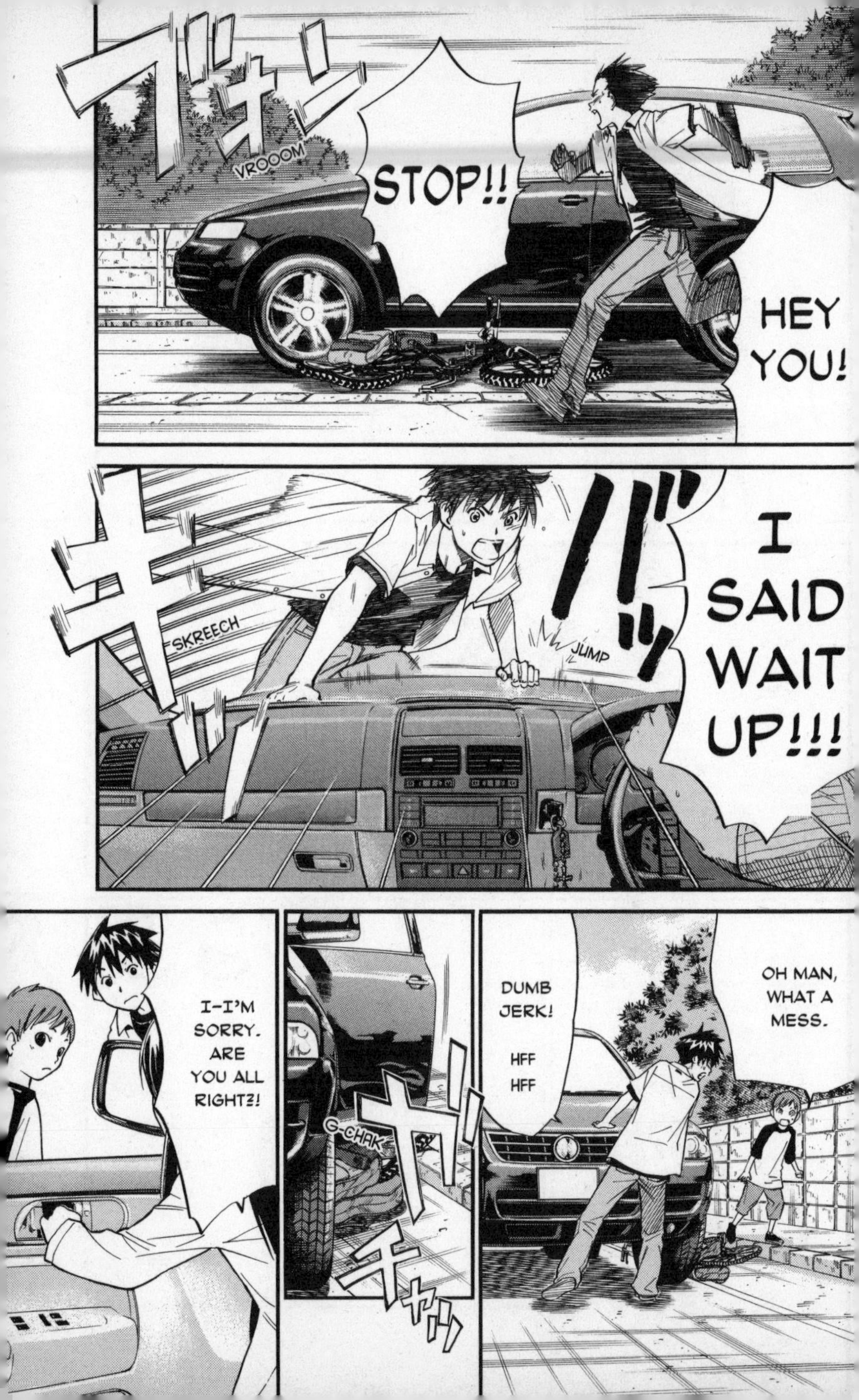
HEY YOU!
STOP!!
VROOOM
I SAID WAIT UP!!!
JUMP
SKREECH
OH MAN, WHAT A MESS.
DUMB JERK!
HFF HFF
G-CHAK
I-I'M SORRY. ARE YOU ALL RIGHT?!

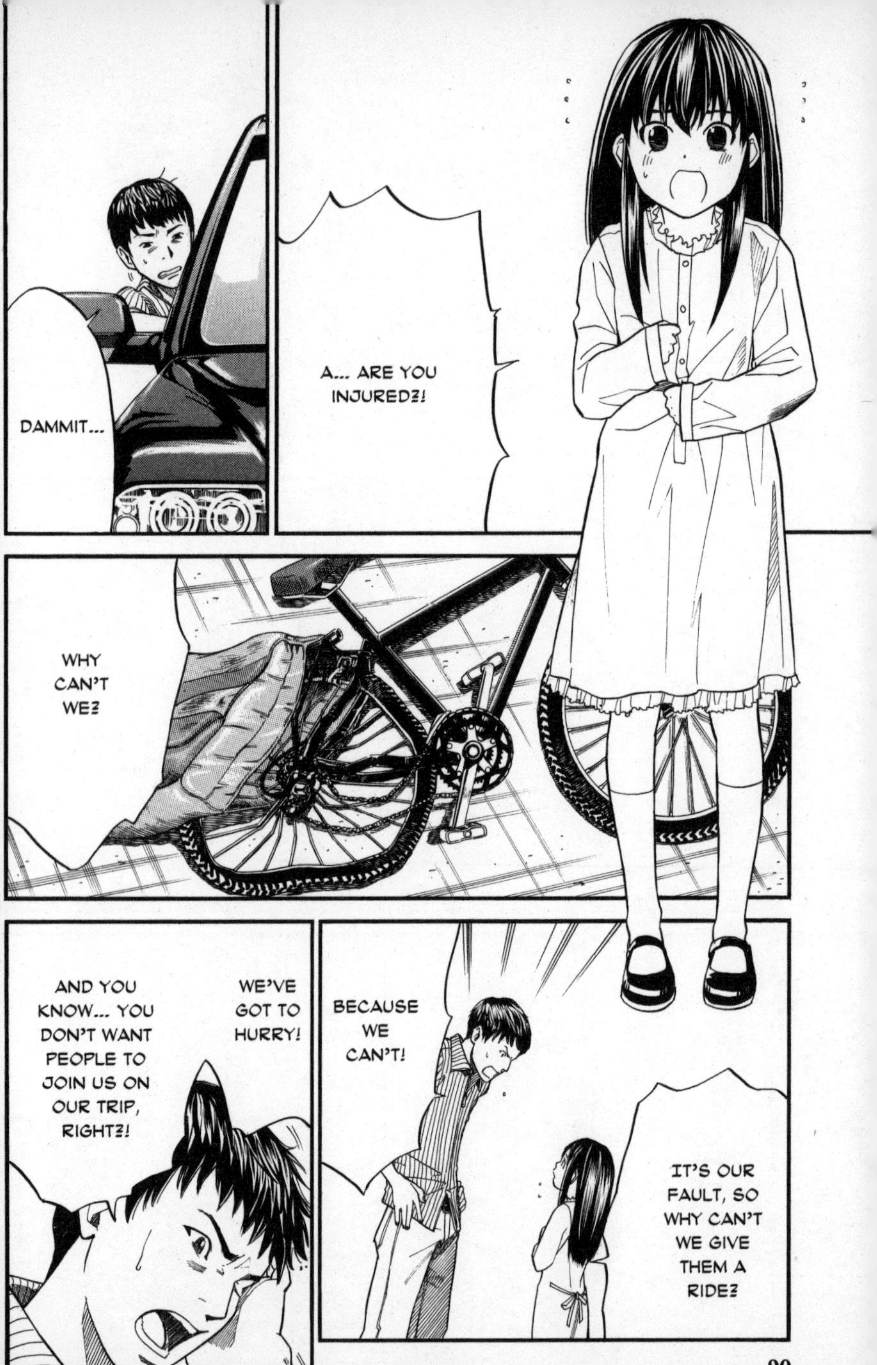
A... ARE YOU INJURED?!
DAMMIT...
WHY CAN'T WE?
IT'S OUR FAULT, SO WHY CAN'T WE GIVE THEM A RIDE?
BECAUSE WE CAN'T!
WE'VE GOT TO HURRY!
AND YOU KNOW... YOU DON'T WANT PEOPLE TO JOIN US ON OUR TRIP, RIGHT?!

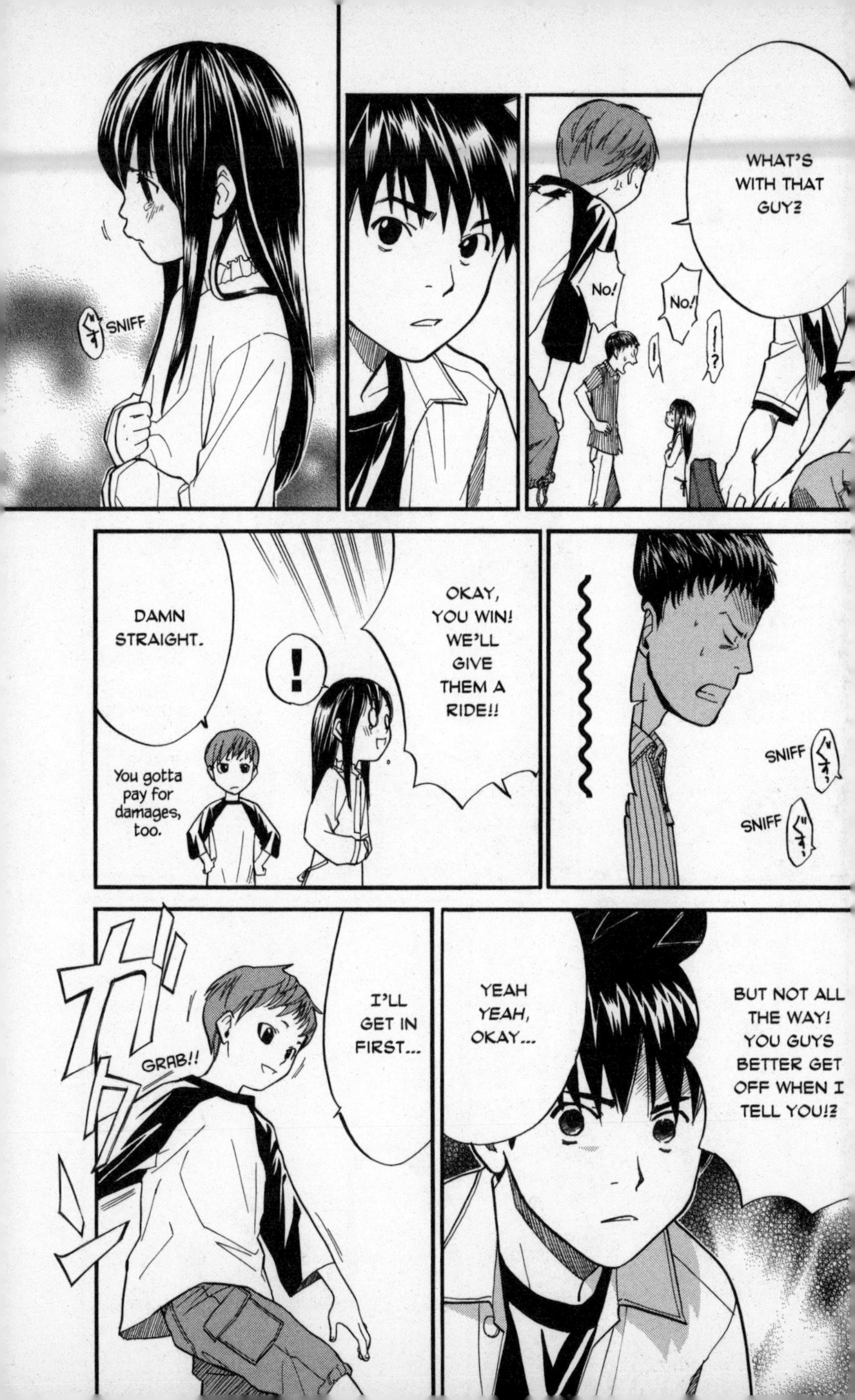
WHAT'S WITH THAT GUY!?
No!
No!
!
!?
SNIFF
SNIFF
SNIFF
OKAY, YOU WIN! WE'LL GIVE THEM A RIDE!!
!
DAMN STRAIGHT.
You gotta pay for damages, too.
BUT NOT ALL THE WAY! YOU GUYS BETTER GET OFF WHEN I TELL YOU!?
YEAH YEAH, OKAY...
I'LL GET IN FIRST...
GRAB!!

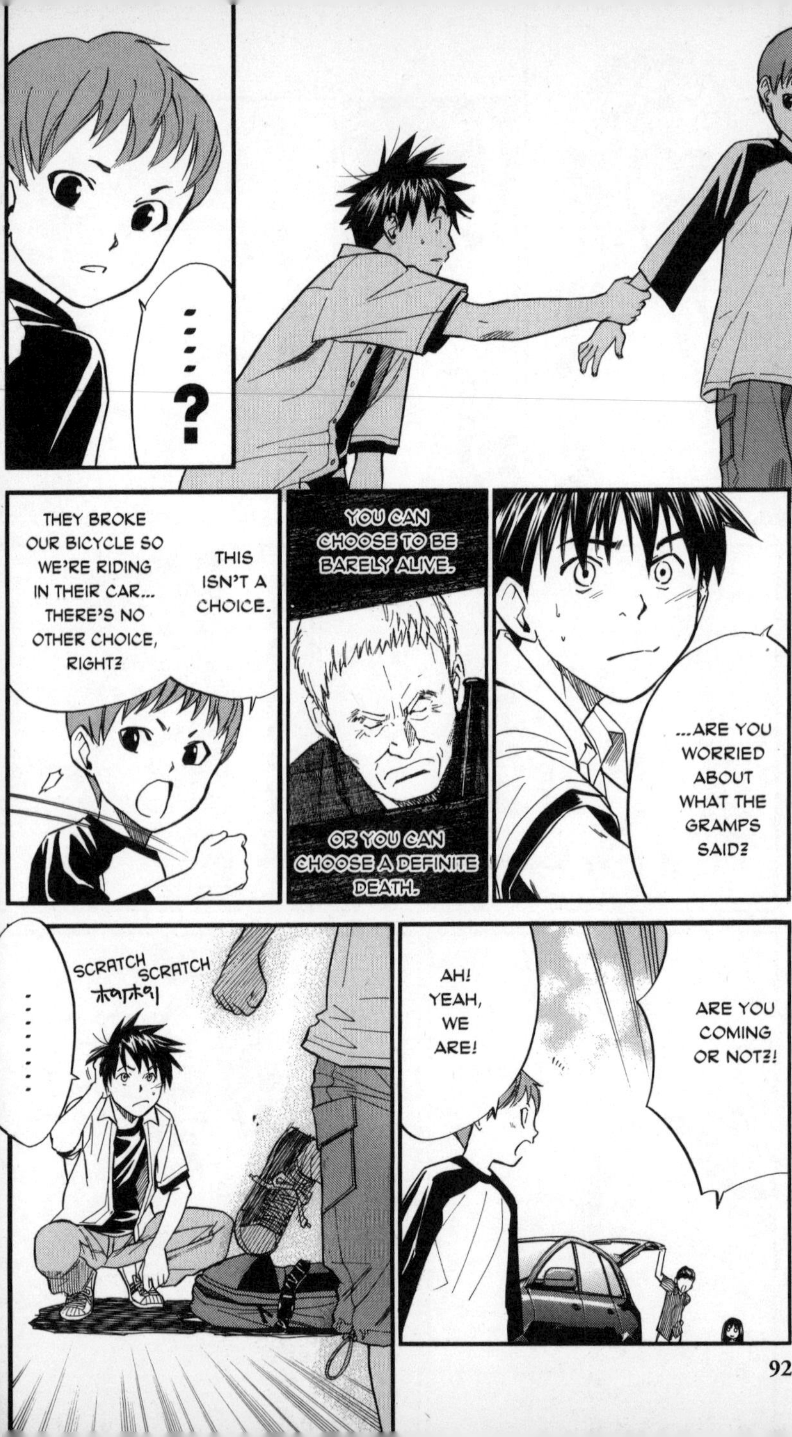
....?
...ARE YOU WORRIED ABOUT WHAT THE GRAMPS SAID?
YOU CAN CHOOSE TO BE BARELY ALIVE.
OR YOU CAN CHOOSE A DEFINITE DEATH.
THEY BROKE OUR BICYCLE SO WE'RE RIDING IN THEIR CAR... THERE'S NO OTHER CHOICE, RIGHT?
THIS ISN'T A CHOICE.
ARE YOU COMING OR NOT?!
AH! YEAH, WE ARE!
SCRATCH SCRATCH
ホリホリ
....

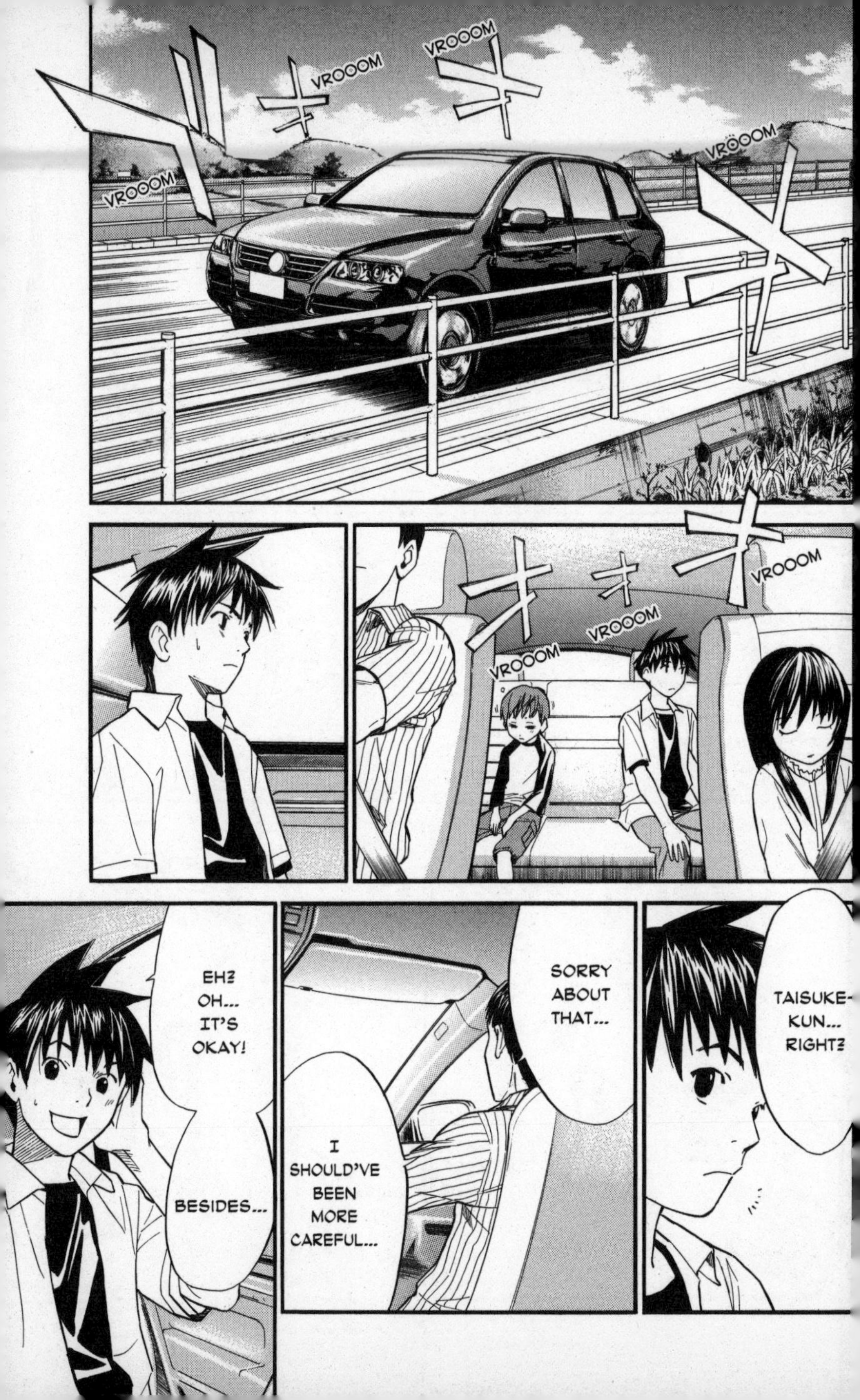
VROOOM
VROOOM
VROOOM
VROOOM
VROOOM
VROOOM
VROOOM
TAISUKE-KUN... RIGHT?
SORRY ABOUT THAT...
I SHOULD'VE BEEN MORE CAREFUL...
EH? OH... IT'S OKAY!
BESIDES...

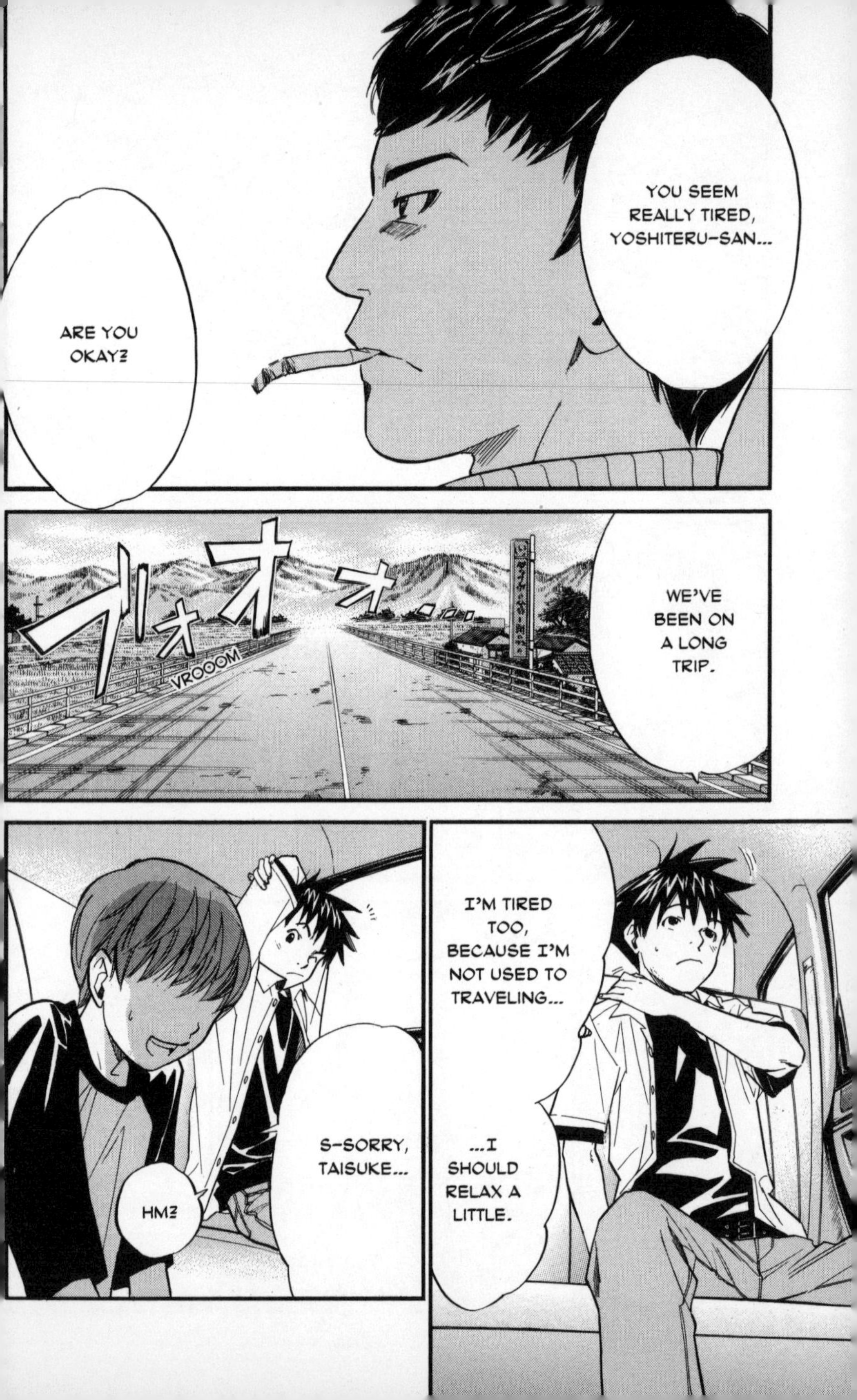
YOU SEEM REALLY TIRED, YOSHITERU-SAN...
ARE YOU OKAY?
WE'VE BEEN ON A LONG TRIP.
VROOOM
I'M TIRED TOO, BECAUSE I'M NOT USED TO TRAVELING...
...I SHOULD RELAX A LITTLE.
S-SORRY, TAISUKE...
HM?

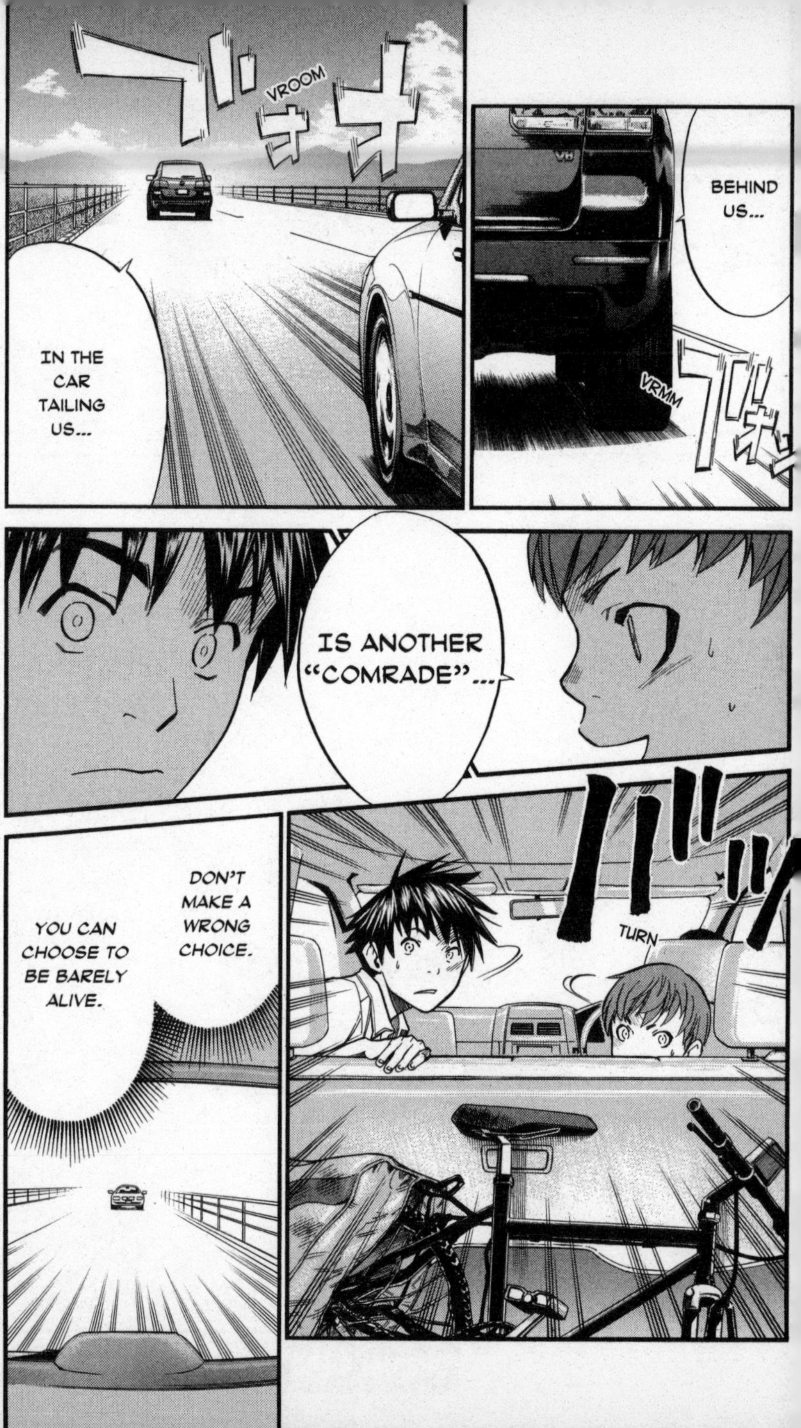
BEHIND US...
VRMM
VROOM
IN THE CAR TAILING US...
IS ANOTHER "COMRADE"...
TURN
DON'T MAKE A WRONG CHOICE.
YOU CAN CHOOSE TO BE BARELY ALIVE.

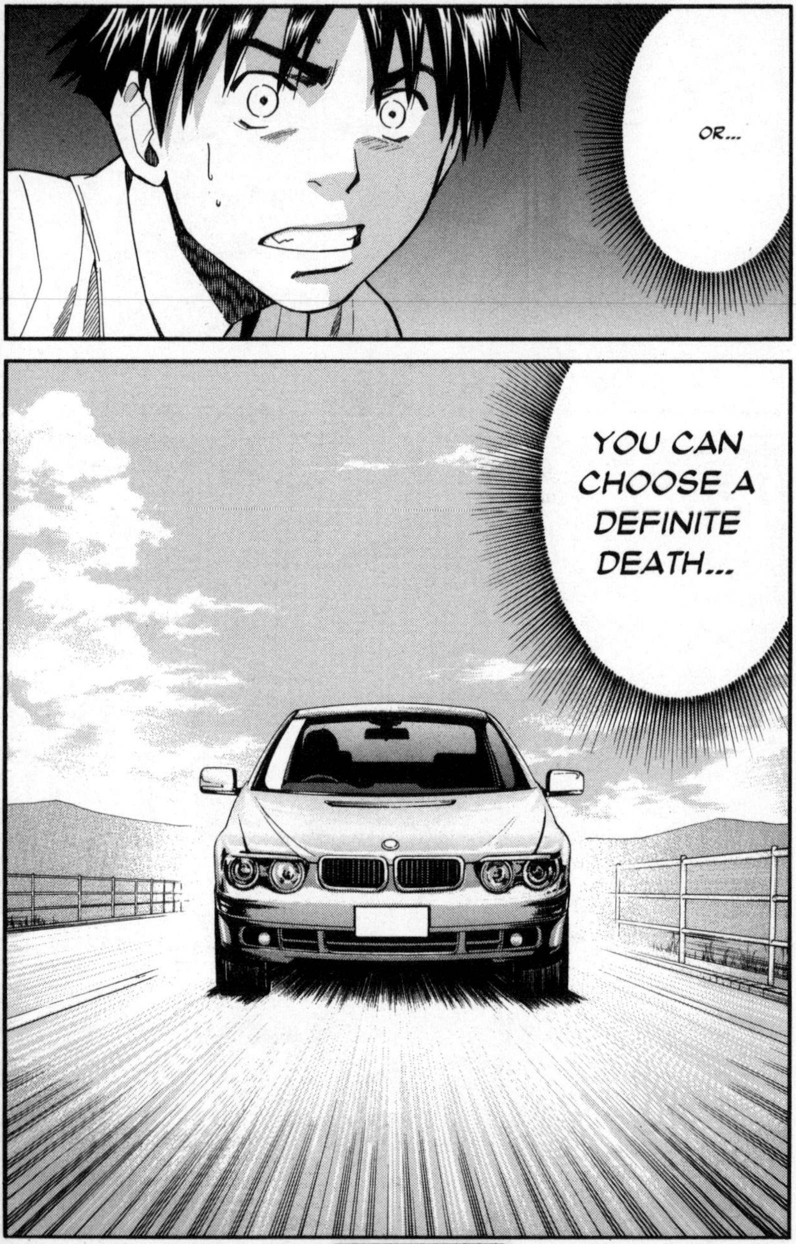
OR...
YOU CAN CHOOSE A DEFINITE DEATH...

Chapter 9/End

最後進化的少年

Alive

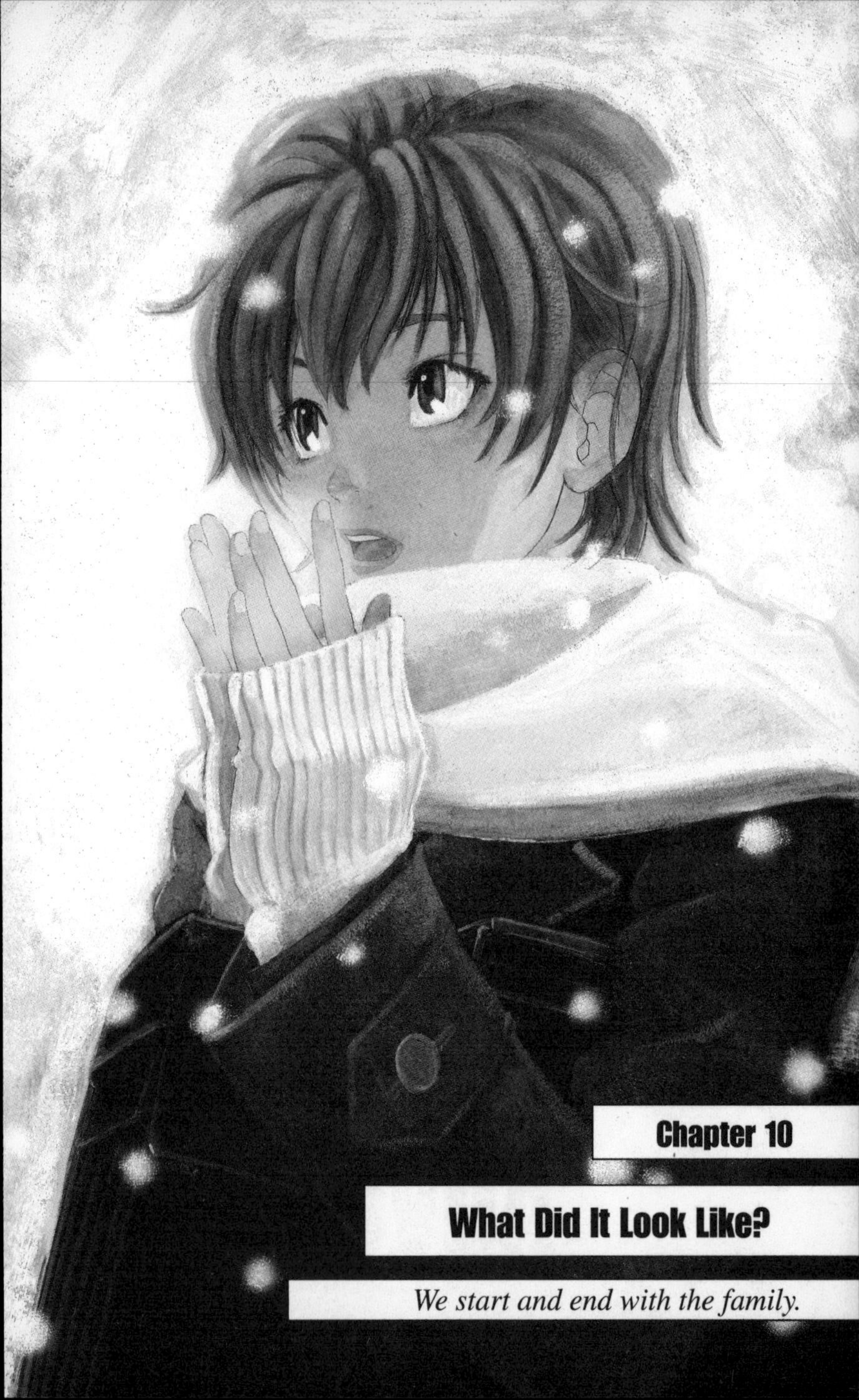

Chapter 10

What Did It Look Like?

We start and end with the family.

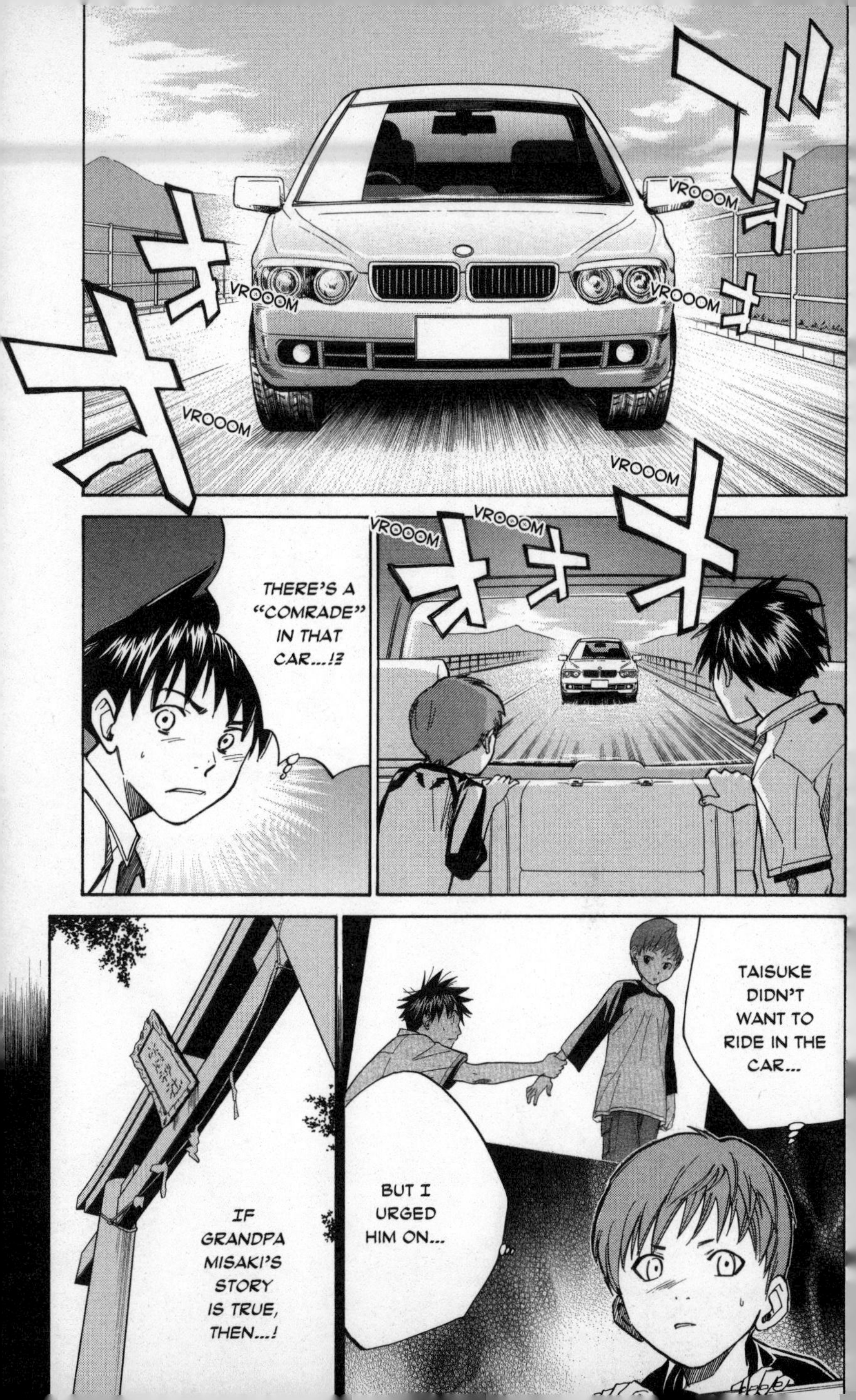
VROOOM
VROOOM
VROOOM
VROOOM
VROOOM
VROOOM
VROOOM
THERE'S A "COMRADE" IN THAT CAR...!?
TAISUKE DIDN'T WANT TO RIDE IN THE CAR...
BUT I URGED HIM ON...
IF GRANDPA MISAKI'S STORY IS TRUE, THEN...!

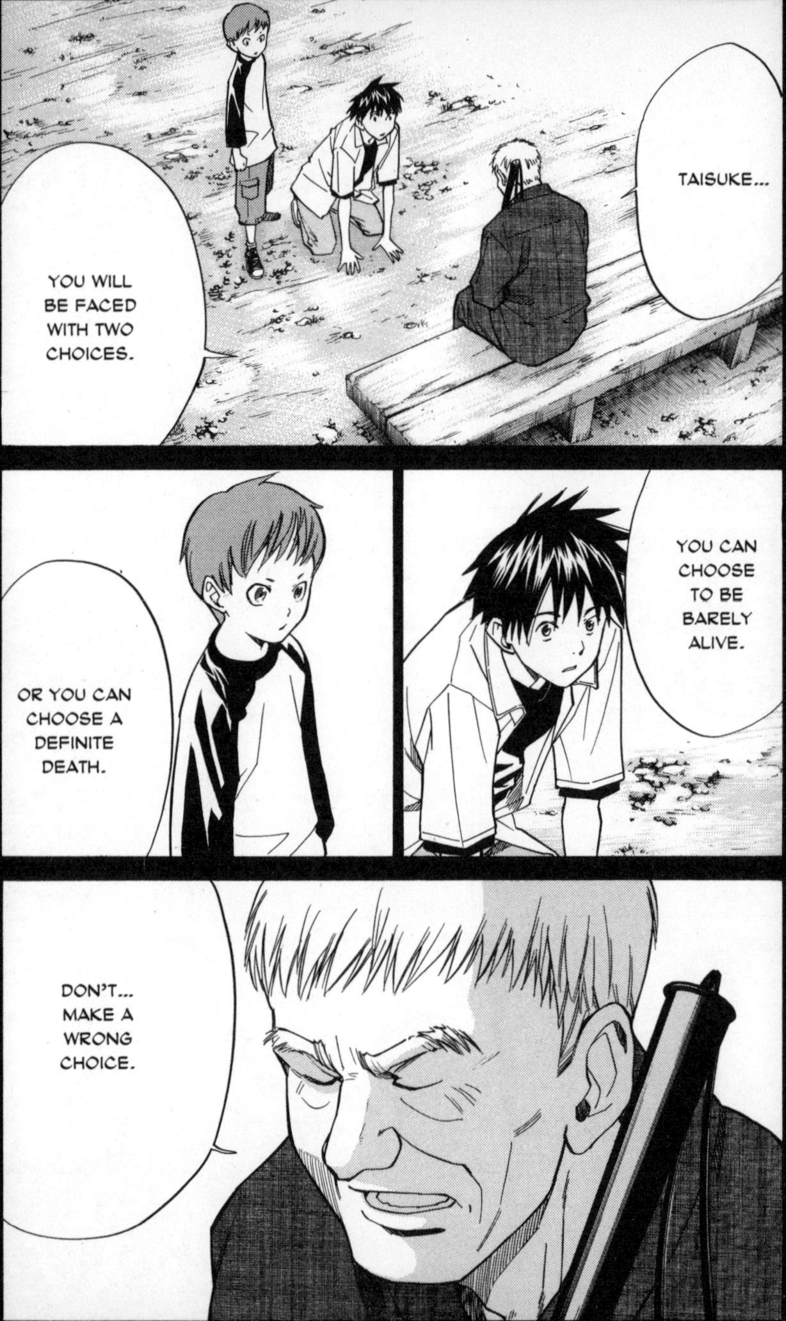
TAISUKE...
YOU WILL BE FACED WITH TWO CHOICES.
YOU CAN CHOOSE TO BE BARELY ALIVE.
OR YOU CAN CHOOSE A DEFINITE DEATH.
DON'T... MAKE A WRONG CHOICE.

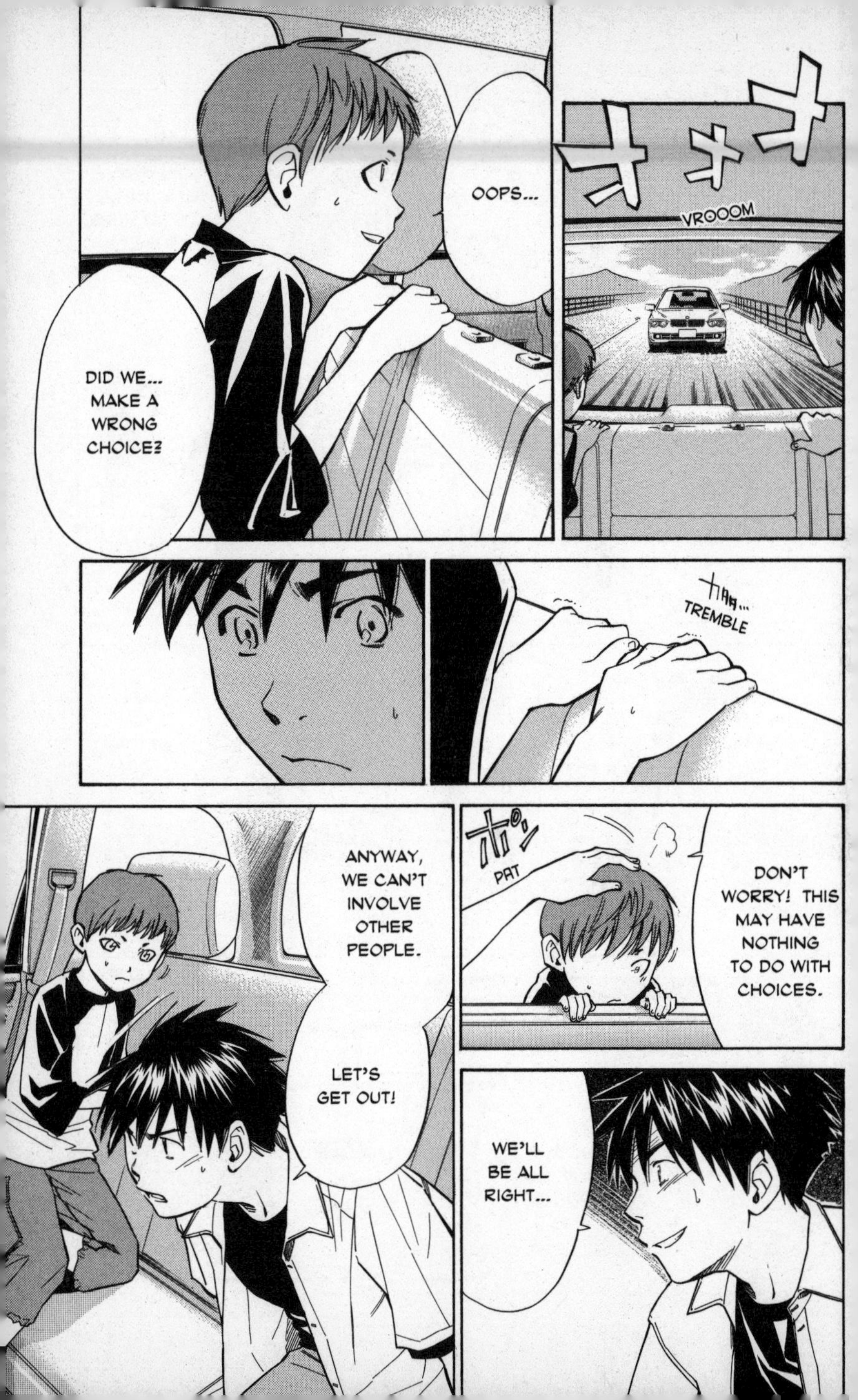
VROOOM
OOPS...
DID WE... MAKE A WRONG CHOICE?
TREMBLE
DON'T WORRY! THIS MAY HAVE NOTHING TO DO WITH CHOICES.
PAT
WE'LL BE ALL RIGHT...
ANYWAY, WE CAN'T INVOLVE OTHER PEOPLE.
LET'S GET OUT!

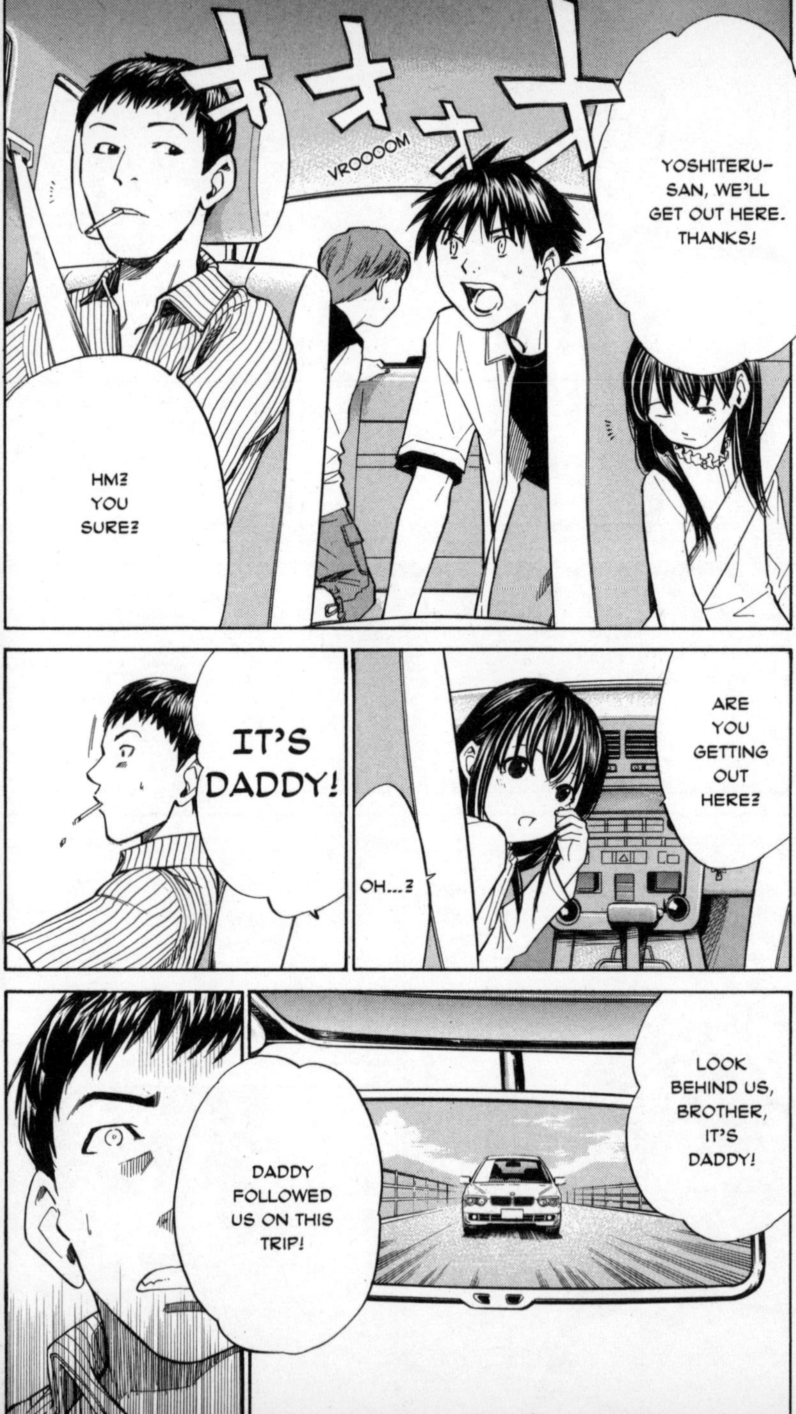
YOSHITERU-SAN, WE'LL GET OUT HERE. THANKS!
VROOOOM
HM? YOU SURE?
ARE YOU GETTING OUT HERE?
OH...?
IT'S DADDY!
LOOK BEHIND US, BROTHER, IT'S DADDY!
DADDY FOLLOWED US ON THIS TRIP!

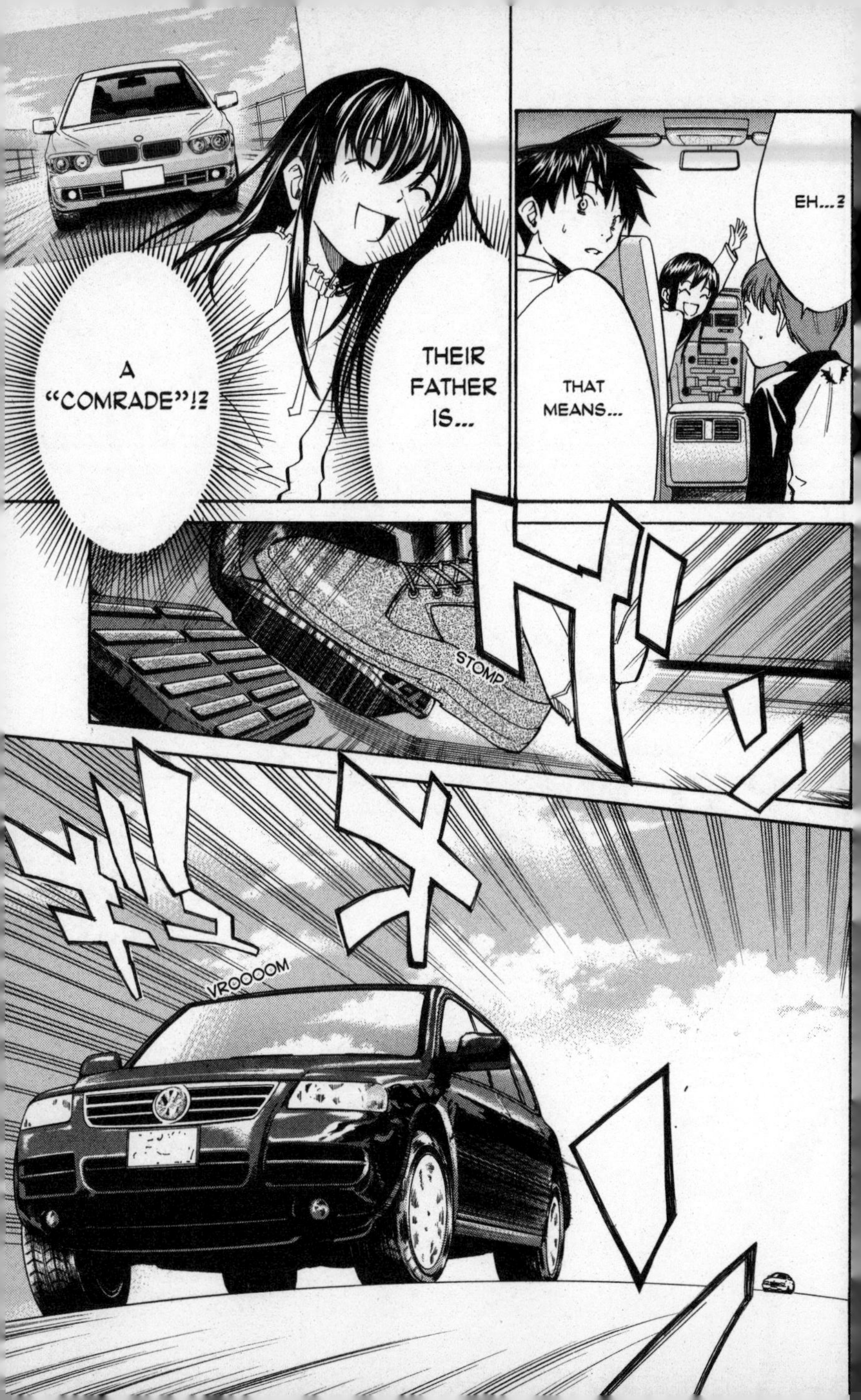
EH...?
THAT MEANS...
THEIR FATHER IS...
A "COMRADE"!?
STOMP
VROOOOM

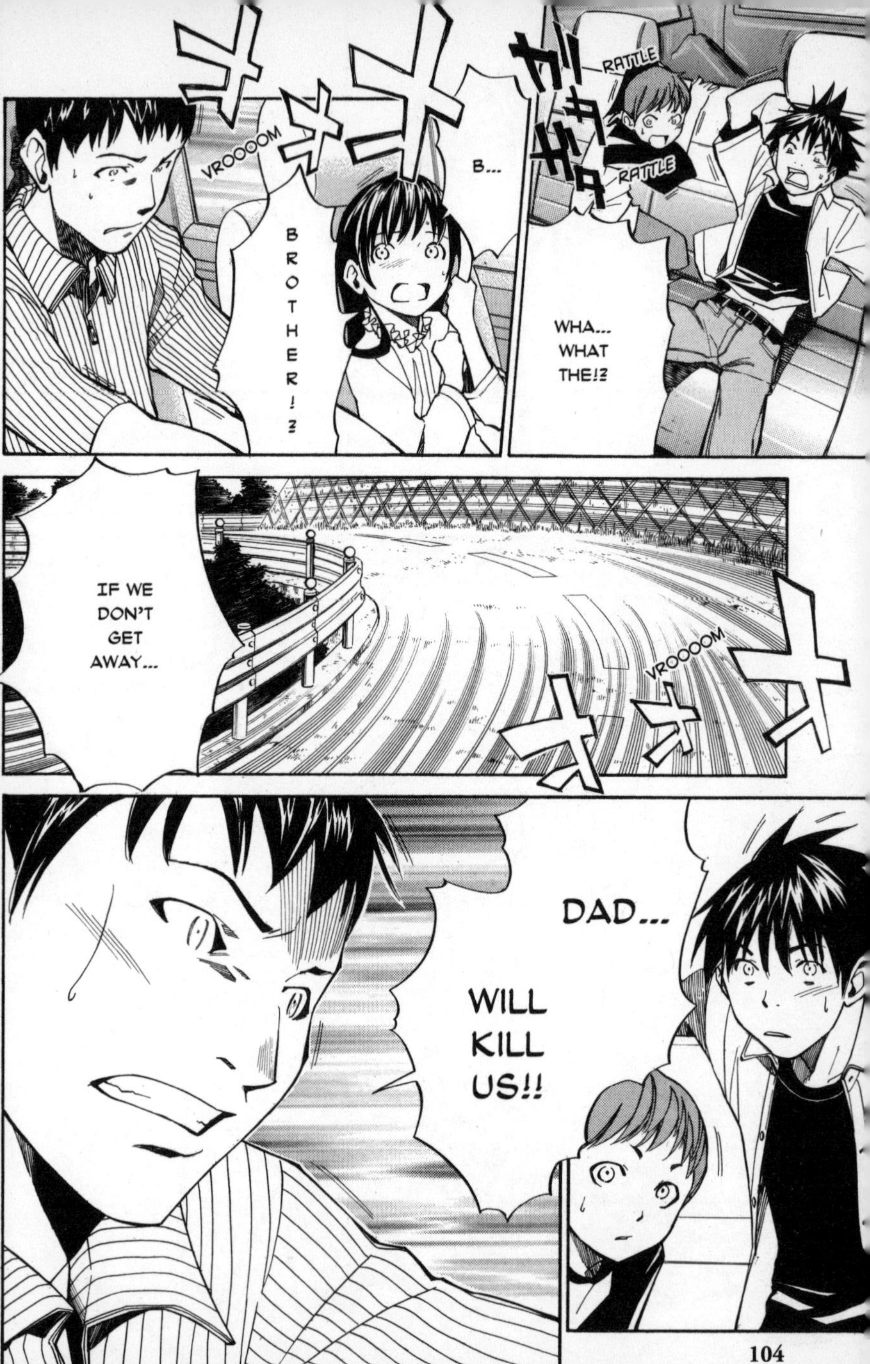
RATTLE
RATTLE
WHA... WHAT THE!?
VROOOOM
B...
BROTHER!?
VROOOOM
IF WE DON'T GET AWAY...
DAD...
WILL KILL US!!

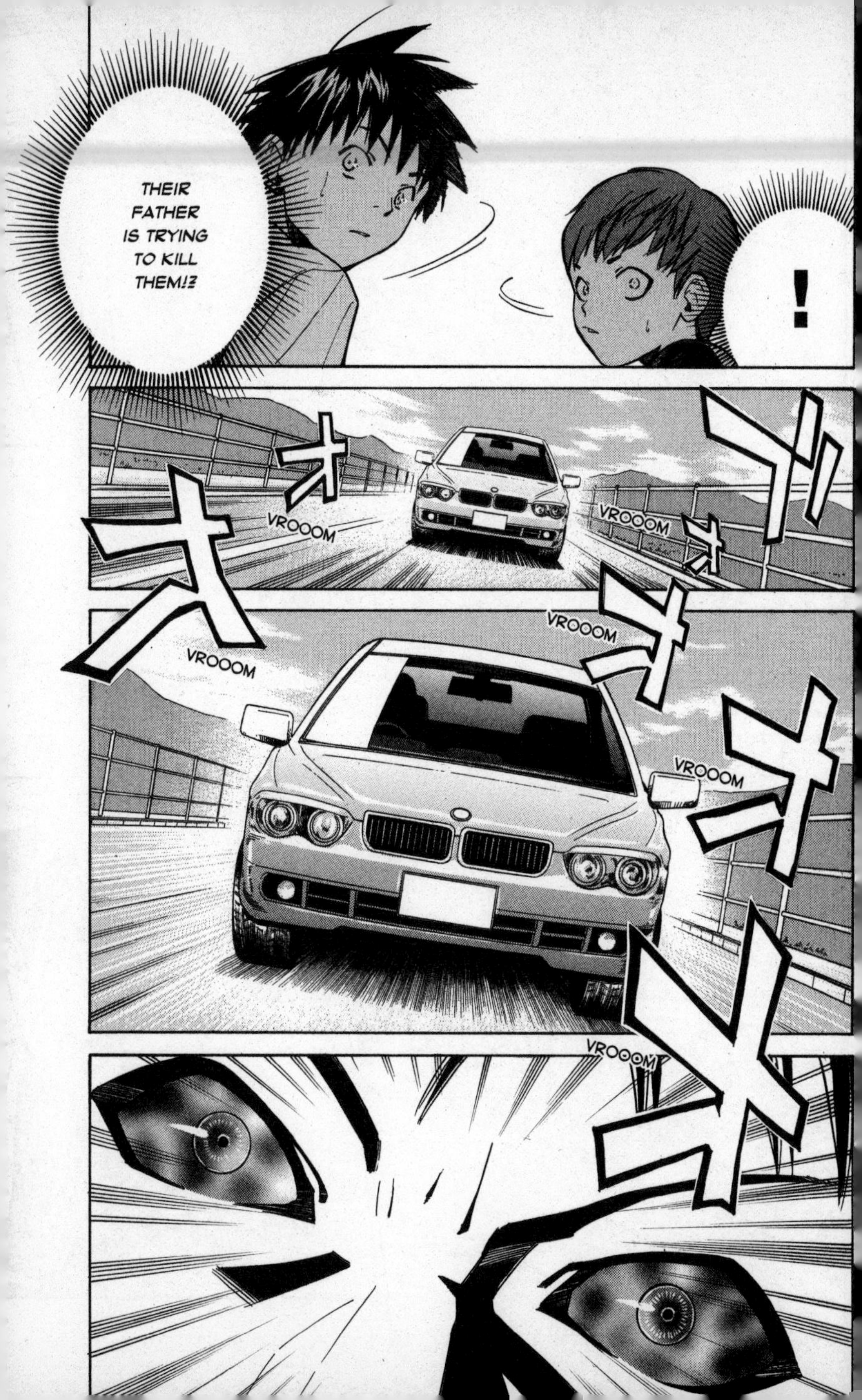
!
THEIR FATHER IS TRYING TO KILL THEM!?
VROOOM
VROOOM
VROOOM
VROOOM
VROOOM
VROOOM

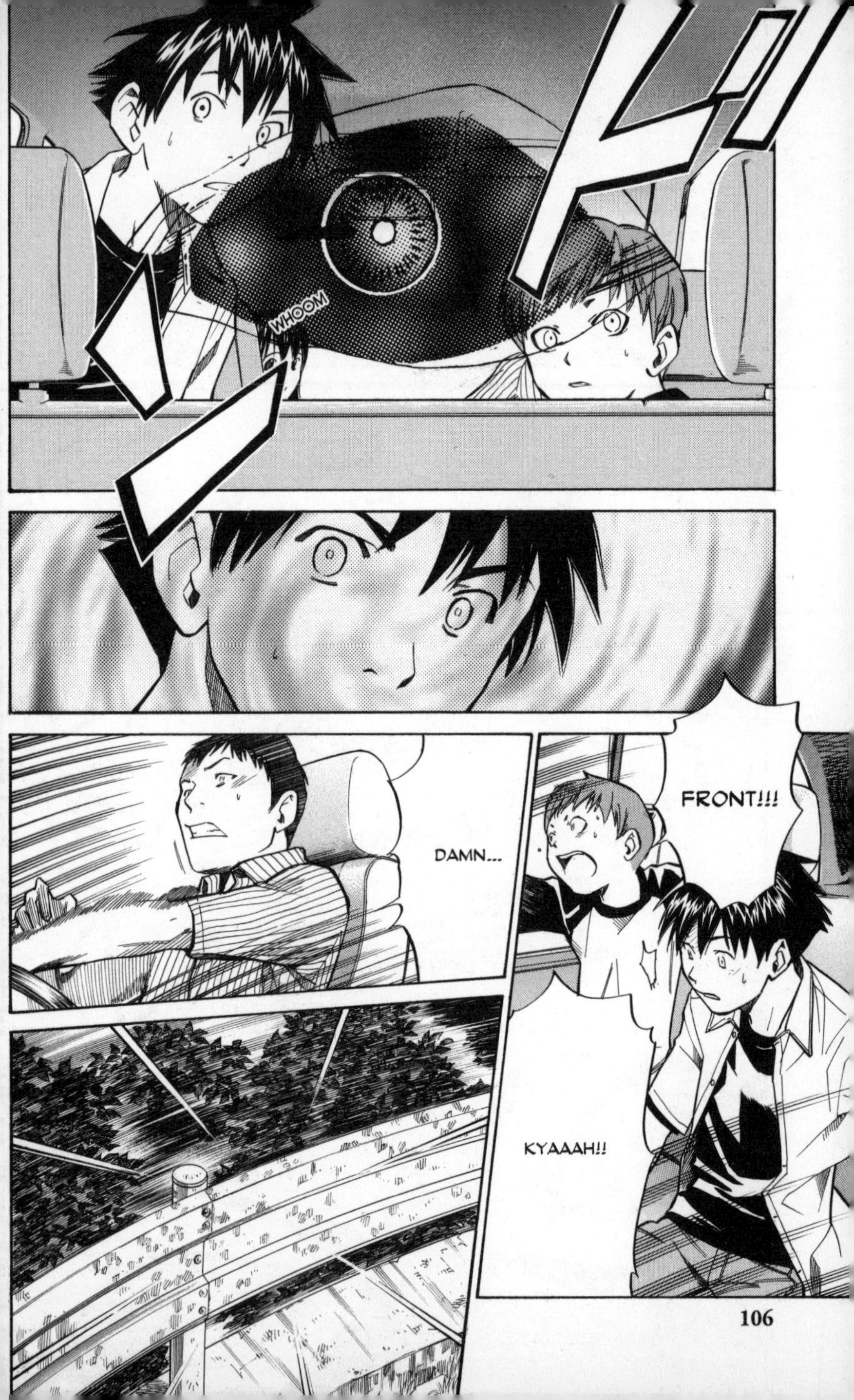
WHOOM
FRONT!!!
KYAAAH!!
DAMN...

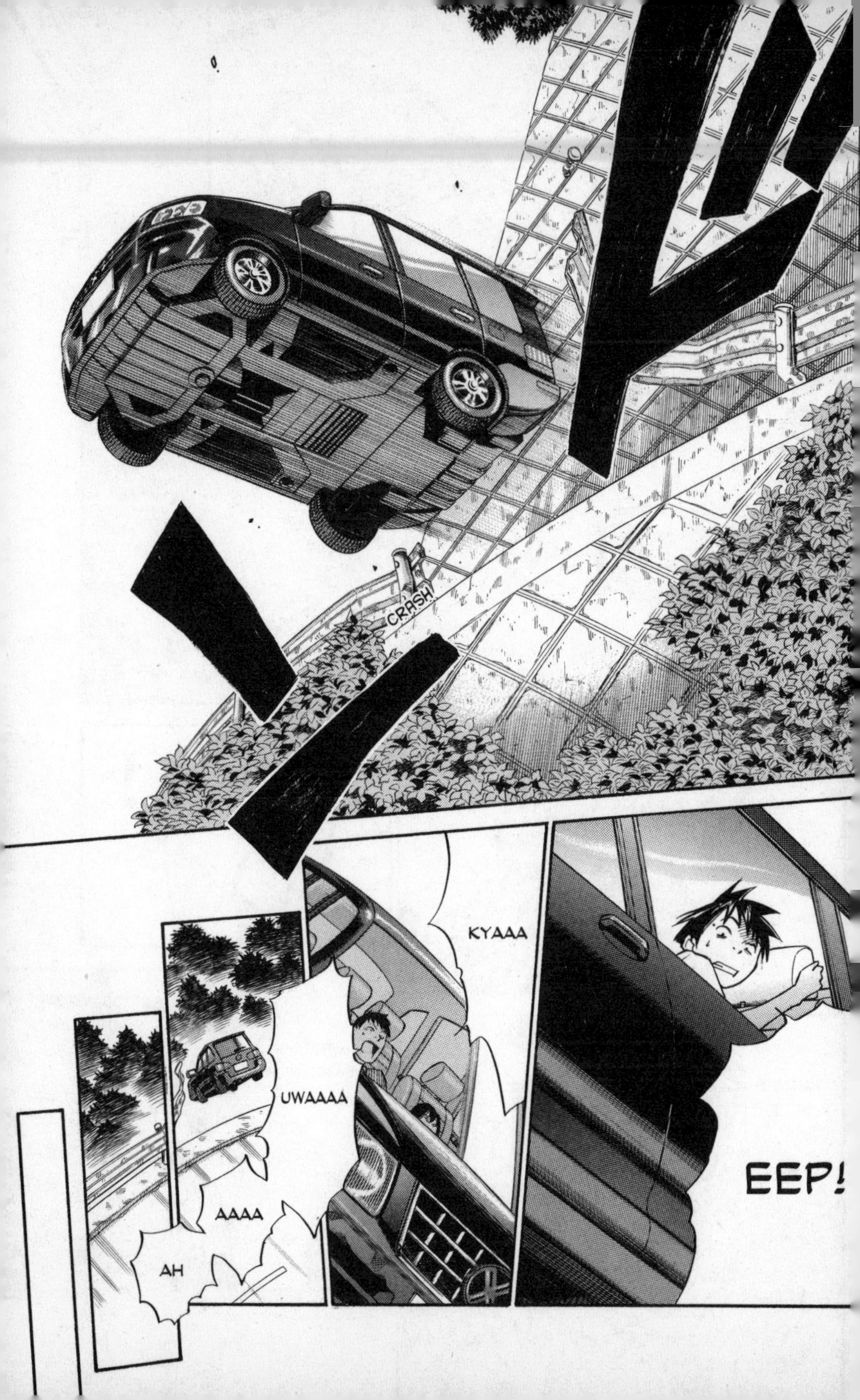

CRASH
EEP!
KYAAA
UWAAAA
AAAA
AH

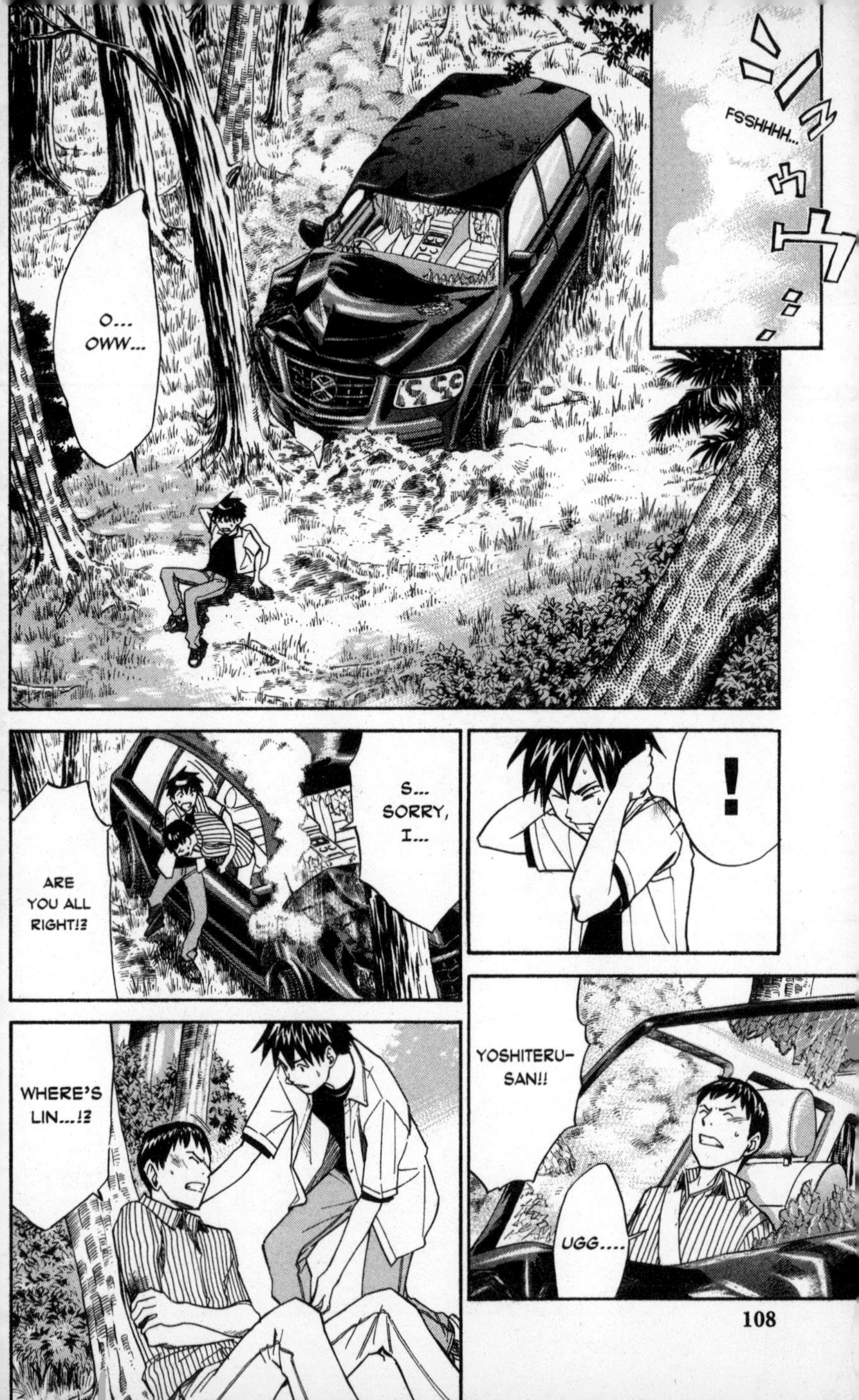
FSSHHHH...
O... OWW...
!
S... SORRY, I...
ARE YOU ALL RIGHT!?
YOSHITERU-SAN!!
UGG....
WHERE'S LIN...!?

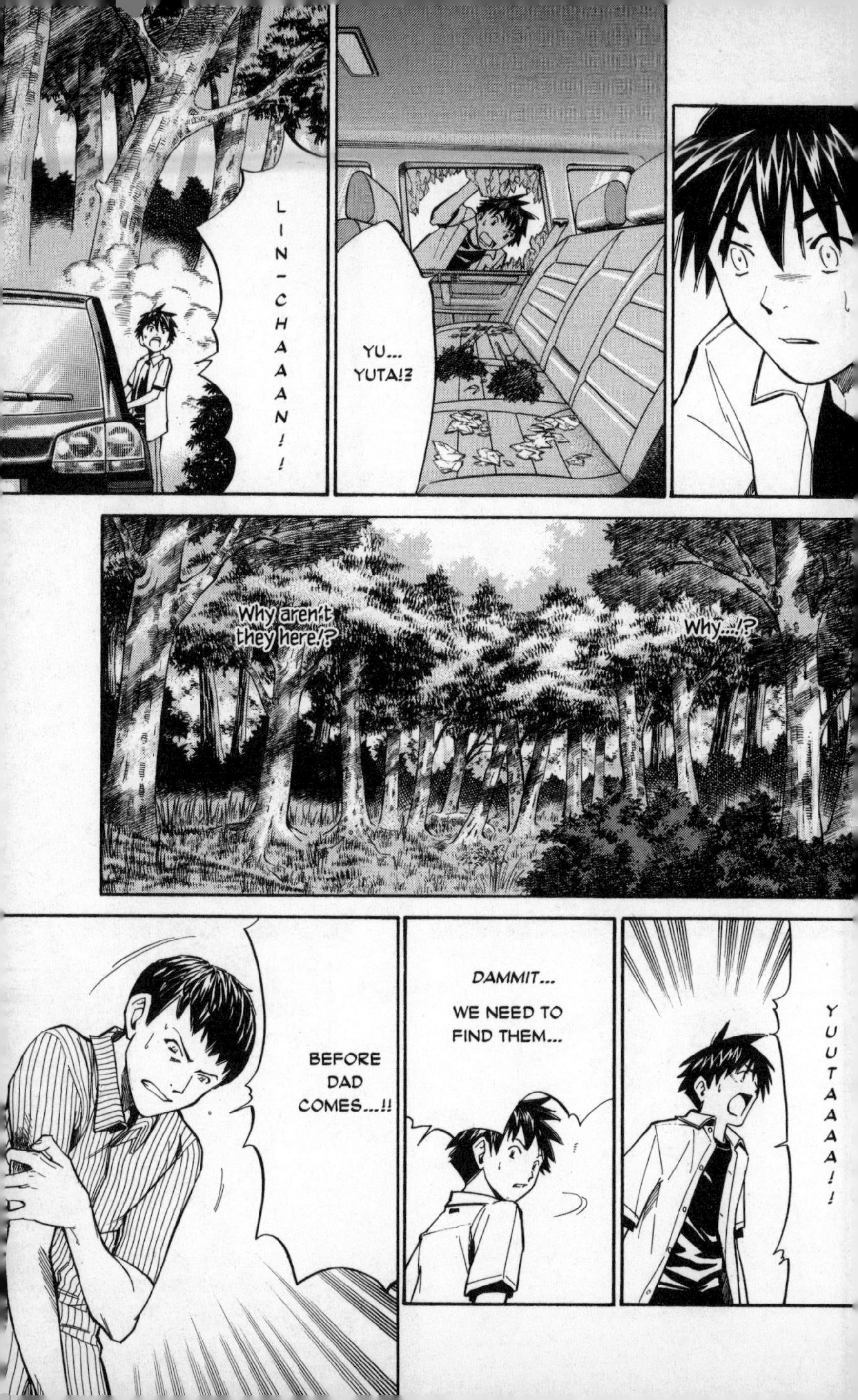
YU... YUTA!?
LIN-CHAAAN!!
Why...!?
Why aren't they here!?
YUUTAAAA!!
DAMMIT...
WE NEED TO FIND THEM...
BEFORE DAD COMES...!!

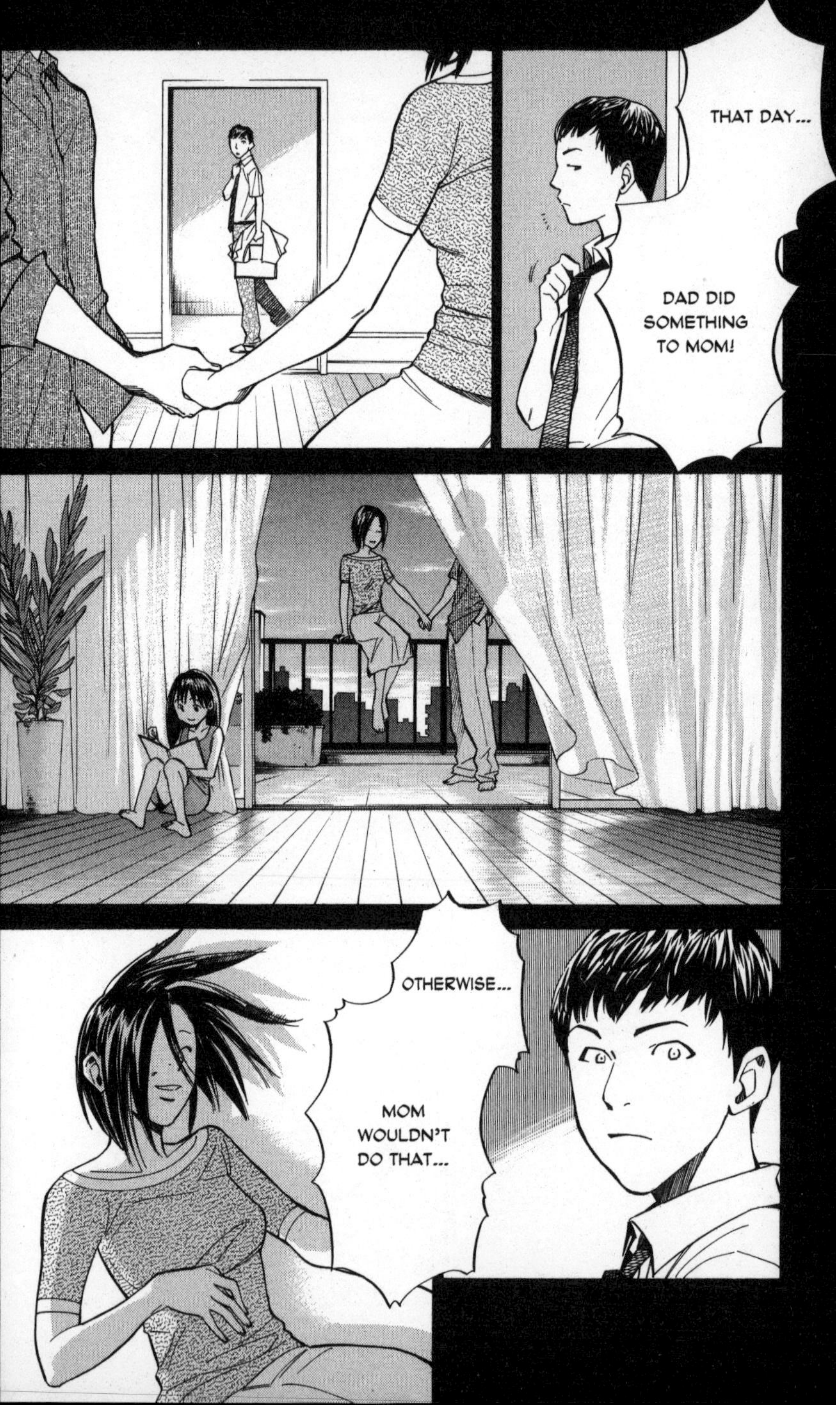
THAT DAY...
DAD DID SOMETHING TO MOM!
OTHERWISE...
MOM WOULDN'T DO THAT...

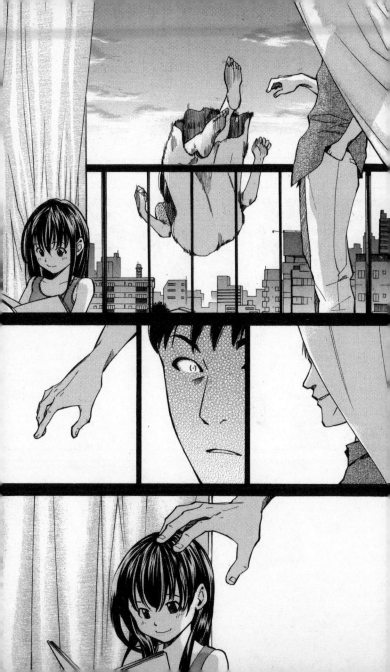

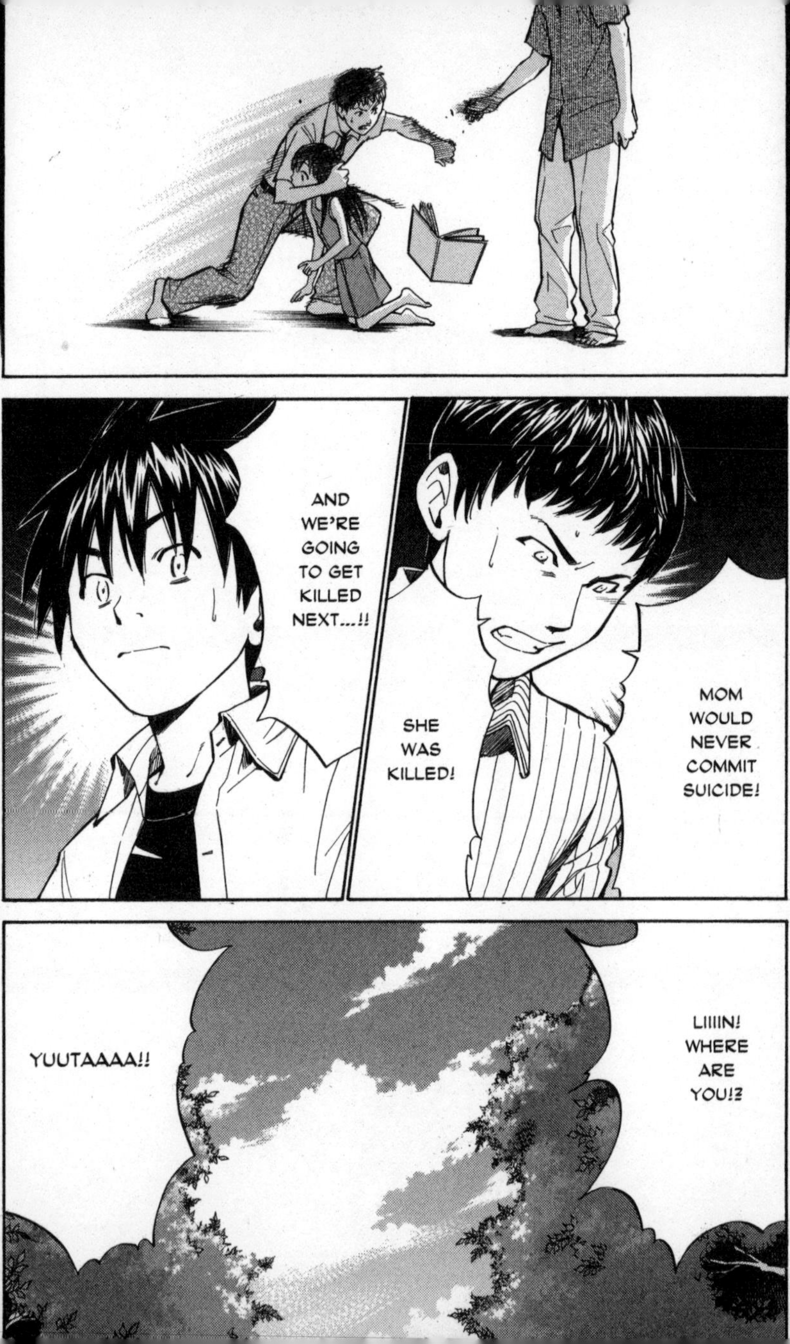
MOM WOULD NEVER COMMIT SUICIDE!
SHE WAS KILLED!
AND WE'RE GOING TO GET KILLED NEXT...!!
LIIIN! WHERE ARE YOU!?
YUUTAAAA!!

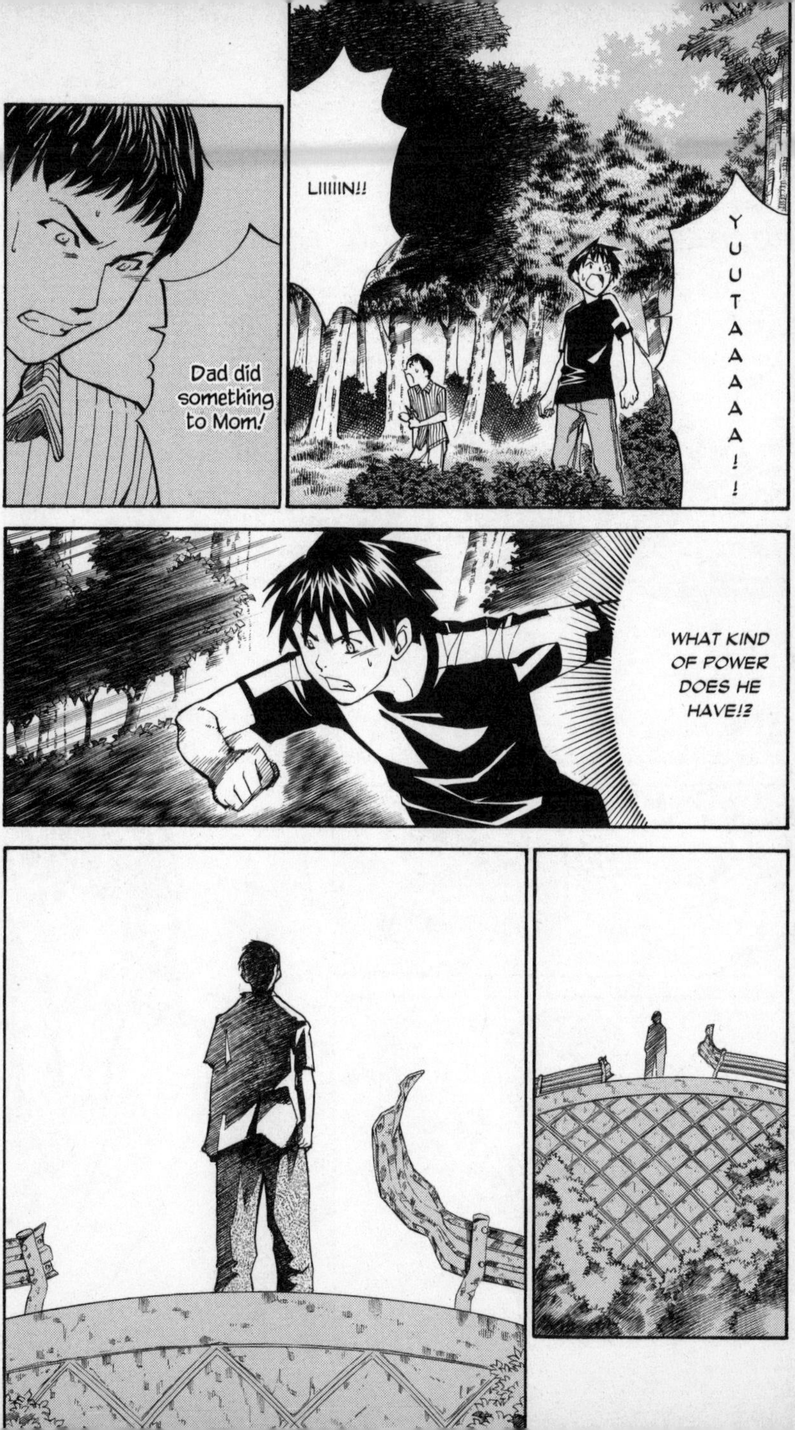
YUUTAAAAA!!
LIIIIN!!
Dad did something to Mom!
WHAT KIND OF POWER DOES HE HAVE!?

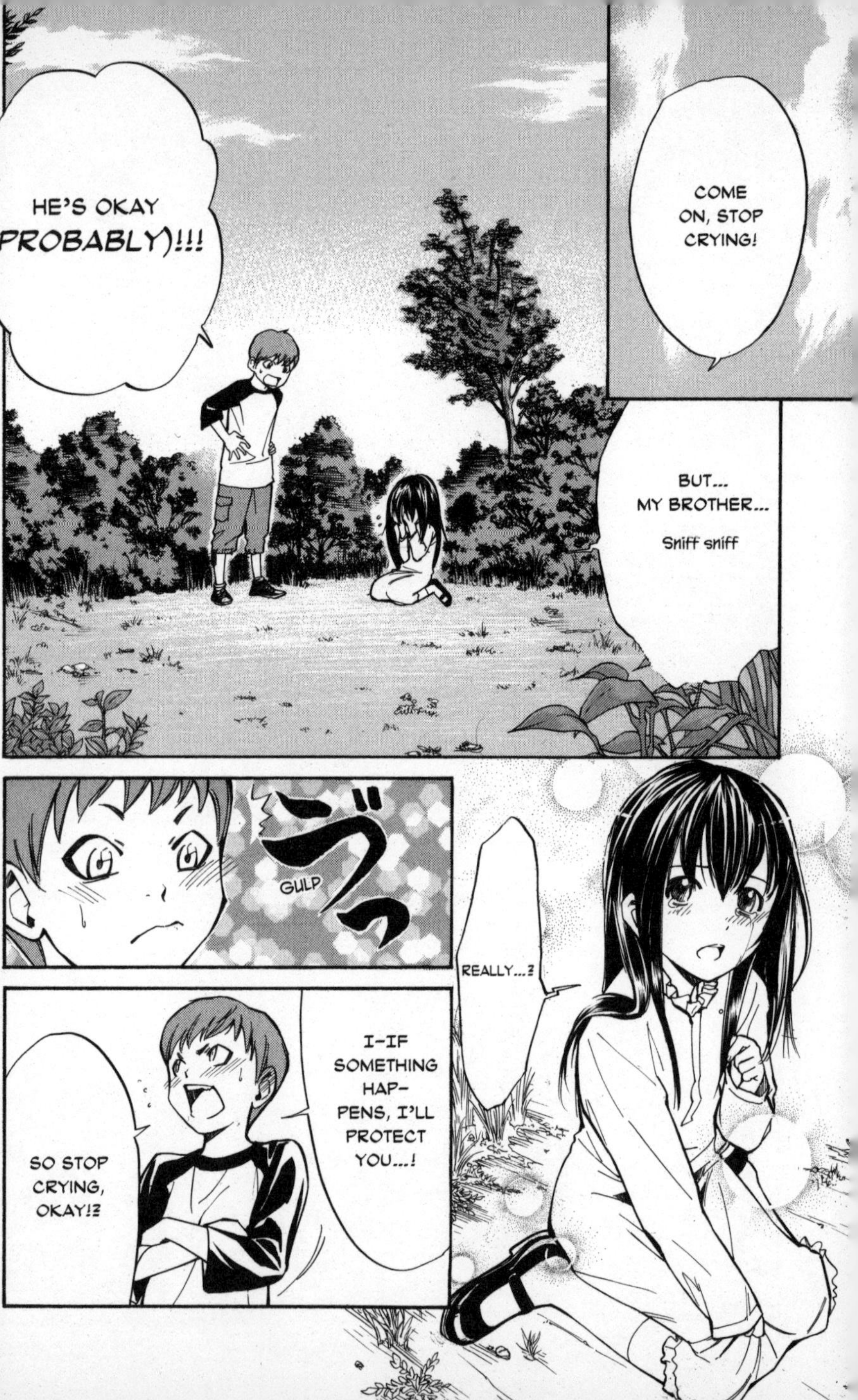
COME ON, STOP CRYING!
BUT... MY BROTHER...
Sniff sniff
HE'S OKAY (PROBABLY)!!!
REALLY...!?
GULP
I-IF SOMETHING HAP-PENS, I'LL PROTECT YOU...!
SO STOP CRYING, OKAY!?

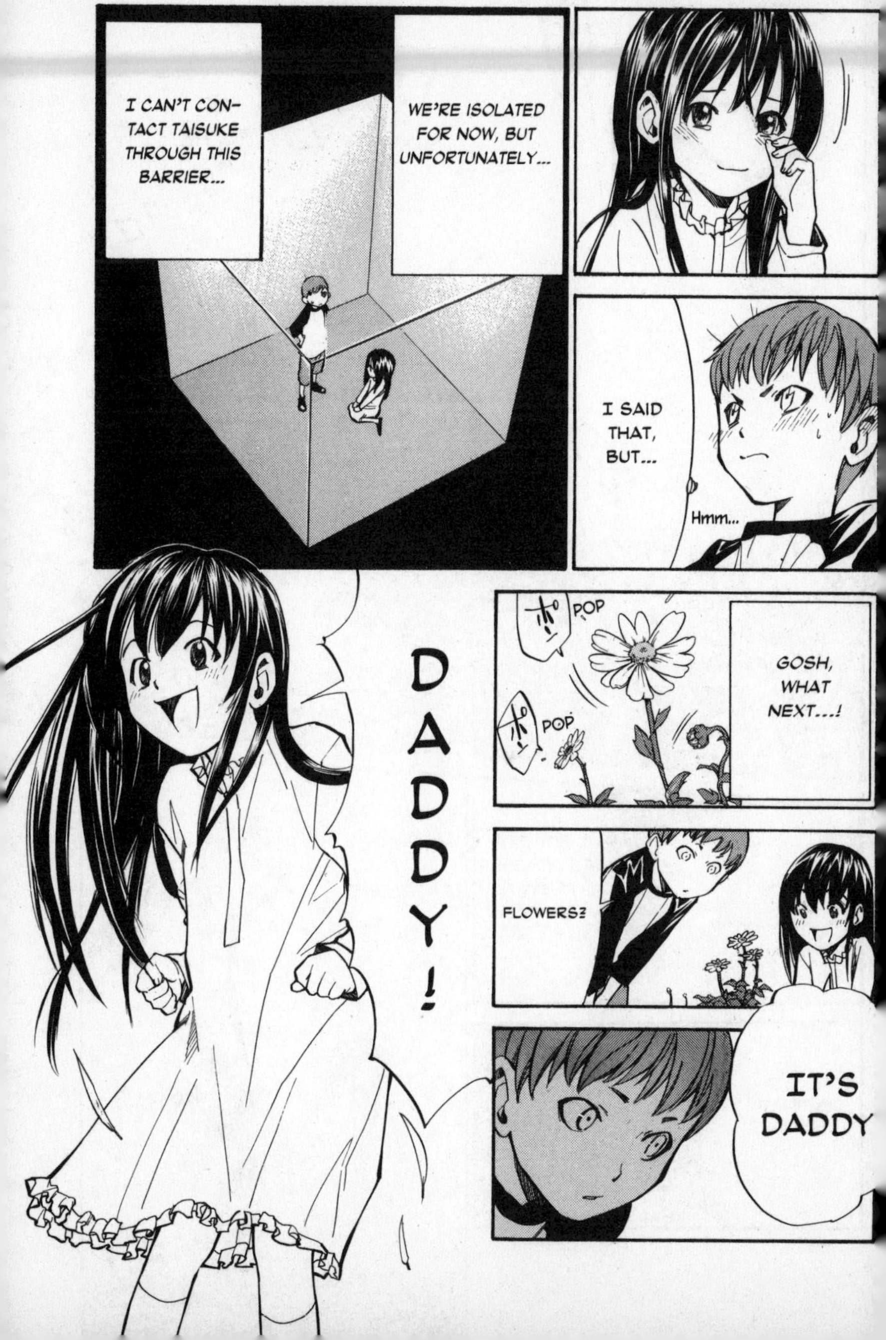
I SAID THAT, BUT...
Hmm...
WE'RE ISOLATED FOR NOW, BUT UNFORTUNATELY...
I CAN'T CONTACT TAISUKE THROUGH THIS BARRIER...
GOSH, WHAT NEXT...!
POP
POP
FLOWERS?
IT'S DADDY
DADDY!

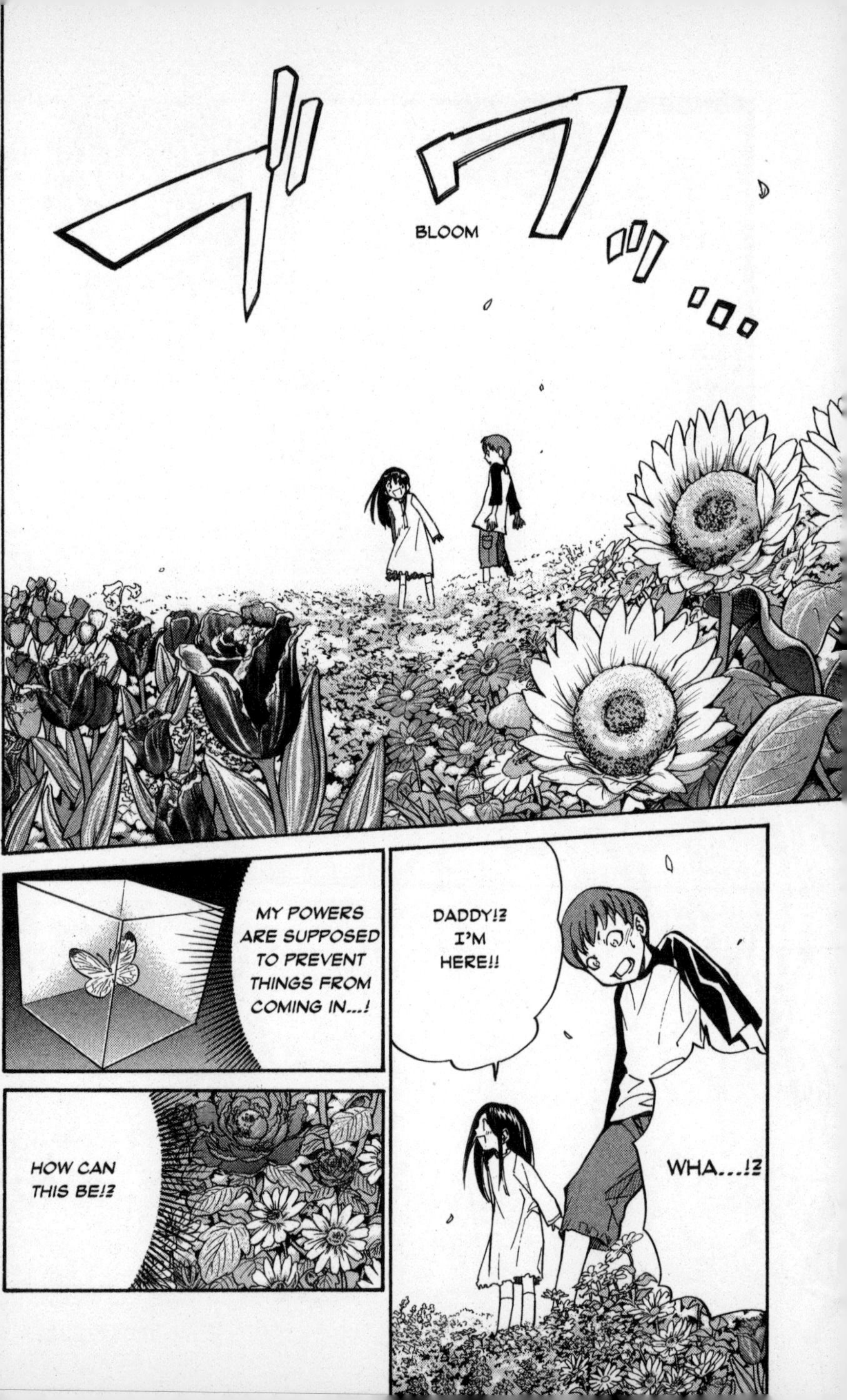
BLOOM
DADDY!? I'M HERE!!
WHA...!?
MY POWERS ARE SUPPOSED TO PREVENT THINGS FROM COMING IN...!
HOW CAN THIS BE!?

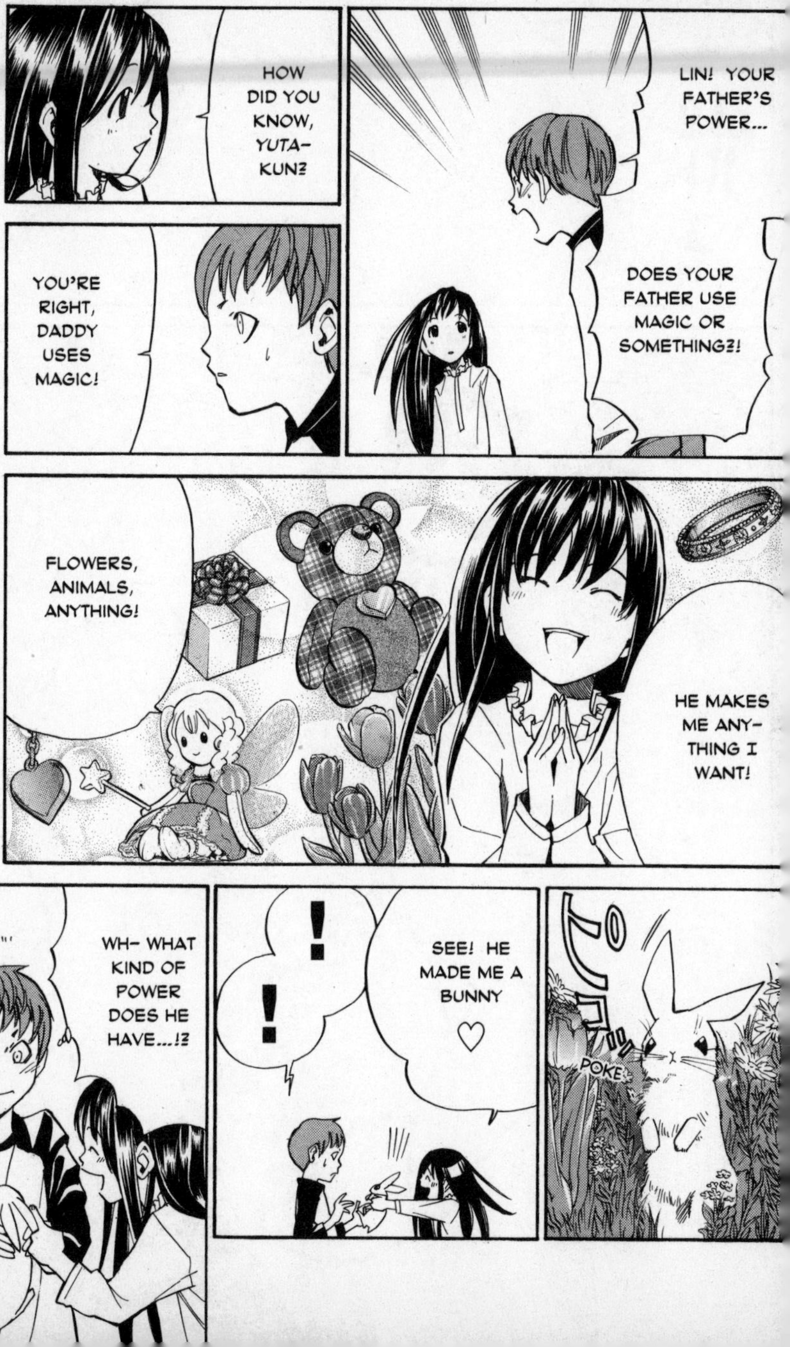
LIN! YOUR FATHER'S POWER...
DOES YOUR FATHER USE MAGIC OR SOMETHING?!
HOW DID YOU KNOW, YUTA-KUN?
YOU'RE RIGHT, DADDY USES MAGIC!
HE MAKES ME ANYTHING I WANT!
FLOWERS, ANIMALS, ANYTHING!
POKE
SEE! HE MADE ME A BUNNY ♡
!
!
WH- WHAT KIND OF POWER DOES HE HAVE...!?

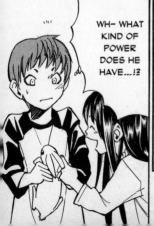

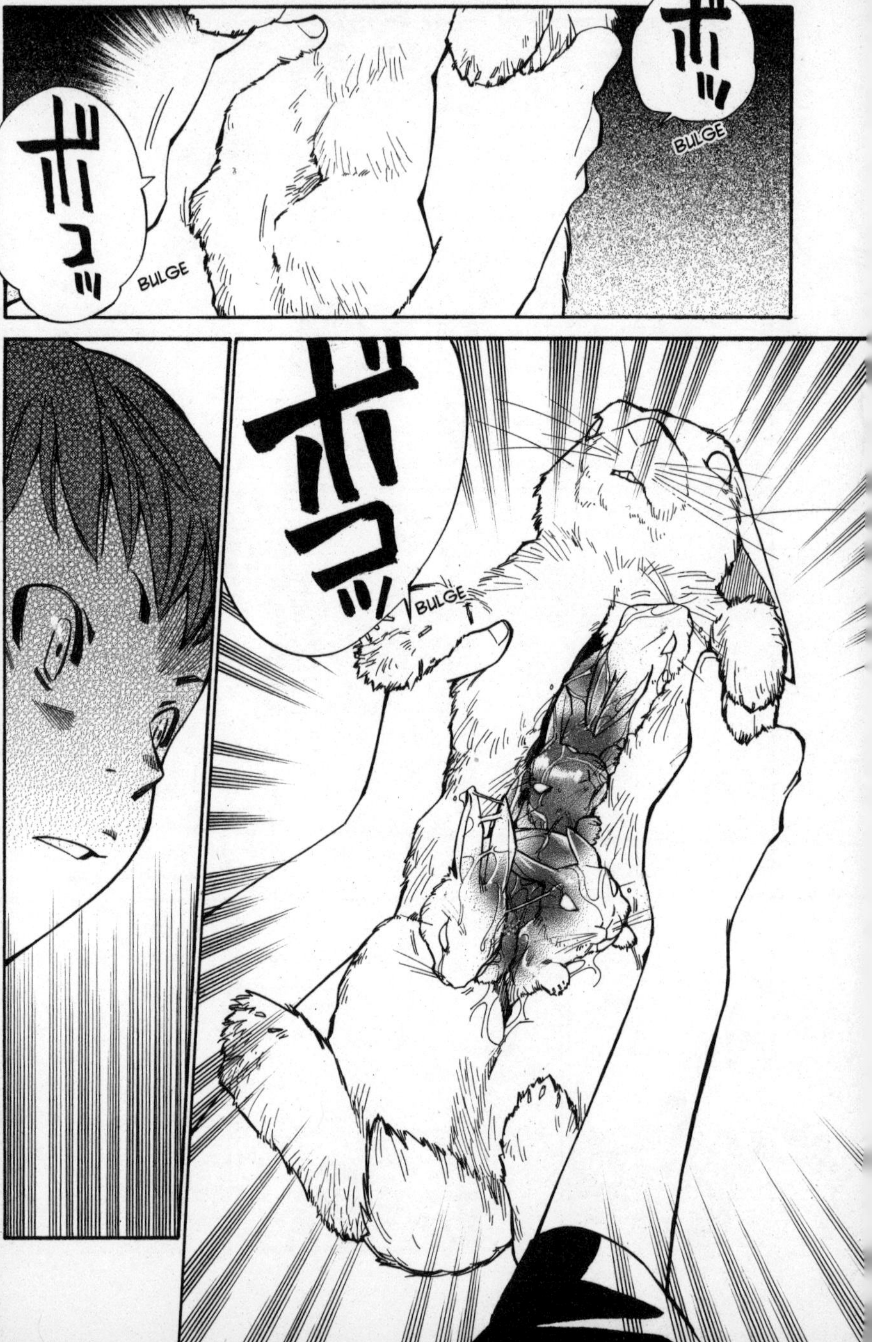
ボッ
BULGE
ボコッ
BULGE
ボコッ
BULGE

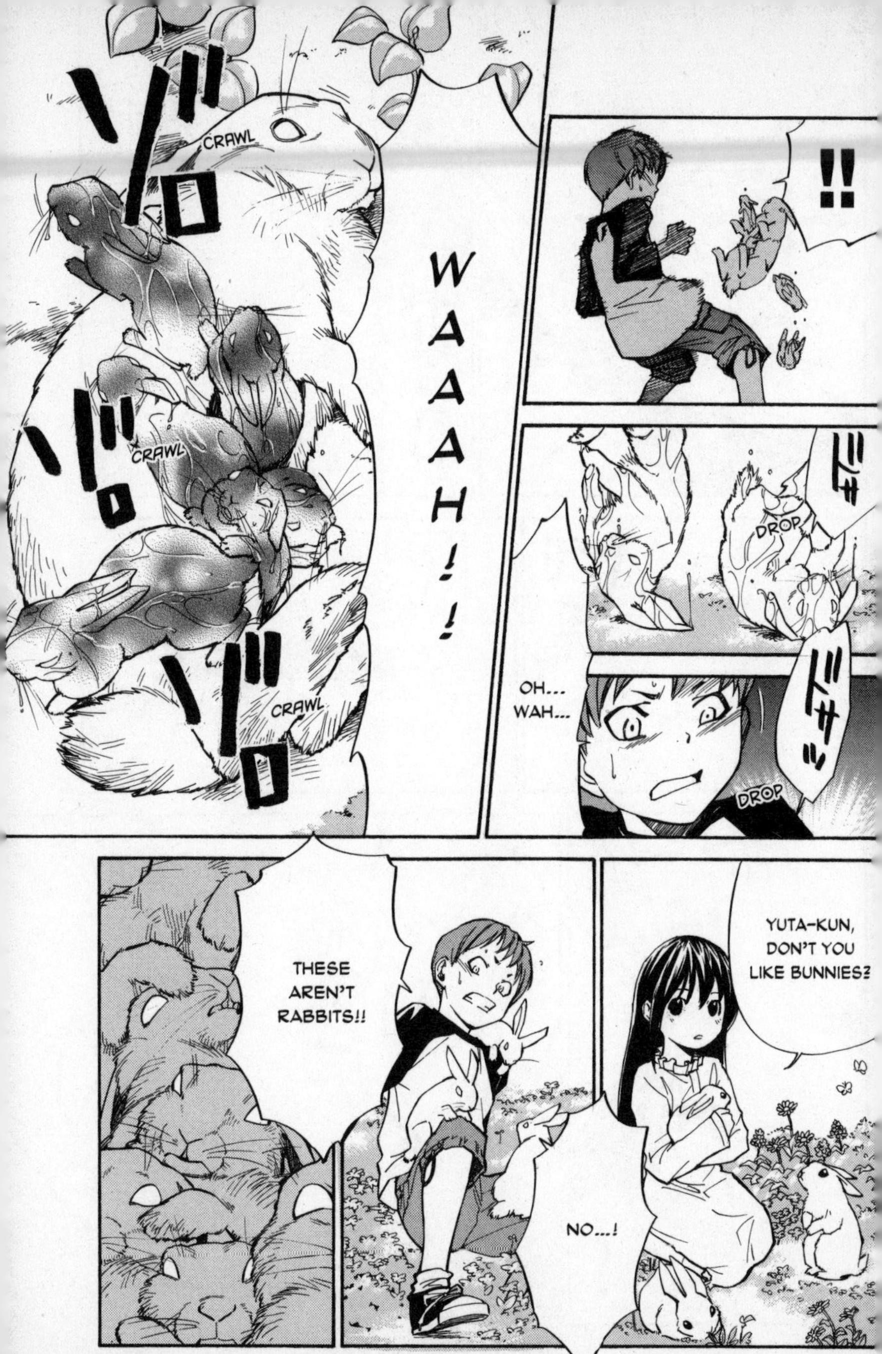
!!
DROP
OH... WAH...
ドサッ
DROP
ゾロ
CRAWL
ゾロ
CRAWL
ゾロ
CRAWL
WAAAAH!!!
YUTA-KUN, DON'T YOU LIKE BUNNIES?
NO...!
THESE AREN'T RABBITS!!

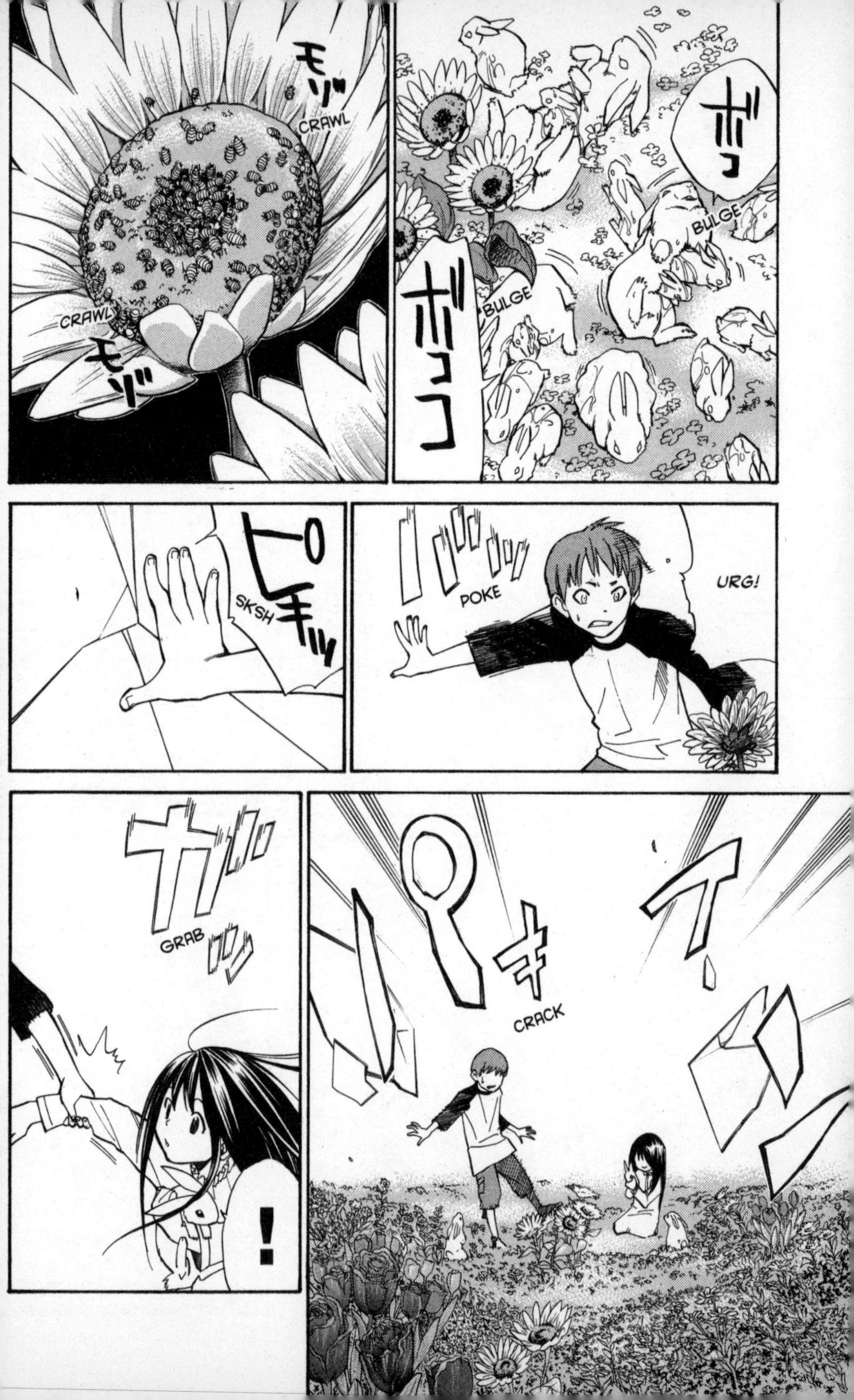
BULGE
BULGE
CRAWL
CRAWL
URG!
POKE
SKSH
CRACK
GRAB
!

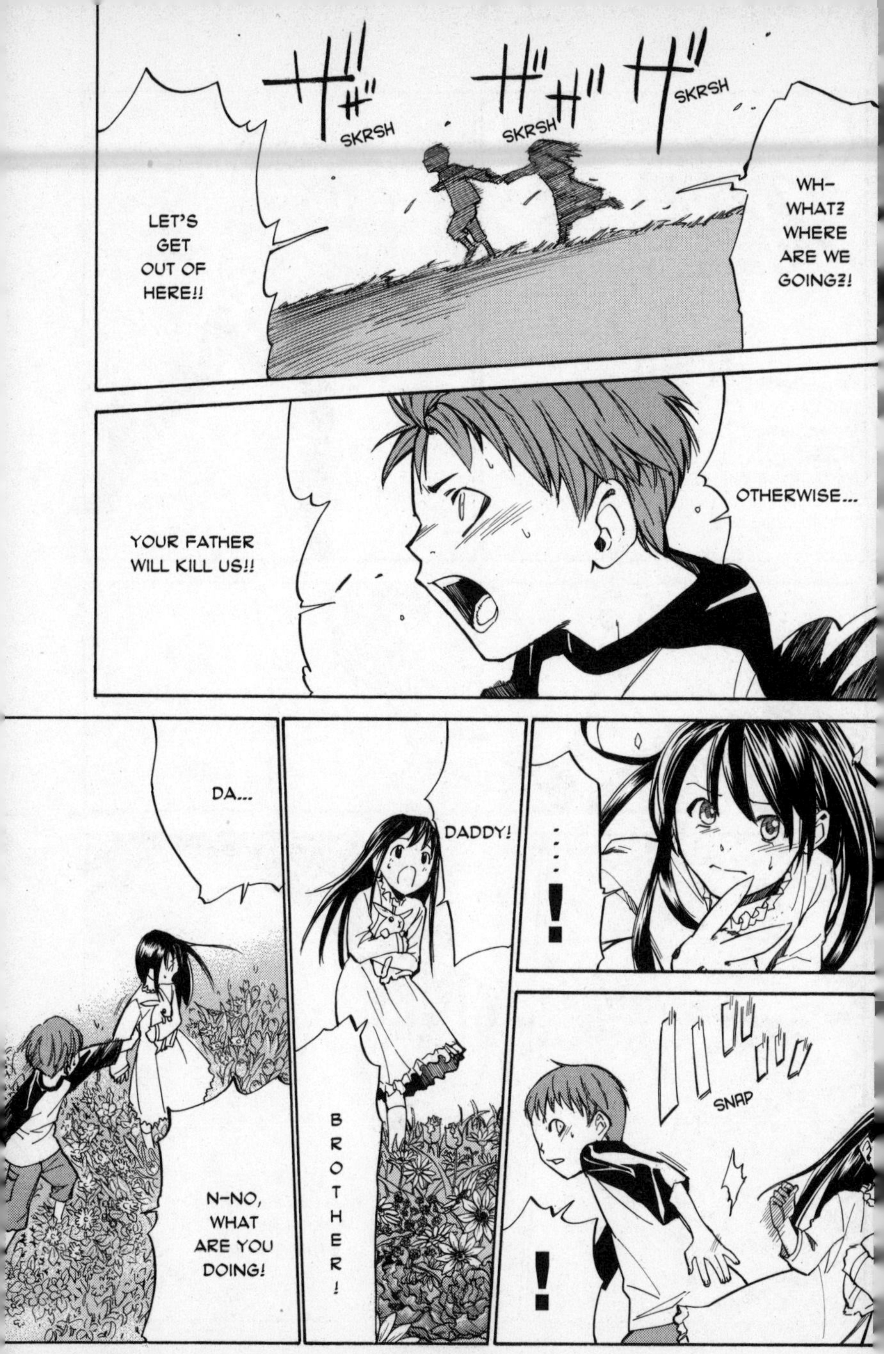
SKRSH
WH- WHAT? WHERE ARE WE GOING?!
SKRSH
SKRSH
LET'S GET OUT OF HERE!!
OTHERWISE...
YOUR FATHER WILL KILL US!!
...!
SNAP
!
DADDY!
BROTHER!
DA...
N-NO, WHAT ARE YOU DOING!

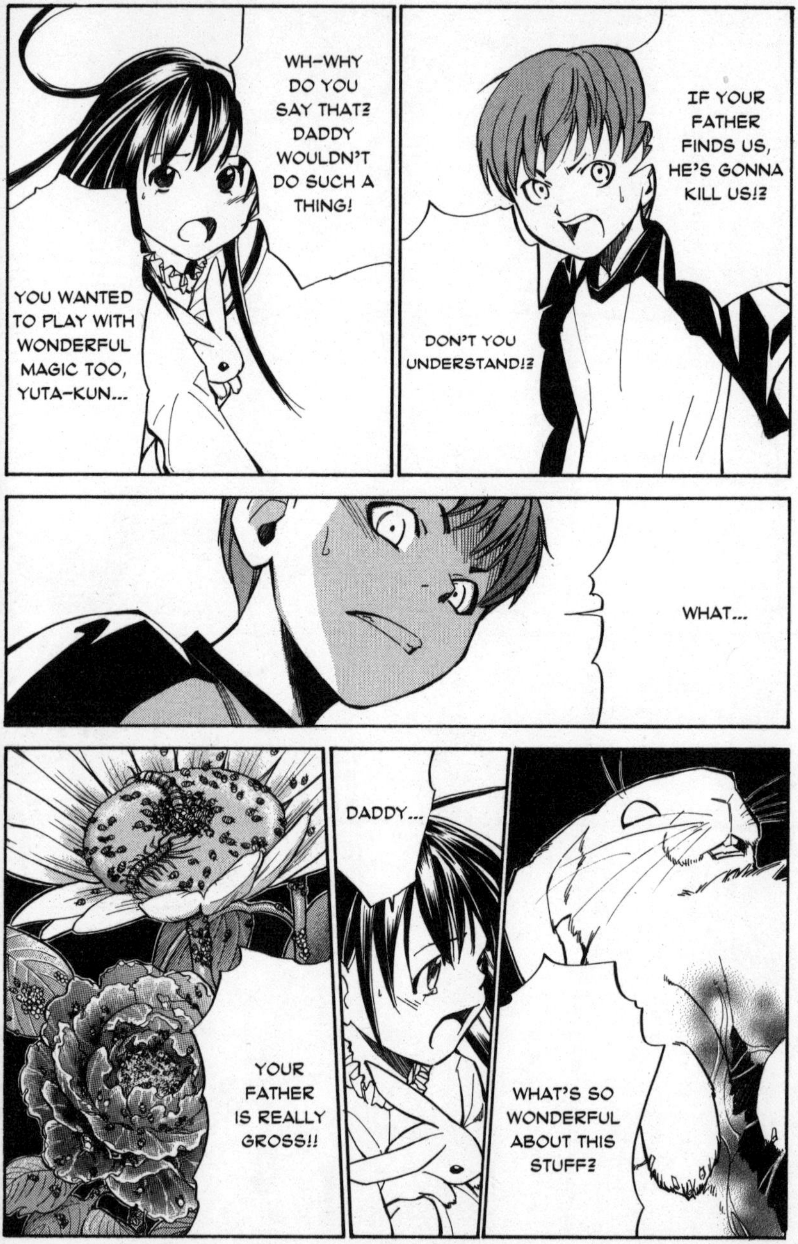
IF YOUR FATHER FINDS US, HE'S GONNA KILL US!?
DON'T YOU UNDERSTAND!?
WH-WHY DO YOU SAY THAT? DADDY WOULDN'T DO SUCH A THING!
YOU WANTED TO PLAY WITH WONDERFUL MAGIC TOO, YUTA-KUN...
WHAT...
WHAT'S SO WONDERFUL ABOUT THIS STUFF?
DADDY...
YOUR FATHER IS REALLY GROSS!!

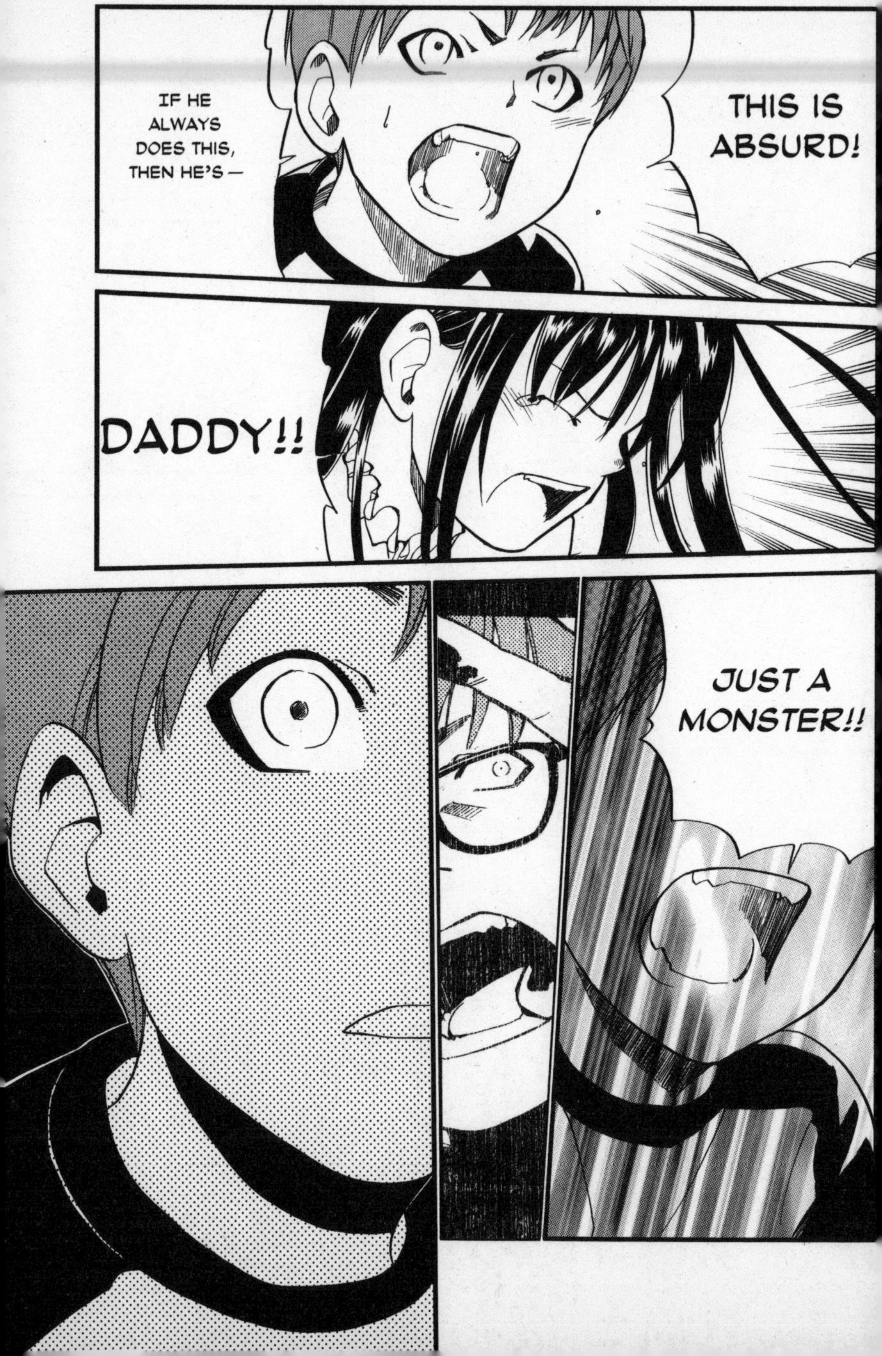
THIS IS ABSURD!
IF HE ALWAYS DOES THIS, THEN HE'S —
DADDY!!
JUST A MONSTER!!

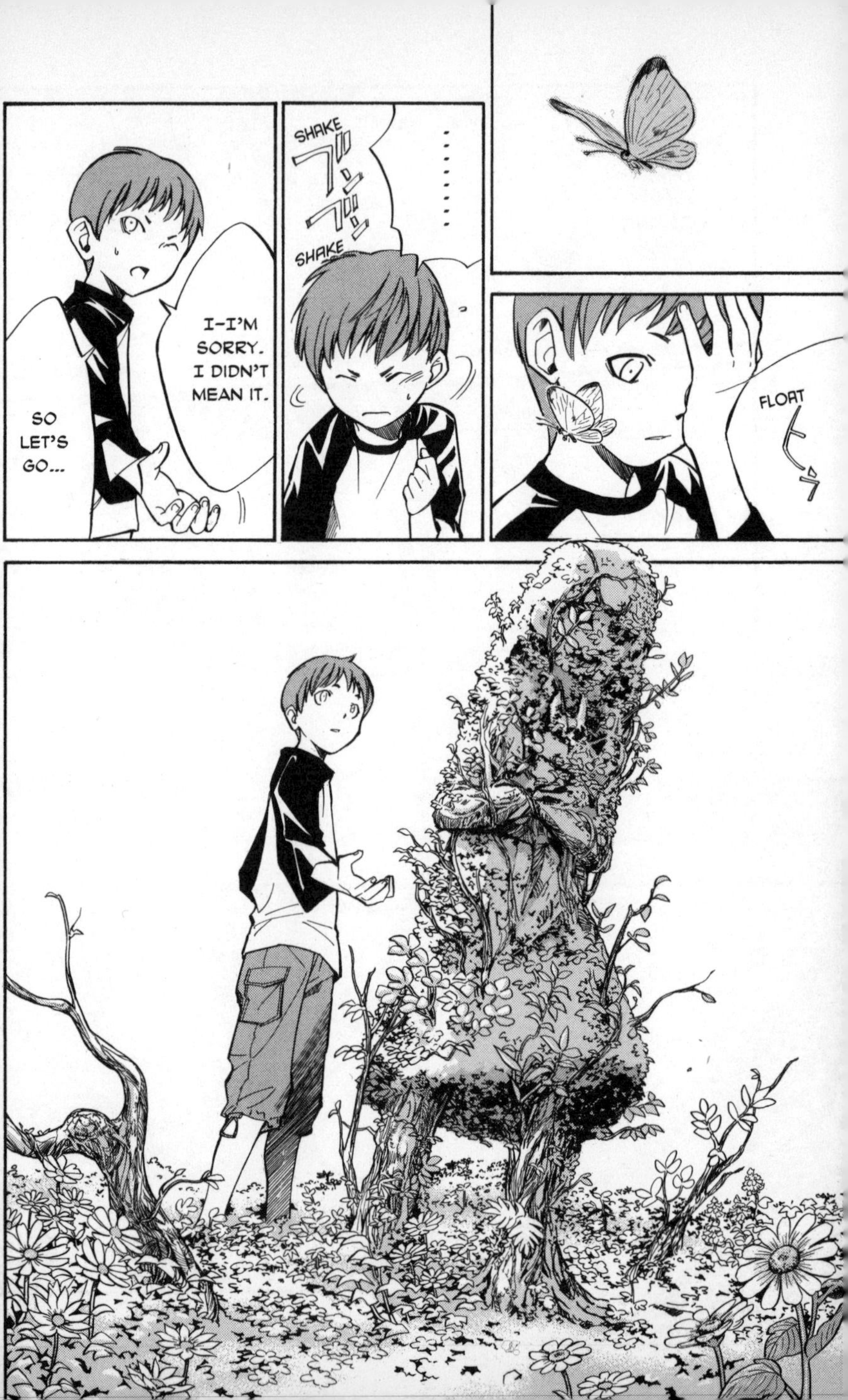

FLOAT
SHAKE
......
SHAKE
I-I'M SORRY. I DIDN'T MEAN IT.
SO LET'S GO...

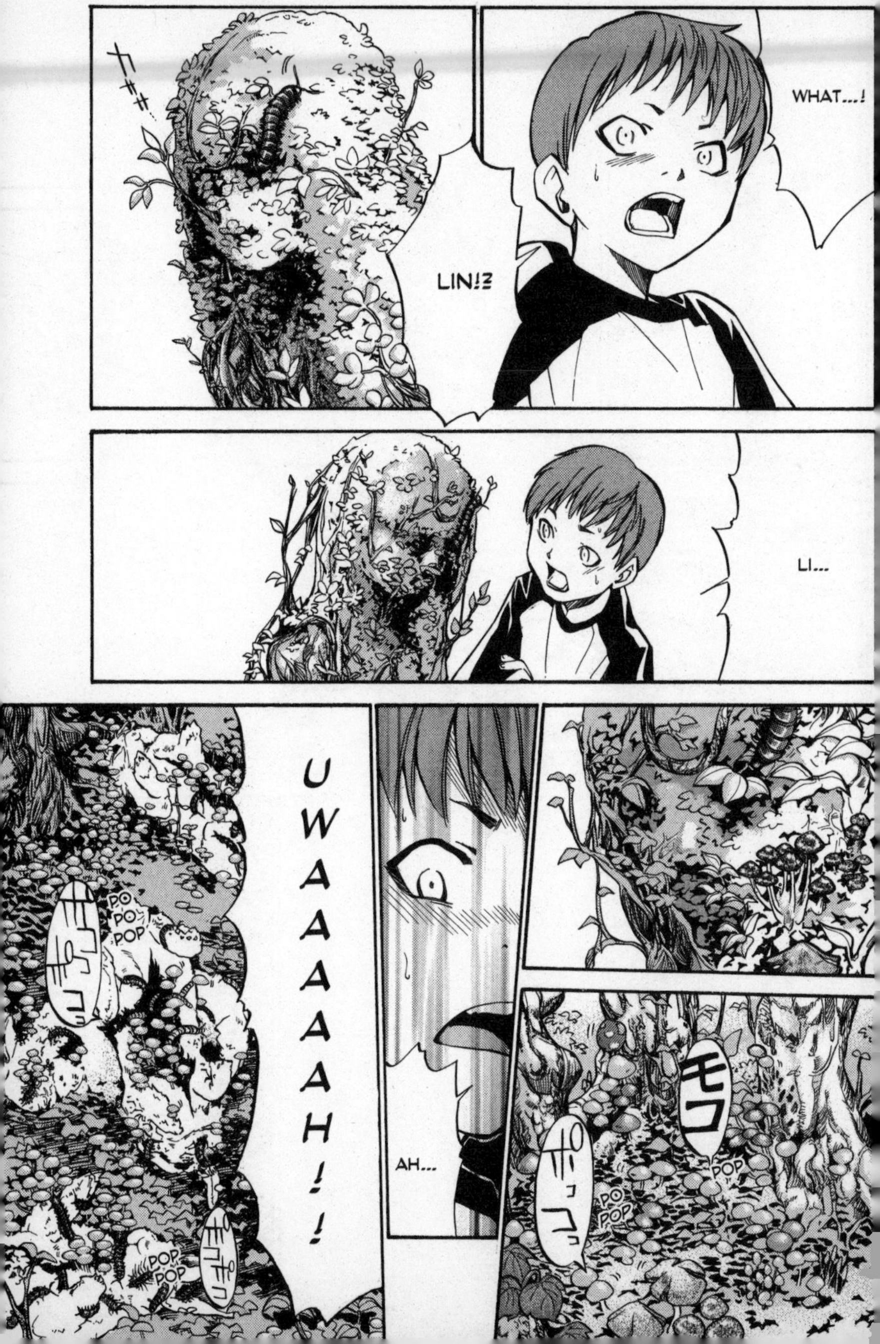
WHAT...!
LIN!?
LI...
モコ
POP
PO POP
AH...
UWAAAAAAH!!!
PO PO POP
POP POP

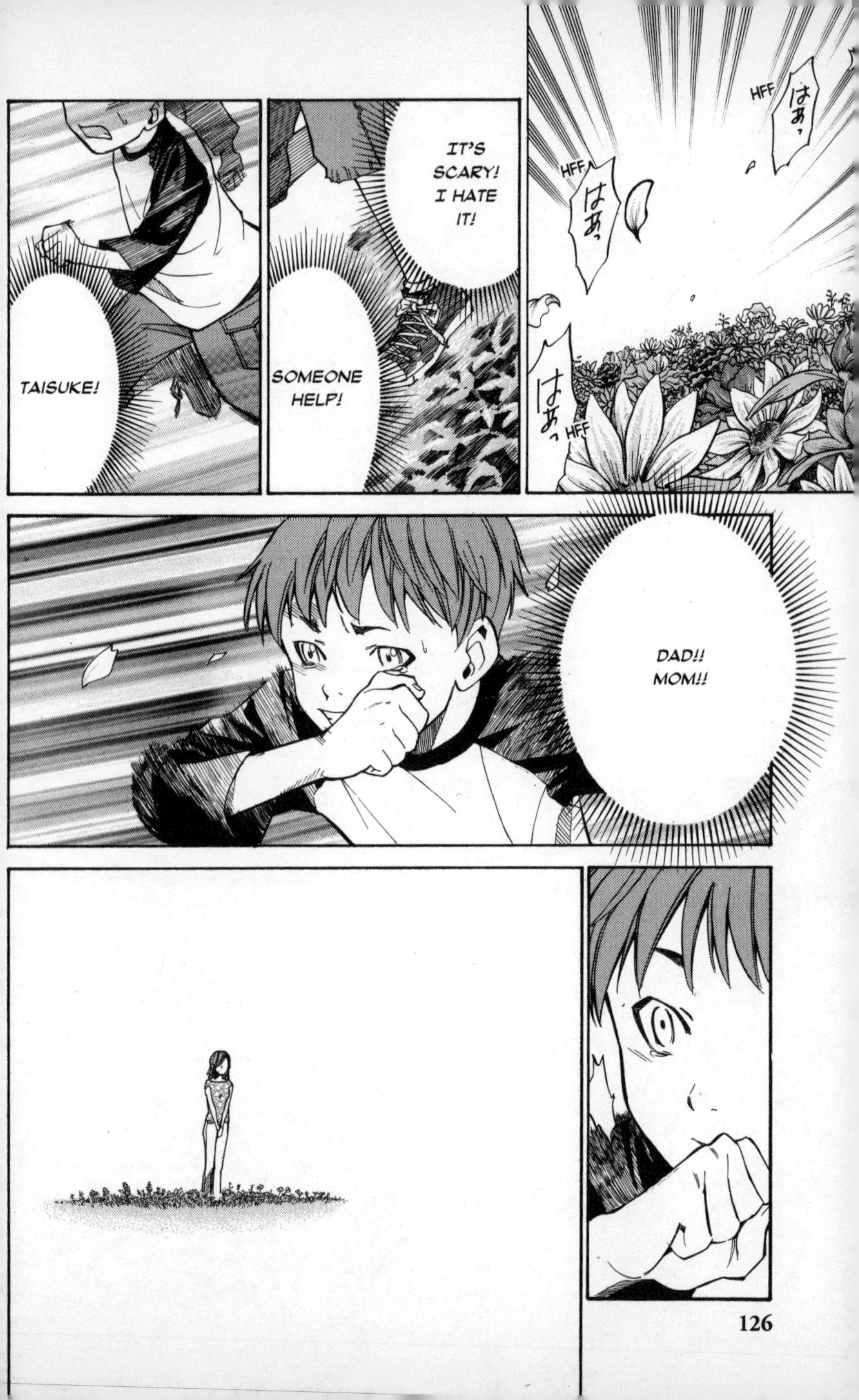
HFF
はぁっ
HFF
はぁっ
はぁっ
HFF
IT'S SCARY! I HATE IT!
SOMEONE HELP!
TAISUKE!
DAD!! MOM!!

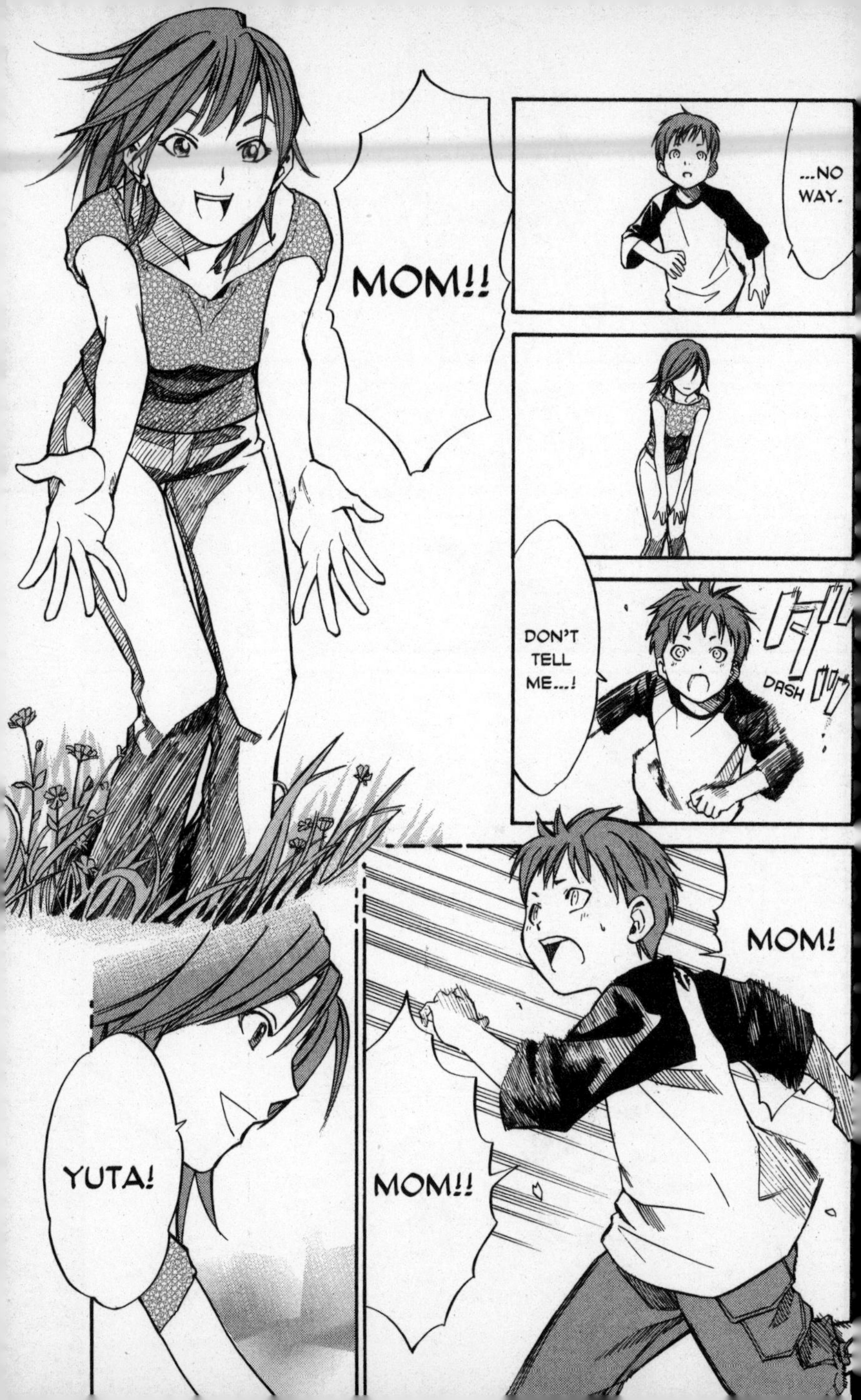
...NO WAY.
DON'T TELL ME...!
DASH
MOM!!
MOM!
MOM!!
YUTA!

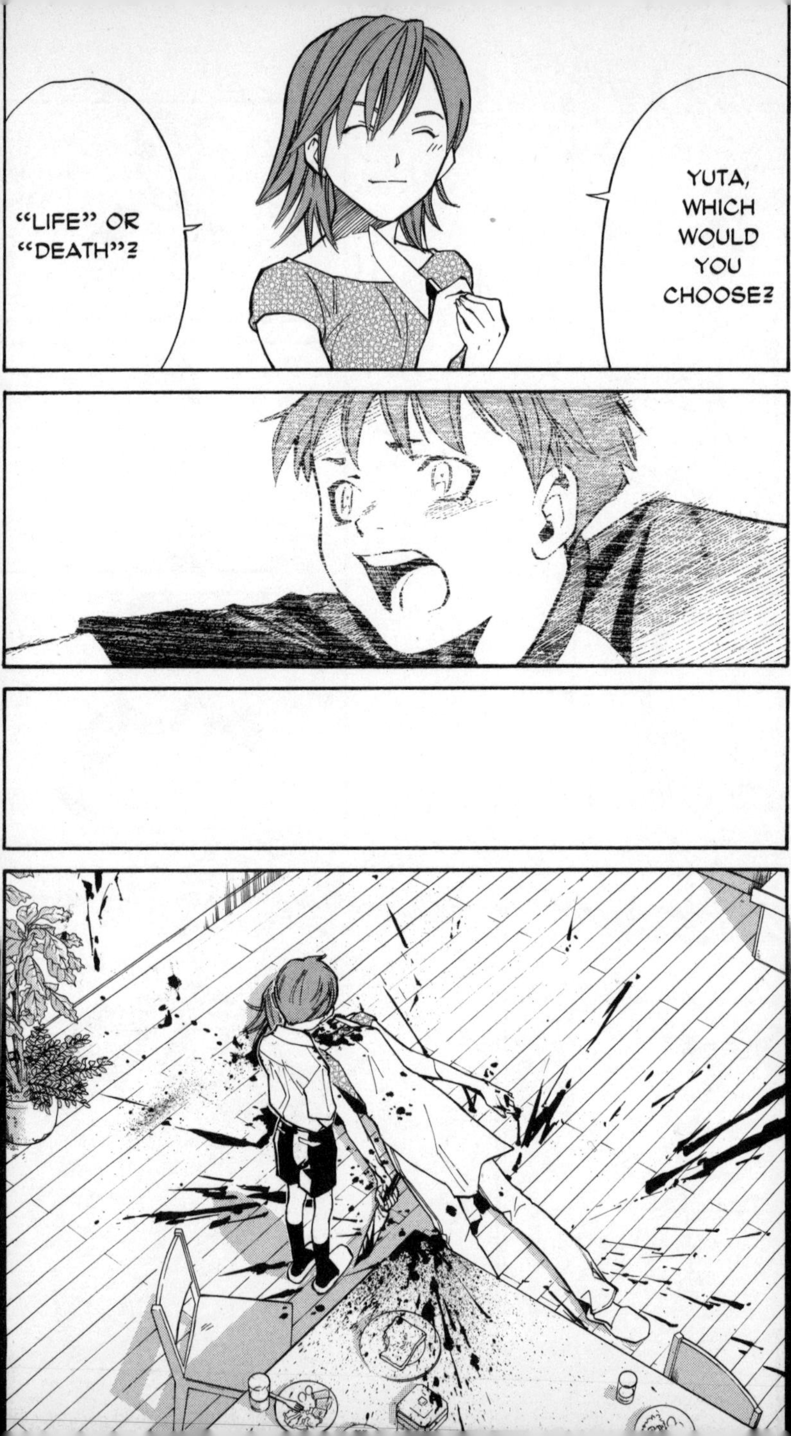
YUTA, WHICH WOULD YOU CHOOSE?
"LIFE" OR "DEATH"?

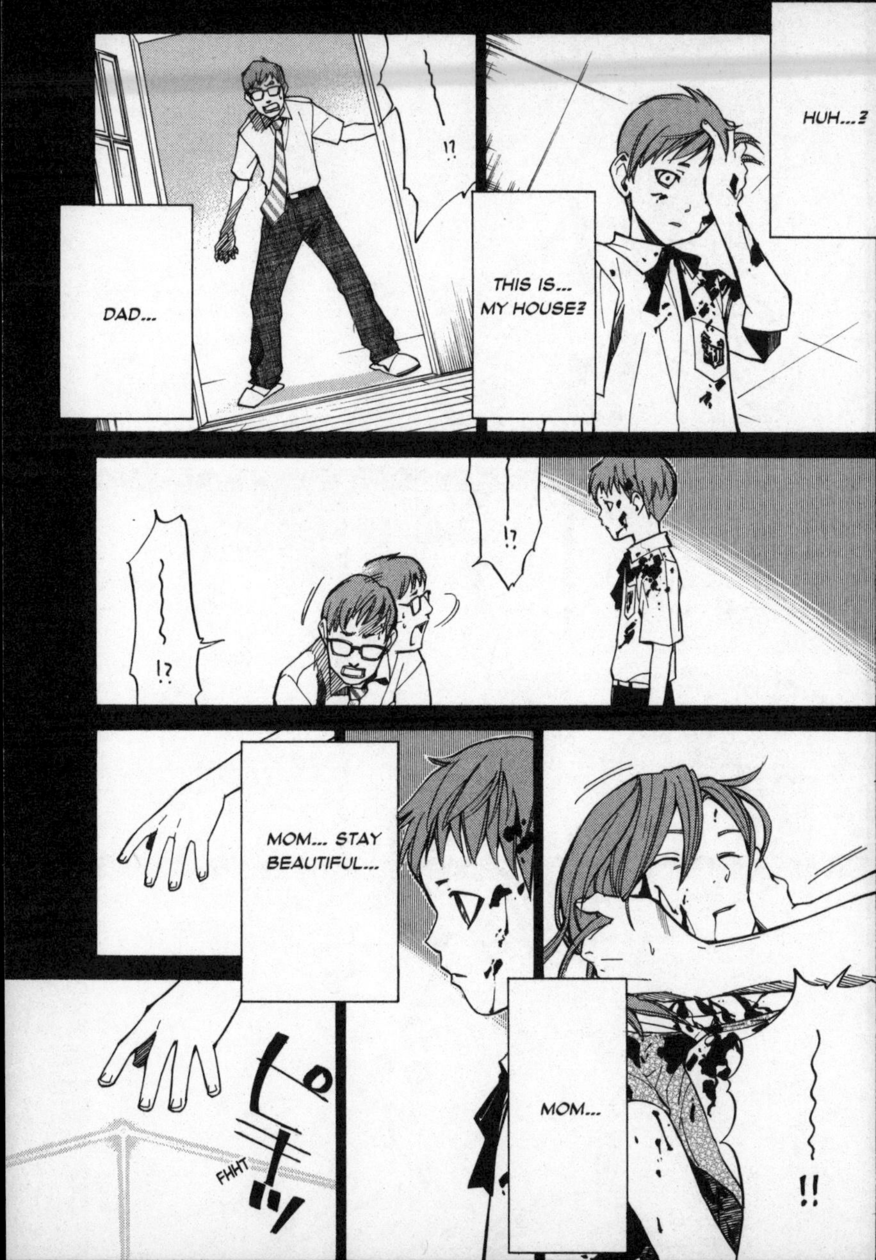
HUH...?
THIS IS... MY HOUSE?
!?
DAD...
!?
!?
!!
MOM...
MOM... STAY BEAUTIFUL...
FHHT

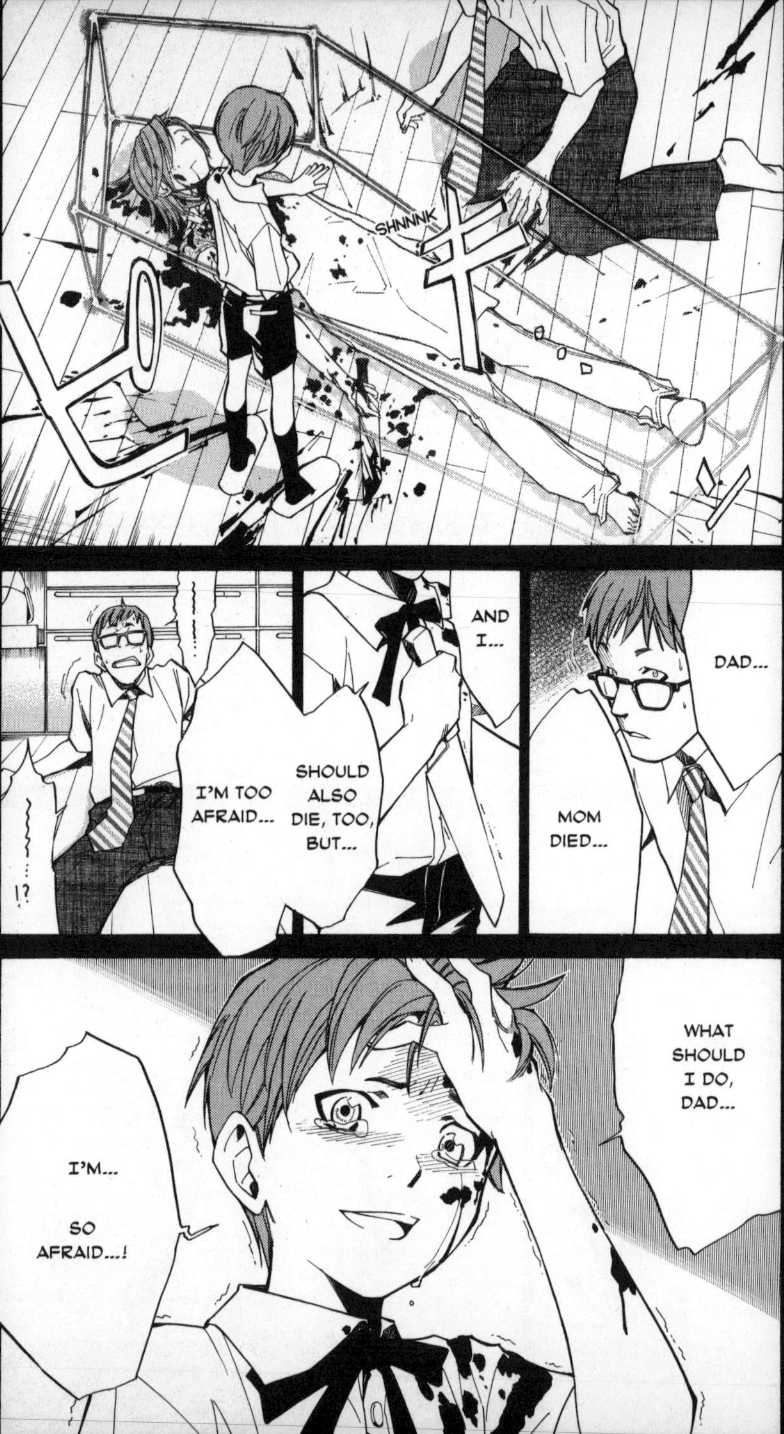
SHNNNK
DAD...
MOM DIED...
AND I...
SHOULD ALSO DIE, TOO, BUT...
I'M TOO AFRAID...
......
......!?
WHAT SHOULD I DO, DAD...
I'M...
SO AFRAID...!

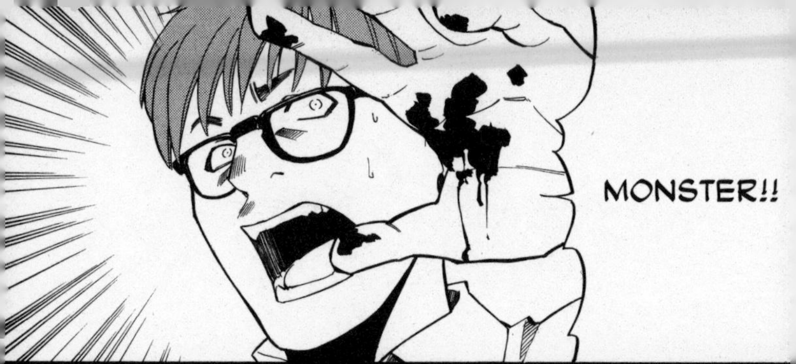
MONSTER!!
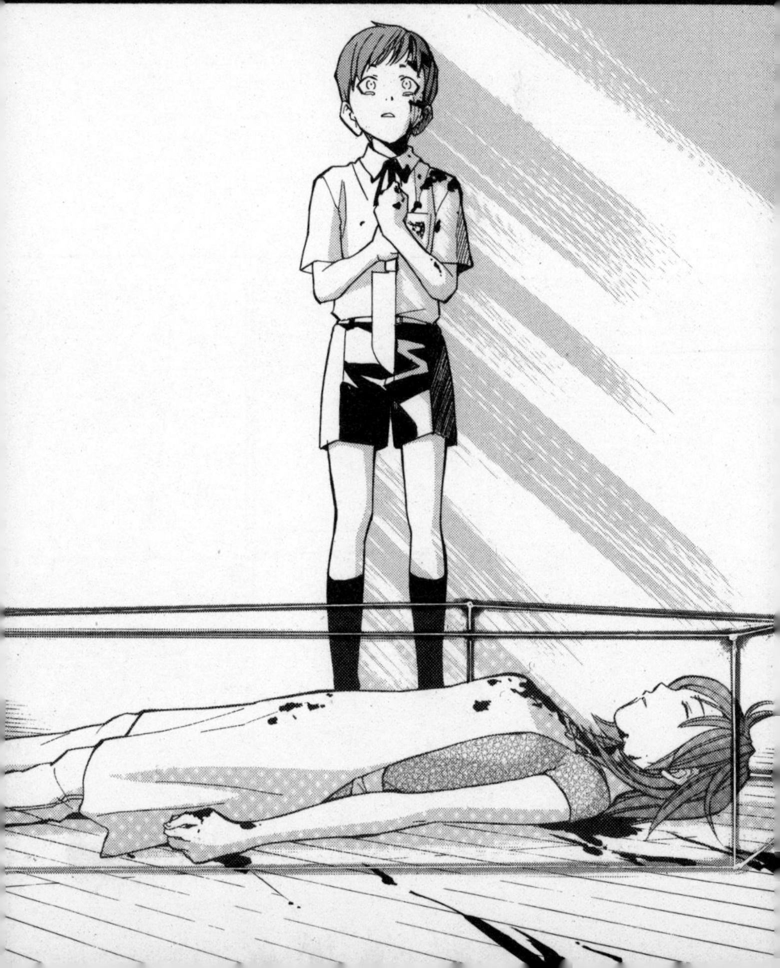

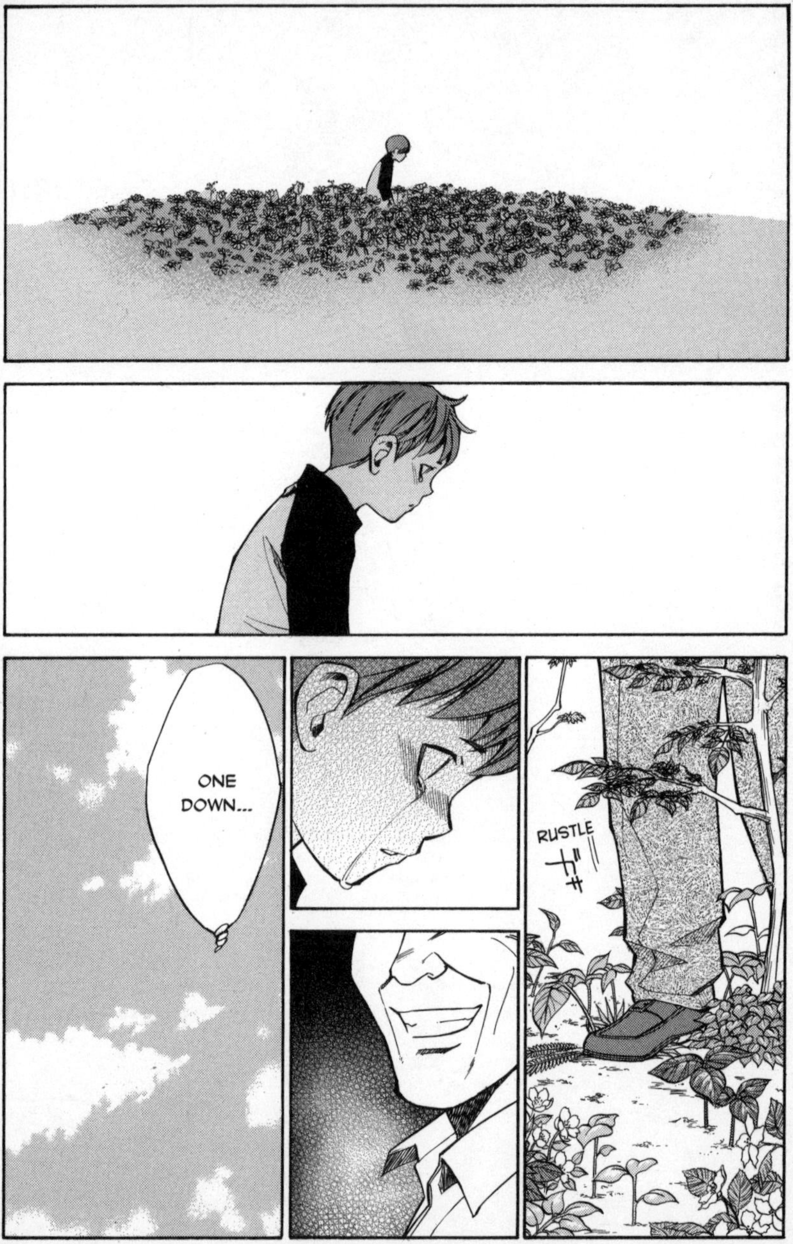
RUSTLE
ガサ
ONE DOWN...

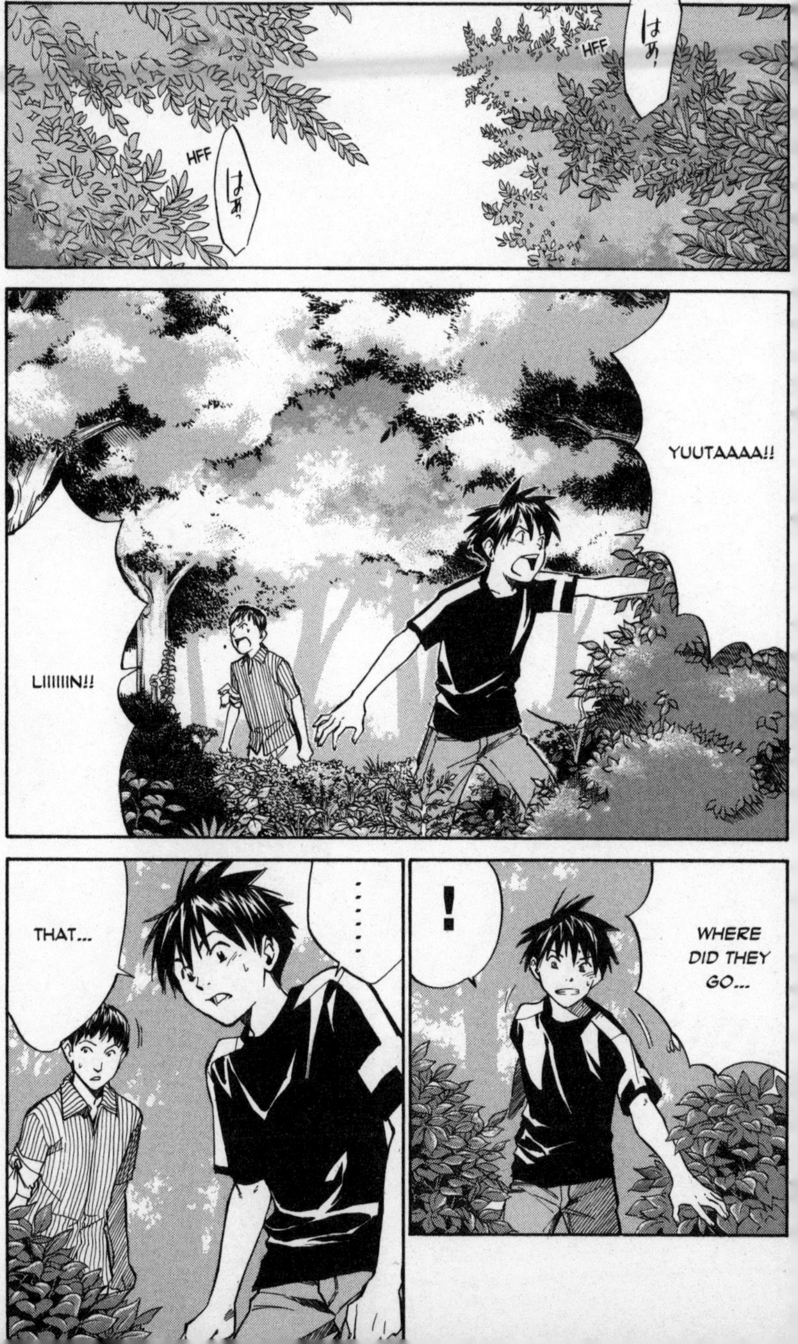
はぁ、
HFF
HFF
はぁっ
YUUTAAAA!!
LIIIIIN!!
WHERE DID THEY GO...
!
......
THAT...

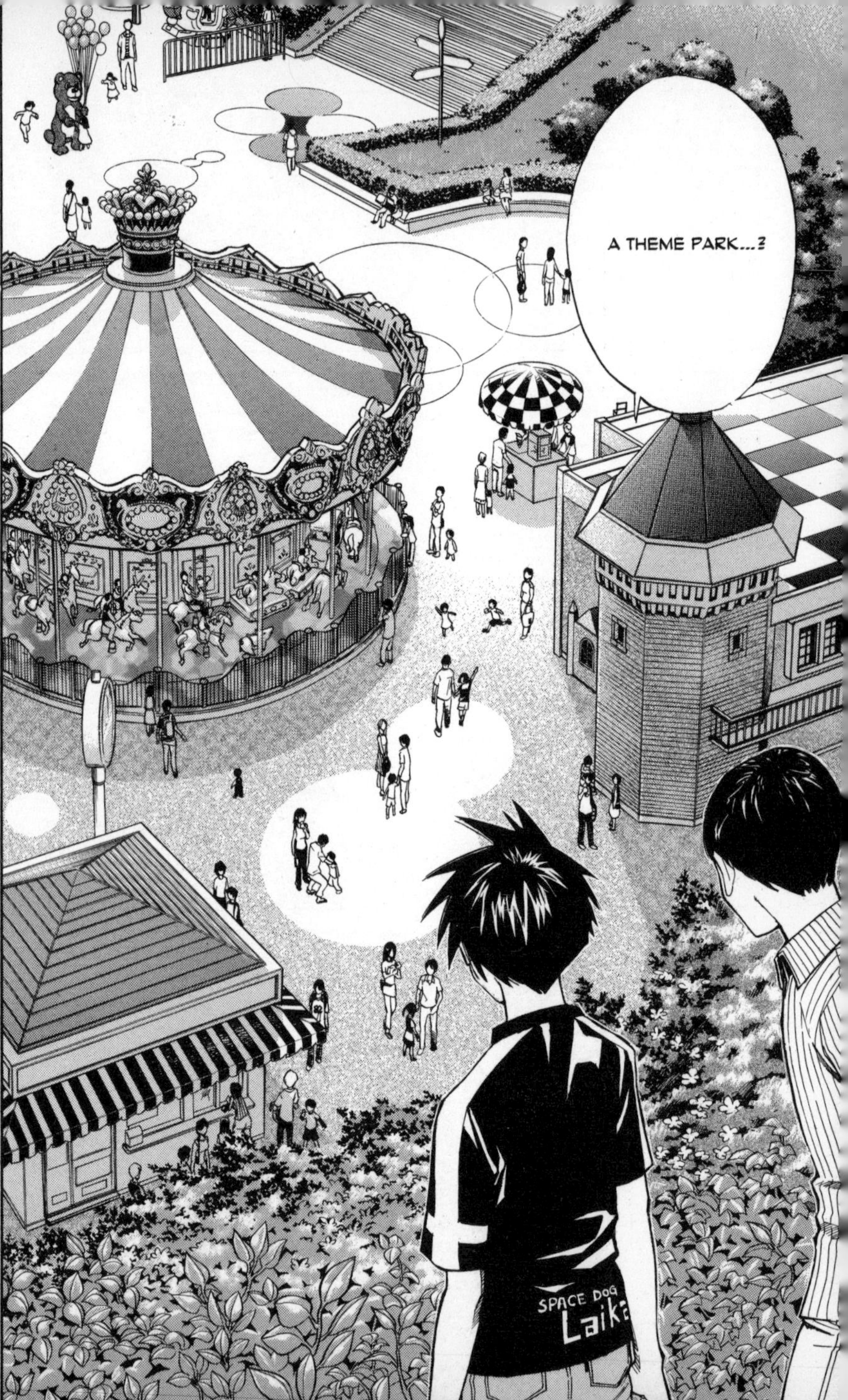
A THEME PARK...?
SPACE DOG
Laika

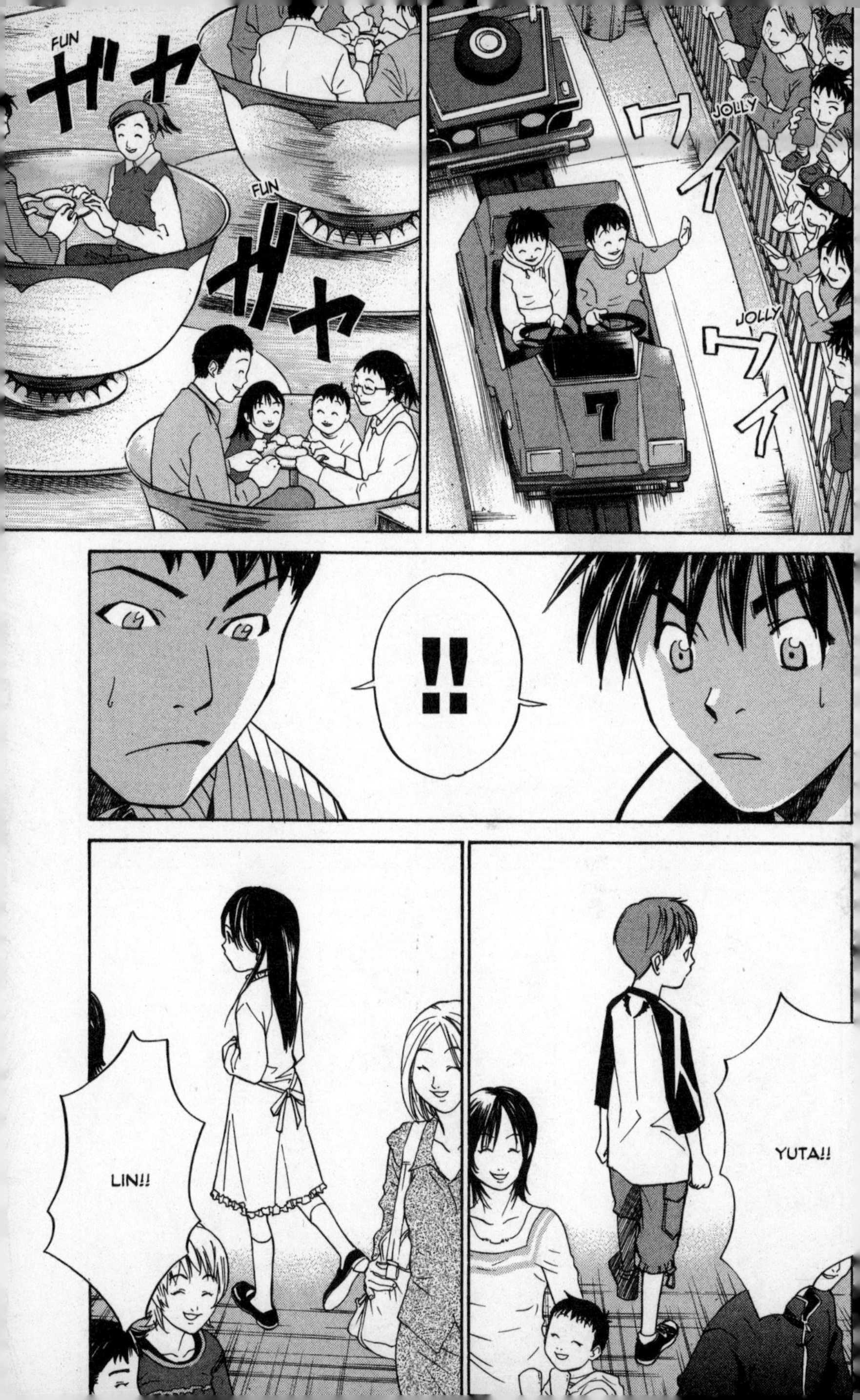
ワイ
JOLLY
ワイ
JOLLY
FUN
ガヤ
FUN
ガヤ
!!
YUTA!!
LIN!!

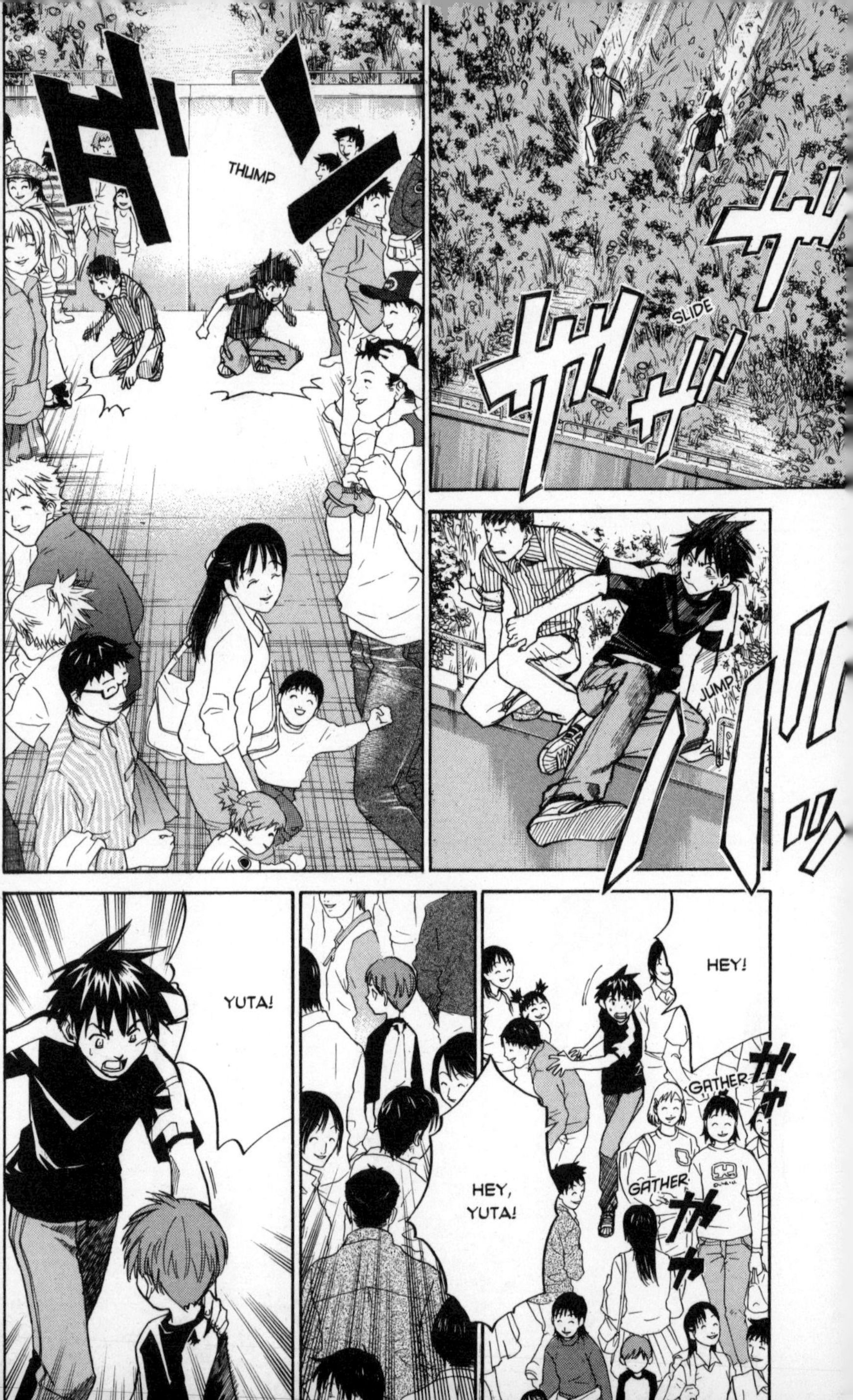
SLIDE
JUMP
THUMP
HEY!
GATHER
GATHER
HEY, YUTA!
YUTA!

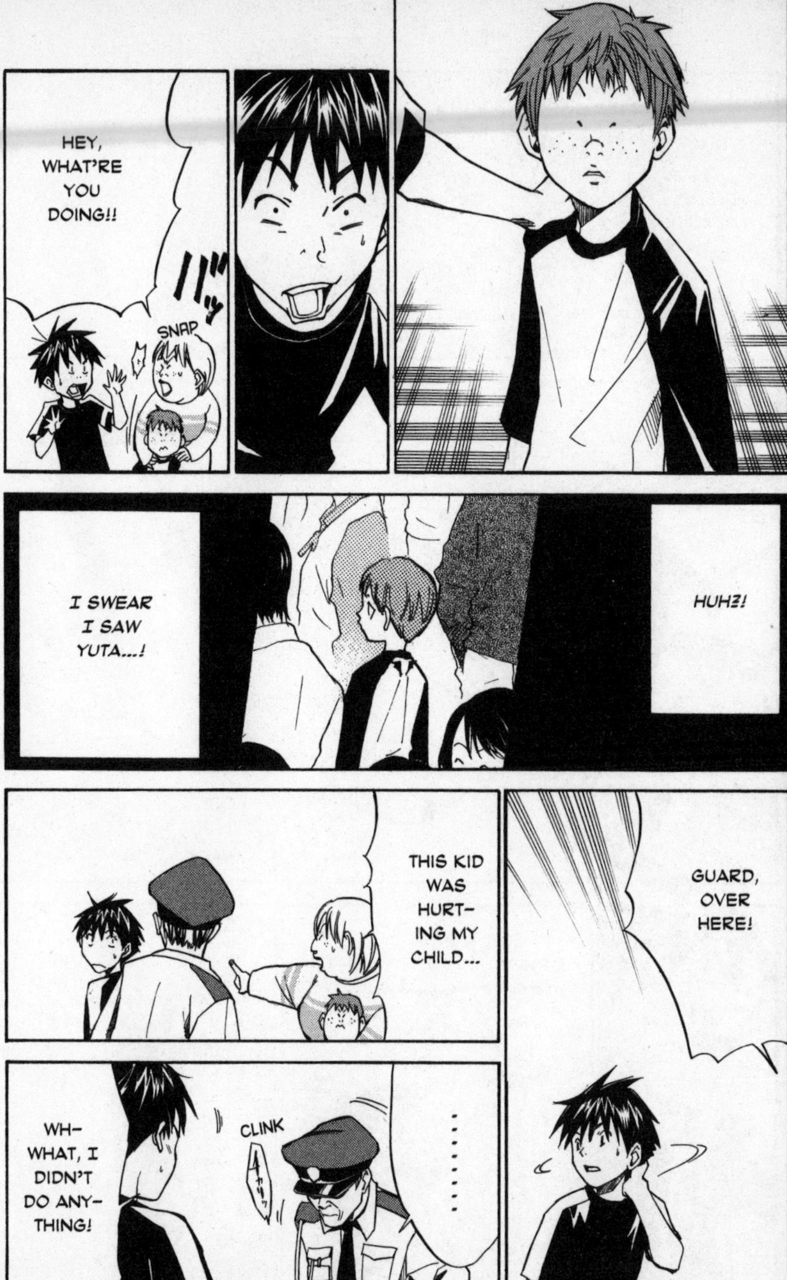
HEY, WHAT'RE YOU DOING!!
SNAP
HUH?!
I SWEAR I SAW YUTA...!
GUARD, OVER HERE!
THIS KID WAS HURT-ING MY CHILD...
......
CLINK
WH-WHAT, I DIDN'T DO ANY-THING!

I REALLY DIDN'T DO—

HOLD IT, KID!

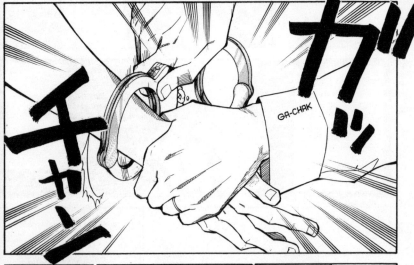

GA-CHAK

COME HERE.

WHOAAAH, JUST WAIT A SEC!!

RANT

LET ME EXPLAIN—

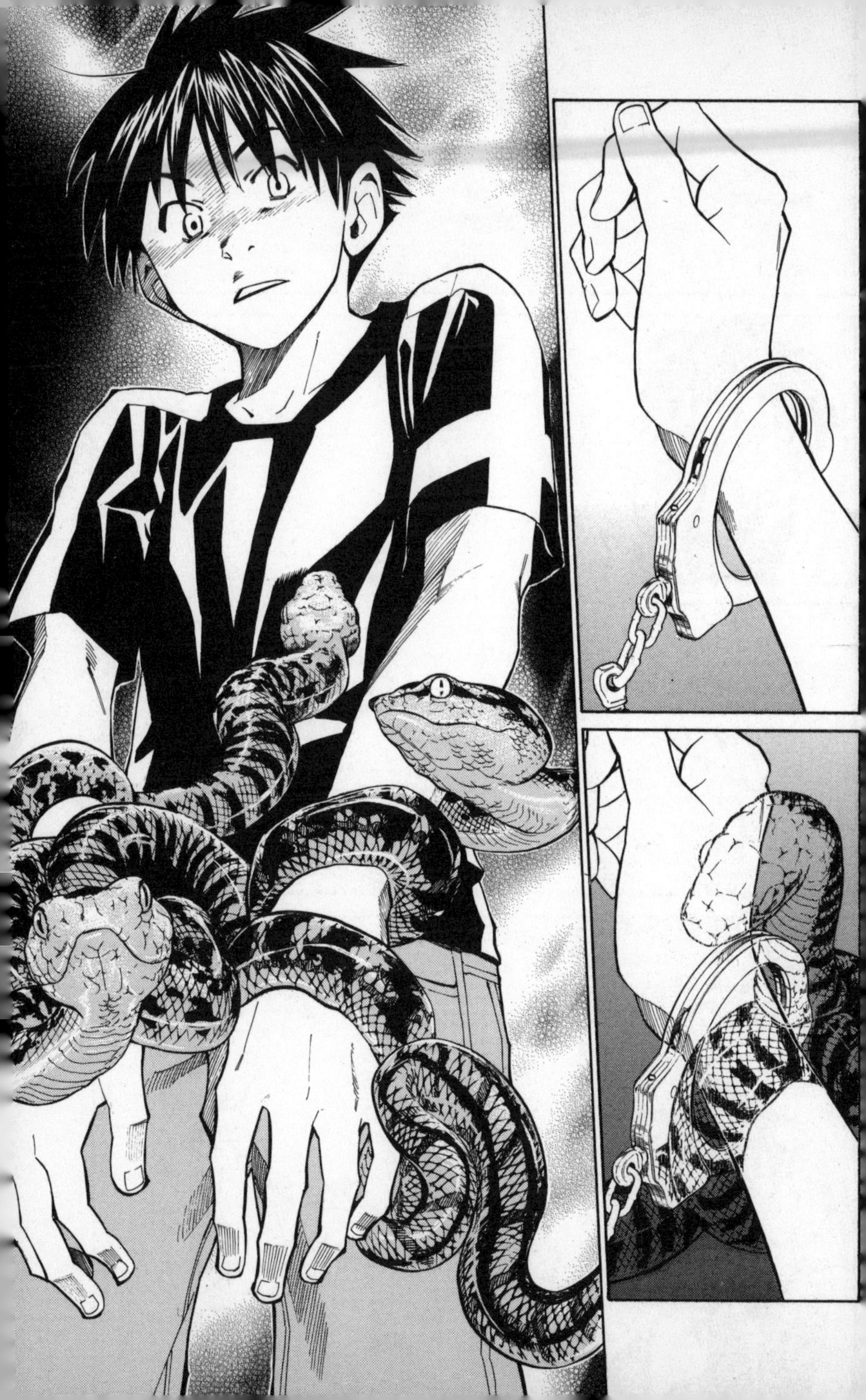

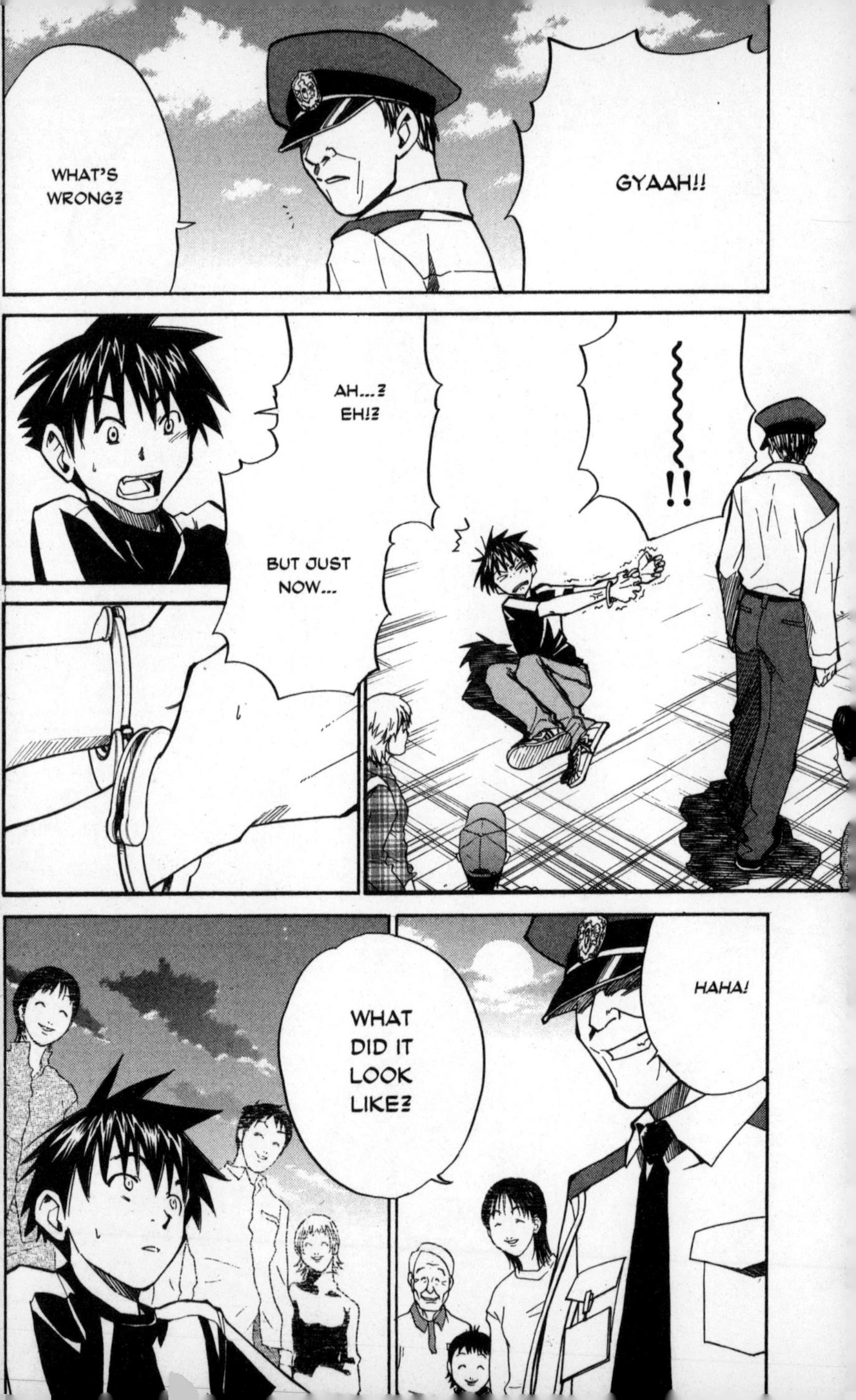
GYAAH!!
WHAT'S WRONG?
~~~~!!
AH...? EH!?
BUT JUST NOW...
HAHA!
WHAT DID IT LOOK LIKE?
~~~~

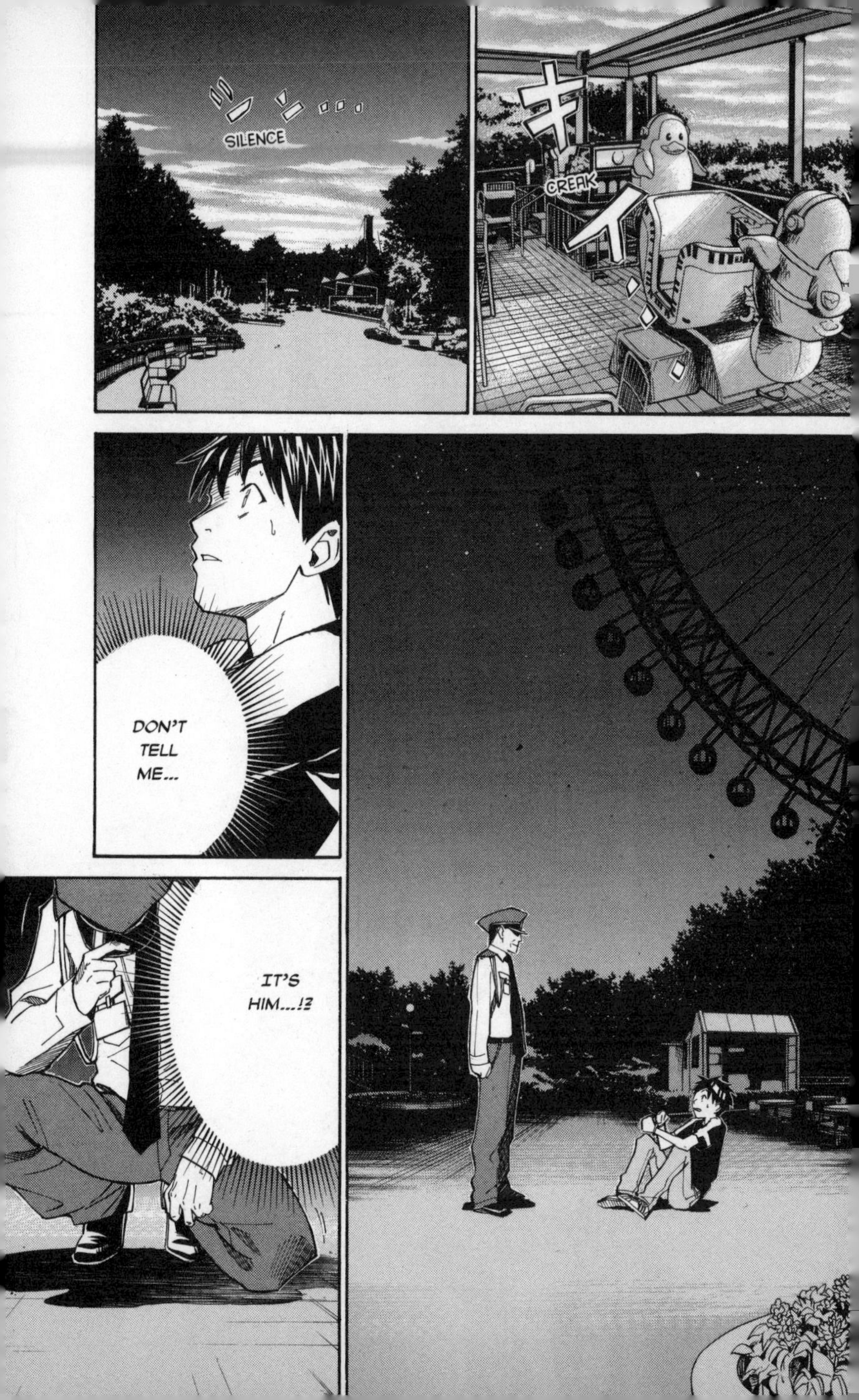
CREAK
SILENCE
DON'T TELL ME...
IT'S HIM...!?

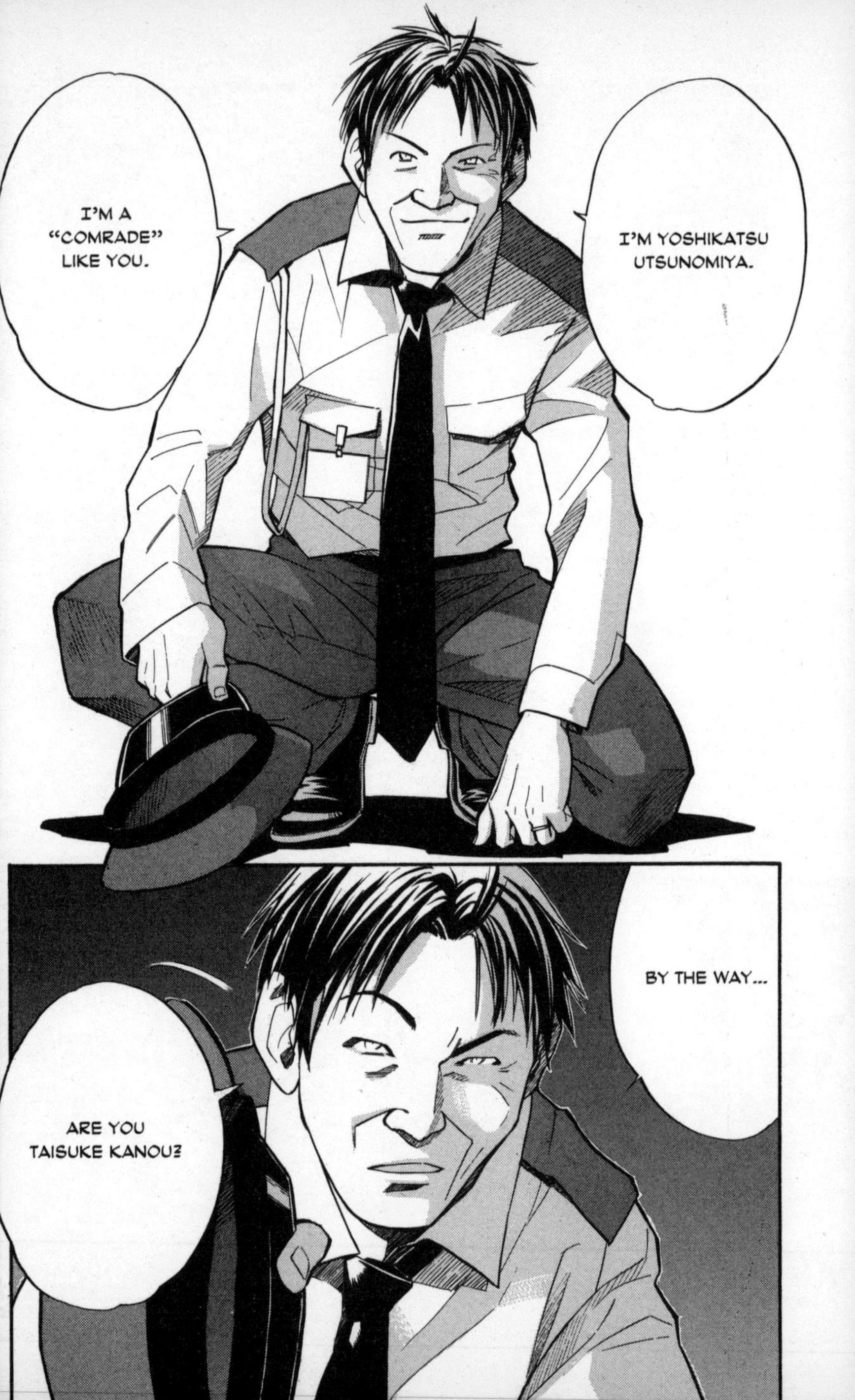
I'M YOSHIKATSU UTSUNOMIYA.
I'M A "COMRADE" LIKE YOU.
BY THE WAY...
ARE YOU TAISUKE KANOU?

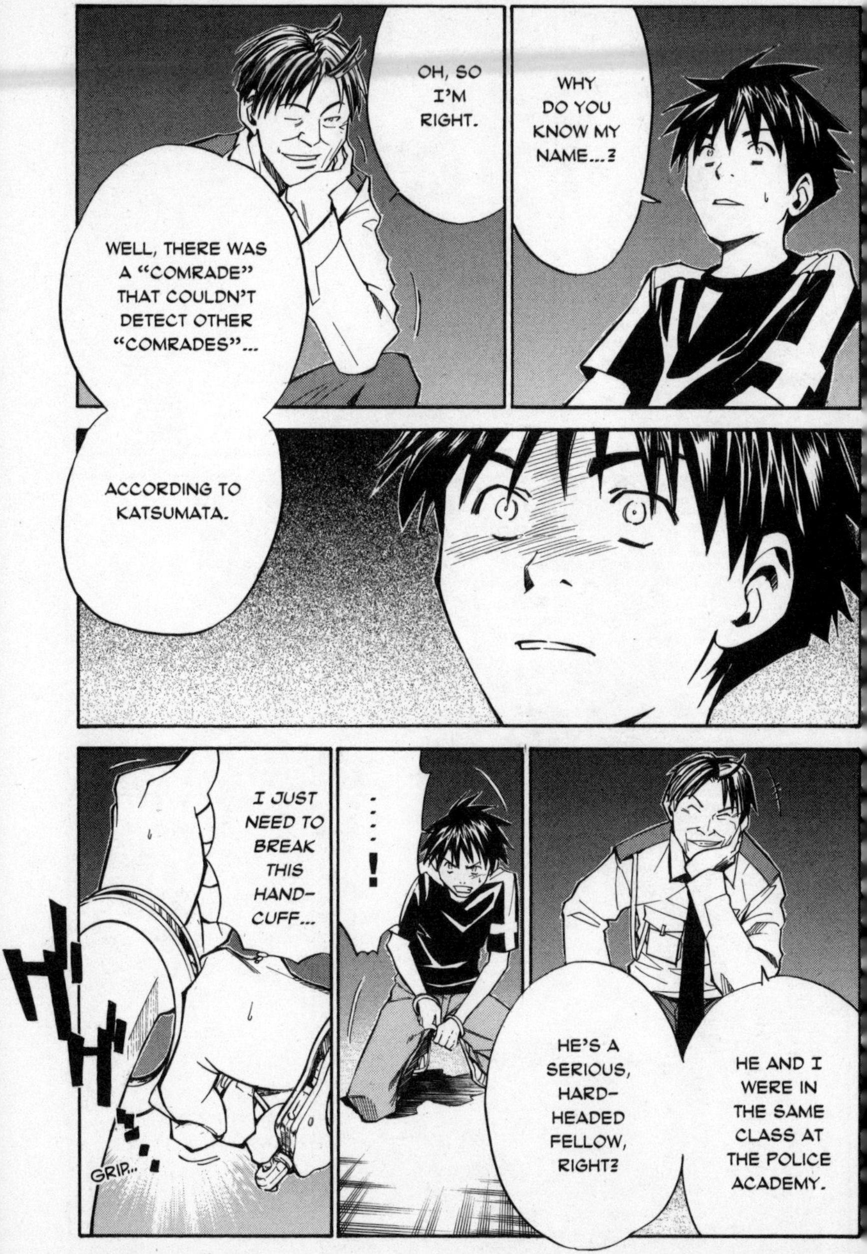
WHY DO YOU KNOW MY NAME...?
OH, SO I'M RIGHT.
WELL, THERE WAS A "COMRADE" THAT COULDN'T DETECT OTHER "COMRADES"...
ACCORDING TO KATSUMATA.
HE AND I WERE IN THE SAME CLASS AT THE POLICE ACADEMY.
HE'S A SERIOUS, HARD-HEADED FELLOW, RIGHT?
...!
I JUST NEED TO BREAK THIS HAND-CUFF...
GRIP..

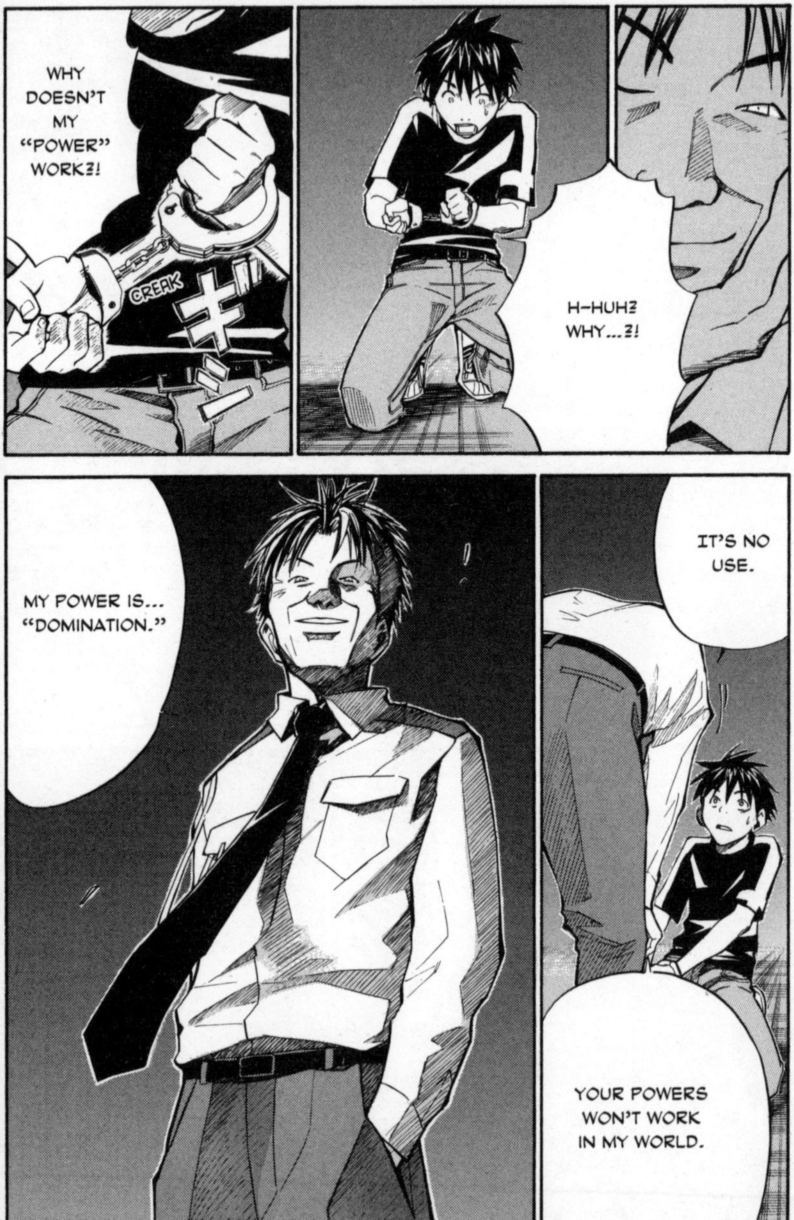
H-HUH? WHY...?!
WHY DOESN'T MY "POWER" WORK?!
CREAK
IT'S NO USE.
YOUR POWERS WON'T WORK IN MY WORLD.
MY POWER IS... "DOMINATION."

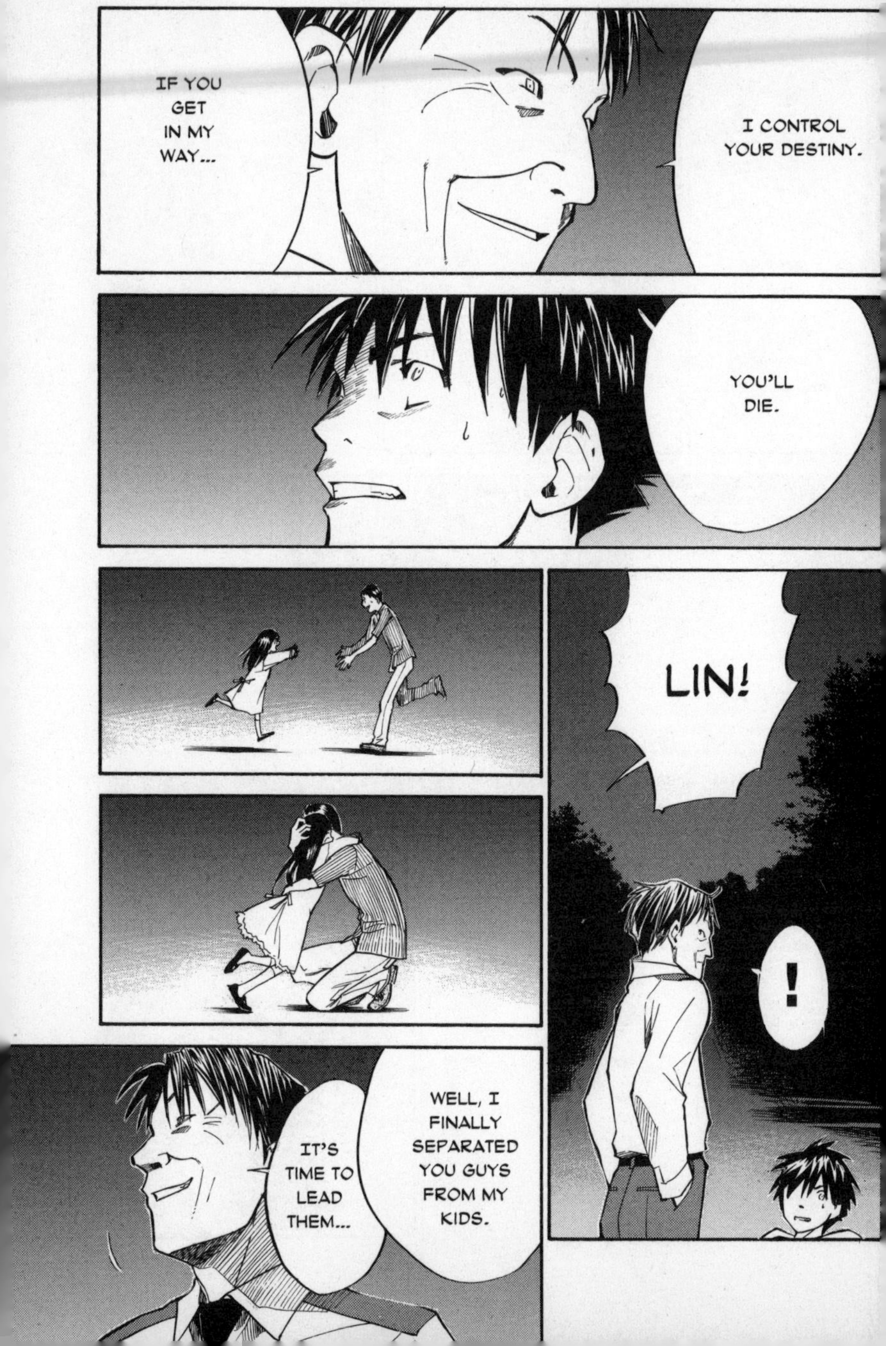
I CONTROL YOUR DESTINY.
IF YOU GET IN MY WAY...
YOU'LL DIE.
LIN!
!
WELL, I FINALLY SEPARATED YOU GUYS FROM MY KIDS.
IT'S TIME TO LEAD THEM...

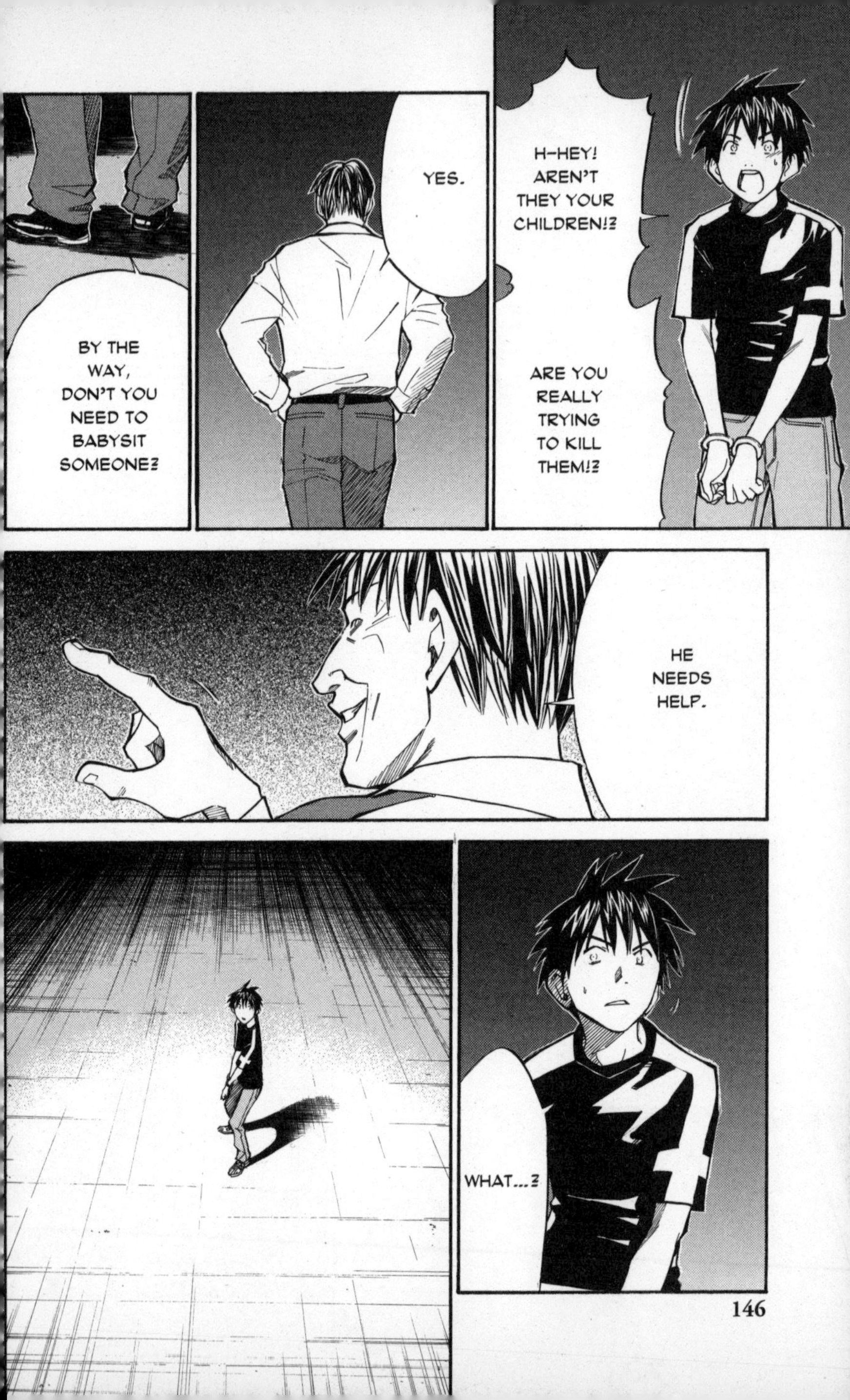
H-HEY! AREN'T THEY YOUR CHILDREN!?
ARE YOU REALLY TRYING TO KILL THEM!?
YES.
BY THE WAY, DON'T YOU NEED TO BABYSIT SOMEONE?
HE NEEDS HELP.
WHAT...?

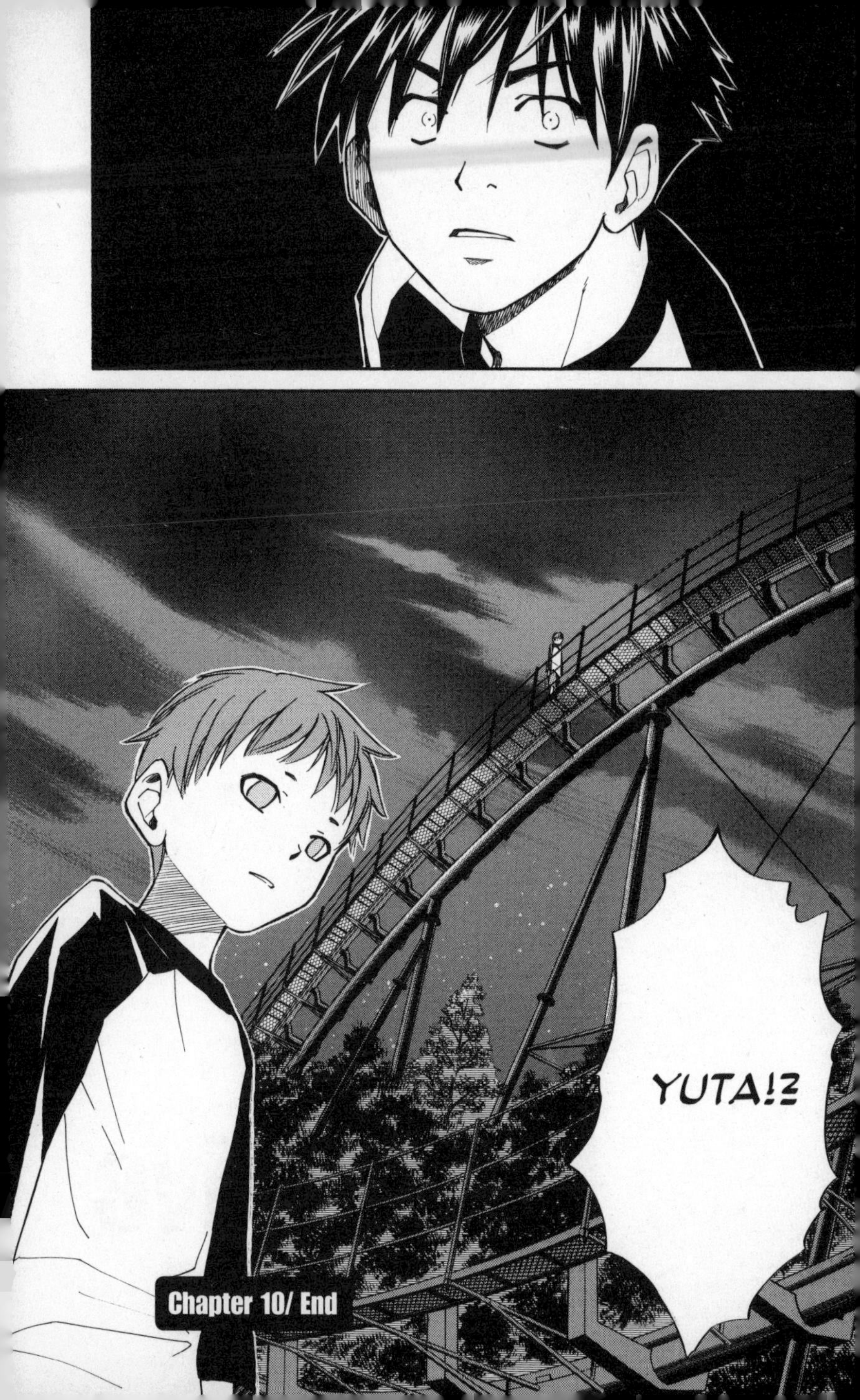
YUTA!?
Chapter 10/ End

Alive

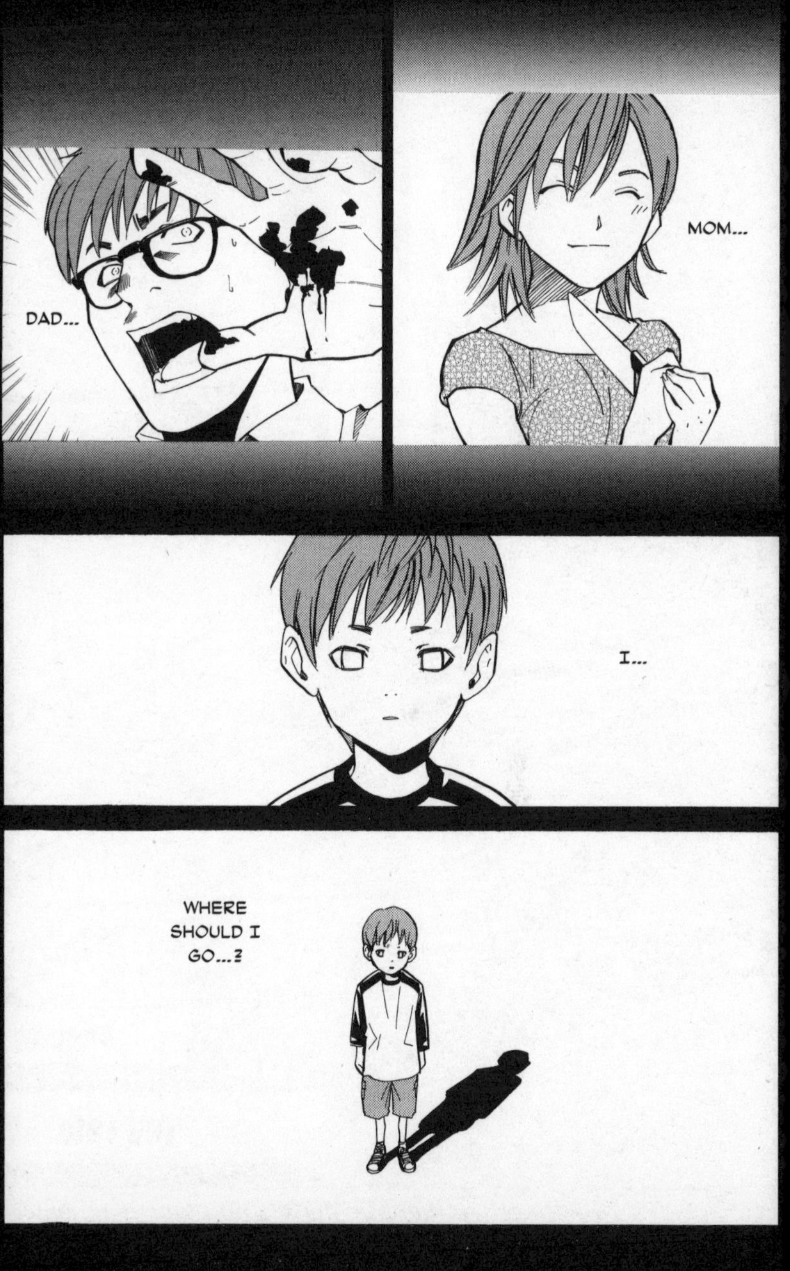
MOM...
DAD...
I...
WHERE SHOULD I GO...?

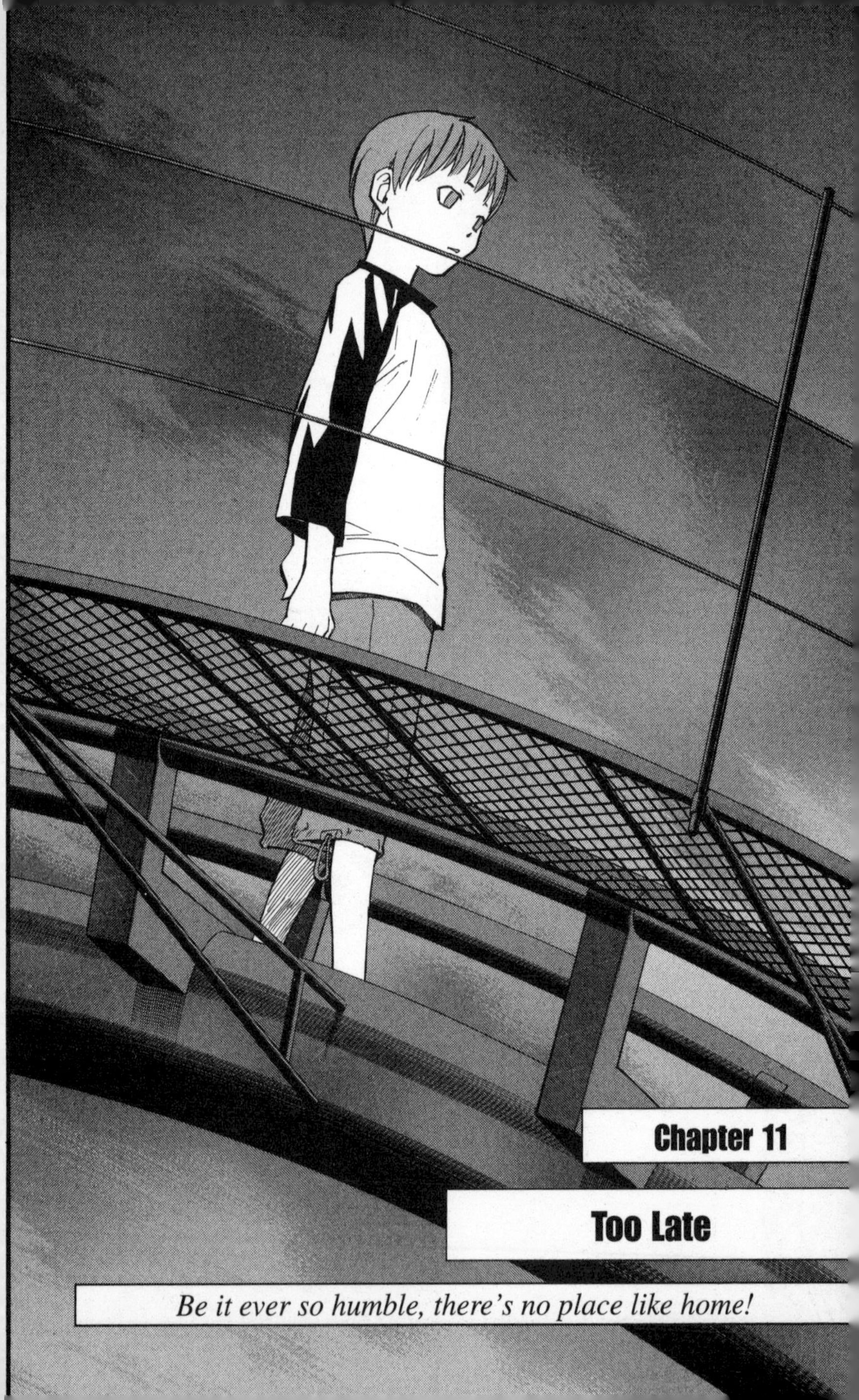
Chapter 11
Too Late
Be it ever so humble, there's no place like home!

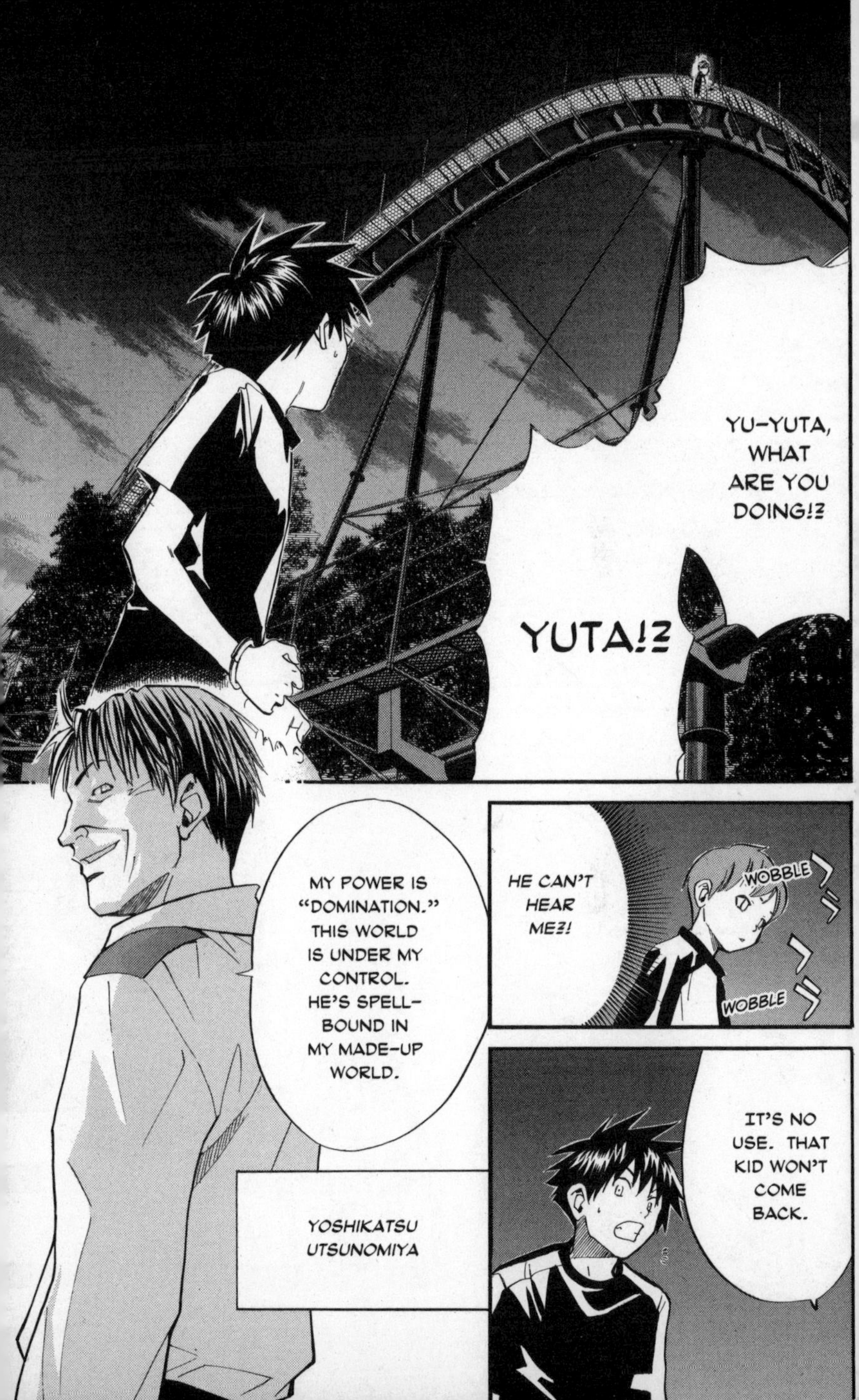
YU-YUTA, WHAT ARE YOU DOING!?
YUTA!?
HE CAN'T HEAR ME?!
WOBBLE
WOBBLE
IT'S NO USE. THAT KID WON'T COME BACK.
MY POWER IS "DOMINATION." THIS WORLD IS UNDER MY CONTROL. HE'S SPELL-BOUND IN MY MADE-UP WORLD.
YOSHIKATSU UTSUNOMIYA

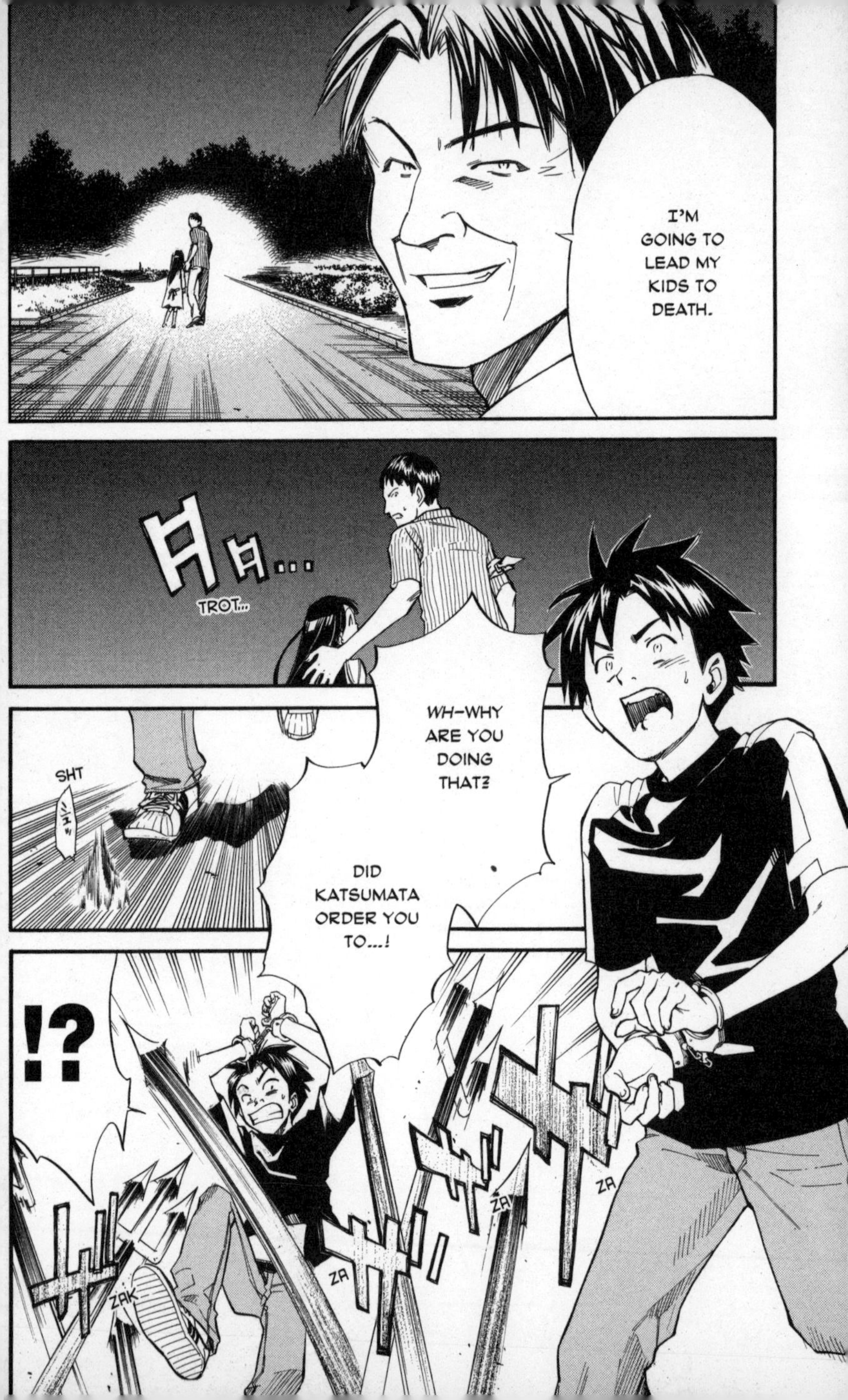
I'M GOING TO LEAD MY KIDS TO DEATH.
TROT...
WH-WHY ARE YOU DOING THAT?
DID KATSUMATA ORDER YOU TO...!
SHT
ZA
ZA
!?
ZA
ZAK

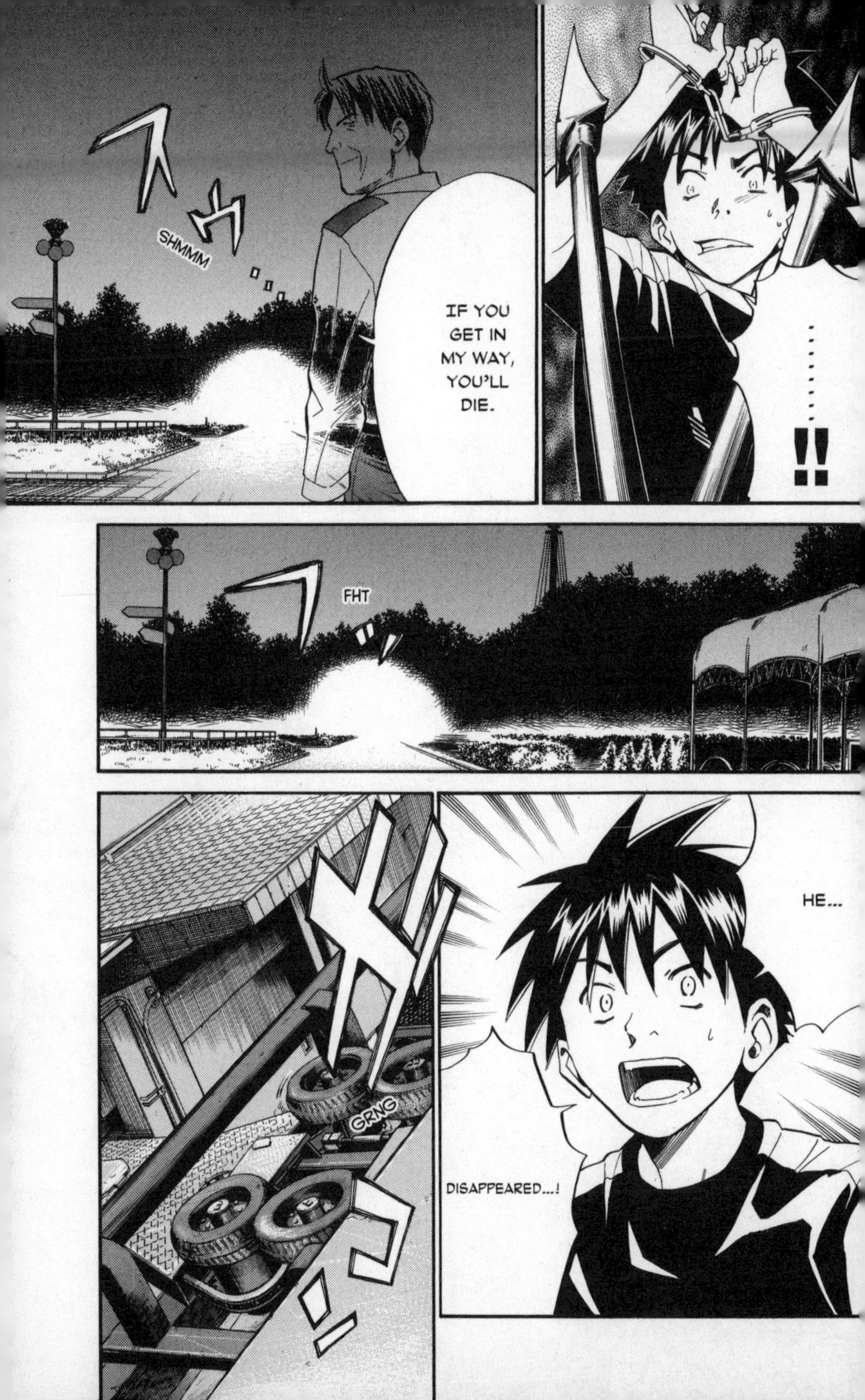
......!!
IF YOU GET IN MY WAY, YOU'LL DIE.
SHMMM
FHT
HE...
DISAPPEARED...!
GRNG

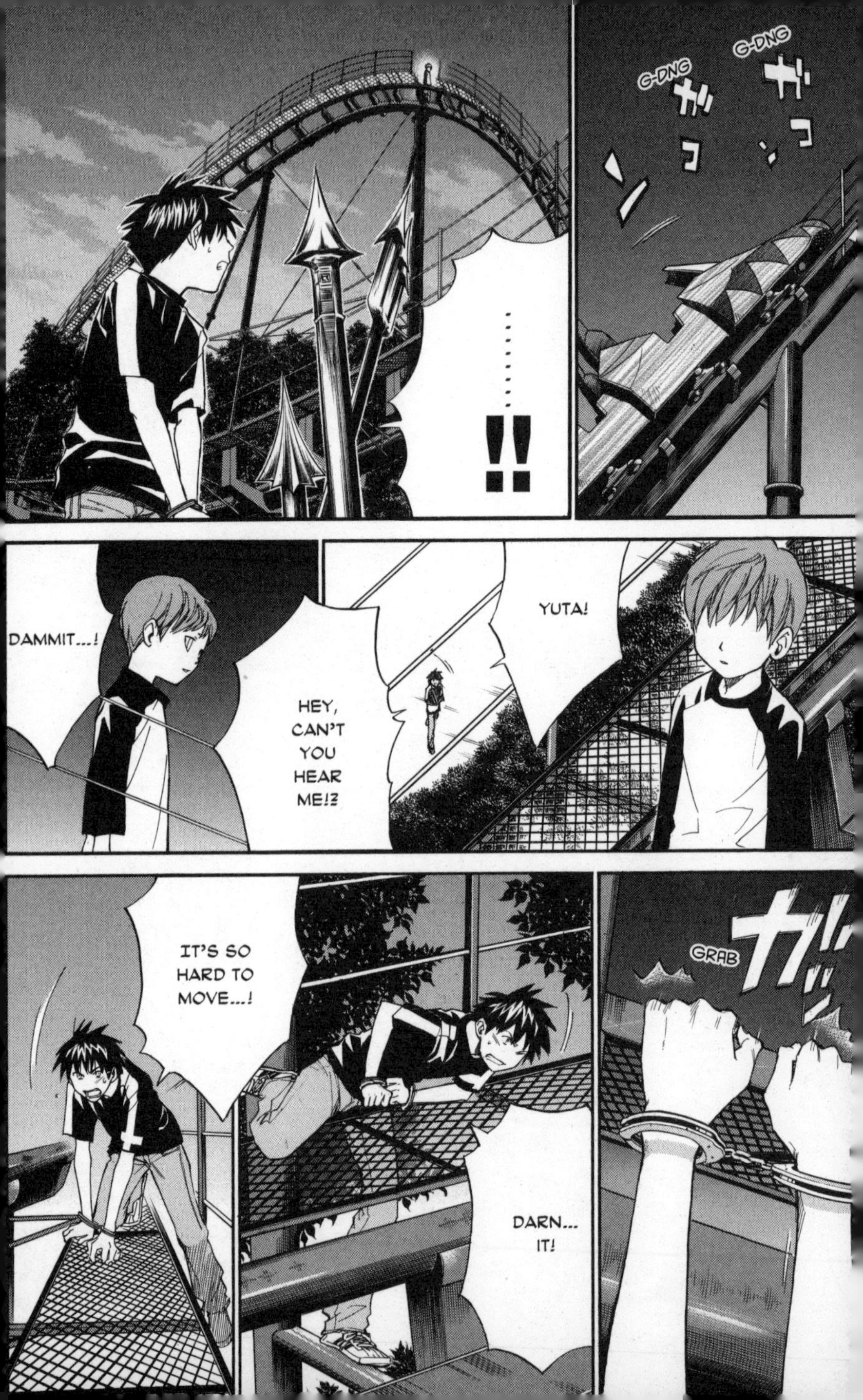
G-DNG
ガコン
G-DNG
ガコン
......
!!
YUTA!
HEY, CAN'T YOU HEAR ME!?
DAMMIT...!
GRAB
DARN... IT!
IT'S SO HARD TO MOVE...!

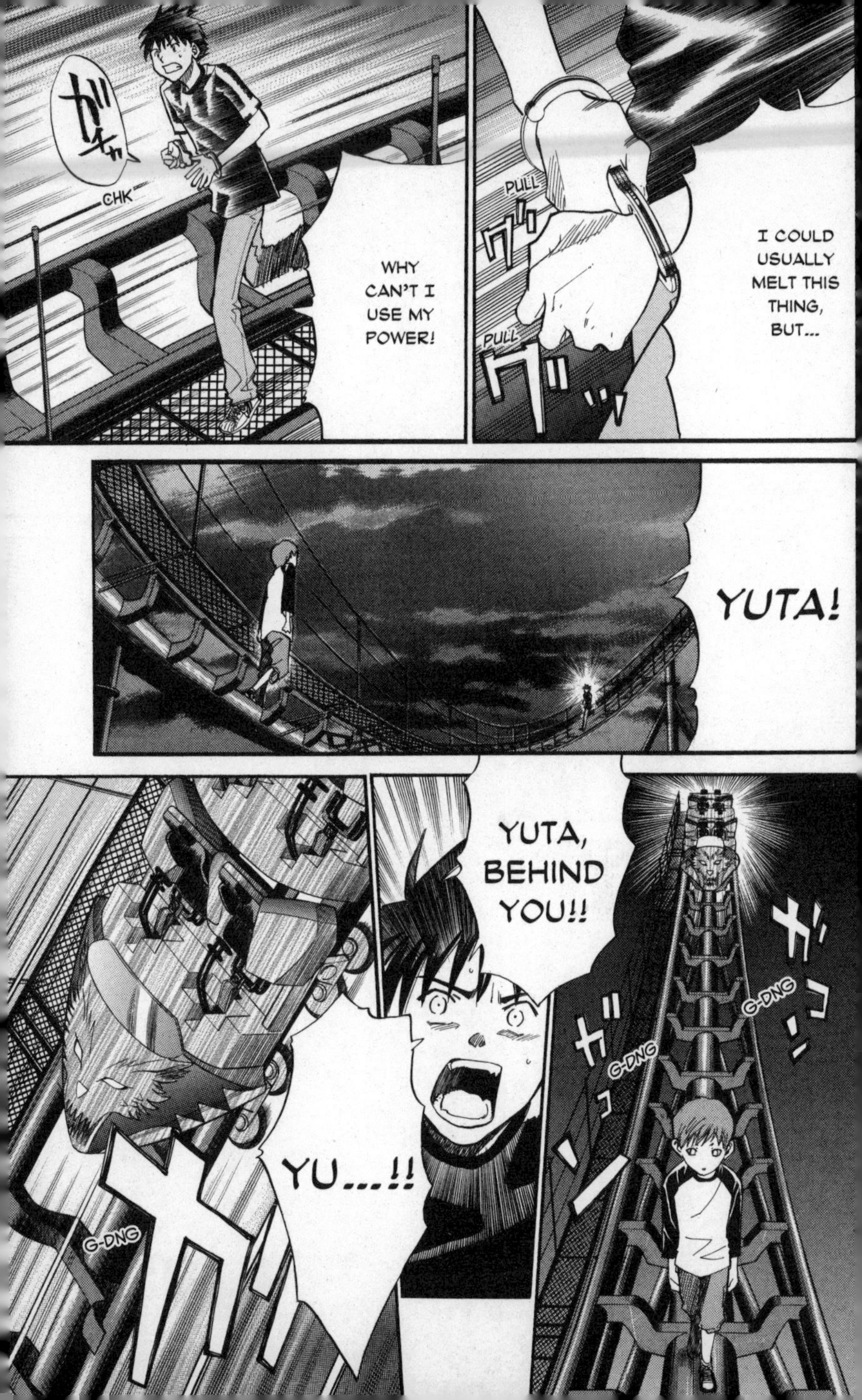

I COULD USUALLY MELT THIS THING, BUT...
PULL
PULL
WHY CAN'T I USE MY POWER!
CHK
YUTA!
G-DNG
G-DNG
YUTA, BEHIND YOU!!
YU...!!
G-DNG

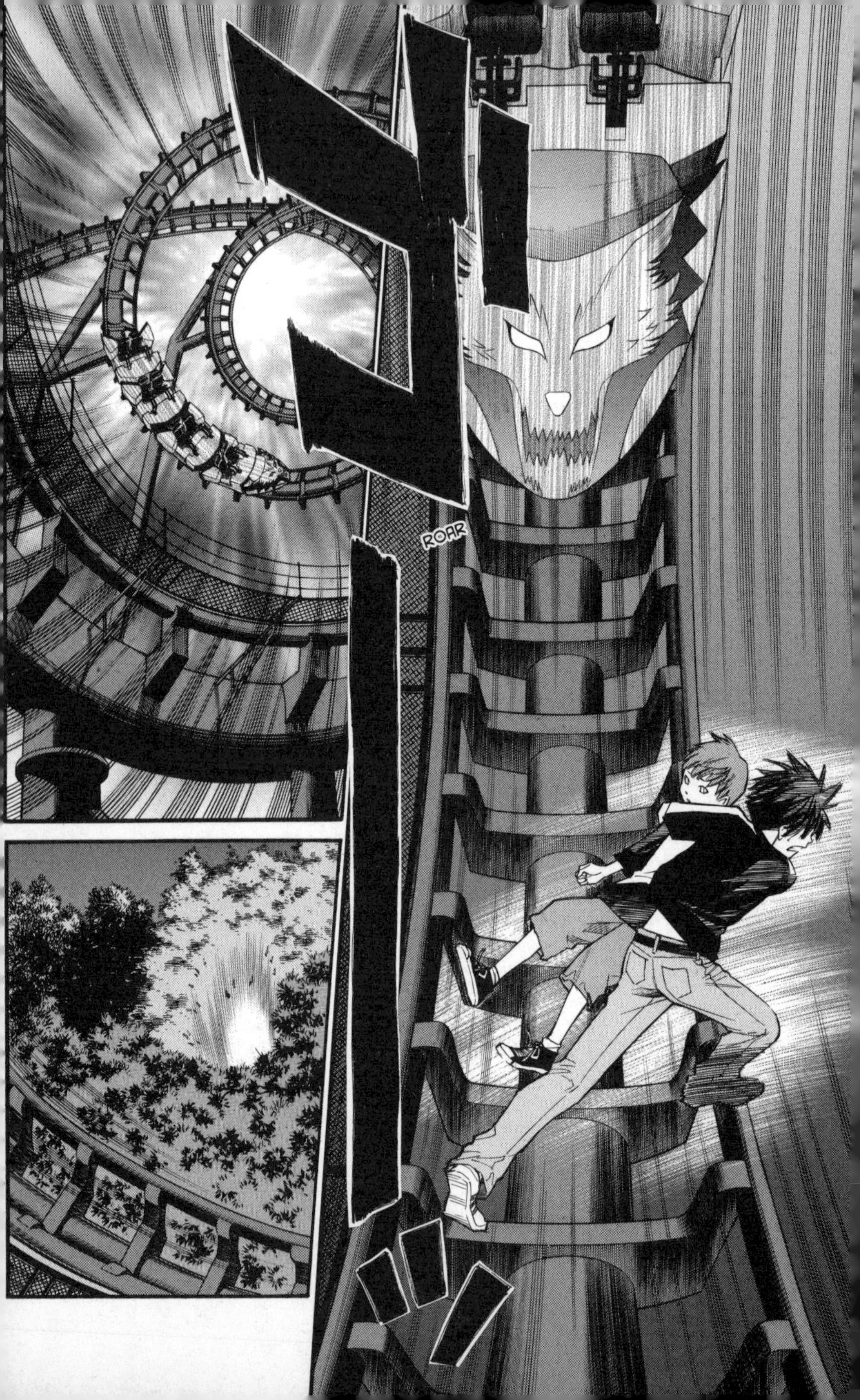
ROAR

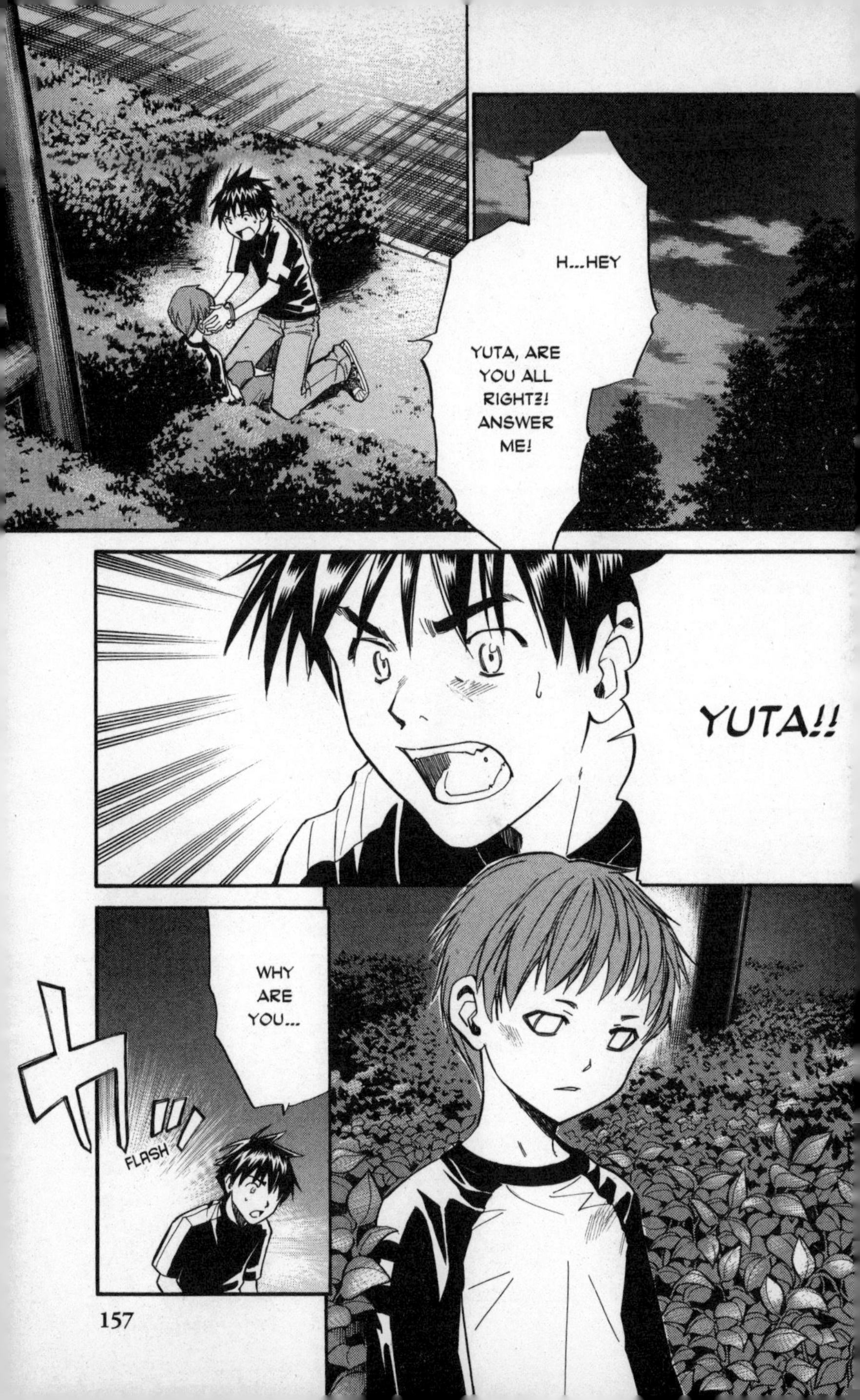
H...HEY
YUTA, ARE YOU ALL RIGHT?! ANSWER ME!
YUTA!!
WHY ARE YOU...
FLASH

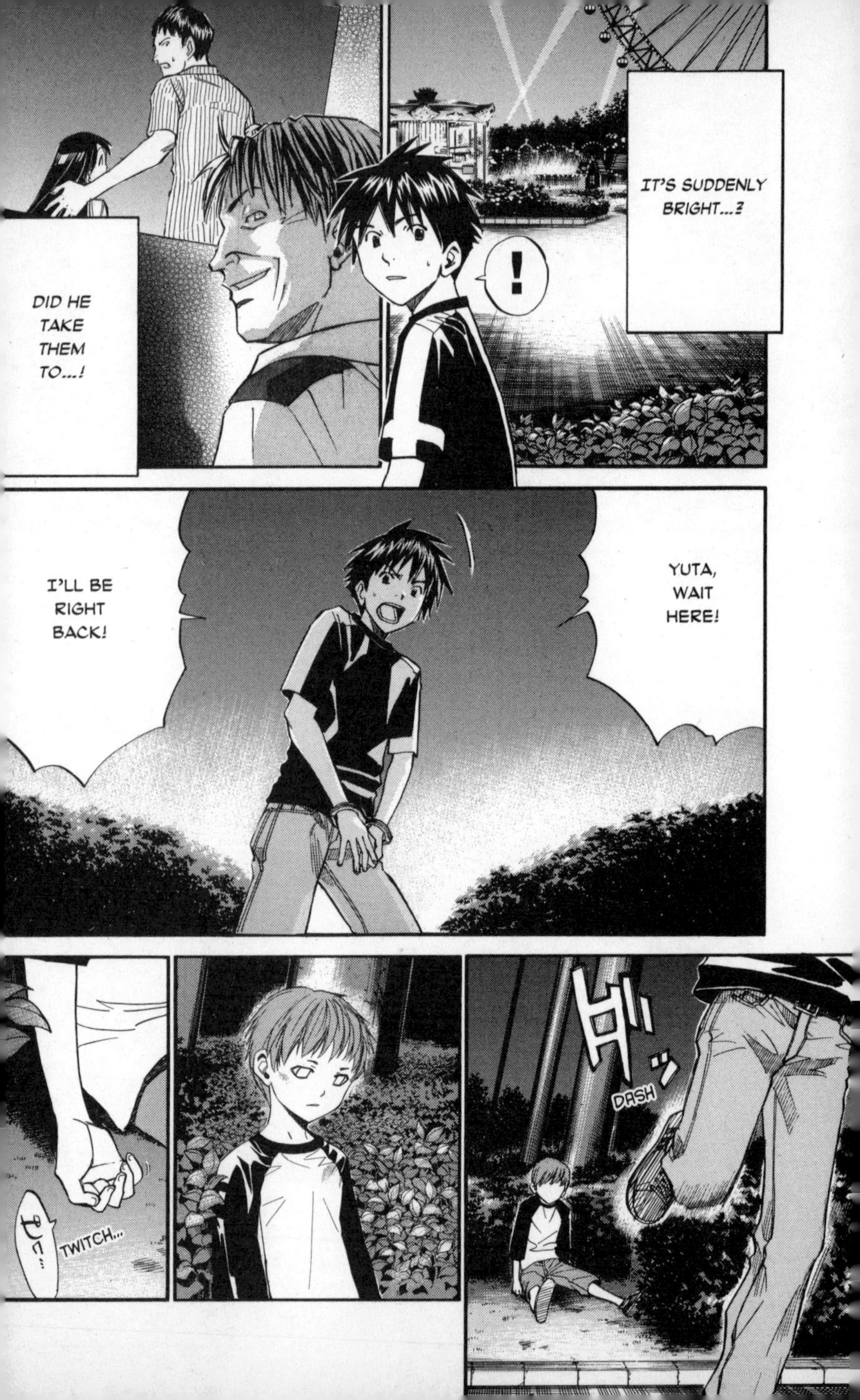
IT'S SUDDENLY BRIGHT...?
!
DID HE TAKE THEM TO...!
YUTA, WAIT HERE!
I'LL BE RIGHT BACK!
ダッ
DASH
ピク…
TWITCH...

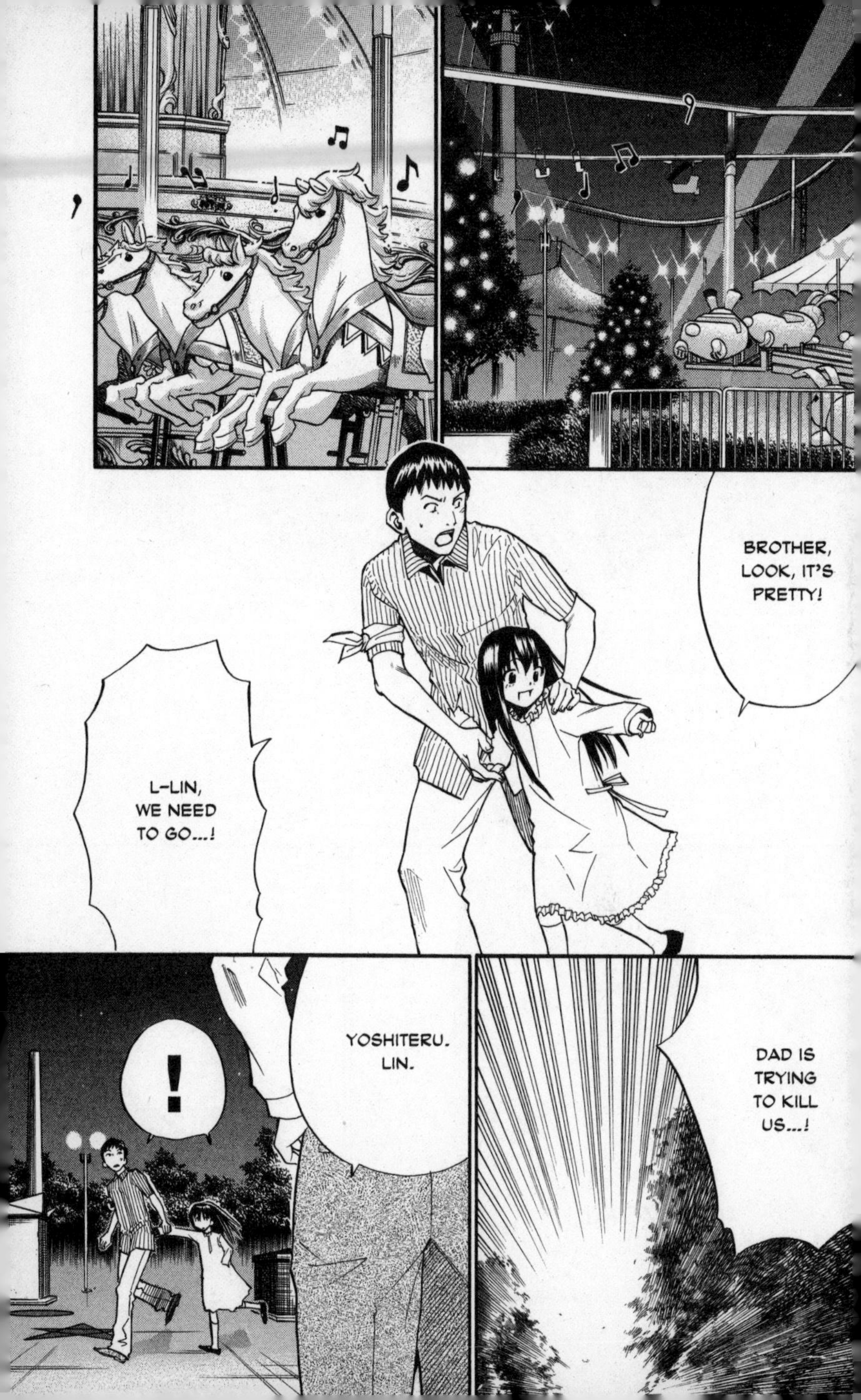
BROTHER, LOOK, IT'S PRETTY!
L-LIN, WE NEED TO GO...!
DAD IS TRYING TO KILL US...!
YOSHITERU. LIN.
!

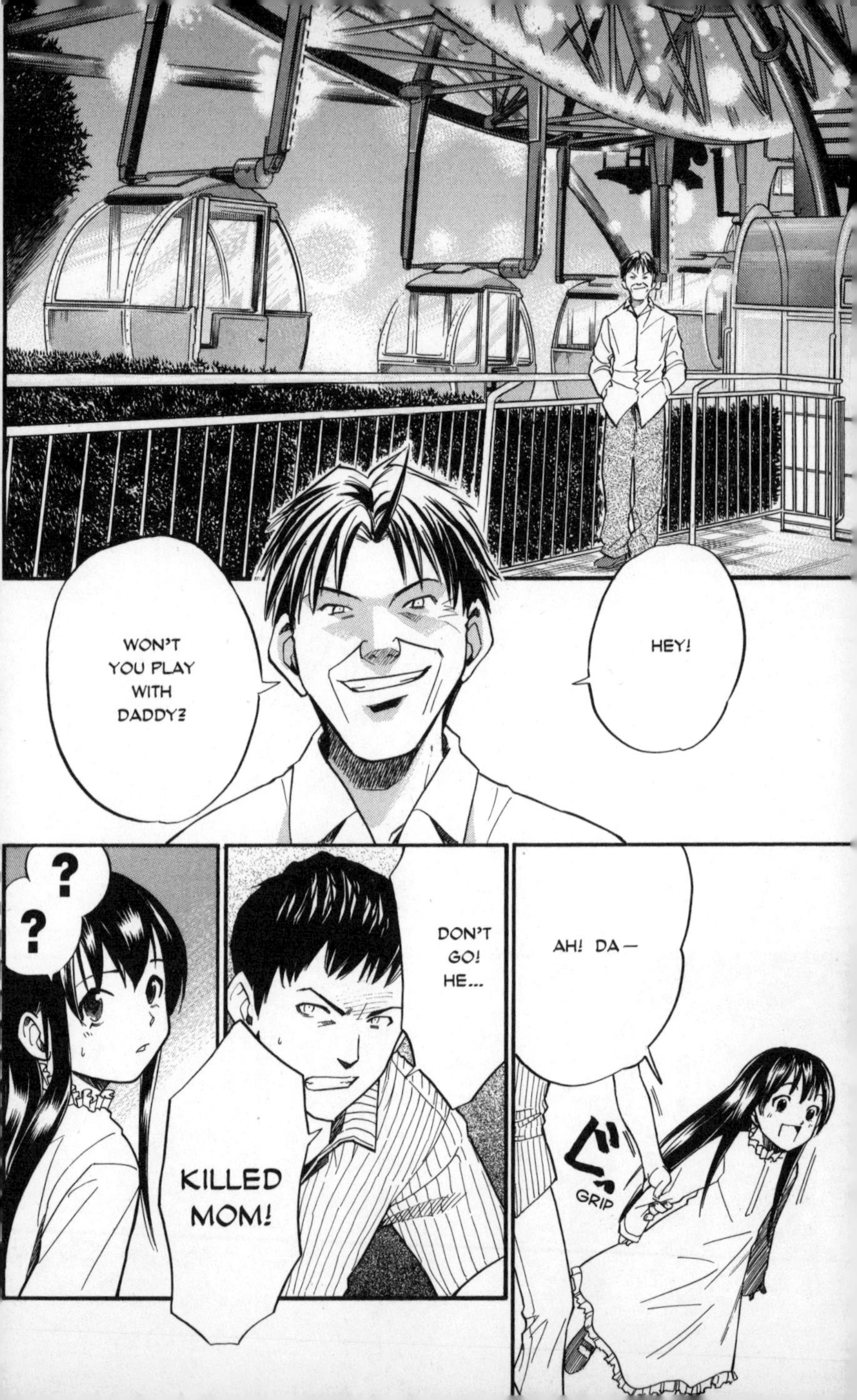
HEY!
WON'T YOU PLAY WITH DADDY?
AH! DA—
ぐっ
GRIP
DON'T GO! HE...
KILLED MOM!
? ?

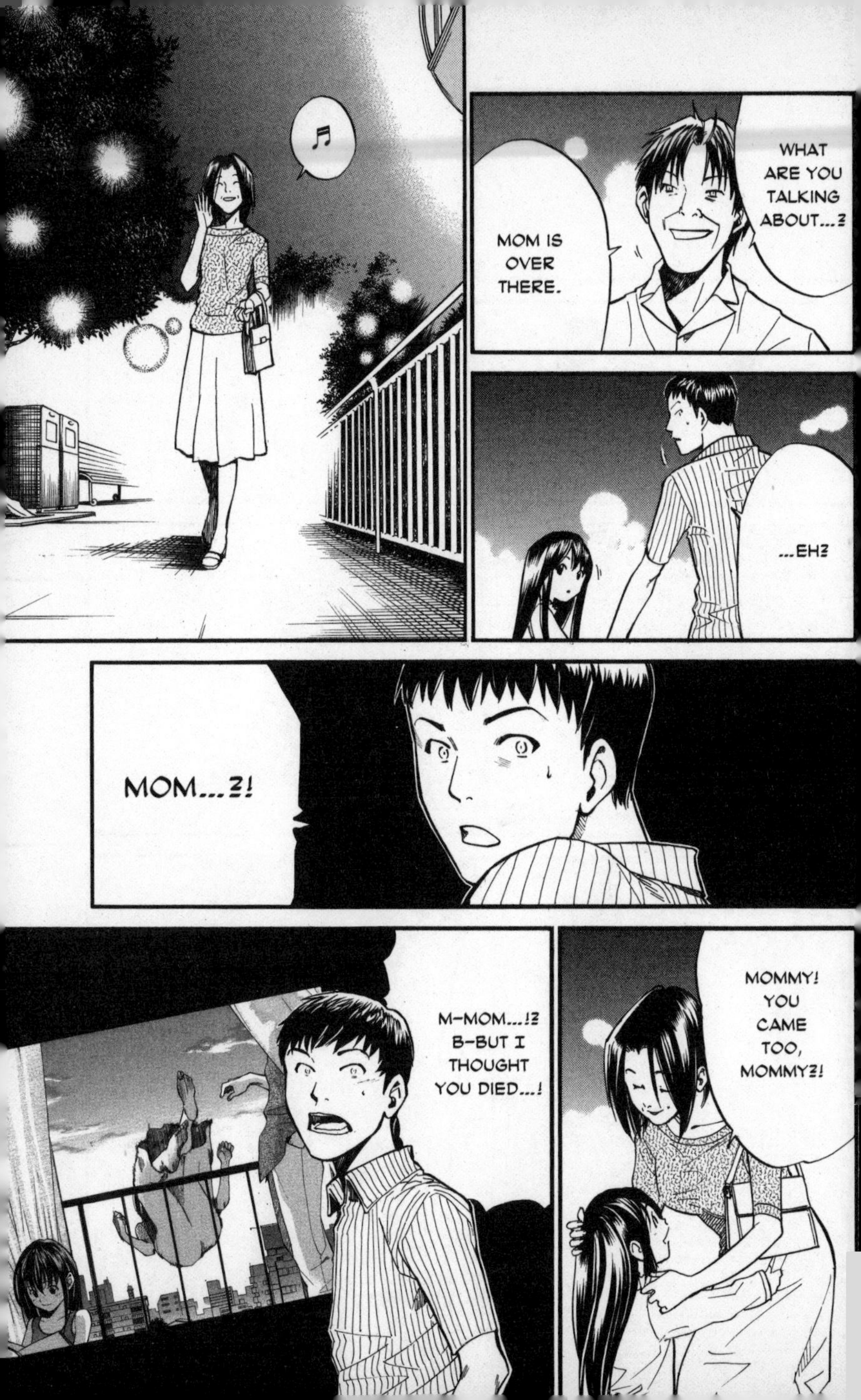
WHAT ARE YOU TALKING ABOUT...?
MOM IS OVER THERE.
♬
...EH?
MOM...?!
MOMMY! YOU CAME TOO, MOMMY?!
M-MOM...!? B-BUT I THOUGHT YOU DIED...!

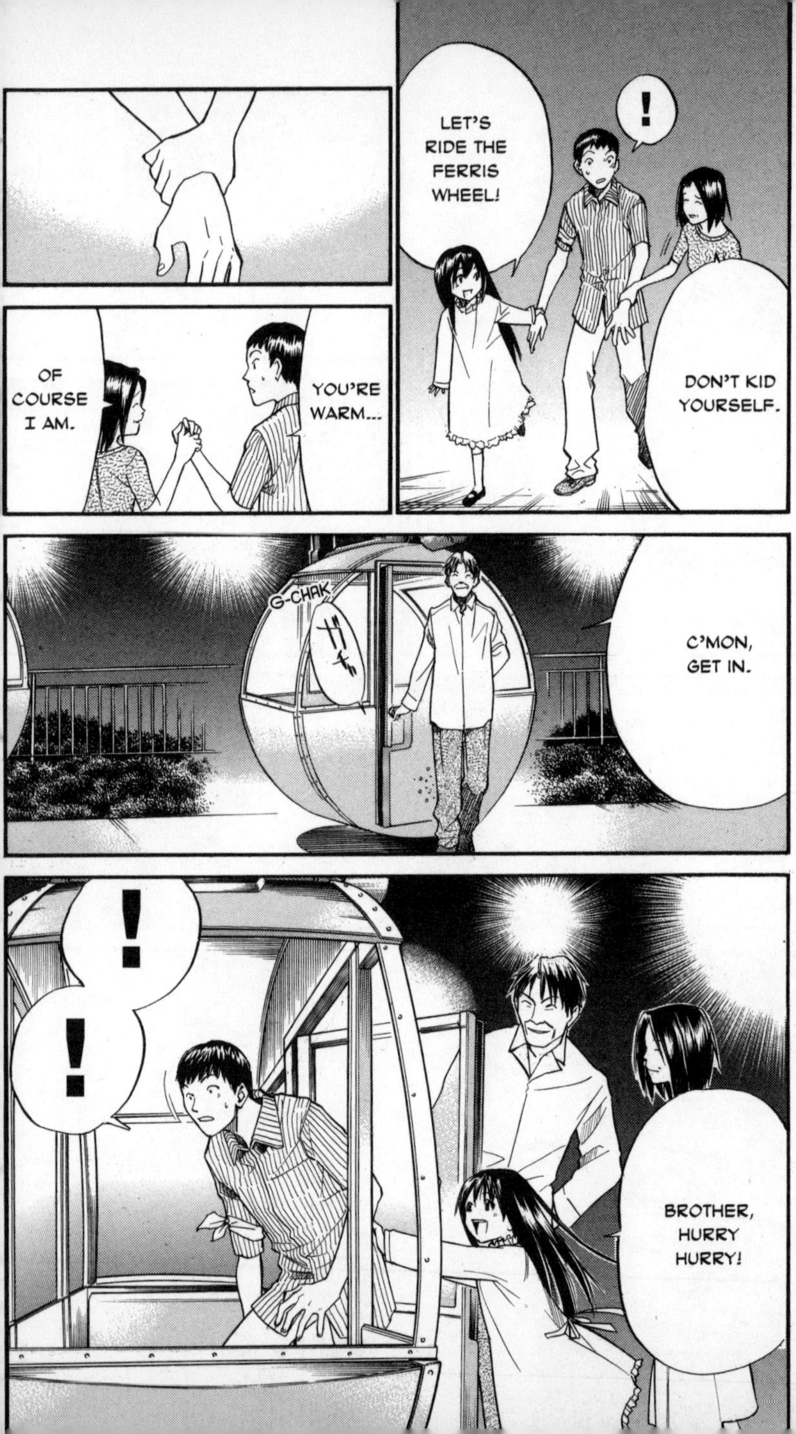
LET'S RIDE THE FERRIS WHEEL!
!
DON'T KID YOURSELF.
YOU'RE WARM...
OF COURSE I AM.
C'MON, GET IN.
G-CHAK
ガチャ
BROTHER, HURRY HURRY!
!
!

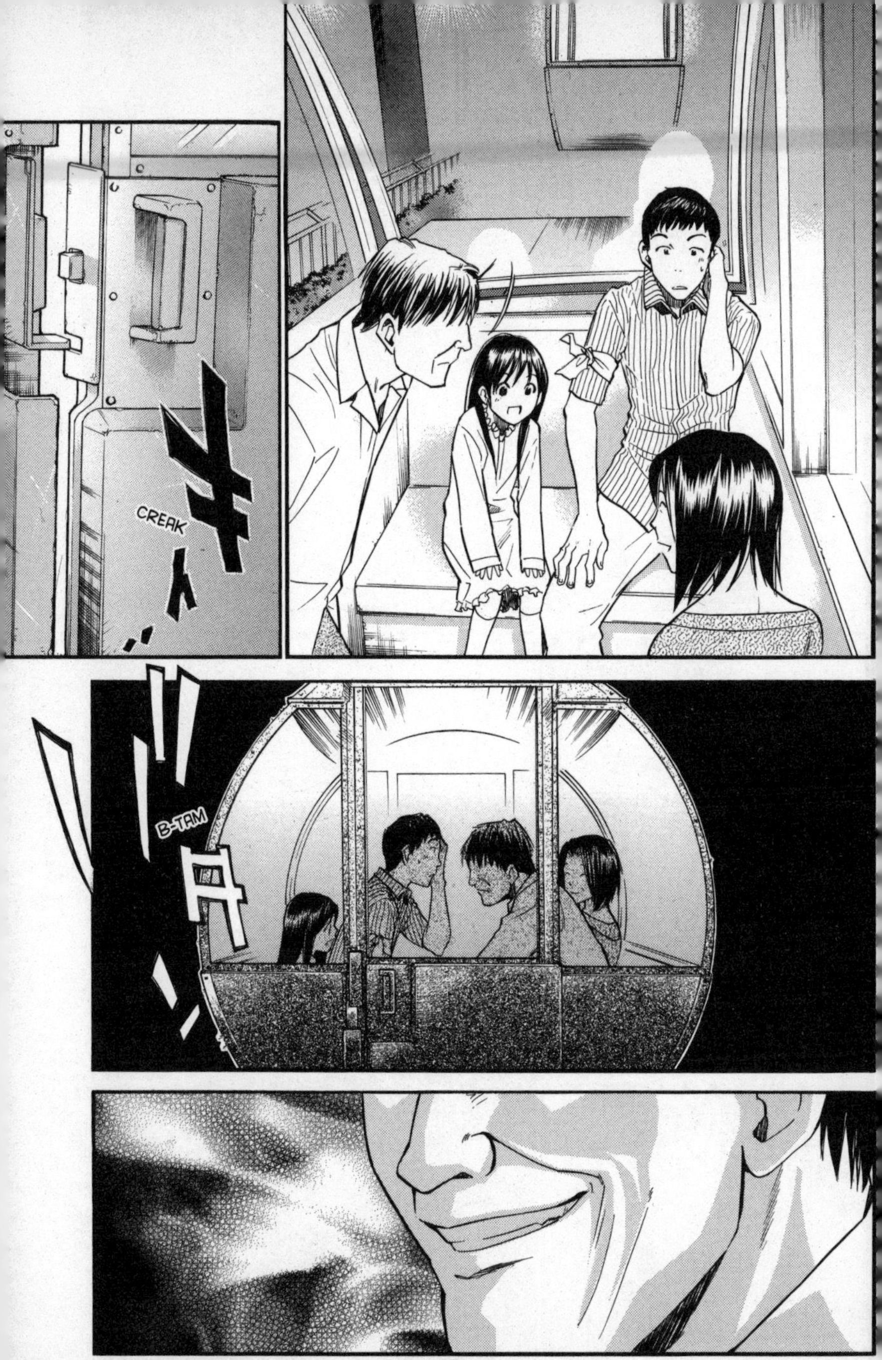
CREAK
B-TAM

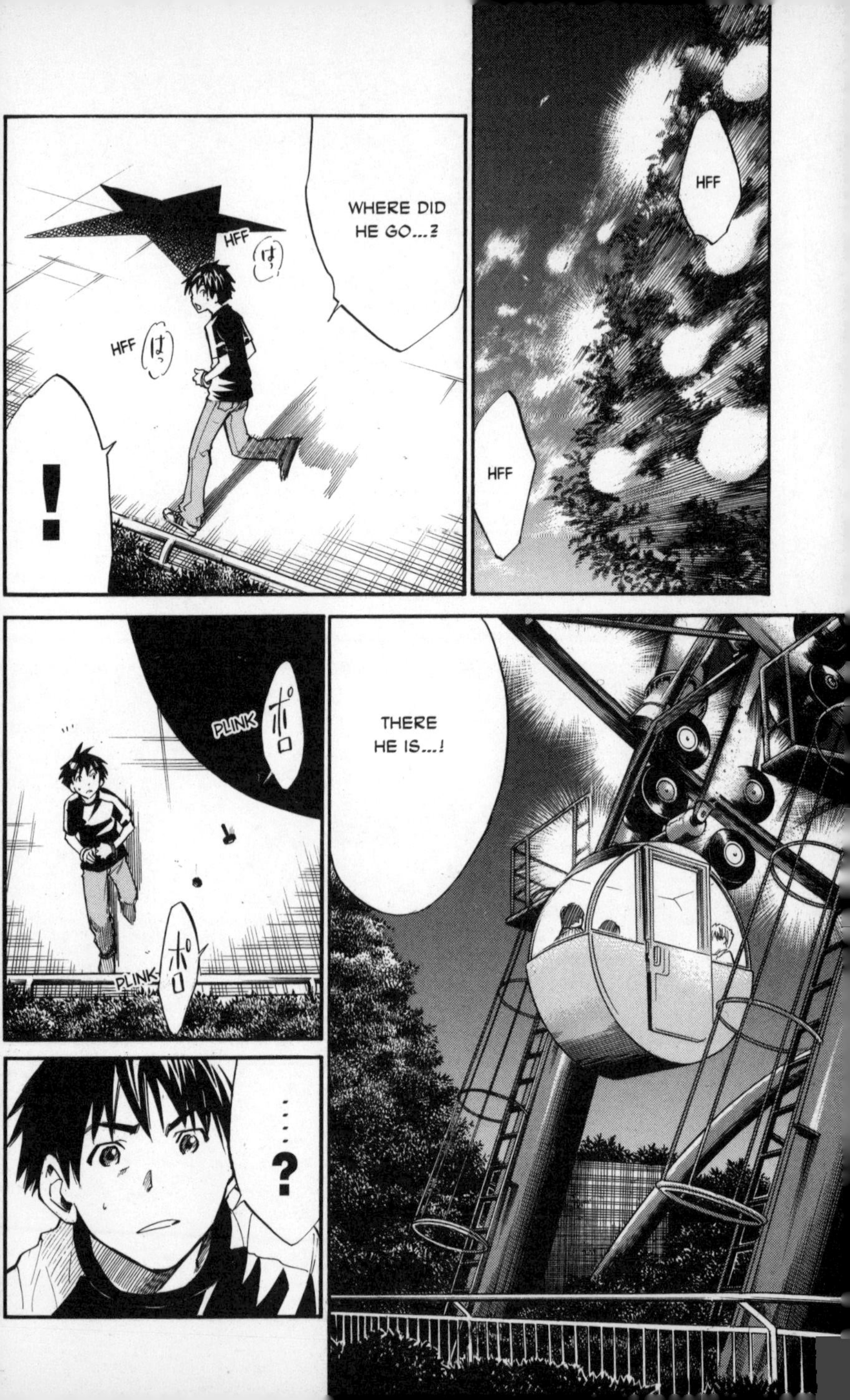
HFF
HFF
WHERE DID HE GO...?
HFF
はっ
HFF
はっ
!
THERE HE IS...!
PLINK
ポロ
PLINK
ポロ
...
?

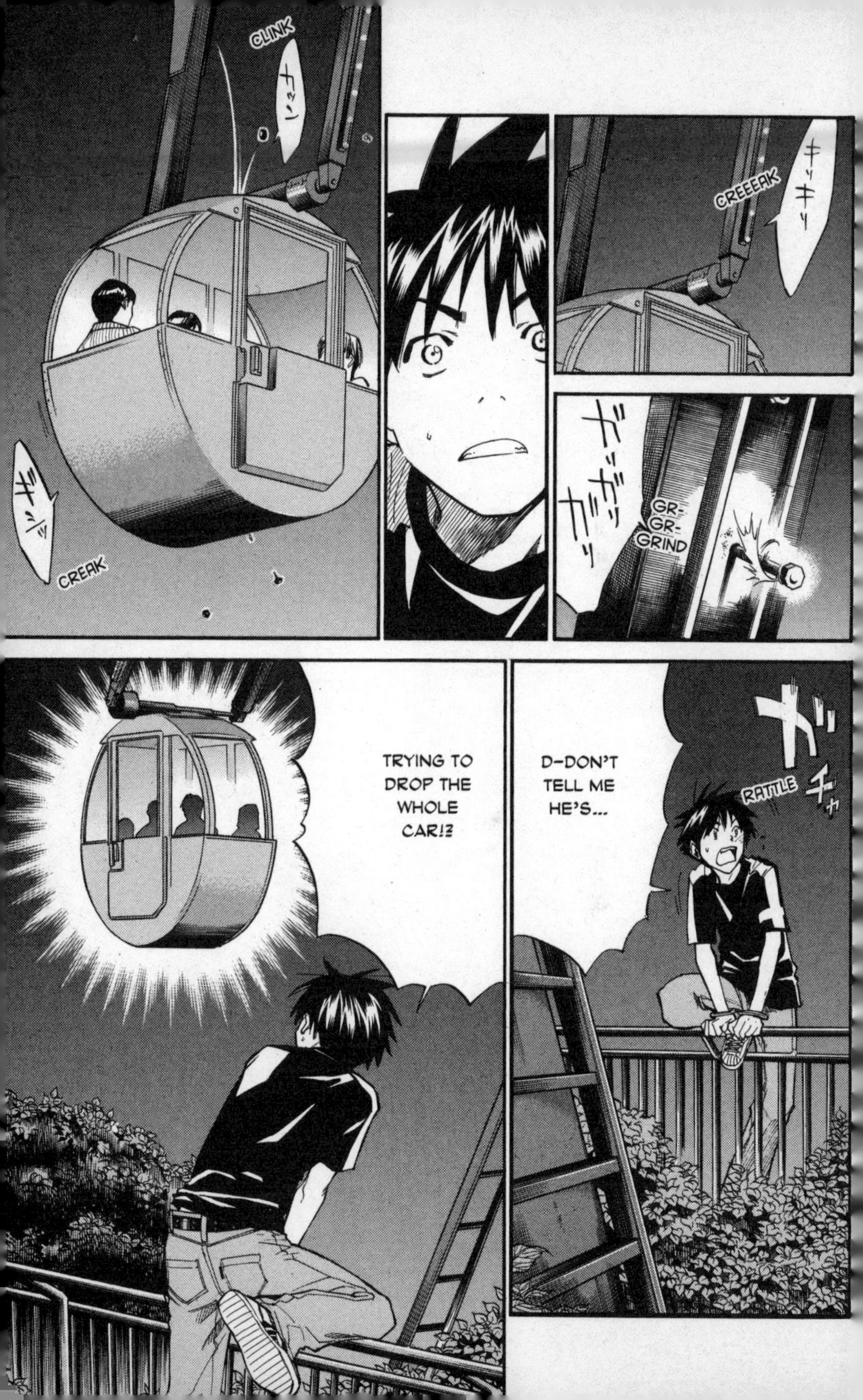
キッキッ
CREEEAK
GR-GR-GRIND
CLINK
CREAK
RATTLE
D-DON'T TELL ME HE'S...
TRYING TO DROP THE WHOLE CAR!?

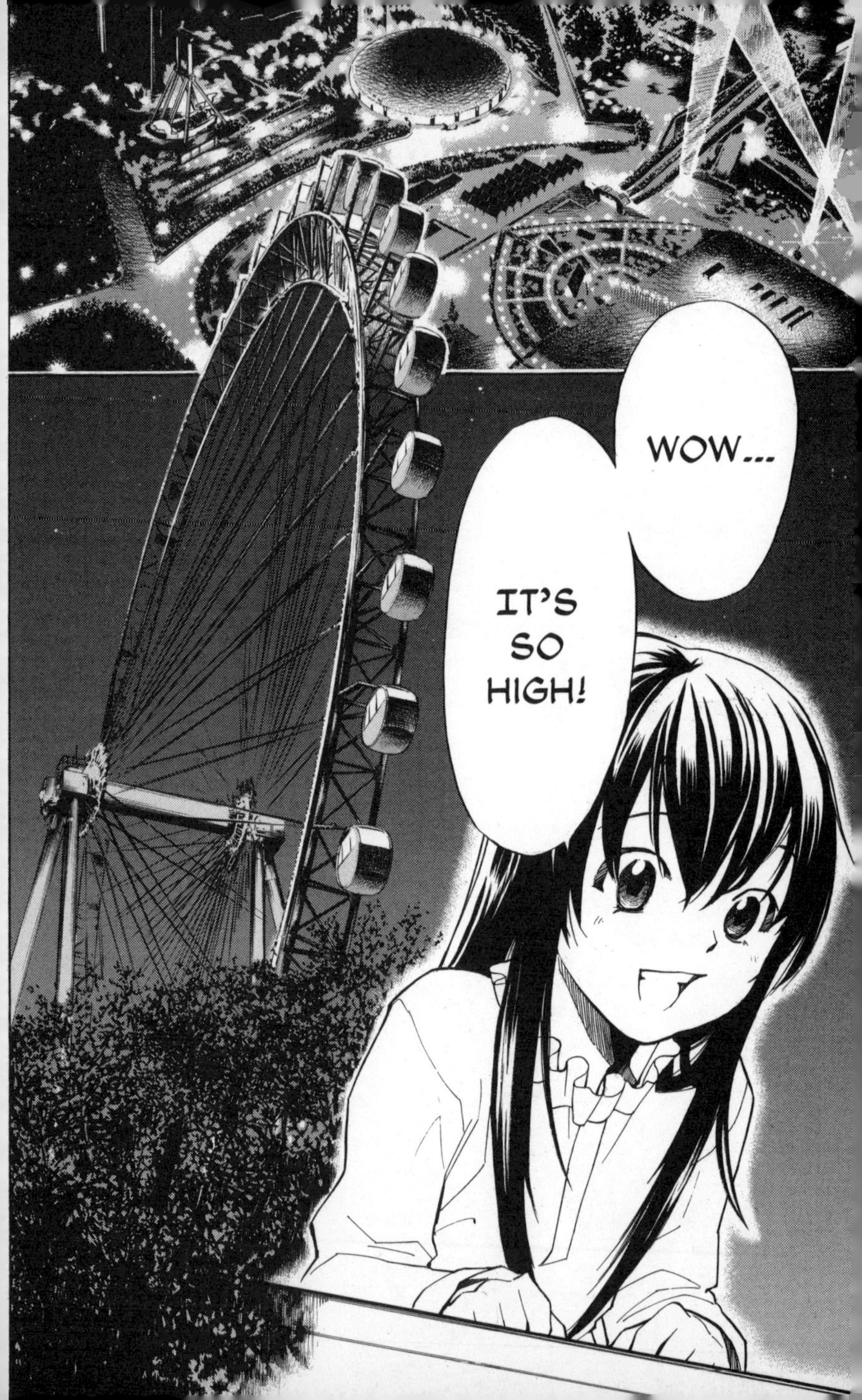
WOW...
IT'S SO HIGH!

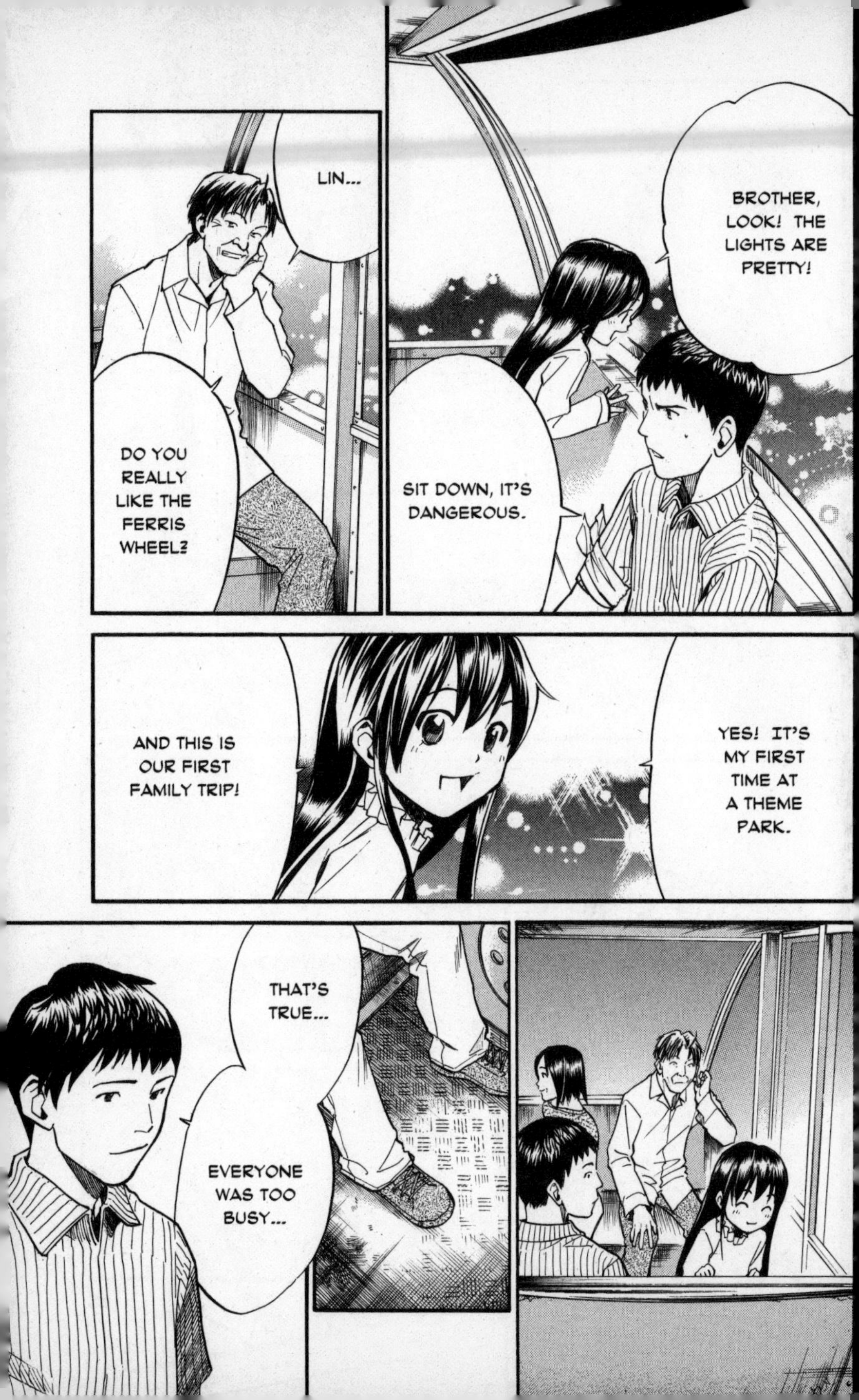
BROTHER, LOOK! THE LIGHTS ARE PRETTY!
SIT DOWN, IT'S DANGEROUS.
LIN...
DO YOU REALLY LIKE THE FERRIS WHEEL?
YES! IT'S MY FIRST TIME AT A THEME PARK.
AND THIS IS OUR FIRST FAMILY TRIP!
THAT'S TRUE...
EVERYONE WAS TOO BUSY...

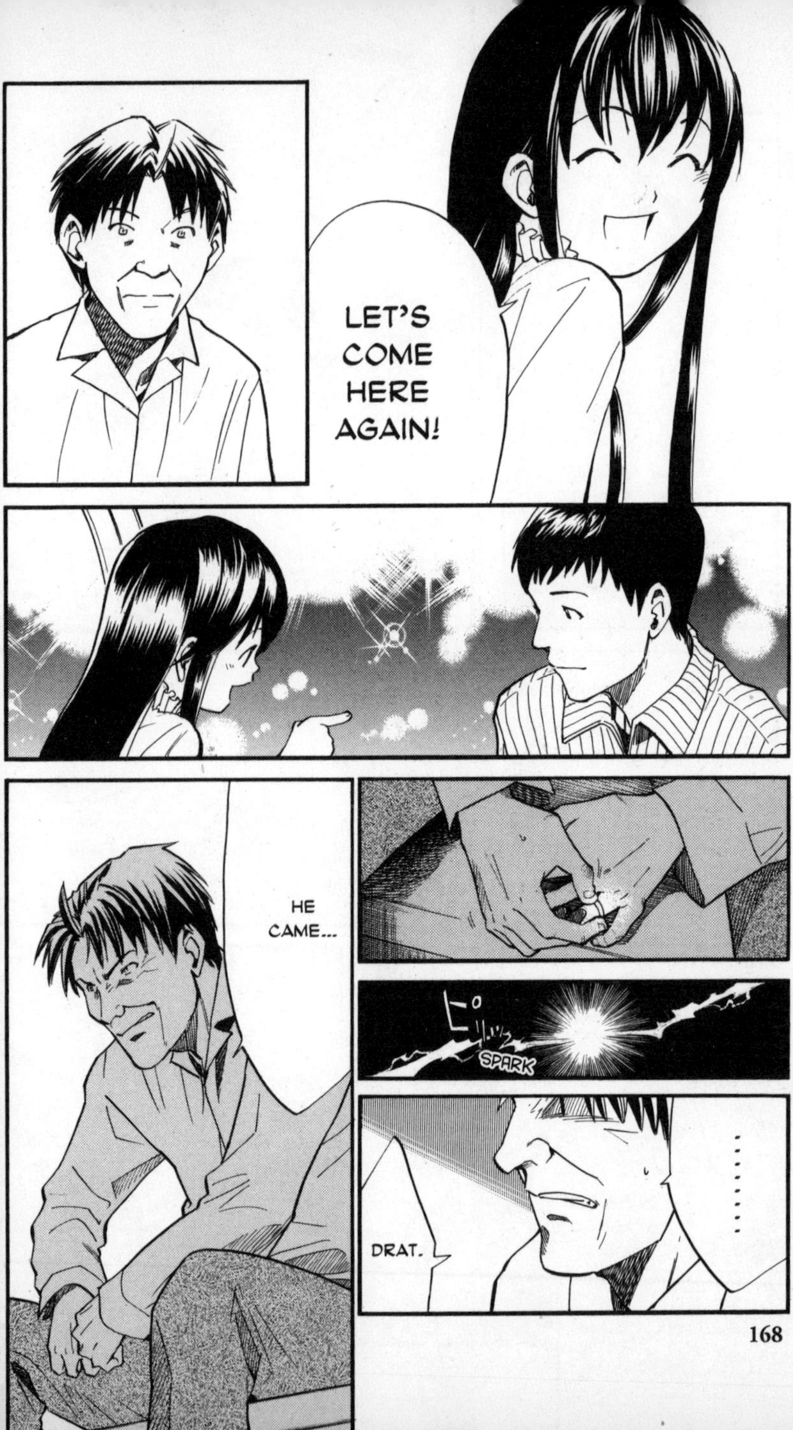
LET'S COME HERE AGAIN!
SPARK
......
DRAT.
HE CAME...

AAAAH

GYAAAA

SHUDDER

PHEW

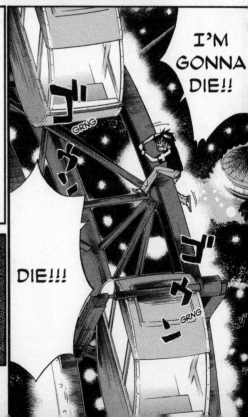

I'M GONNA DIE!!

GRNG

DIE!!!

GRNG

!?

G-CHAK

169

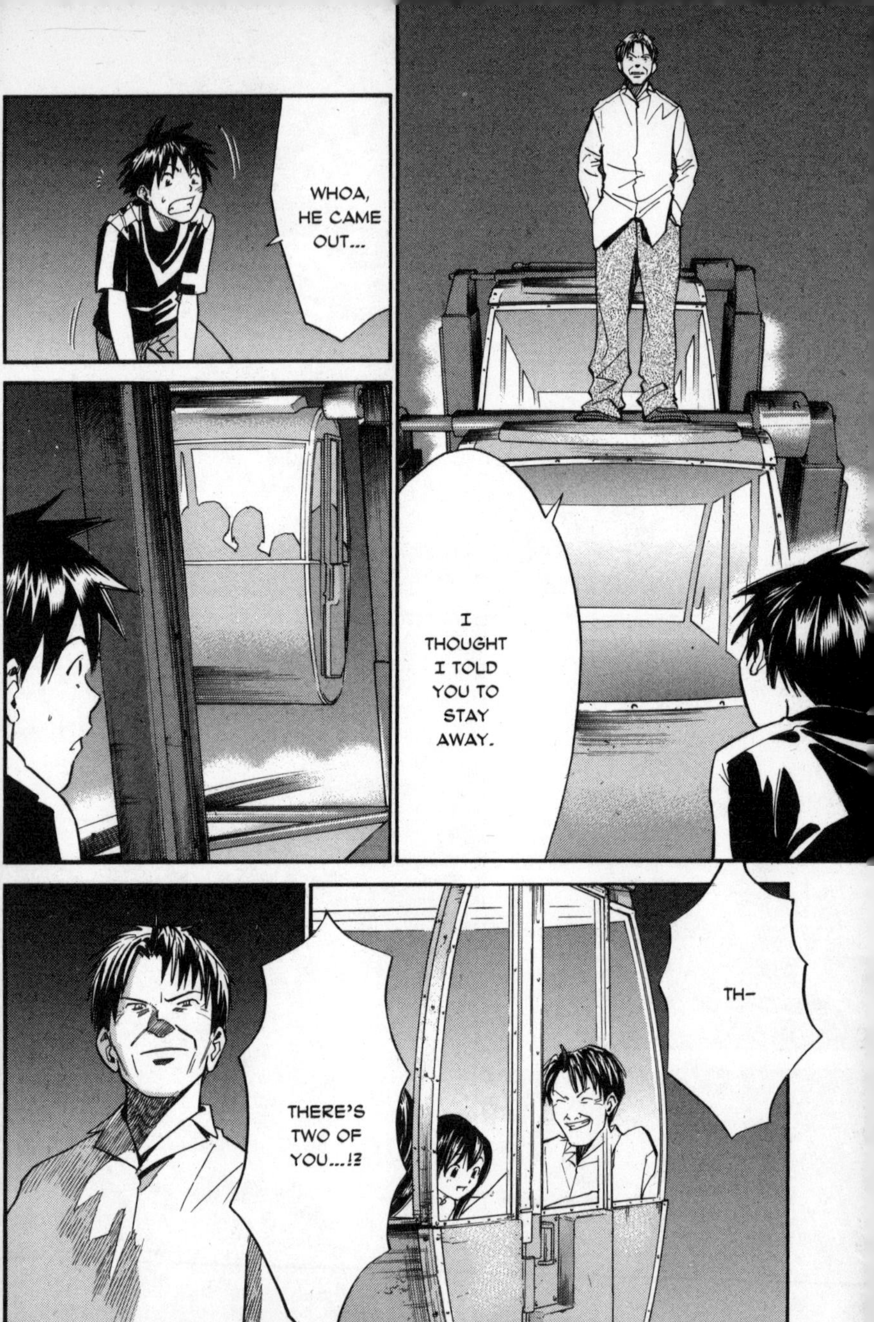
I THOUGHT I TOLD YOU TO STAY AWAY.
WHOA, HE CAME OUT...
TH-
THERE'S TWO OF YOU...!?

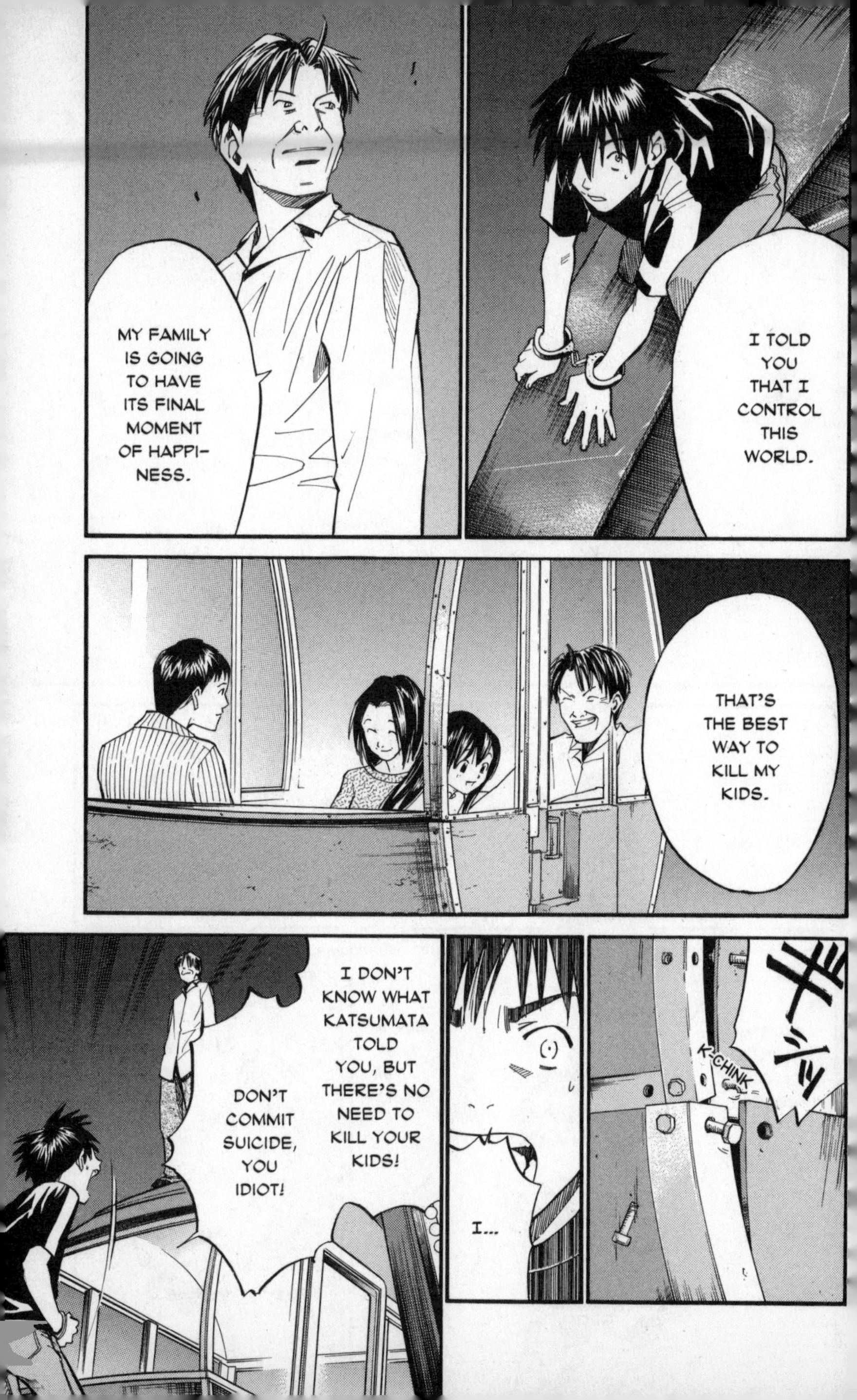
I TOLD YOU THAT I CONTROL THIS WORLD.
MY FAMILY IS GOING TO HAVE ITS FINAL MOMENT OF HAPPINESS.
THAT'S THE BEST WAY TO KILL MY KIDS.
ギシッ
K-CHINK
I...
I DON'T KNOW WHAT KATSUMATA TOLD YOU, BUT THERE'S NO NEED TO KILL YOUR KIDS!
DON'T COMMIT SUICIDE, YOU IDIOT!

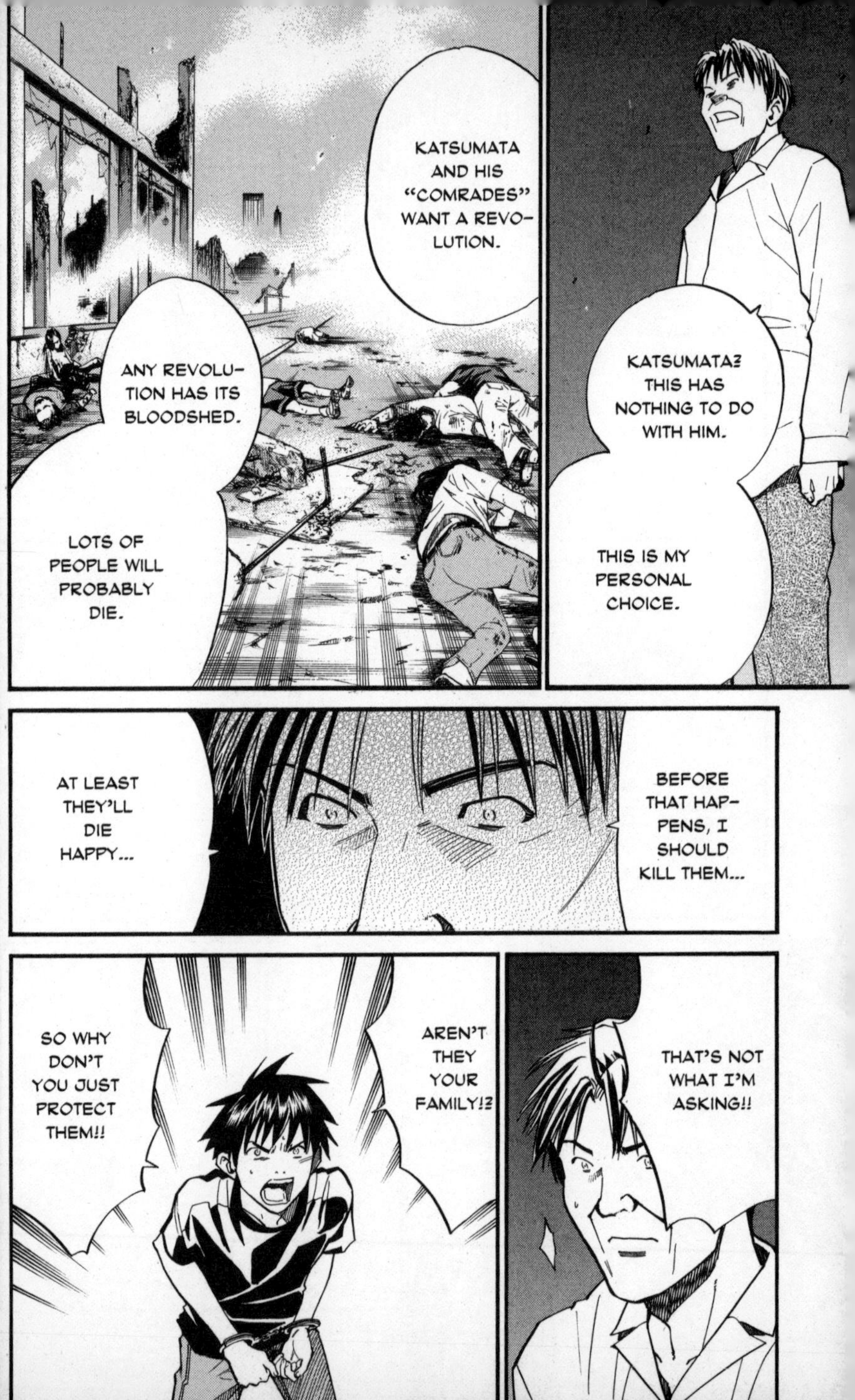
KATSUMATA? THIS HAS NOTHING TO DO WITH HIM.
THIS IS MY PERSONAL CHOICE.
KATSUMATA AND HIS "COMRADES" WANT A REVOLUTION.
ANY REVOLUTION HAS ITS BLOODSHED.
LOTS OF PEOPLE WILL PROBABLY DIE.
BEFORE THAT HAPPENS, I SHOULD KILL THEM...
AT LEAST THEY'LL DIE HAPPY...
THAT'S NOT WHAT I'M ASKING!!
AREN'T THEY YOUR FAMILY!?
SO WHY DON'T YOU JUST PROTECT THEM!!

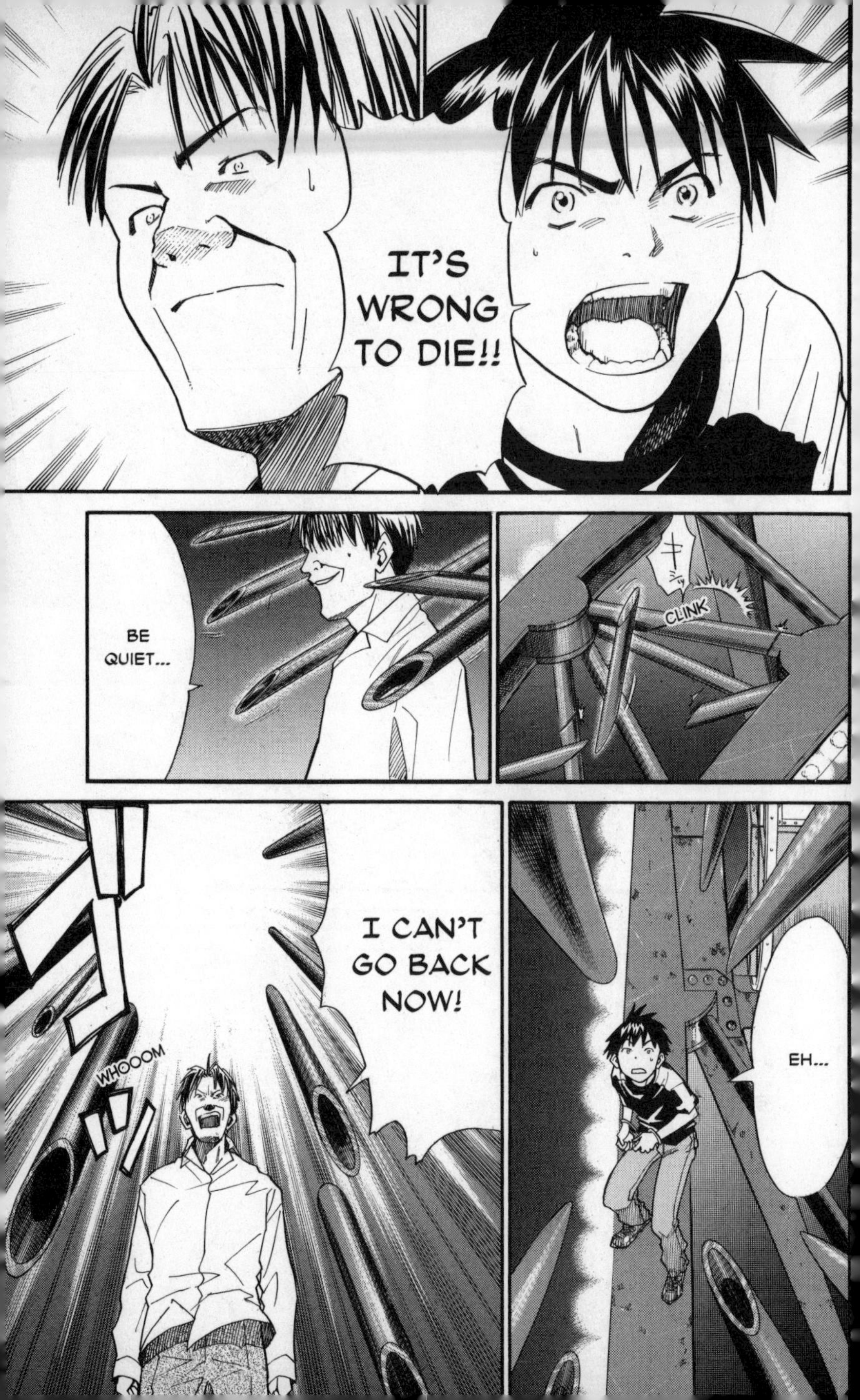
IT'S WRONG TO DIE!!
CLINK
BE QUIET...
EH...
I CAN'T GO BACK NOW!
WHOOOM

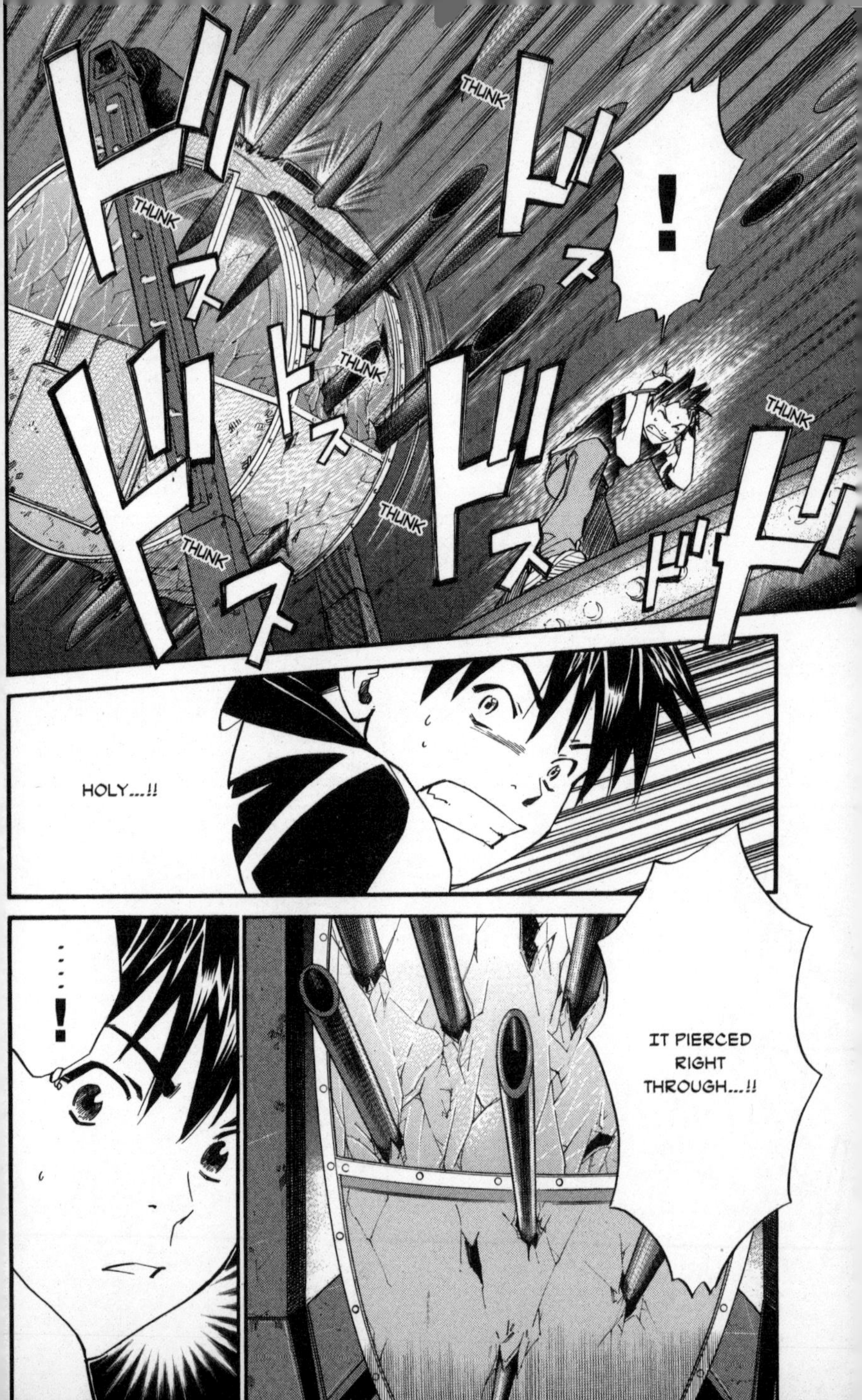
!
THUNK
THUNK
THUNK
THUNK
THUNK
THUNK
HOLY...!!
IT PIERCED RIGHT THROUGH...!!
....!

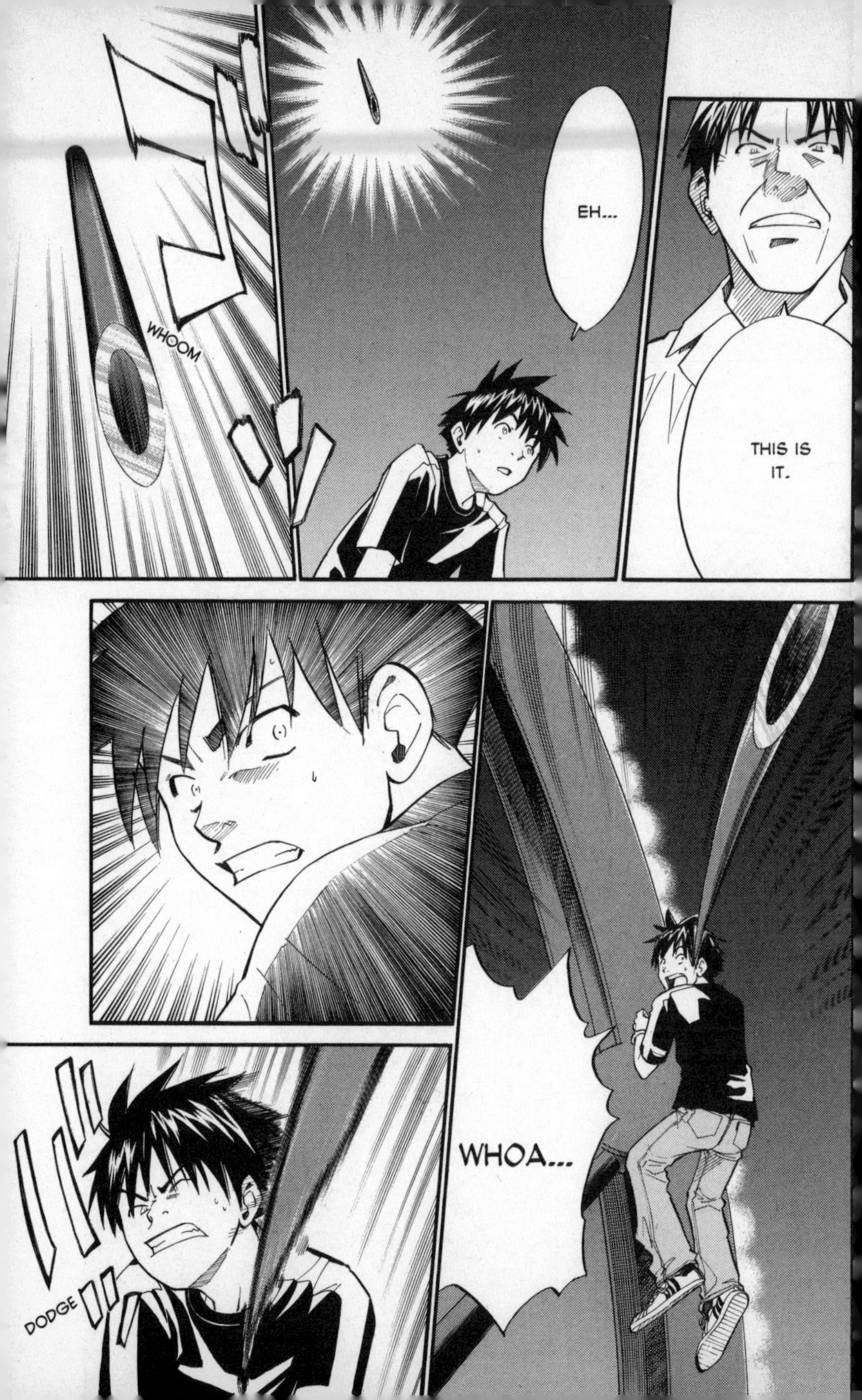
THIS IS IT.
EH...
WHOOM
WHOA...
DODGE

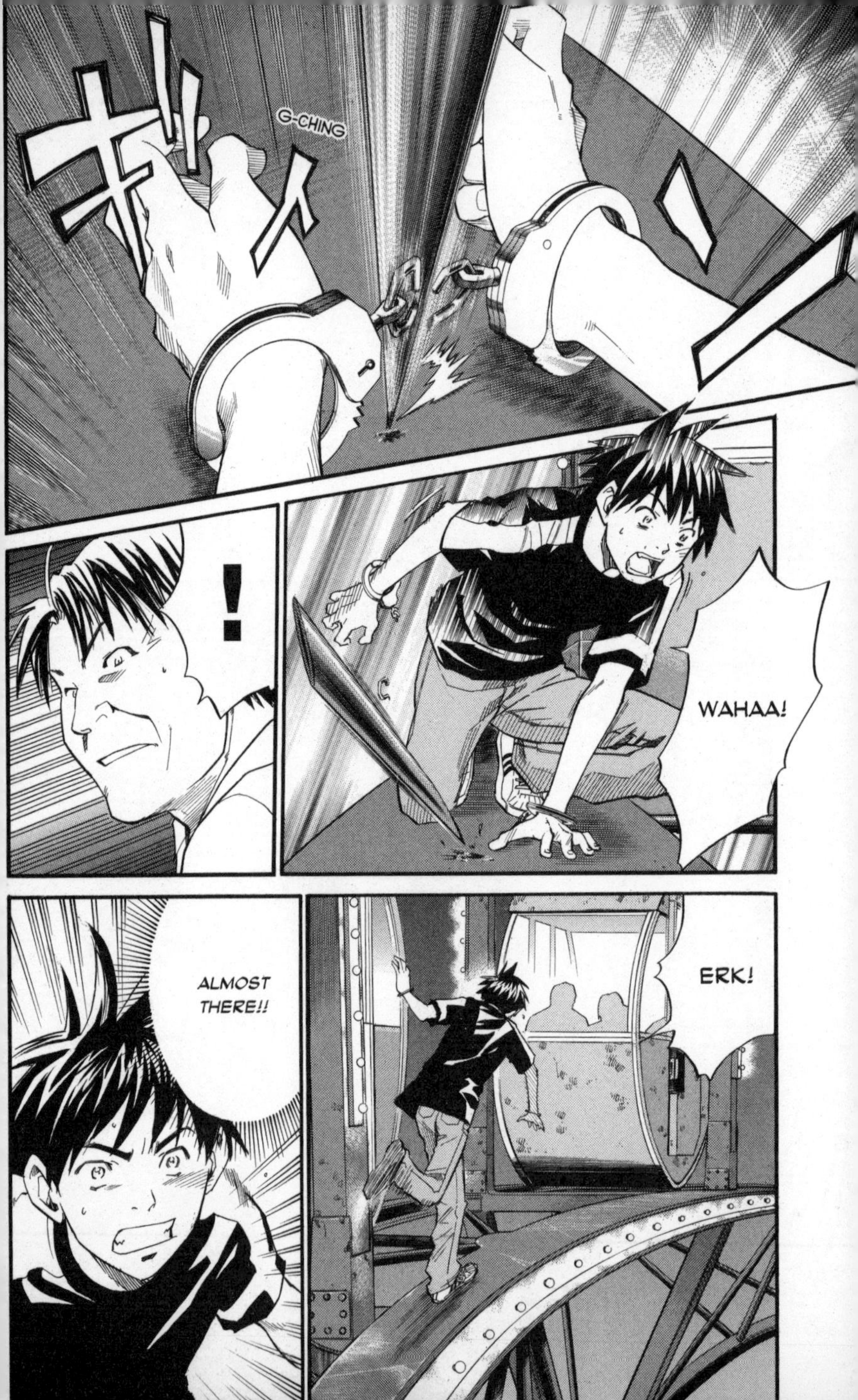
G-CHING
WAHAA!
!
ERK!
ALMOST THERE!!

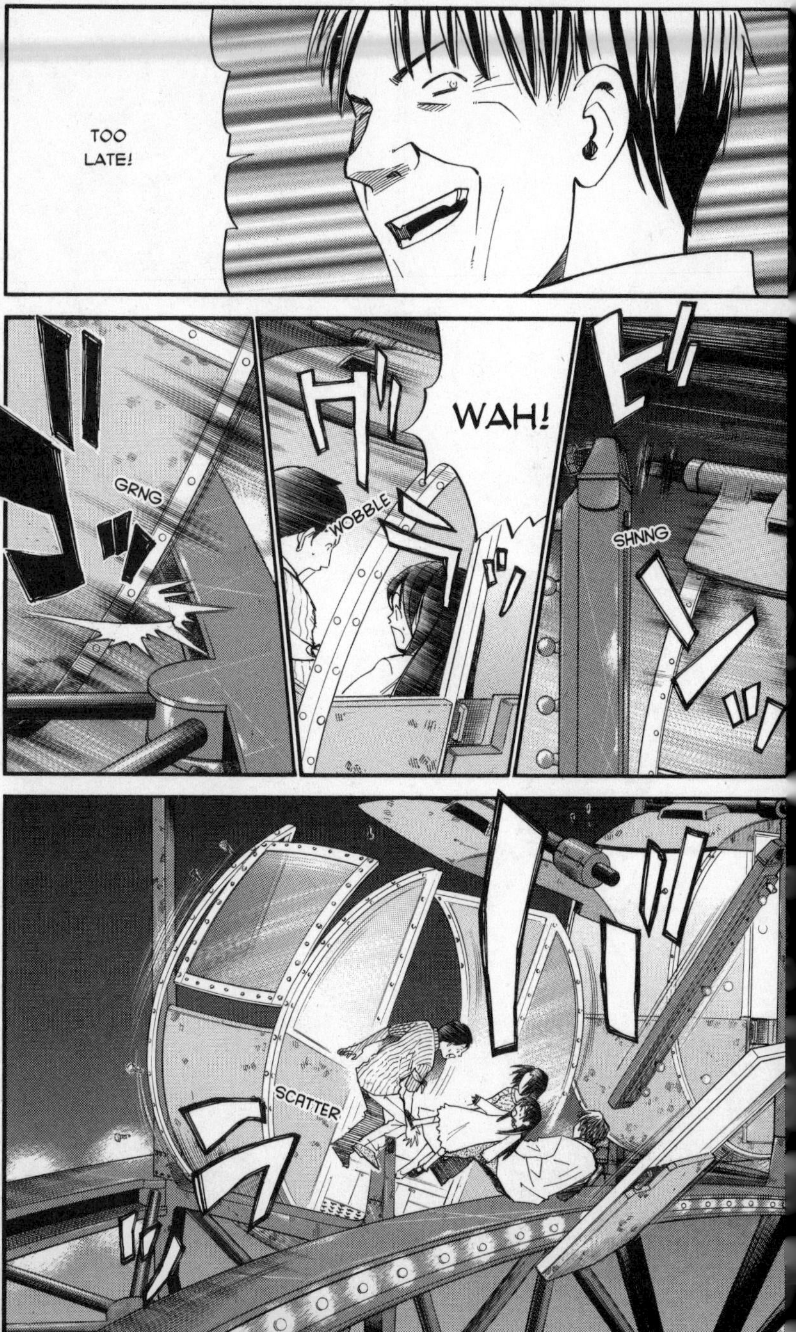
TOO LATE!
SHNNG
WAH!
WOBBLE
GRNG
SCATTER

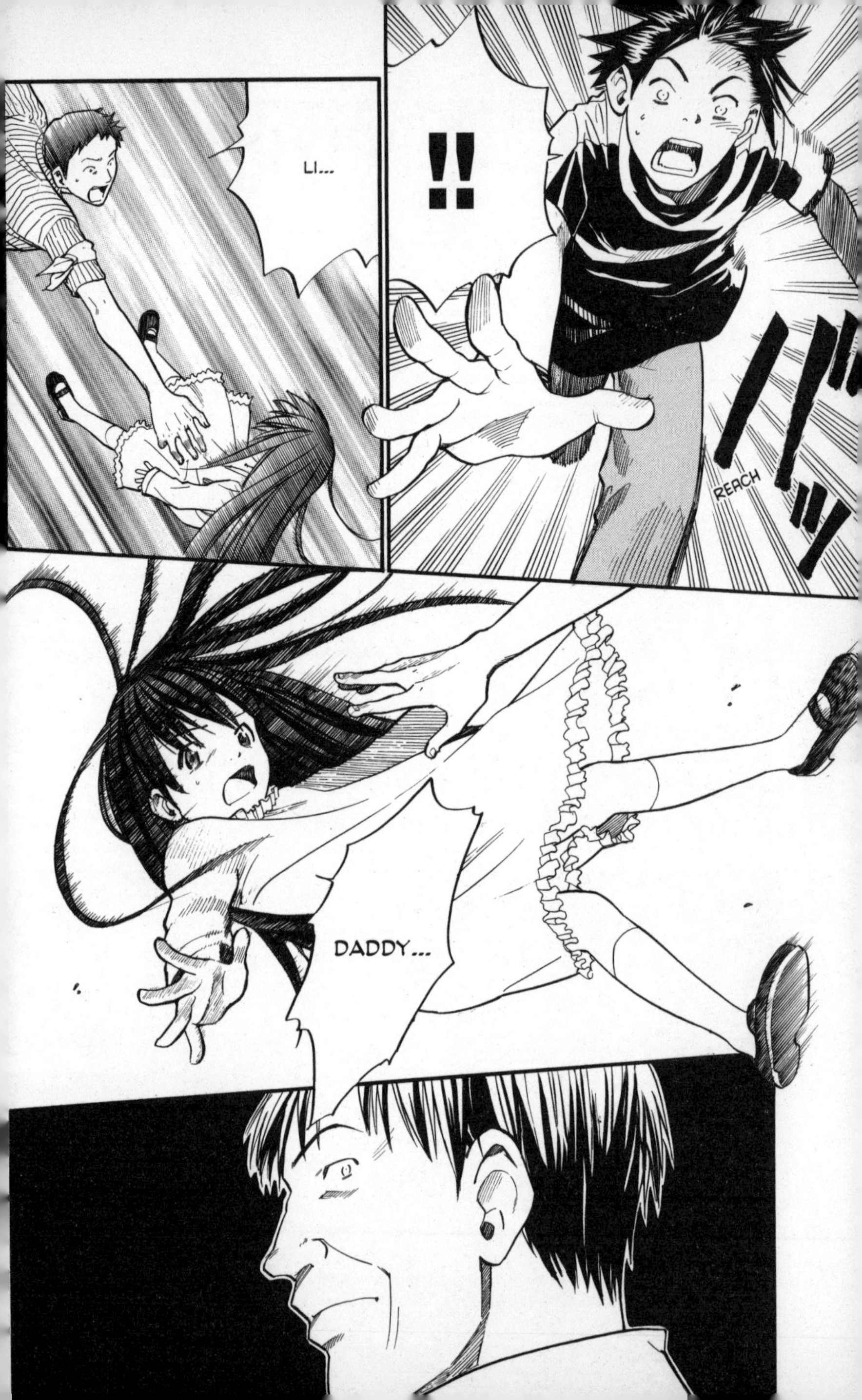
!!
REACH
LI...
DADDY...

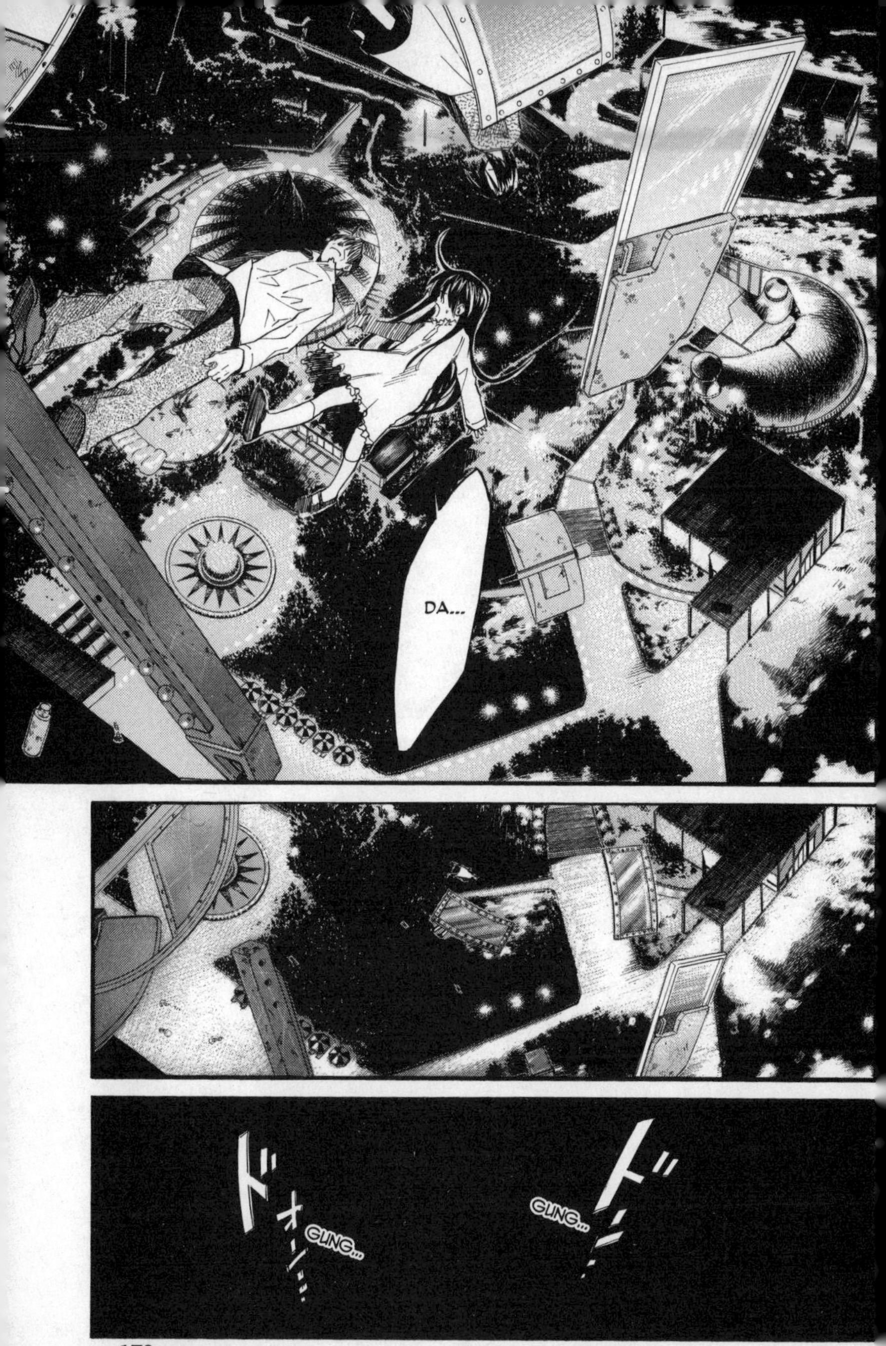
DA...
ドン…
GUNG...
ドォーン…
GUNG...

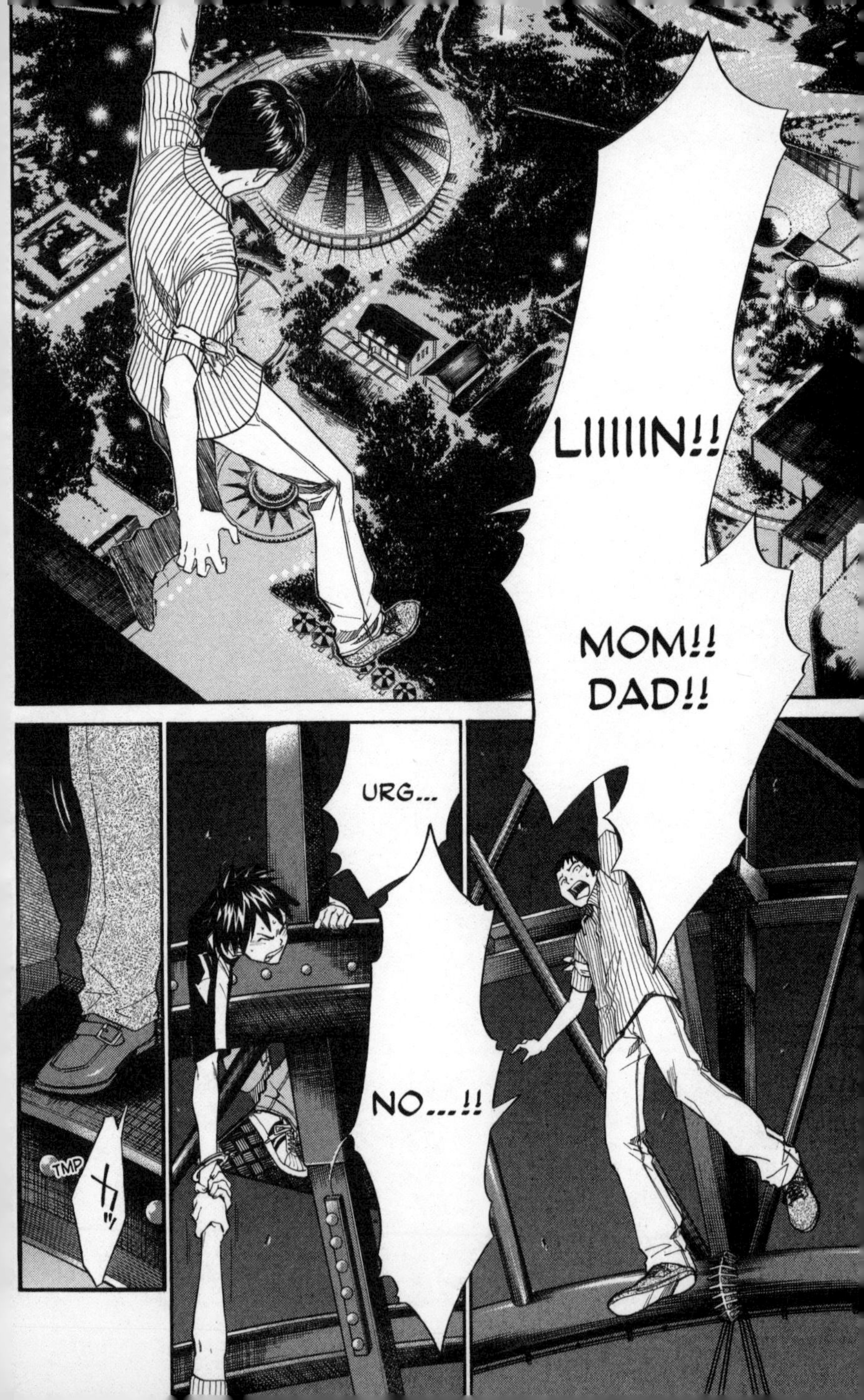
LIIIIIN!!
MOM!!
DAD!!
URG...
NO...!!
TMP

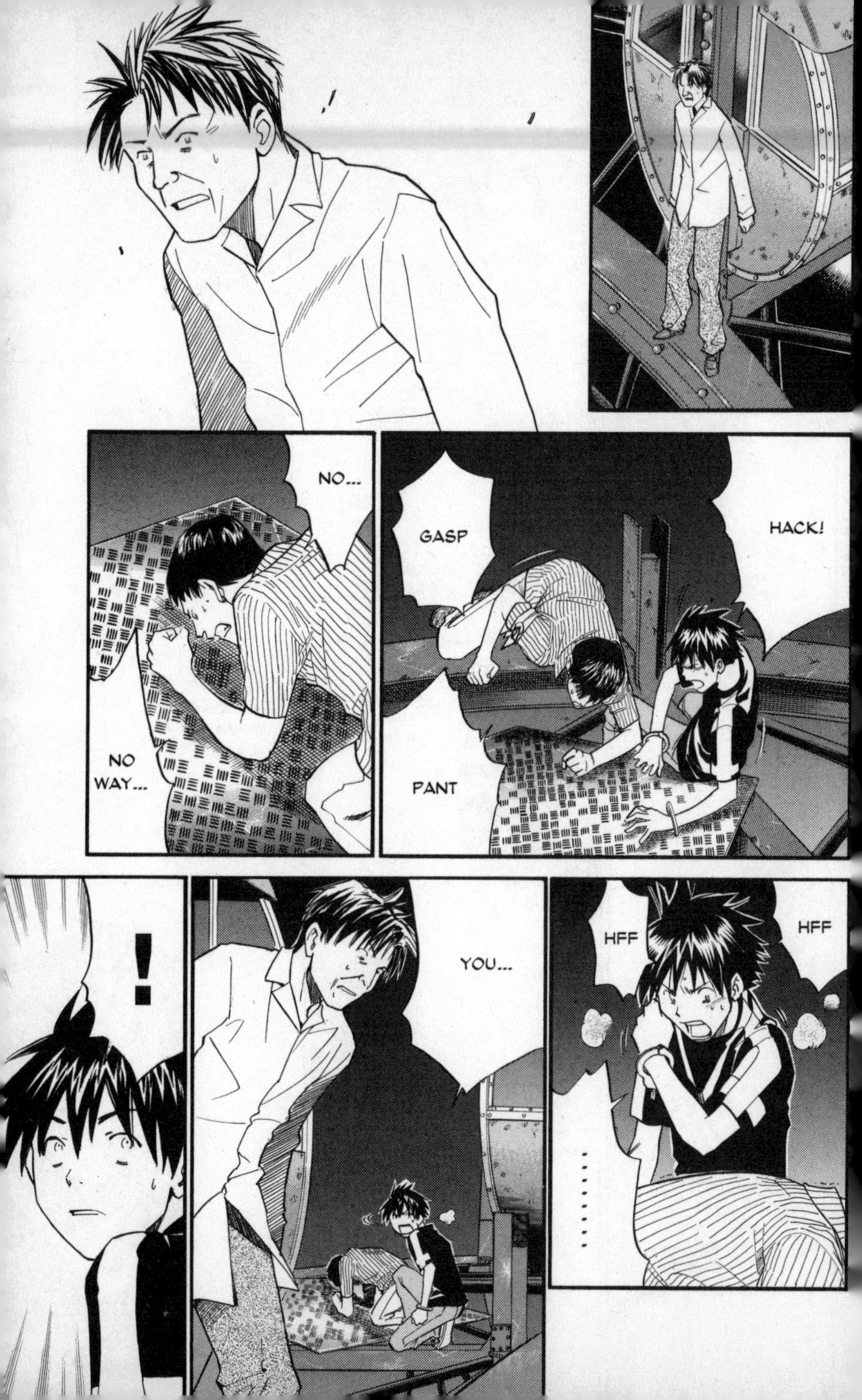
HACK!
GASP
PANT
NO...
NO WAY...
HFF
HFF
......
YOU...
!

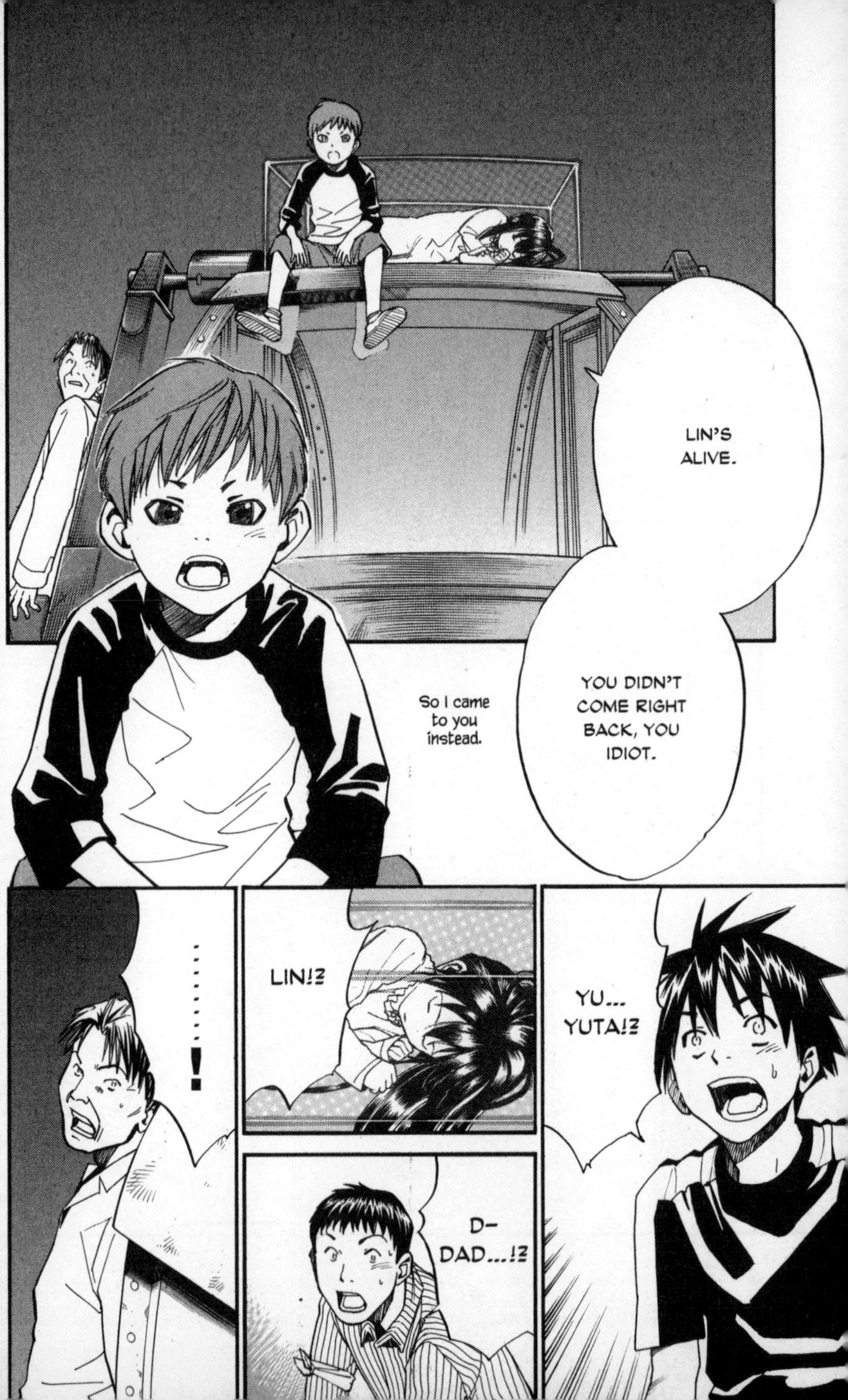
LIN'S ALIVE.
YOU DIDN'T COME RIGHT BACK, YOU IDIOT.
So I came to you instead.
YU... YUTA!?
LIN!?
D- DAD...!?
......!

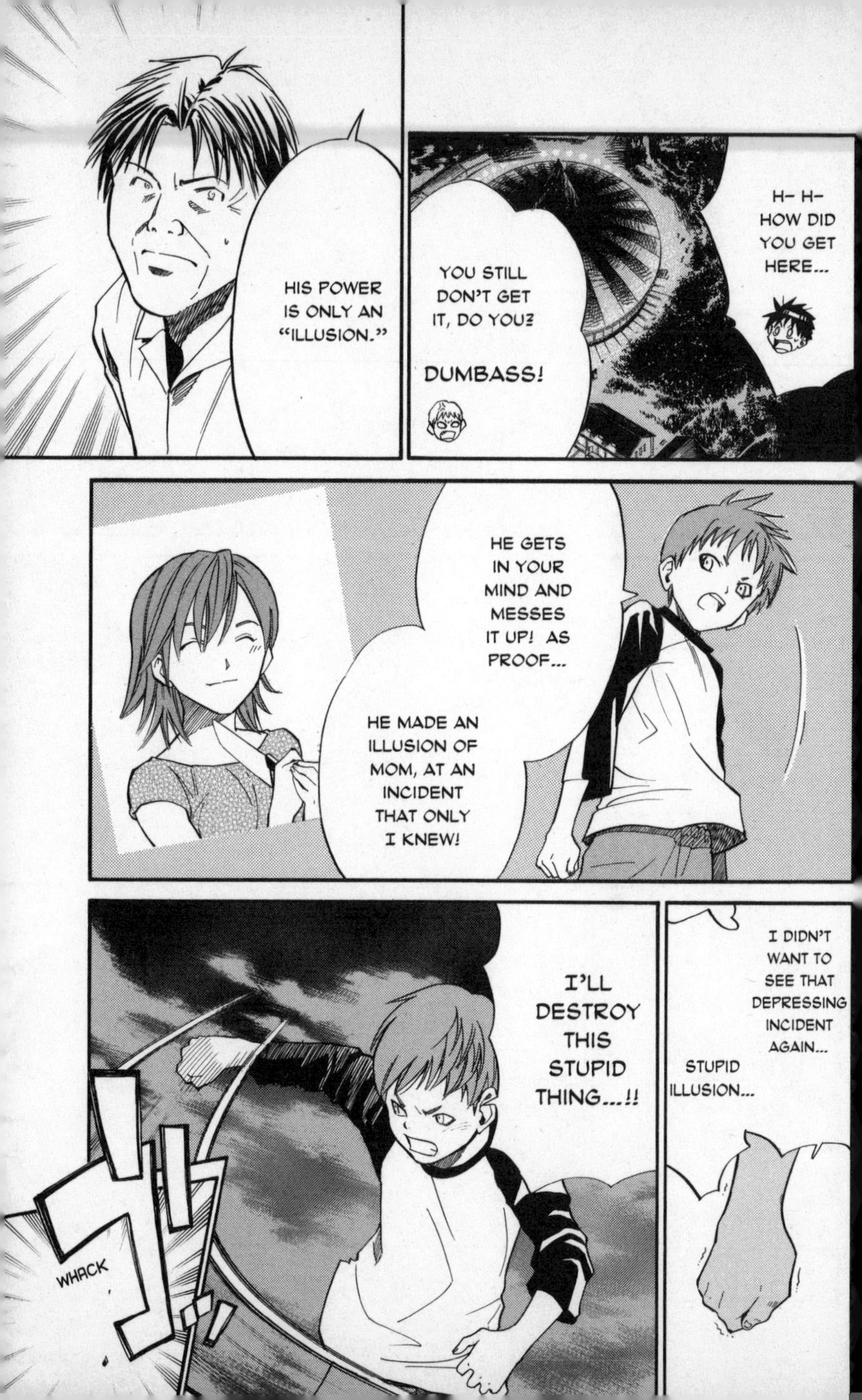
H- H- HOW DID YOU GET HERE...
YOU STILL DON'T GET IT, DO YOU?
DUMBASS!
HIS POWER IS ONLY AN "ILLUSION."
HE GETS IN YOUR MIND AND MESSES IT UP! AS PROOF...
HE MADE AN ILLUSION OF MOM, AT AN INCIDENT THAT ONLY I KNEW!
I DIDN'T WANT TO SEE THAT DEPRESSING INCIDENT AGAIN...
STUPID ILLUSION...
I'LL DESTROY THIS STUPID THING...!!
WHACK

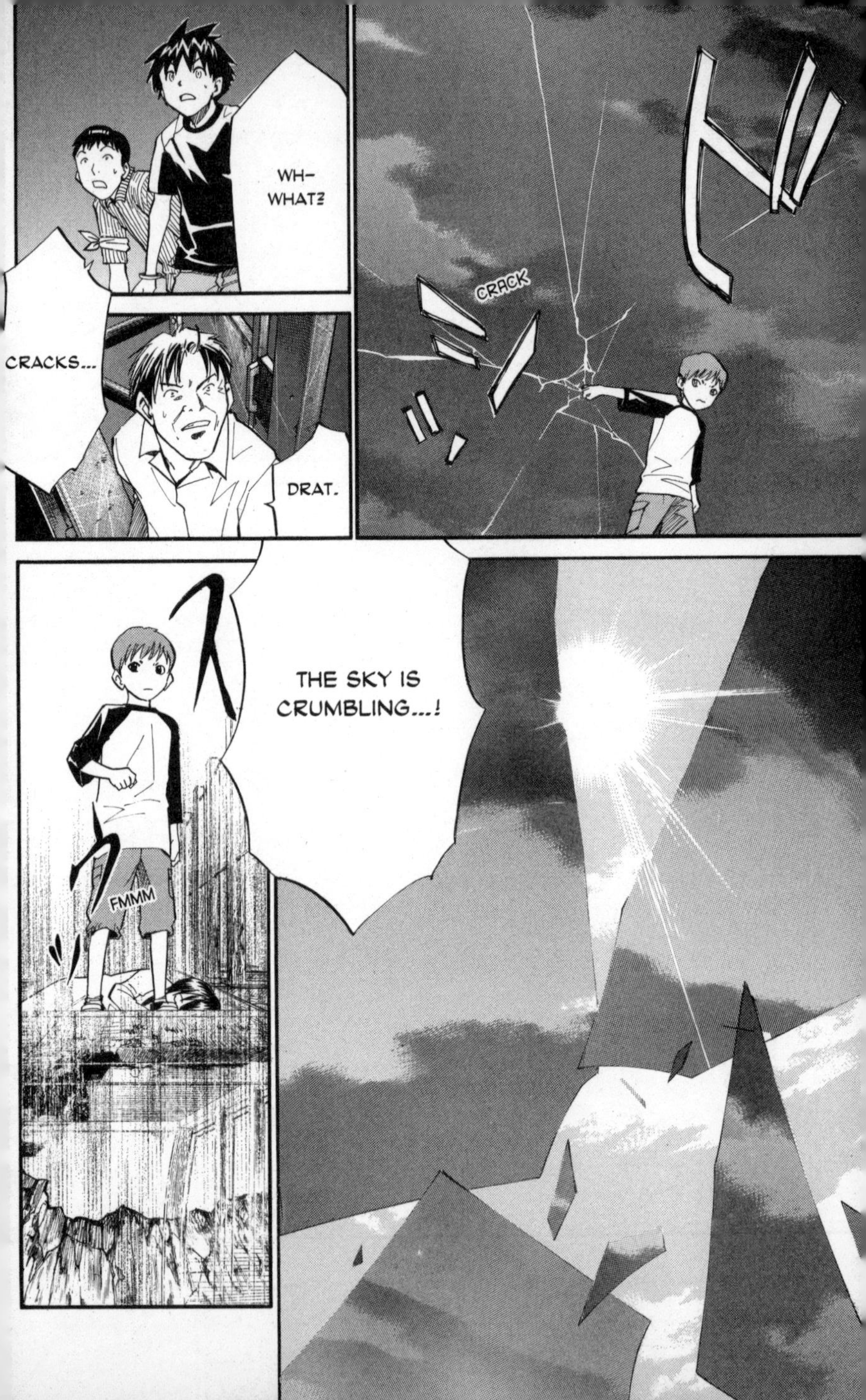
CRACK
WH- WHAT!?
CRACKS...
DRAT.
THE SKY IS CRUMBLING...!
FMMM

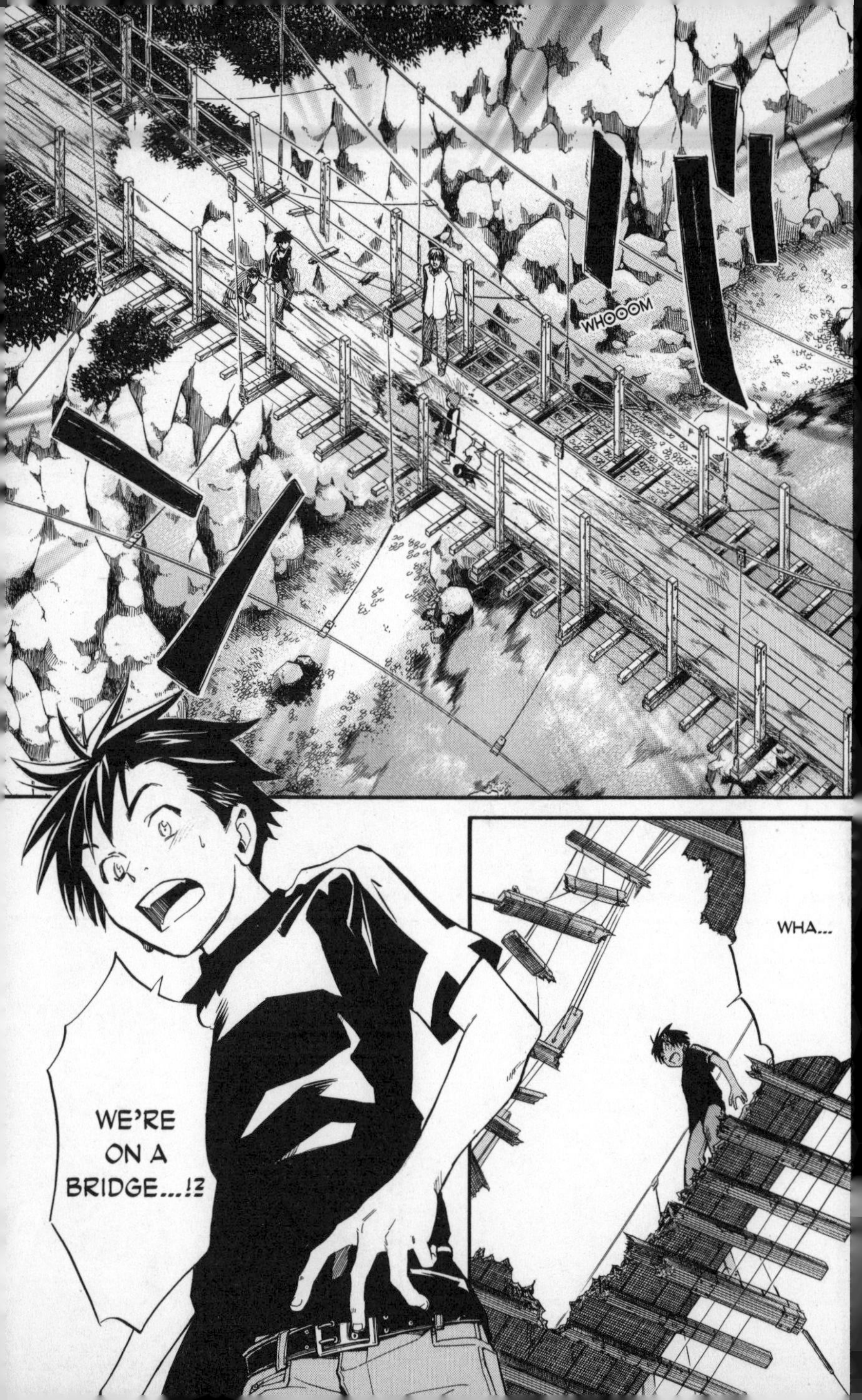
WHOOOM
WHA...
WE'RE ON A BRIDGE...!?

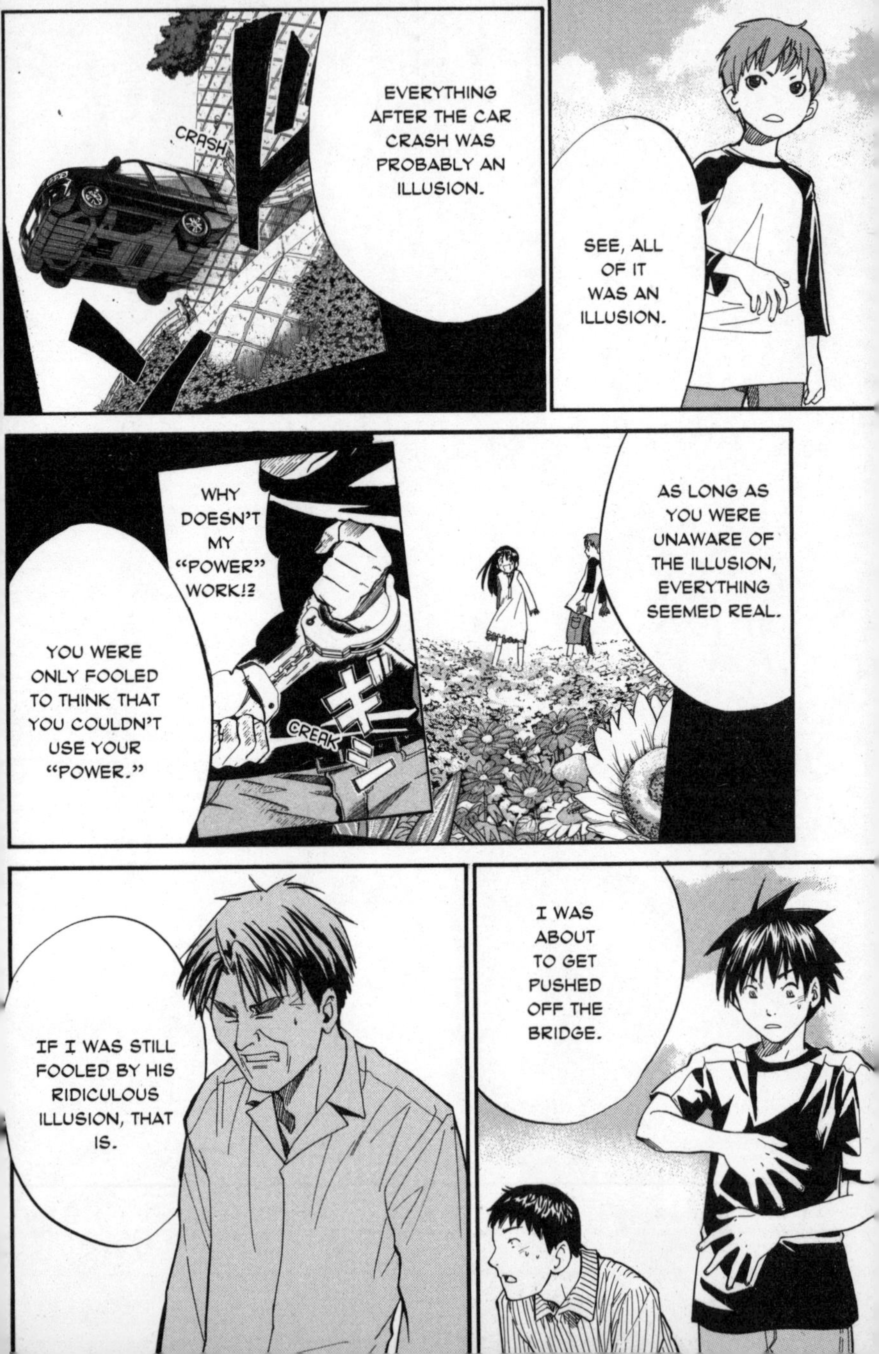
SEE, ALL OF IT WAS AN ILLUSION.
EVERYTHING AFTER THE CAR CRASH WAS PROBABLY AN ILLUSION.
CRASH
AS LONG AS YOU WERE UNAWARE OF THE ILLUSION, EVERYTHING SEEMED REAL.
WHY DOESN'T MY "POWER" WORK!?
CREAK
YOU WERE ONLY FOOLED TO THINK THAT YOU COULDN'T USE YOUR "POWER."
I WAS ABOUT TO GET PUSHED OFF THE BRIDGE.
IF I WAS STILL FOOLED BY HIS RIDICULOUS ILLUSION, THAT IS.

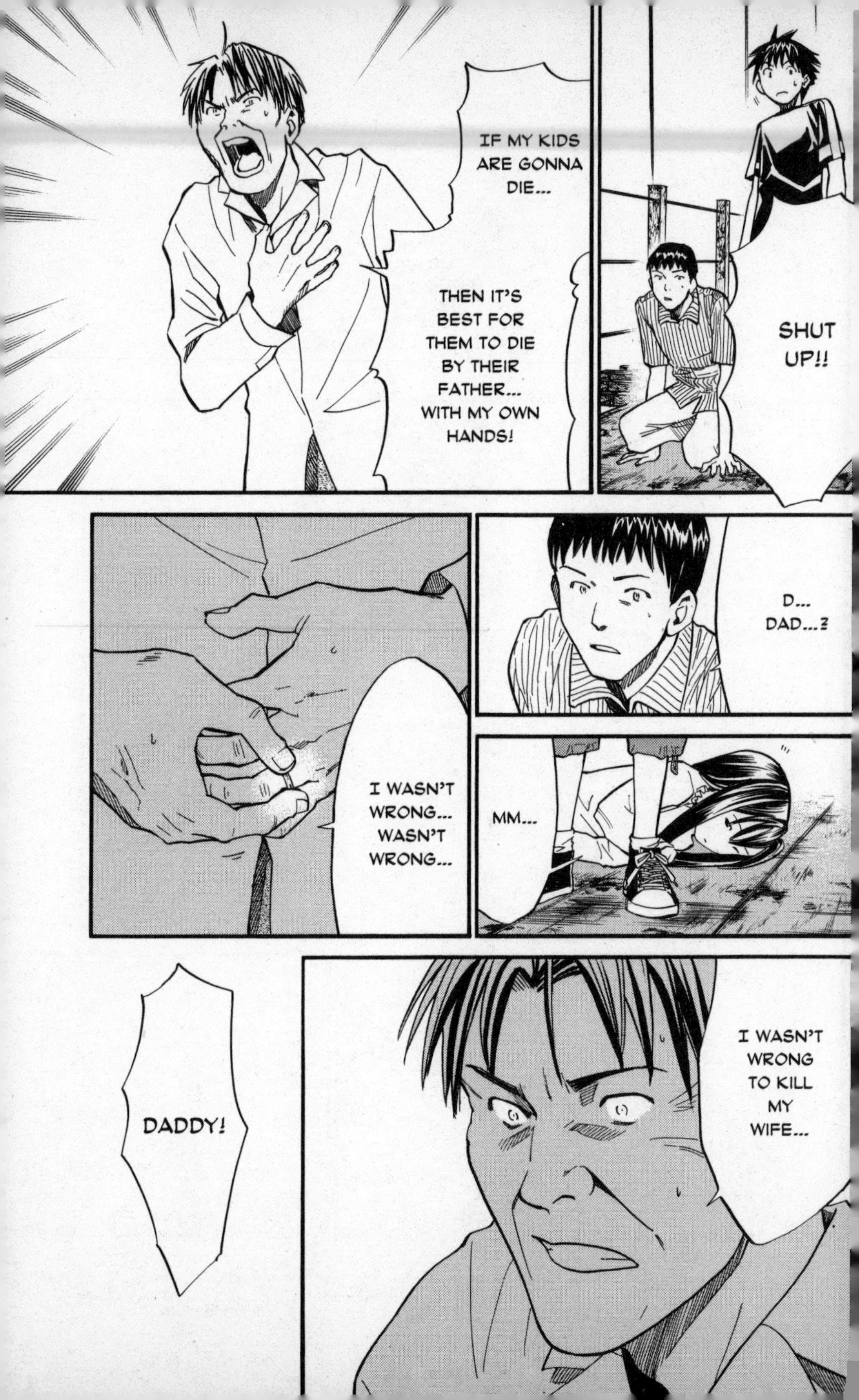
SHUT UP!!
IF MY KIDS ARE GONNA DIE...
THEN IT'S BEST FOR THEM TO DIE BY THEIR FATHER... WITH MY OWN HANDS!
D... DAD...?
MM...
I WASN'T WRONG... WASN'T WRONG...
I WASN'T WRONG TO KILL MY WIFE...
DADDY!

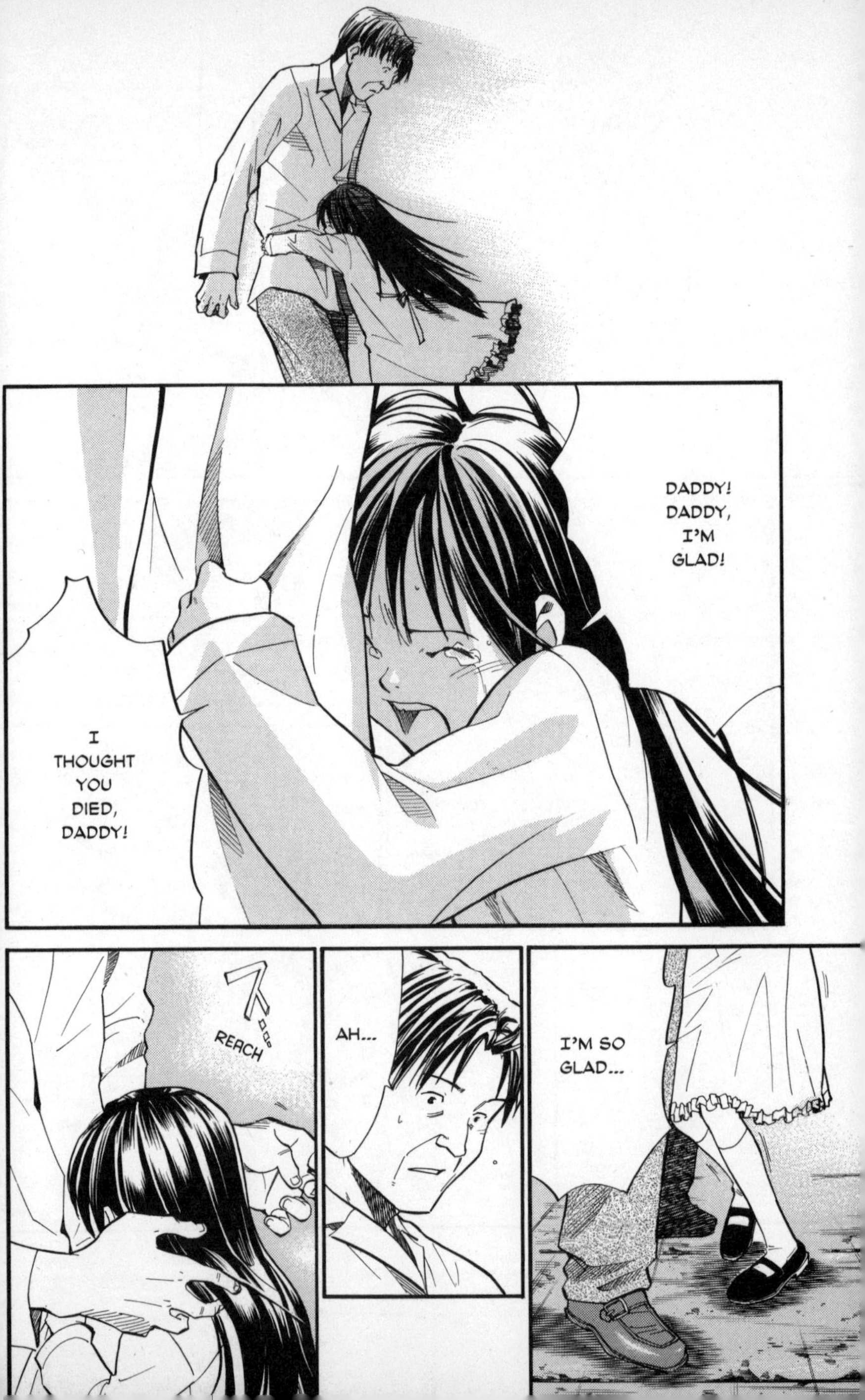
DADDY! DADDY, I'M GLAD!
I THOUGHT YOU DIED, DADDY!
I'M SO GLAD...
AH...
REACH

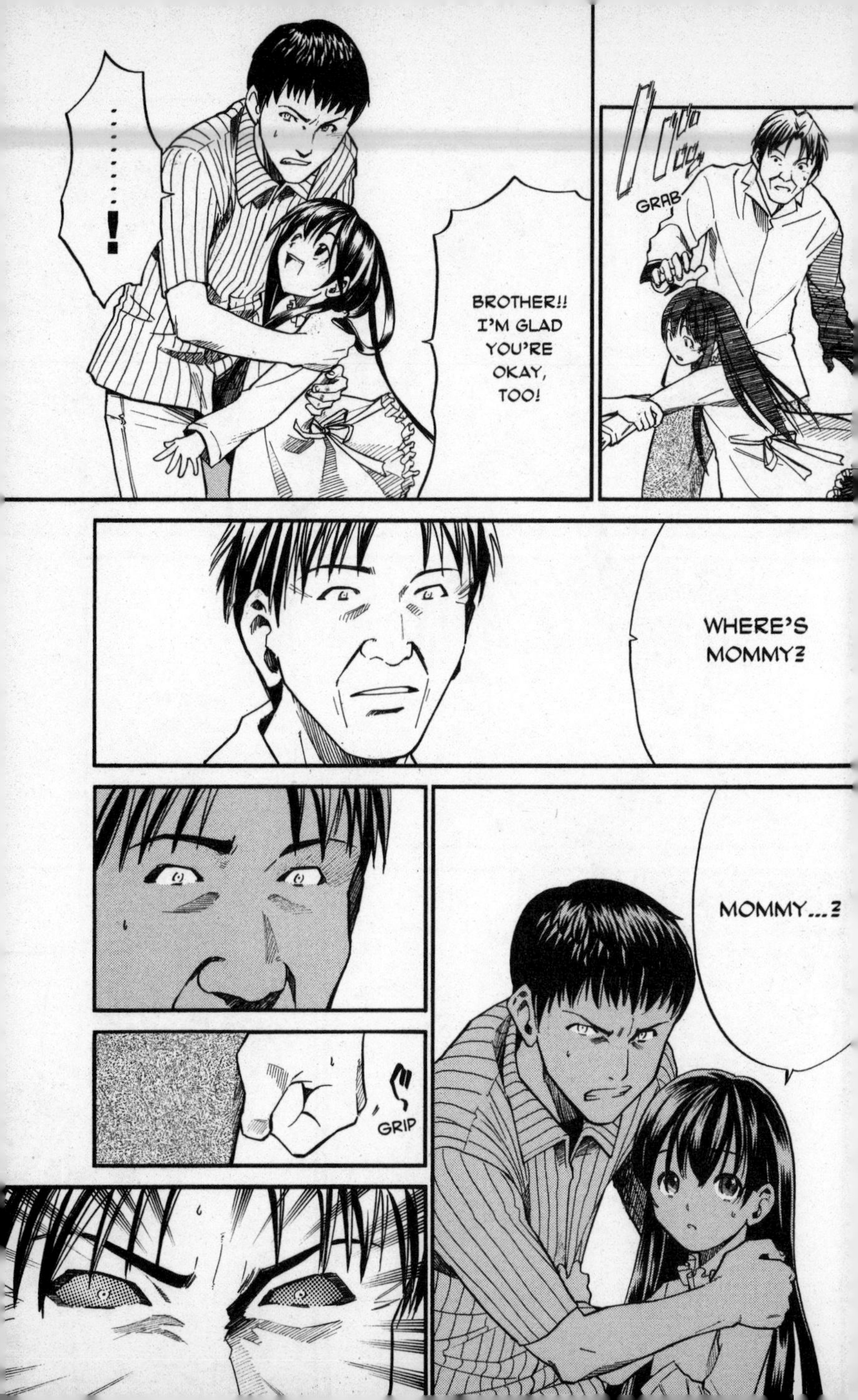
GRAB
BROTHER!! I'M GLAD YOU'RE OKAY, TOO!
......!
WHERE'S MOMMY?
MOMMY...?
GRIP

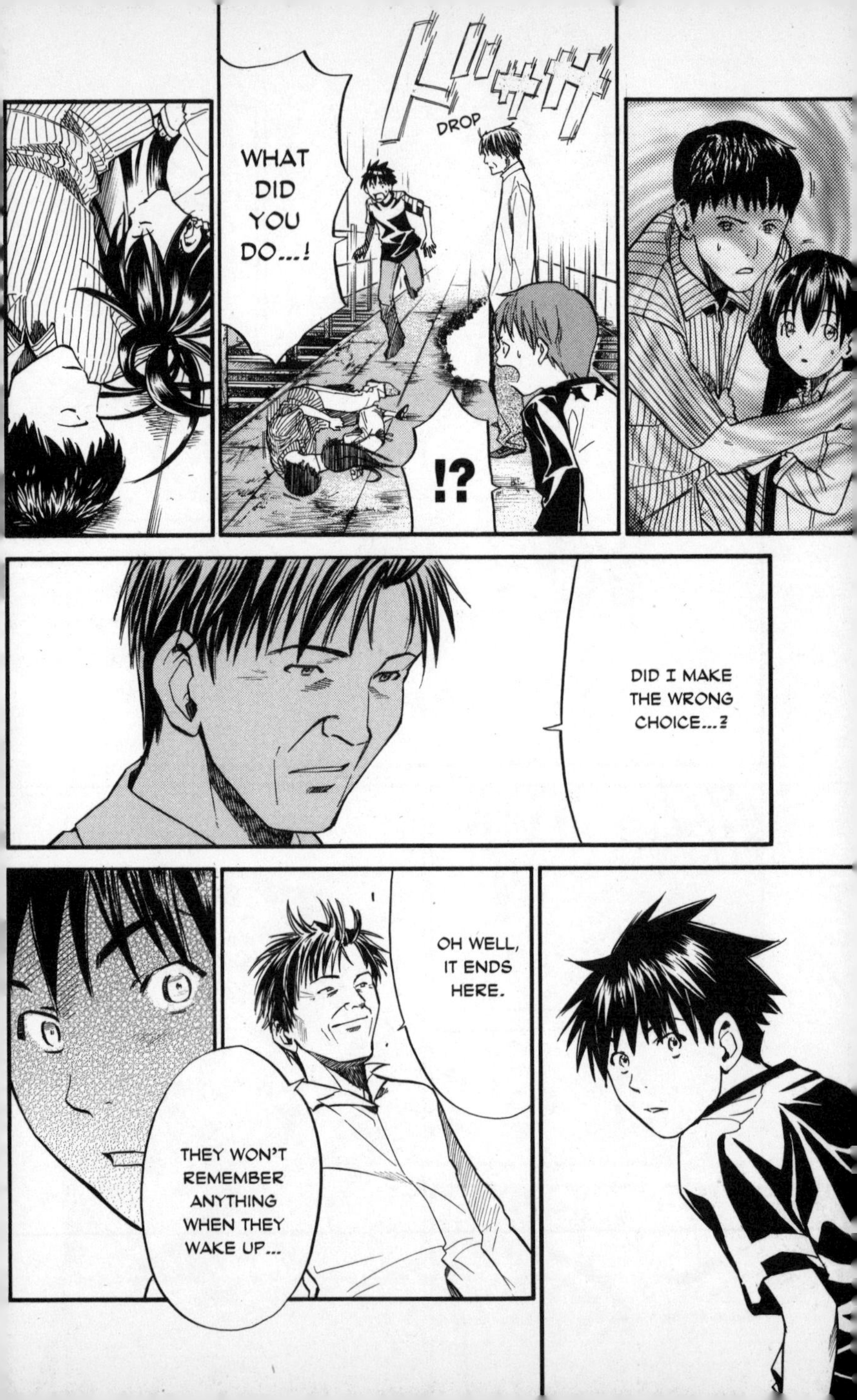
DROP
WHAT DID YOU DO...!
!?
DID I MAKE THE WRONG CHOICE...?
OH WELL, IT ENDS HERE.
THEY WON'T REMEMBER ANYTHING WHEN THEY WAKE UP...

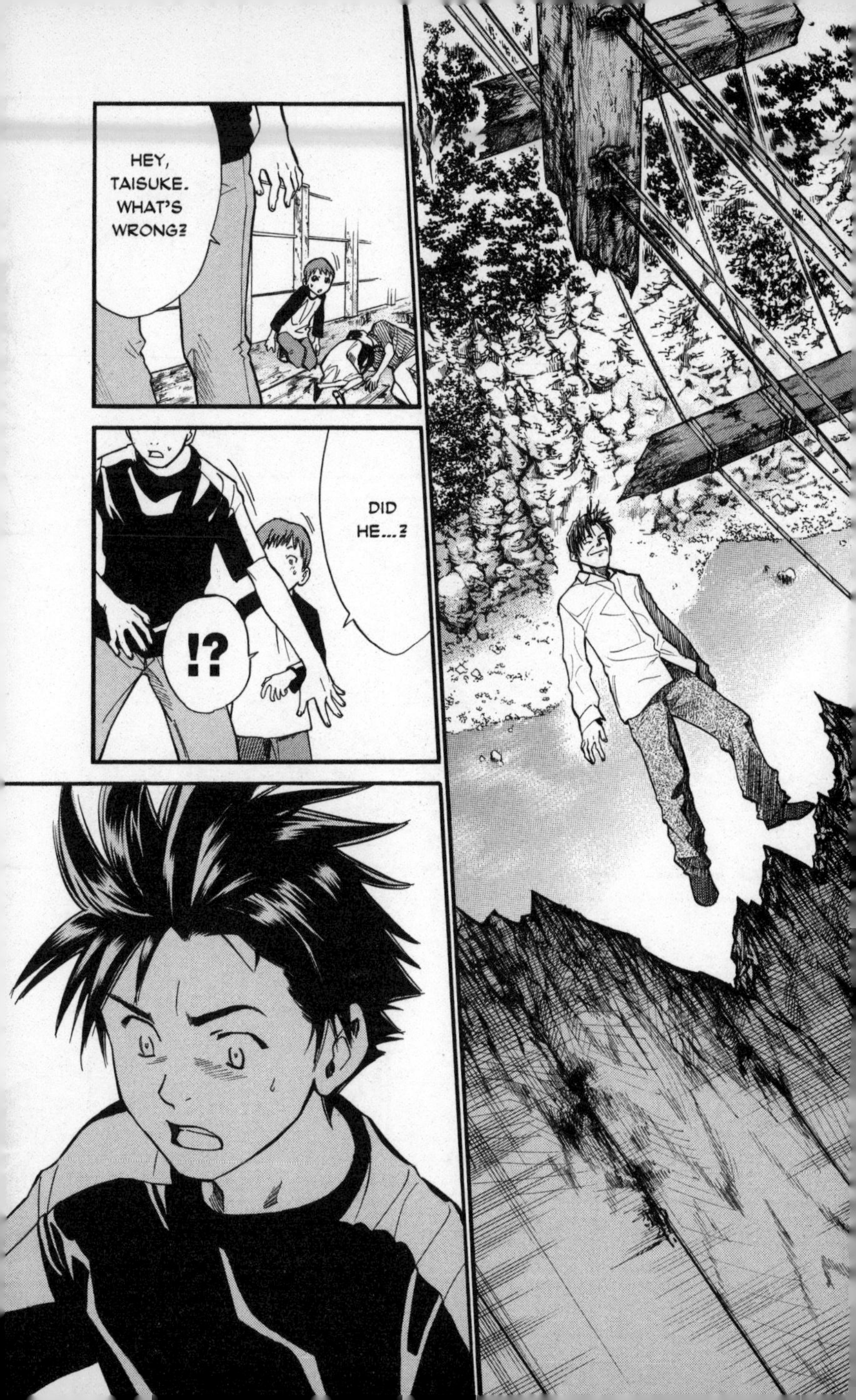
HEY, TAISUKE. WHAT'S WRONG?
DID HE...?
!?

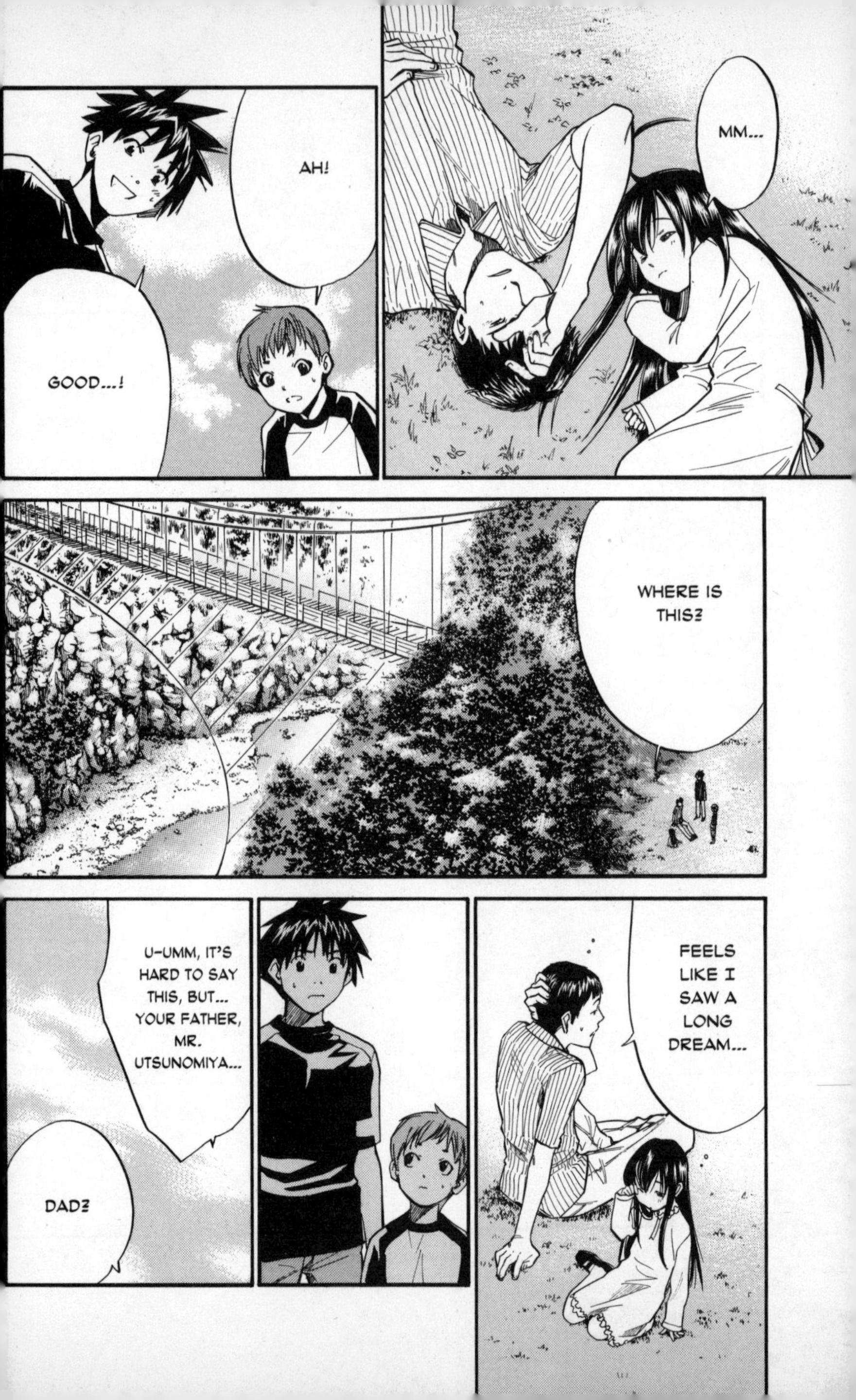
MM...
AH!
GOOD...!
WHERE IS THIS?
FEELS LIKE I SAW A LONG DREAM...
U-UMM, IT'S HARD TO SAY THIS, BUT... YOUR FATHER, MR. UTSUNOMIYA...
DAD?

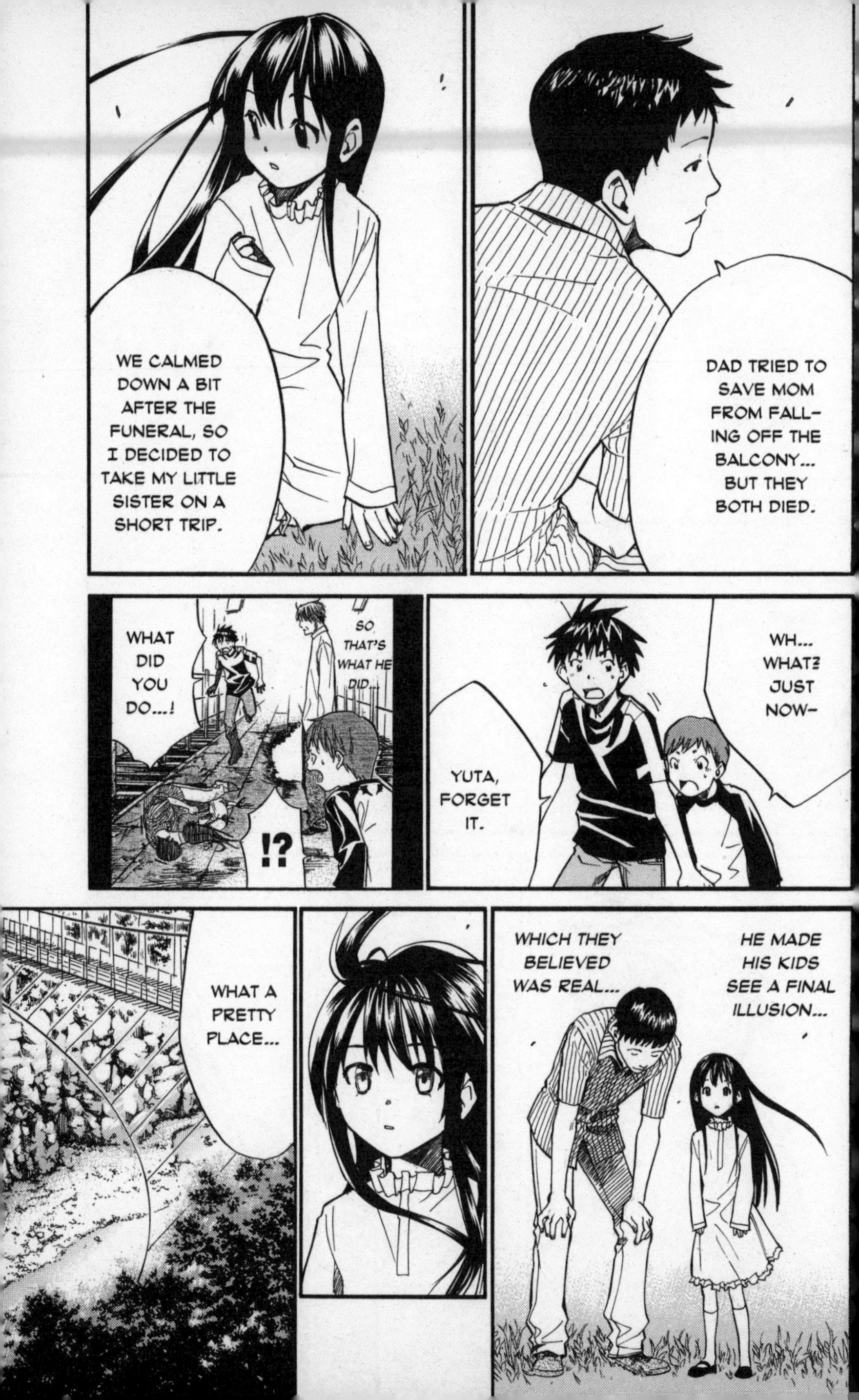
DAD TRIED TO SAVE MOM FROM FALL-ING OFF THE BALCONY... BUT THEY BOTH DIED.
WE CALMED DOWN A BIT AFTER THE FUNERAL, SO I DECIDED TO TAKE MY LITTLE SISTER ON A SHORT TRIP.
WH... WHAT? JUST NOW-
YUTA, FORGET IT.
SO THAT'S WHAT HE DID...
WHAT DID YOU DO...!
!?
HE MADE HIS KIDS SEE A FINAL ILLUSION...
WHICH THEY BELIEVED WAS REAL...
WHAT A PRETTY PLACE...

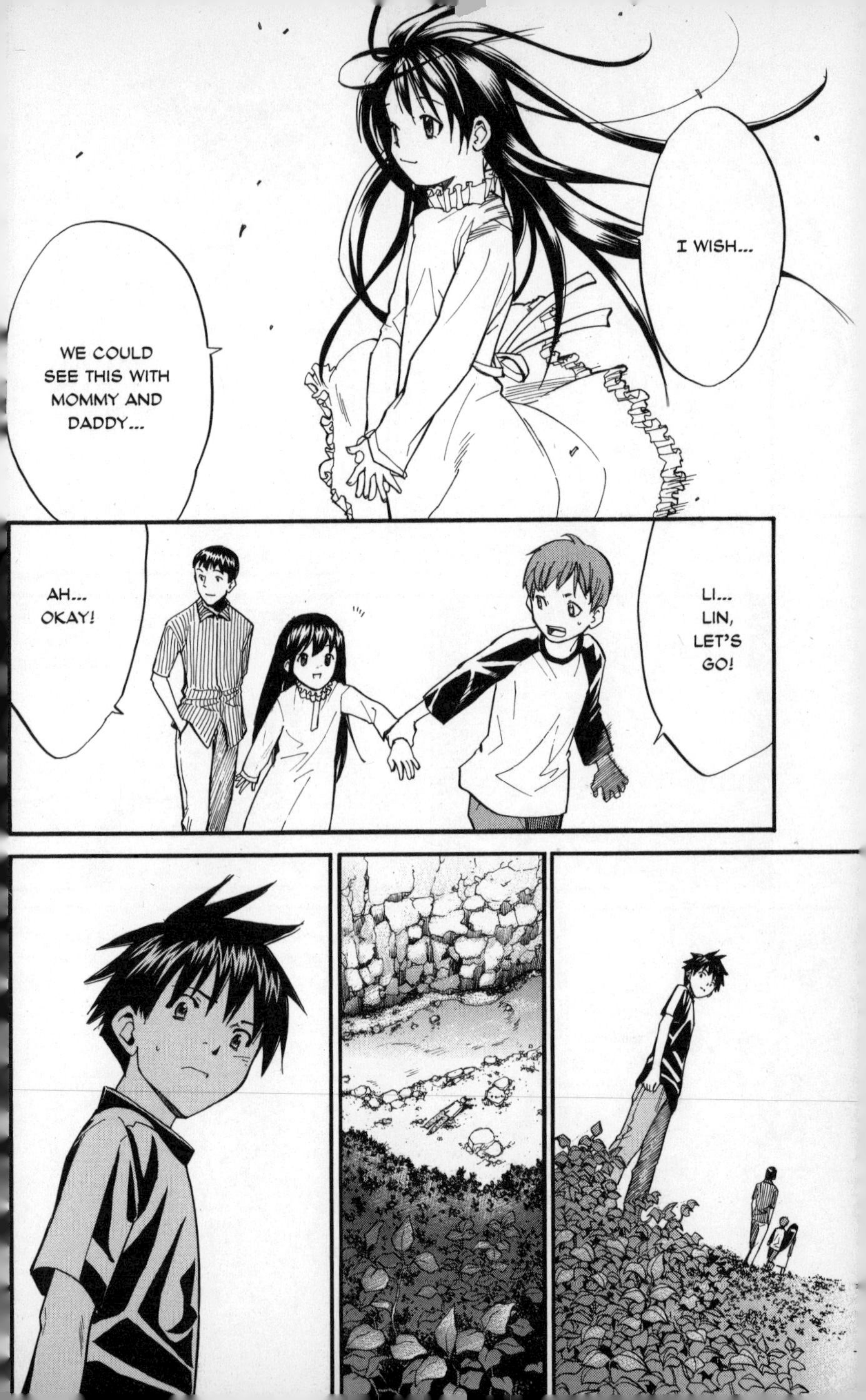
I WISH...
WE COULD SEE THIS WITH MOMMY AND DADDY...
LI... LIN, LET'S GO!
AH... OKAY!

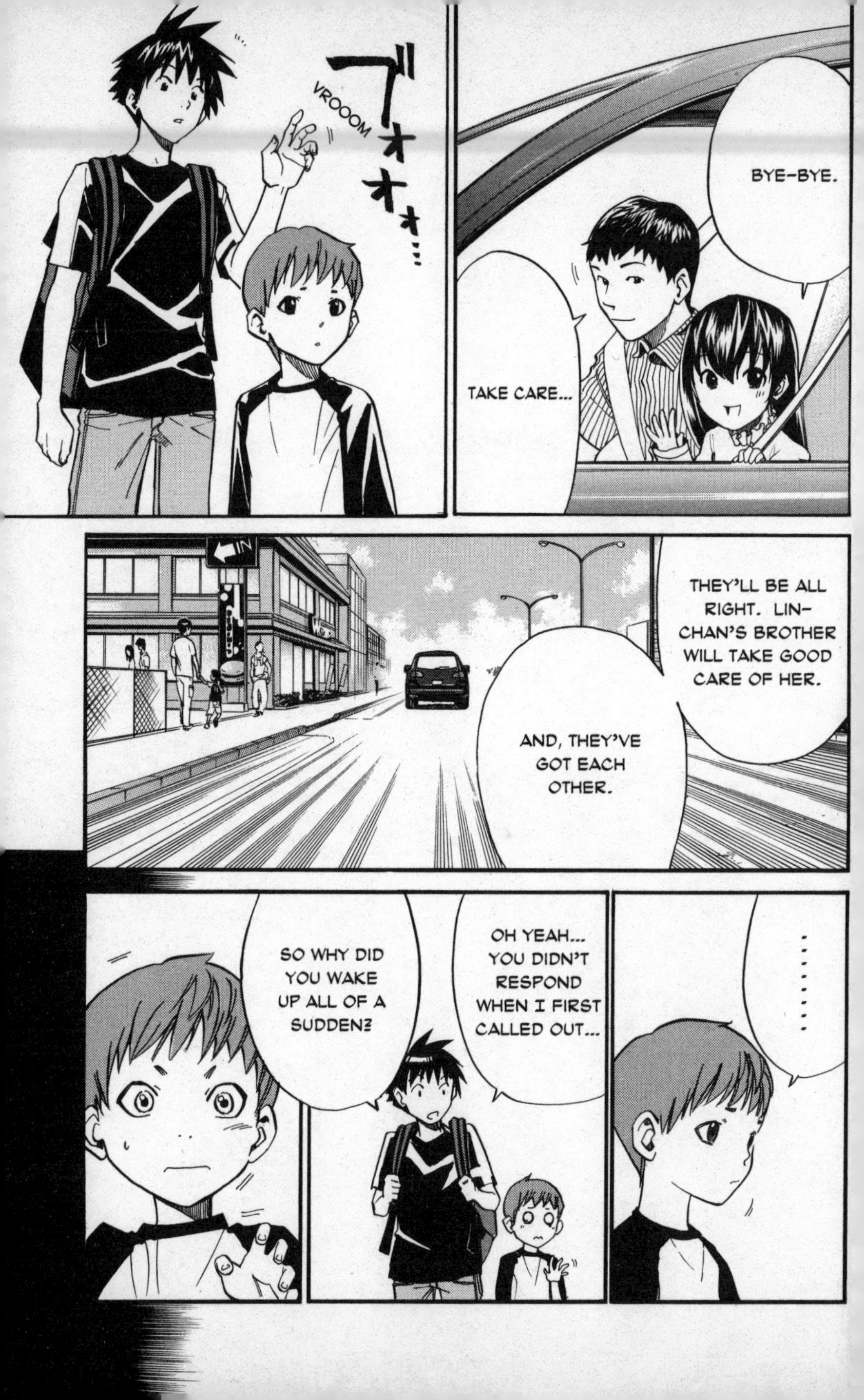
BYE-BYE.
TAKE CARE...
ブオオォ…
VROOOM
THEY'LL BE ALL RIGHT. LIN-CHAN'S BROTHER WILL TAKE GOOD CARE OF HER.
AND, THEY'VE GOT EACH OTHER.
......
OH YEAH... YOU DIDN'T RESPOND WHEN I FIRST CALLED OUT...
SO WHY DID YOU WAKE UP ALL OF A SUDDEN?

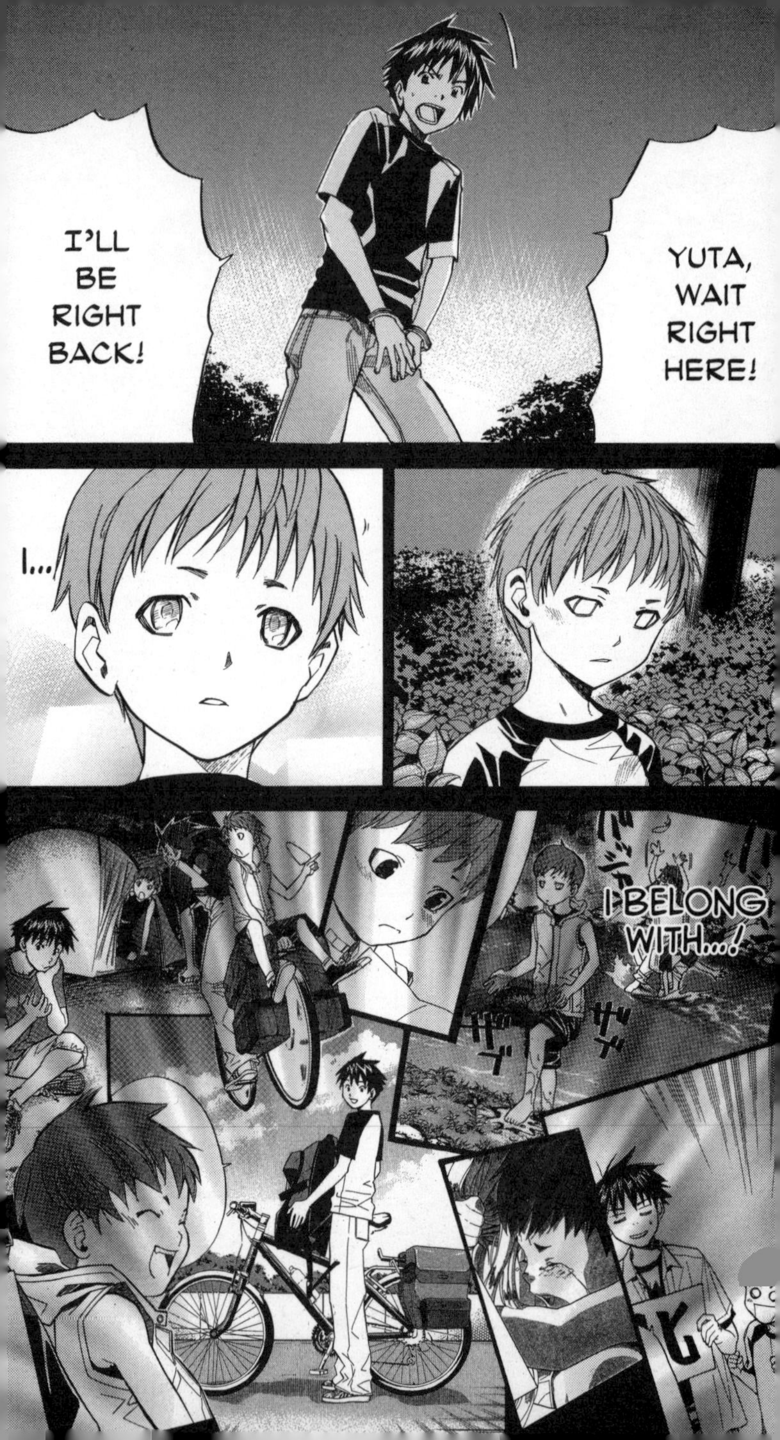
YUTA, WAIT RIGHT HERE!
I'LL BE RIGHT BACK!
I...
I BELONG WITH...!

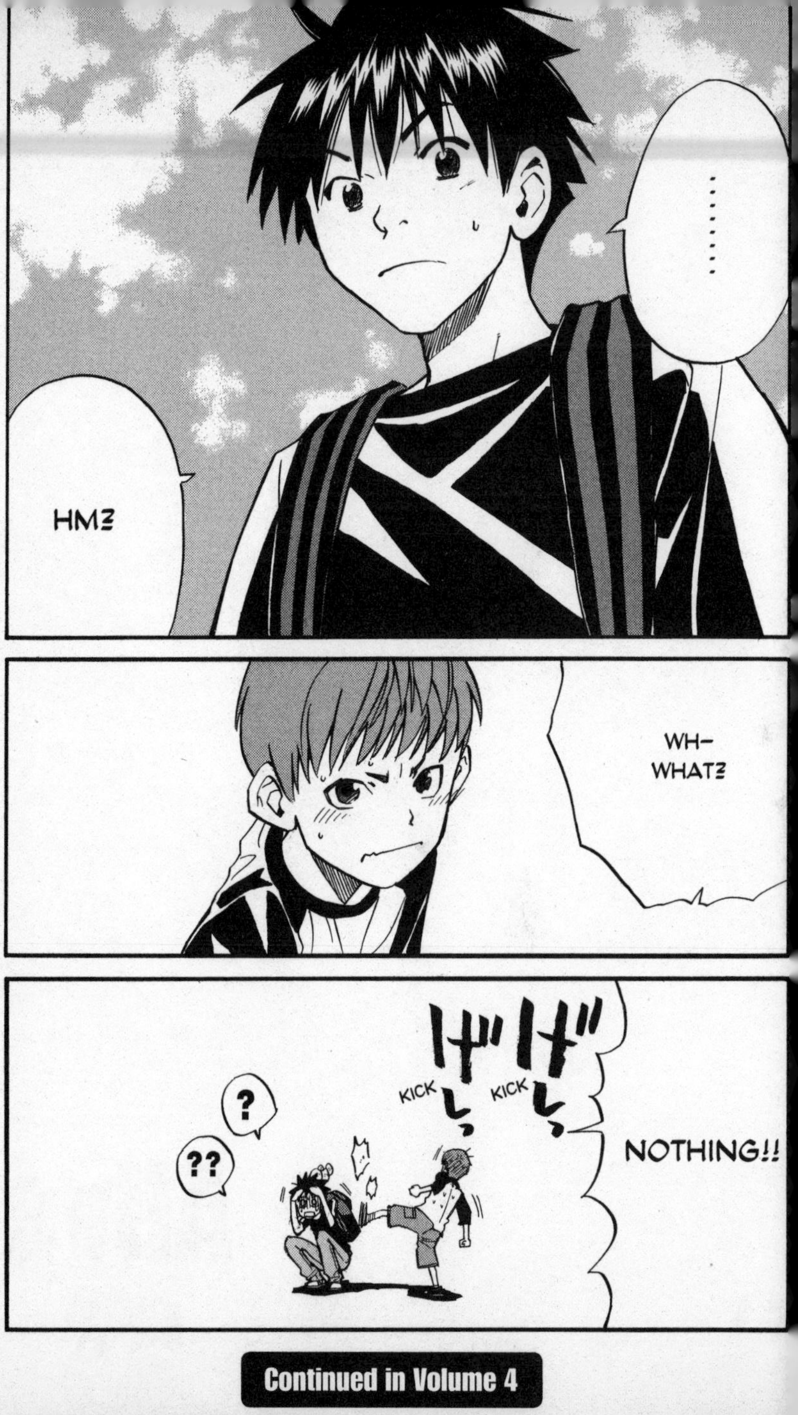

......
HM?
WH-WHAT?
NOTHING!!
げしっ
KICK
げしっ
KICK
?
??

Continued in Volume 4

Alive

Light Visual Manga

3

CRUNCH
Hah!
H-HEY!? WAIT UP!!
CRU-CRUNCH
HEY YOU!
VROOOM
STOP!
I SAID WAIT UP!!
JUMP
OH MAN, WHAT A MESS.
OH GOSH!!

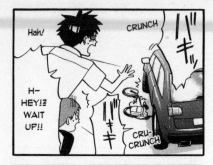

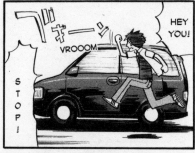

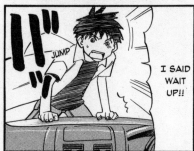

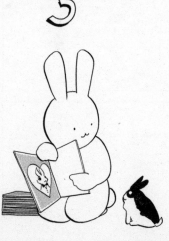

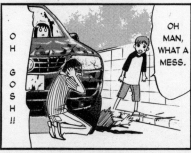

ALIVE... THE END!

RICE COOKING BOY

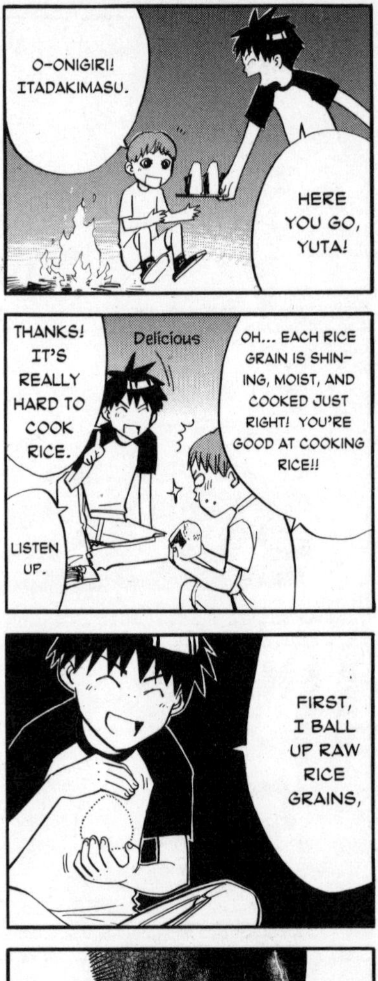
HERE YOU GO, YUTA!
O-ONIGIRI! ITADAKIMASU.
OH... EACH RICE GRAIN IS SHIN-ING, MOIST, AND COOKED JUST RIGHT! YOU'RE GOOD AT COOKING RICE!!
Delicious
THANKS! IT'S REALLY HARD TO COOK RICE.
LISTEN UP.
FIRST, I BALL UP RAW RICE GRAINS,
THEN I SLOWLY BURN IT...
Sigh
DON'T TELL ME...!!
CRUMBLE CRUMBLE

KATTSUN'S JOB

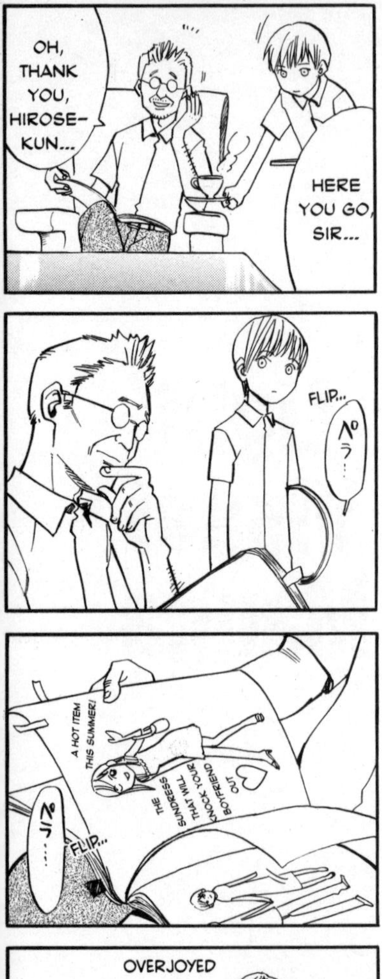
HERE YOU GO, SIR...
OH, THANK YOU, HIROSE-KUN...
FLIP...
A HOT ITEM THIS SUMMER!
THE SUNDRESS THAT WILL KNOCK YOUR BOYFRIEND OUT
FLIP...
YOU'RE AWESOME, KATSUMATA-SAN.
OVERJOYED
THE CLOTHES YOU CHOOSE MAKE OCHIAI-SAN LOOK EVEN CUTER...

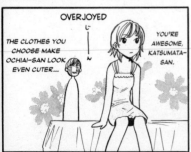

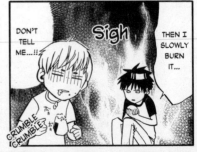

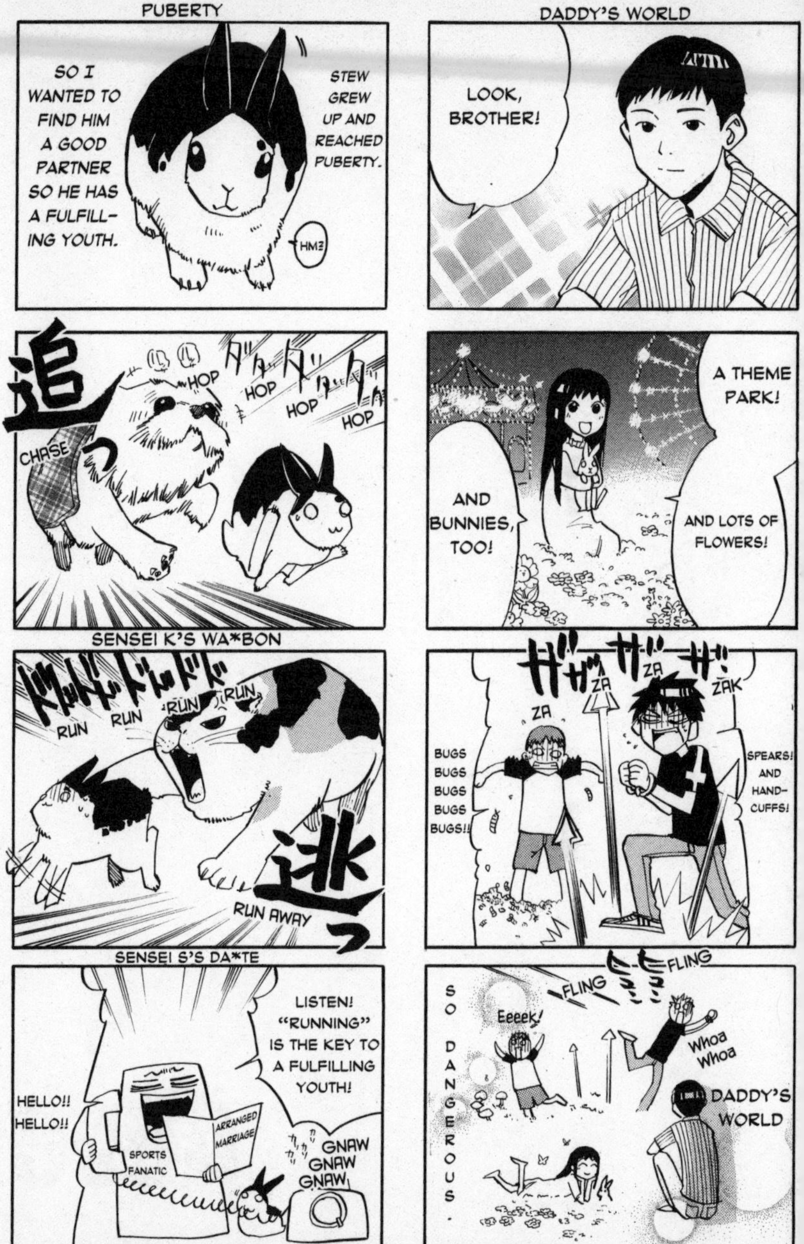
DADDY'S WORLD
LOOK, BROTHER!
A THEME PARK!
AND LOTS OF FLOWERS!
AND BUNNIES, TOO!
ZAK
ZA
ZA
ZA
SPEARS! AND HAND-CUFFS!
BUGS BUGS BUGS BUGS BUGS!!
FLING
FLING
Whoa Whoa
DADDY'S WORLD
Eeeek!
SO DANGEROUS.
PUBERTY
STEW GREW UP AND REACHED PUBERTY.
SO I WANTED TO FIND HIM A GOOD PARTNER SO HE HAS A FULFILLING YOUTH.
HM?
HOP
HOP
HOP
HOP
追っ
CHASE
SENSEI K'S WA*BON
RUN
RUN
RUN
RUN
逃っ
RUN AWAY
SENSEI S'S DA*TE
LISTEN! "RUNNING" IS THE KEY TO A FULFILLING YOUTH!
GNAW GNAW GNAW
ARRANGED MARRIAGE
SPORTS FANATIC
HELLO!! HELLO!!

THANK YOU FOR READING UP TO THIS POINT!

Alive

Translation Notes

Japanese is a tricky language for most Westerners, and translation is often more art than science. For your edification and reading pleasure, here are notes on some of the places where we could have gone in a different direction in our translation of the work, or where a Japanese cultural reference is used.

Kamaitachi, page 3

Kamaitachi is a mythical phenomenon, where winds would mysteriously cut or slice people and objects like a *kama* (sickle). It was thought to be caused by an *itachi* (weasel), so the term *kamaitachi* (sickle weasel) came about.

Kenichirou Morio

One of Katsumata's comrades. Controls wind to create sharp blades of air like a *kamaitachi* to slice humans. Ordered by Katsumata to kill Taisuke.

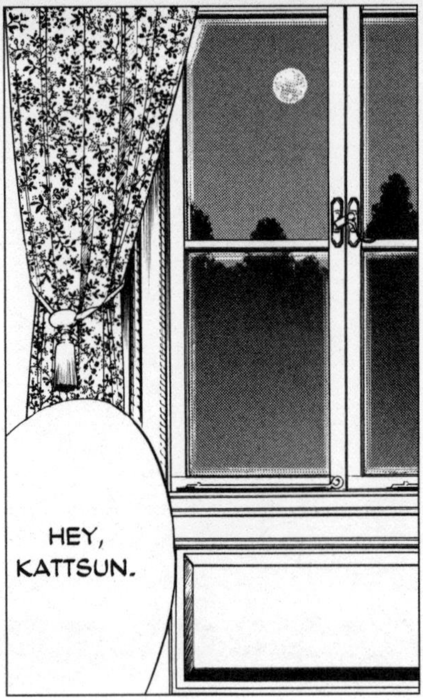
HEY,
KATTSUN.

Kattsun, page 30

Kattsun is a nickname Yura uses for Katsumata.

***kimasu*, page 200**

masu is a Japanese
g said before meals
g "Thank you for this

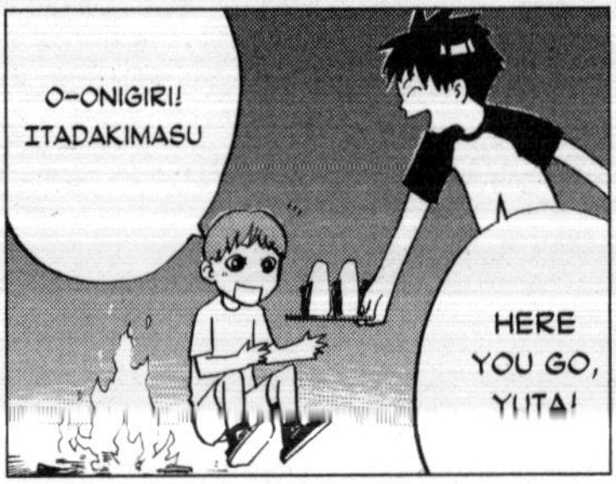
HERE YOU GO, YUTA!
O-ONIGIRI! ITADAKIMASU

page 200

Onigiri is a Japanese rice ball, sometimes triangular in shape.

Sensei, page 201

Sensei is "teacher" or "master" in Japanese. Schoolteachers, masters of martial arts, and specialized professionals, such as artists and politicians, are often called *Sensei*.

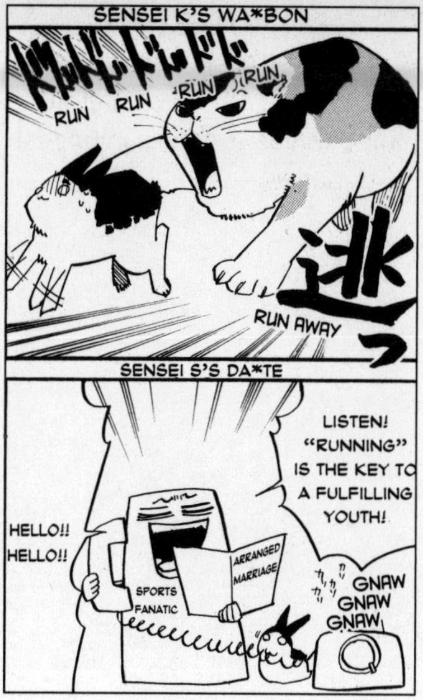
SENSEI K'S WA*BON
RUN
RUN
RUN
RUN
RUN AWAY
SENSEI S'S DA*TE
LISTEN! "RUNNING" IS THE KEY TO A FULFILLING YOUTH!
GNAW GNAW GNAW
ARRANGED MARRIAGE
SPORTS FANATIC
HELLO!! HELLO!!

We're pleased to present you a preview from volume 4. Please check our website (www.delreymanga.com) to see when this volume will be available in English. For now you'll have to make do with Japanese!

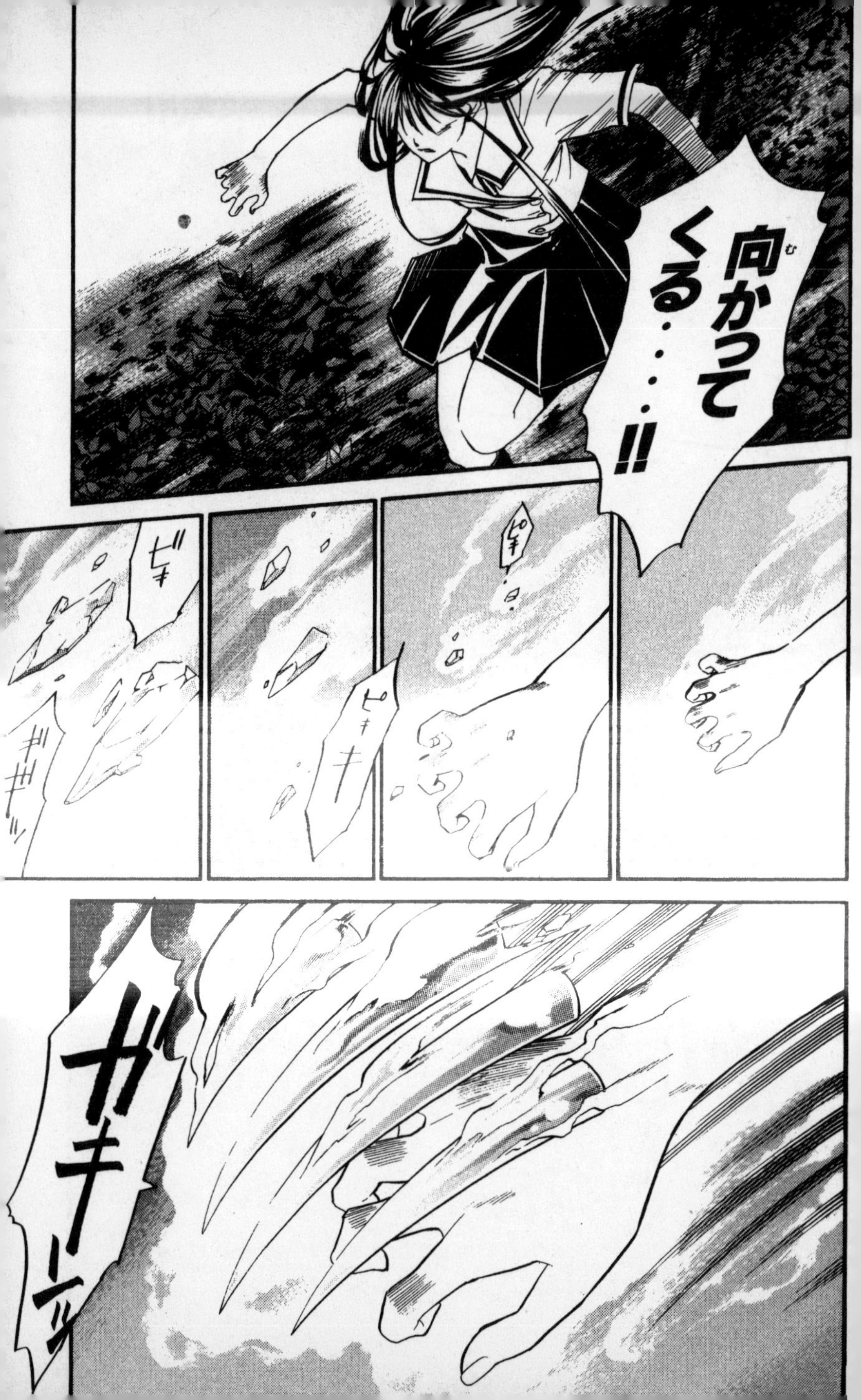

向かってくる……!!
ピキ
ピキキ
ビキ
ギギギッ
ガキーンッ

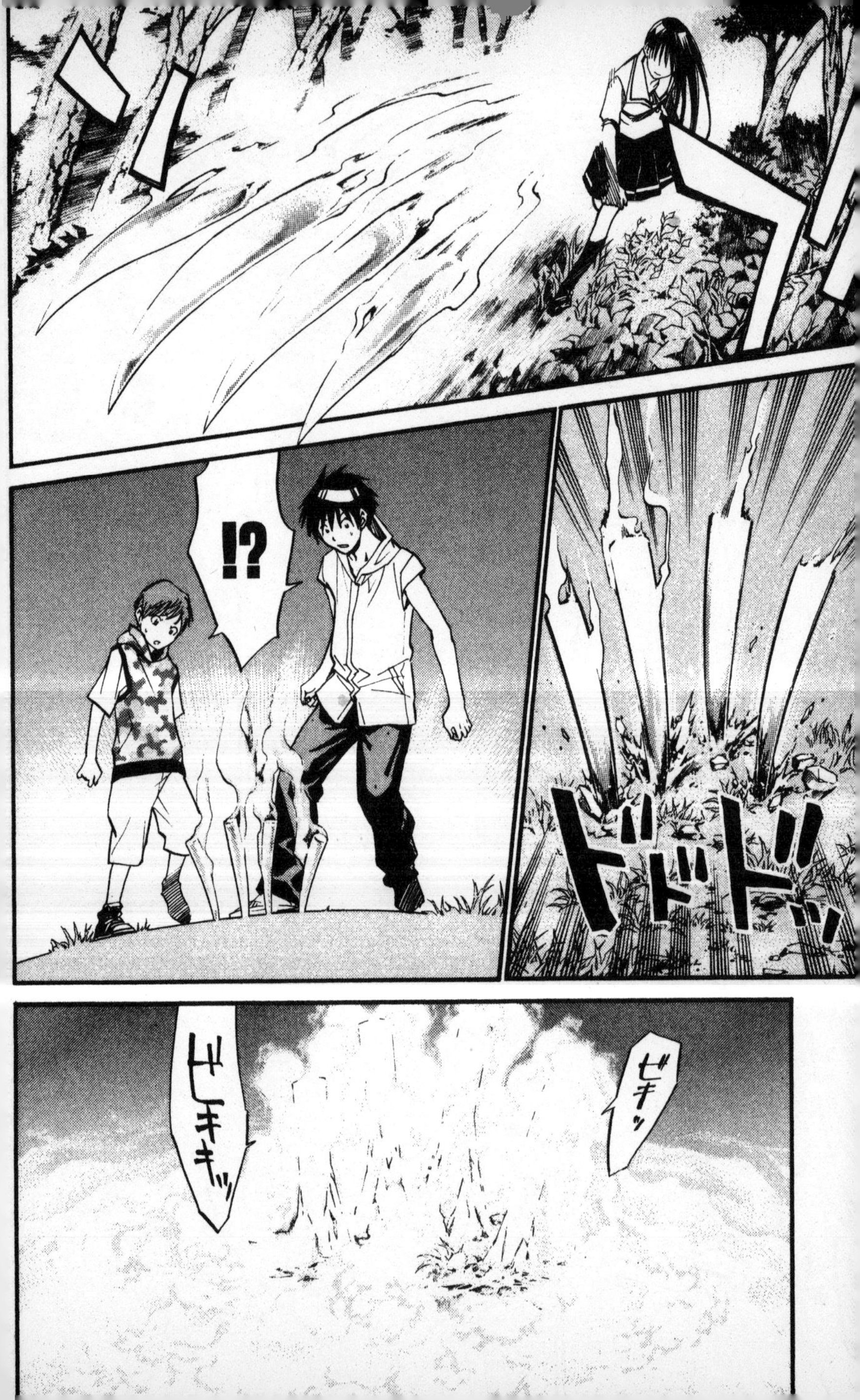

ドドドッ
!?
ビキッ
ビキキッ

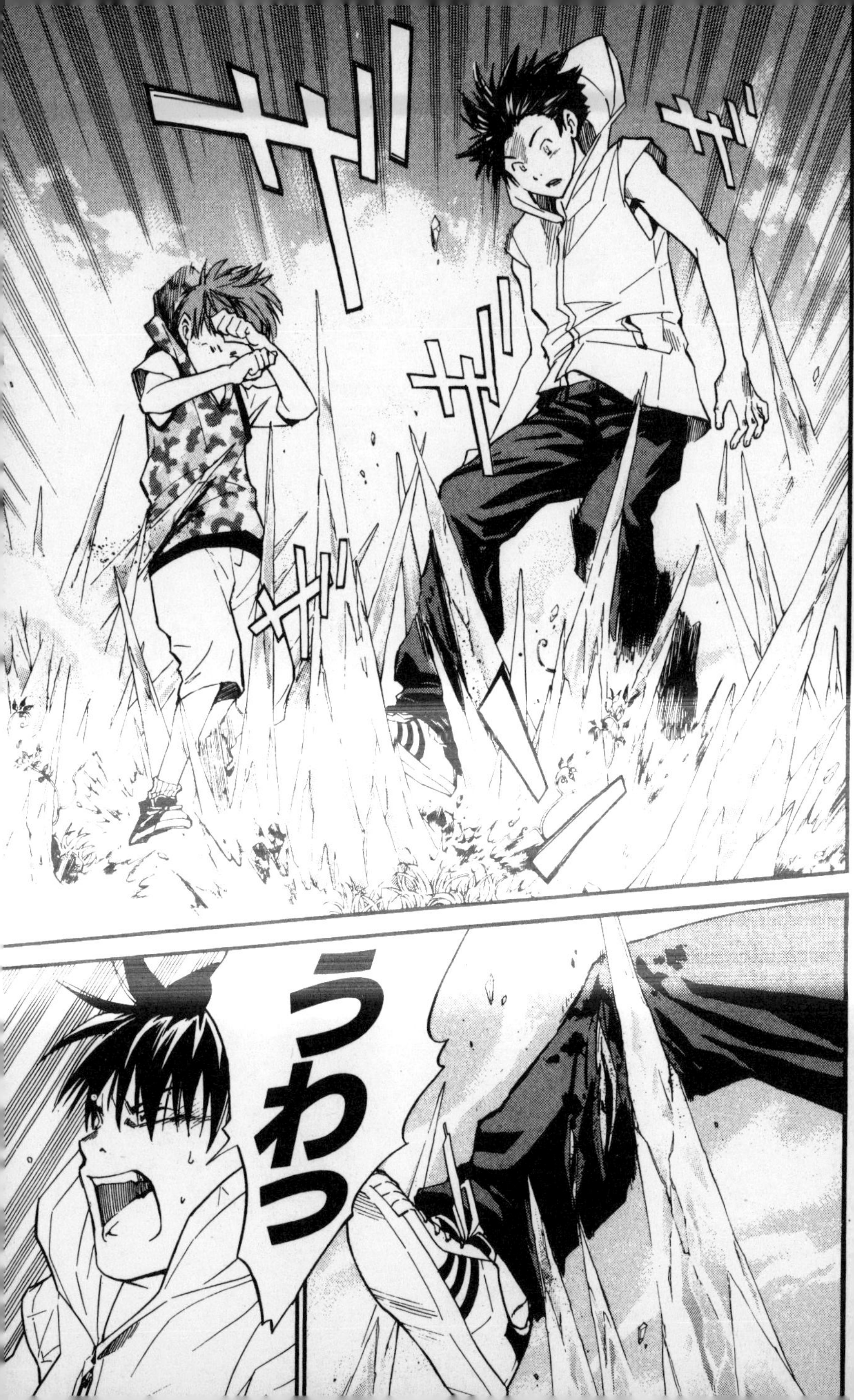
ザ
ザ
ザ
ザ
うわっ

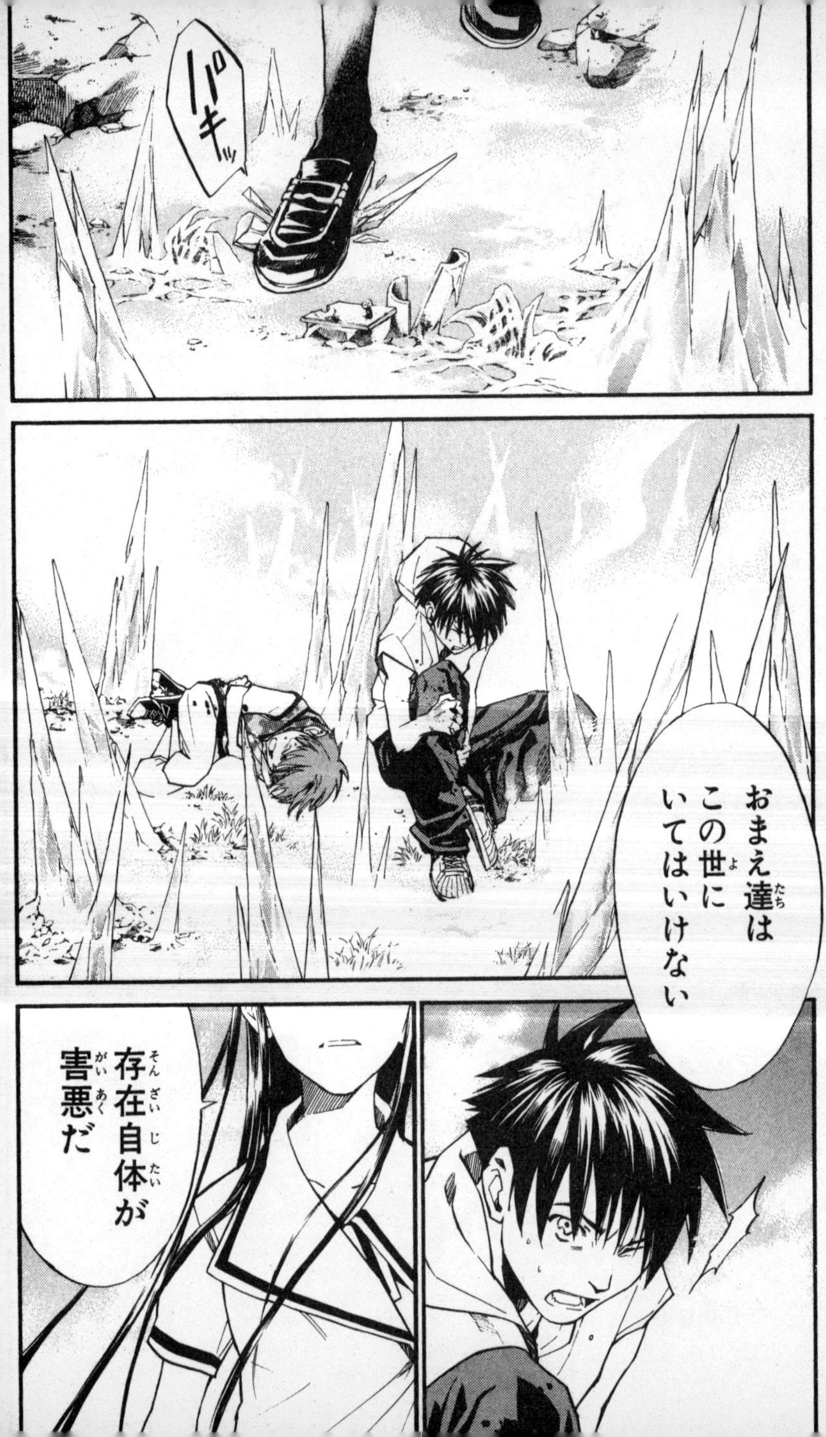
パキッ
おまえ達はこの世にいてはいけない
存在自体が害悪だ

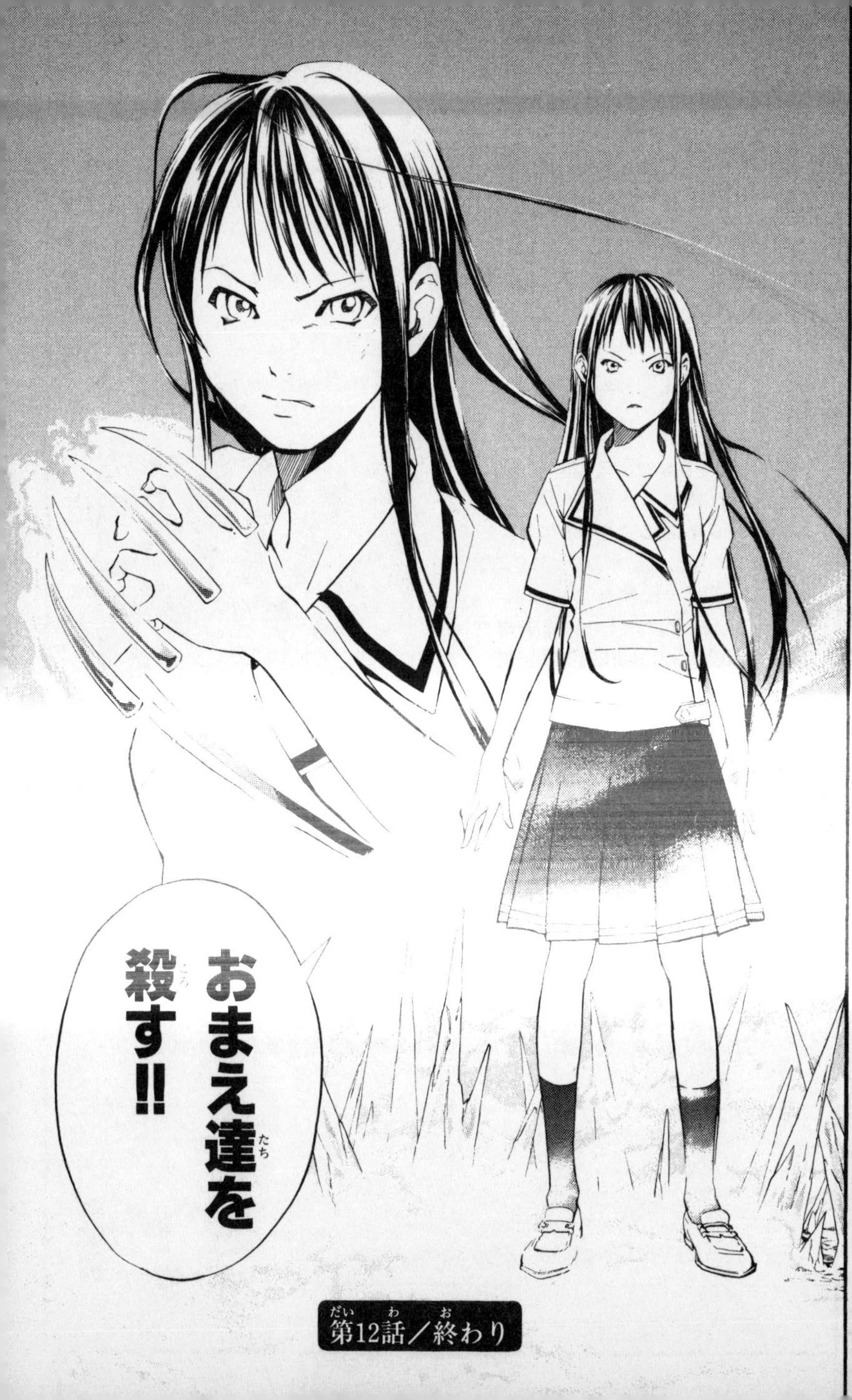

おまえ達を殺す!!
第12話／終わり

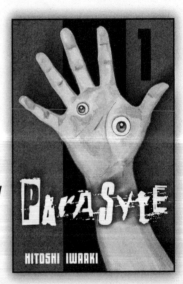

You are going the wrong way!

Manga is a completely different type of reading experience.

To start at the *beginning*, go to the *end*!

That's right! Authentic manga is read the traditional Japanese way—from right to left. Exactly the *opposite* of how American books are read. It's easy to follow: Just go to the other end of the book, and read each page—and each panel—from right side to left side, starting at the top right. Now you're experiencing manga as it was meant to be.